AWS® For Developers

by John Paul Mueller

AWS® For Developers For Dummies®

Published by: **John Wiley & Sons, Inc.**, 111 River Street, Hoboken, NJ 07030-5774, www.wiley.com

Copyright © 2017 by John Wiley & Sons, Inc., Hoboken, New Jersey

Media and software compilation copyright © 2017 by John Wiley & Sons, Inc. All rights reserved.

Published simultaneously in Canada

For general information on our other products and services, please contact our Customer Care Department within the U.S. at 877-762-2974, outside the U.S. at 317-572-3993, or fax 317-572-4002. For technical support, please visit https://hub.wiley.com/community/support/dummies.

Wiley publishes in a variety of print and electronic formats and by print-on-demand. Some material included with standard print versions of this book may not be included in e-books or in print-on-demand. If this book refers to media such as a CD or DVD that is not included in the version you purchased, you may download this material at http://booksupport.wiley.com. For more information about Wiley products, visit www.wiley.com.

Library of Congress Control Number: 2017946597

ISBN: 978-1-119-37184-7

ISBN 978-1-119-37189-2 (ebk); ISBN ePDF 978-1-119-37186-1 (ebk)

Manufactured in the United States of America

10 9 8 7 6 5 4 3 2 1

Table of Contents

Introduction

With the availability of cloud-based resources, developers today have an unprecedented opportunity to create amazing applications that previously weren't possible. Amazon Web Services (AWS) enables developers to interact with the entire world, even when their application supports the smallest of organizations. The access to services in the cloud is amazing enough, but the access to data and other resources is now at mind-boggling levels. Unfortunately, many developers are indeed overawed by the sheer size and scope of cloud-based development, which is why you need *AWS For Developers For Dummies*.

This book is about making things simple. You don't have to try to understand the entire cloud or even just AWS in a single sitting; instead, *AWS For Developers For Dummies* breaks down all the concepts into smaller chunks. If you want to create imaginative applications, this books helps you do so without spending frustrating hours learning the arcane AWS API beforehand. Life is short. With this book, you can create an application in just a few hours and become productive more quickly, freeing you from the drudgery of learning quite a lot to do only a little.

About This Book

The purpose of *AWS For Developers For Dummies* is to help you get up and running quickly. You build a test environment and install tools that let you experiment with many of the major services without a lot of effort. The focus of this book is to get you started doing something by using just a few of the services. One of the hardest parts of working with AWS is that so many services are available (more than 100 of them) that a developer might go nuts just trying to figure out where to begin. This book relieves you of that problem.

Most of the book examples focus on three kinds of AWS interaction: through the console, through the Command Line Interface (CLI), and programmatically. In most cases, these are the three ways developers begin working with AWS. The console lets you see how AWS works from an administrative level. Using CLI helps you understand the AWS functionality at a deeper level, plus you can use it to create scripts. Finally, this book uses Python Notebooks to make experimentation very easy. You don't have to write complete applications to see something happen;

just a few lines of code will do. So, in contrast to other programming projects, in which you spent hours writing code just to see the project die because of the smallest typo, this book helps you attain something significant without much typing at all.

To help you absorb the concepts, this book uses the following conventions:

>> Text that you're meant to type just as it appears in the book is in **bold**. The exception is when you're working through a step list: Because each step is bold, the text to type is not bold.

>> Words for you to type that are also in *italics* are meant as placeholders; you need to replace them with something that works for you. For example, if you see "Type **Your Name** and press Enter," you need to replace *Your Name* with your actual name.

>> I also use *italics* for terms I define. This means that you don't have to rely on other sources to provide the definitions you need.

>> Web addresses and programming code appear in monofont. If you're reading a digital version of this book on a device connected to the Internet, you can click the live link to visit a website, like this: http://www.dummies.com.

>> When you need to click command sequences, you see them separated by a special arrow, like this: File ➪ New File, which tells you to click File and then New File.

Foolish Assumptions

You might have a hard time believing that I've assumed anything about you — after all, I haven't even met you yet! Although most assumptions are indeed foolish, I made certain assumptions to provide a starting point for the book.

The first assumption is that you're familiar with the platform you want to use, because the book doesn't offer any guidance in this regard. This book doesn't discuss any platform-specific issues. You really do need to know how to install applications, use applications, and generally work with your chosen platform before you begin working with this book.

You also need to be familiar with your browser and understand how to interact with browser-based applications. Sprinkled throughout are numerous references to online material that can enhance your learning experience. In addition, most of the tasks you perform with AWS require that you work in your browser.

This book is largely platform independent. However, none of the procedures are tested using small mobile devices, such as a smartphone (and some are almost guaranteed not to work on a small device). Differences in appearance do emerge when using a smaller device; a control that appears as a button on a larger device may appear as a link or other control on a smaller device. You need access to the sort of setup that a developer will use to create and configure online applications, which means a larger tablet, notebook, or, better yet, a full desktop system. The various people who worked on this book used desktop systems running the Windows, Linux, and Mac OS X platforms and using a number of common browsers.

Because this is a book about application development, you also need to have some understanding of the development process. Knowledge of Python would be nice, but it's not absolutely necessary because of the way the examples work. You may still need to spend some time with a Python tutorial to understand everything that the examples provide. In addition, you need to know how to work at the command prompt or terminal window. Many of the examples require that you manually type commands rather than work with a GUI. In fact, a few of the examples simply won't work with a GUI because the options are unavailable. (These examples are clearly marked in the book.)

Icons Used in This Book

As you read this book, you encounter icons in the margins that indicate material of special interest (or not, as the case may be!). Here's what the icons mean:

TIP

Tips are nice because they help you save time or perform some task without a lot of extra work. The tips in this book are time-saving techniques or pointers to resources that you should try so that you can get the maximum benefit when performing AWS-related tasks.

WARNING

I don't want to sound like an angry parent or some kind of maniac, but you should avoid doing anything that's marked with a Warning icon. Otherwise, you might find that your configuration fails to work as expected, you get incorrect results from seemingly bulletproof processes, or (in the worst-case scenario) you lose data.

TECHNICAL
STUFF

Whenever you see this icon, think advanced tip or technique. You might find these tidbits of useful information just too boring for words, or they could contain the solution you need to get an AWS service running. Skip these bits of information whenever you like.

REMEMBER

If you don't get anything else out of a particular chapter or section, remember the material marked by this icon. This text usually contains an essential process or a bit of information that you must know to work with AWS, or to perform cloud-based-setup tasks successfully.

Beyond the Book

This book isn't the end of your AWS learning experience — it's really just the beginning. I provide online content to make this book more flexible and better able to meet your needs. That way, as I receive email from you, I can address questions and tell you how updates to AWS or its associated add-ons affect book content. In fact, you gain access to these cool additions:

>> **Cheat sheet:** You remember using crib notes in school to make a better mark on a test, don't you? You do? Well, a cheat sheet is sort of like that. It provides you with some special notes about tasks that you can do with AWS that not every other person knows. To find the cheat sheet for this book, go to www.dummies.com and search for *AWS For Developers For Dummies Cheat Sheet.* On the page that appears, scroll down the page until your cursor turns the AWS For Developers For Dummies Cheat Sheet link blue; then click it. The cheat sheet contains really neat information such as figuring out which service you want to use.

>> **Updates:** Sometimes changes happen. For example, I might not have seen an upcoming change when I looked into my crystal ball during the writing of this book. In the past, this possibility simply meant that the book became outdated and less useful, but you can now find updates to the book at www.dummies.com.

In addition to these updates, check out the blog posts with answers to reader questions and demonstrations of useful book-related techniques at http://blog.johnmuellerbooks.com/.

>> **Companion files:** Hey! Who really wants to type all the code in the book manually? Most readers prefer to spend their time actually working with Python, performing tasks using AWS, and seeing the interesting things they can do, rather than typing. Fortunately for you, the examples used in the book are available for download, so all you need to do is read the book to learn AWS usage techniques. To get the source code, go to www.dummies.com and search *AWS For Developers For Dummies.* Scroll down to the graphic of the book cover and click it. Click the More About This Book box that appears and then the Download tab to find the files.

Where to Go from Here

It's time to start your AWS adventure! If you're completely new to AWS, you should start with Chapter 1 and progress through the book at a pace that allows you to absorb as much of the material as possible. Chapter 2 is especially important because it helps you understand what Amazon means by free-tier services. You should also read Chapter 3, even if you have experience with AWS, because it provides information about the services discussed in the book.

Readers who have some exposure to AWS must still work through the latter half of Chapter 2 because it shows how to obtain your developer key. After that, you can move directly to Chapter 4. You can always go back to earlier chapters as necessary when you have questions. However, you do need to understand how each technique works before moving to the next one. Every technique and procedure has important lessons for you, and you can miss vital content if you start skipping too much information.

1

Discovering the AWS Development Environment

Chapter **1**

Starting Your AWS Adventure

There was a time when business development meant creating software for a single machine or for a workgroup. The client-server architecture, with its emphasis on both local and centralized servers, came next. Developers eventually started creating applications for the Internet as well, enabling people to do things like work from home without losing contact with the organization's database. Browser-based applications actually appear on most desktops today, and you might spend much of your nondevelopment time using one.

As development has moved onward and outward, the tools, techniques, and processes for development have changed as well. Today you deal with the cloud, where the server that holds your application doesn't even reside on the premises. In many respects, everyone is a remote user today. Of course, organizations have a huge investment in existing hardware and software, so you're actually more likely to find yourself working in a hybrid environment with one foot on local resources and the other on someone else's turf. Amazon Web Services (AWS) provides you with a complete development environment, but for many developers, the changes that using AWS require are significant and awkward. This chapter helps you better understand what to expect from AWS and to feel just a little less awkward about the coming changes.

You may also find yourself drowning in a sea of new abbreviations and acronyms. Of course, you can act like you know what all these terms mean, but they're actually important terms, and knowing what they mean gives you an edge over everyone else. This chapter also helps you understand terms like Infrastructure as a Service (IaaS) and discover just what this new term means to you as a developer. If you already work on the Internet, you could possibly skip this part of the chapter, but if you've spent your career working with desktop applications or a local intranet, you definitely want to find out more.

Developers often find that the most frustrating part of creating an application is having the right tool. Development is more than knowing the right procedures and the right function calls — it's a matter of knowing the most efficient manner in which to use them and determining when the tools already in use won't do the job. This chapter closes with some essential information about the platforms that AWS supports. Reading this material will help you avoid some serious trouble later because you can avoid the most serious platform issues at the outset.

Defining the AWS Cloud

As a developer, you need to meet end-user demands with the least amount of effort and in the quickest time. Amazon Web Services (AWS) is a huge array of services that affects consumers, small to medium-sized businesses (SMB), and enterprises. Using AWS, you can do everything from creating applications for remote access to organization data to creating a full-fledged IT department in the cloud. The installed base is immense. You can find case studies of companies like Adobe and Netflix that use AWS at `https://aws.amazon.com/solutions/case-studies/`. (The page also includes a link to create an account, a topic discussed in Chapter 2.) AWS use isn't just for private companies, either — even the government makes use of its services.

The technologies that make all these services possible are simple in conception. Think of a pair of tin cans attached to each other by a string. Amazon holds one tin can and you hold the other. By talking into one tin can, you can hear what is said at the other end. The implementation, however, relies on details that make communication harder than you might initially think. The following sections give you an overview on how the AWS cloud works.

Understanding service-driven application architectures

Service-driven application architectures, sometimes known as Service-Oriented Architectures (SOA), come in many forms. No matter how you view them, *service-driven application architectures* are extensions of the client-server technologies that you may still use when creating localized applications, in that a client makes a request that a server fulfills by performing an action or sending a response.

The request/response implementation details have changed significantly over the years, however, making modern applications far more reliable, flexible, and less reliant on a specific network configuration. The request and response process can involve multiple levels of granularity, with the term *microservice* applied to the smallest request and response pairs. Developers often refer to an application that relies on a service-driven application architecture as a *composite application* because it exists as multiple pieces glued together to form a whole. Service-driven application architectures follow many specific patterns, but in general, they use the following sequence to perform communication tasks:

1. Create a request on the client using whatever message technology the server requires.

2. Package the request, adding security or other information as needed.

3. Send the request using a protocol, such as Simple Object Access Protocol (SOAP), or an architecture, such as REpresentational State Transfer (REST).

TIP

No matter what programming language you use, you need to know how to communicate with web services using your programming language of choice. The "Considering the AWS-Supported Platforms" section of this chapter helps you make a good decision about a language choice. You can discover how SOAP works at http://www.w3schools.com/xml/xml:soap.asp and how REST works at http://www.tutorialspoint.com/restful/. Knowledge of both is required when working with AWS as a developer.

4. Process the request on the server.

5. Perform an action or return data as required by the request.

6. When working with data, process the response on the client and present the results to the user (or other recipient).

REMEMBER

AWS provides a service-driven application architecture in which you choose a specific service, such as Simple Storage Service (S3), to perform specific tasks, such as to store application data in a remote location. In many cases, you must perform setup steps in addition to simply interacting with the service. For example, if you look at the ten-minute tutorial at http://aws.amazon.com/getting-started/tutorials/backup-files-to-amazon-s3/, you find that you must first create a bucket to store the files you want to upload to Amazon. This additional step makes sense because you have to establish a location from which to retrieve the files later, and you don't want your files mixed in with files from other people.

Even though many of the processes you perform with AWS require using an app (so that you have a user interface rather than code to work with), the underlying process is the same. The code provided in the app makes requests and then waits for a response. In some cases, the app must determine the success or failure of an action on the server. Rather than reinvent the wheel, a smart developer will use as many of these apps as possible to perform general configuration tasks. Using the AWS apps places the burden of updating the code on Amazon so that you can focus on custom tasks related to your organization.

Understanding process- and function-driven work flows

In creating apps to help manage underlying services, AWS also defines workflows. A *workflow* is an organized method of accomplishing tasks. For example, when you want to save a file to AWS using S3, you must first create a bucket to hold the file. Only after you create a bucket can you save a file to AWS. In addition, you can't retrieve a file from the bucket until you first save a file there, which makes sense because you can't grab a file out of thin air. In short, a workflow defines a procedure for working with software, and the concept has been around for a long time. (The first workflows appeared in the mid-1970s with simple office automation prototypes at Xerox Parc and the University of Pennsylvania's Wharton School of Business.)

Workflows can consist of additional workflows. In addition, workflows manage the interaction between users and underlying services. A *process* is the aggregation of services managed by workflows into a cohesive whole. The workflows may perform generic tasks, but processes tend to be specific and help users accomplish particular goals. A process-driven workflow is proactive and attempts to circumvent potential problems by

>> Spotting failure patterns and acting on them

>> Looking for trends that tend to lead to failures

>> Locating and extinguishing potential threats

TIP

In looking through the tutorials at http://aws.amazon.com/getting-started/tutorials/, you find that they all involve using some type of user interface. The user interface provides the workflow used to manage the underlying services. Each major tutorial step is a workflow that performs a specific task, such as creating a bucket. When you combine these individual workflows into an aggregate, the process can help a user perform tasks such as moving files between the cloud and the user's system. Creating a cloud file system is an example of a process-driven workflow: The workflow exists to make the process viable. Workflows can become quite complex in large-scale operations, but viewing them helps you understand AWS better. You can find a more detailed discussion of workflows and processes at https://msdn.microsoft.com/library/bb833024.aspx.

A *function* is the reactive use of services managed by workflows to address specific problems in real time. Even though it would be nice if process-driven workflows worked all the time, the reality is that even with 99.999 percent reliability, the process will fail at some point, and a function-driven workflow must be in place to address that failure. Although process-driven workflows focus on flexible completion of tasks, function-driven workflows focus on procedurally attenuating the effect of a failure. In short, function-driven workflows address needs. The AWS services and workflows also deal with this issue through the user interface, such as by manually restoring a backup to mitigate a system failure.

REMEMBER

As a developer, you find yourself involved in a number of tasks that may appear at first to fall outside the realm of development. Development in the cloud isn't quite the same as development at the desktop or development of applications using a browser strategy. When working through development tasks with AWS, you find yourself performing these kinds of tasks in order to implement workflows:

>> Configuring the native functionality of AWS using wizards, AWS-driven scripts, or direct API calls through code

>> Modifying AWS-driven scripts as needed to accomplish specific goals in the least amount of time possible

>> Defining new configuration scenarios to meet workflow requirements by modifying underlying AWS configuration files, scripts, and code

>> Using AWS-supplied tools, such as lambda functions (see https://aws.amazon.com/lambda/), to perform tasks without resorting to hard coding

>> Developing applications that rely on API calls to perform tasks

Discovering IaaS

Even though this book frequently refers to virtual environments and services that you can't physically see, these elements all exist as part of a real computer environment that Amazon hosts on your behalf. You need to understand how these elements work to some extent because they have a physical presence and impact on your personal or business needs. Three technologies enable anyone to create a virtual computer center using AWS:

>> **Infrastructure as a Service (IaaS):** A form of cloud computing that provides virtualized computing resources. You essentially use IaaS to replace physical resources, such as servers, with virtual resources hosted and managed by Amazon.

>> **Software as a Service (SaaS):** A software distribution service that lets you use applications without actually having the applications installed locally. Another term used to describe this service is *software on demand*. The host, Amazon, maintains the software, provides the required licenses, and does all the other work needed to make the software available.

>> **Platform as a Service (PaaS):** A *platform* provides a complete solution for running software in an integrated manner on a particular piece of hardware. For example, Windows is a particular kind of platform. The virtual platform provided by PaaS allows a customer to develop, run, and manage applications of all sorts.

The following sections provide an extended discussion of these three technologies and help you understand how they interact with each other. The point of these sections is that each element performs a different task, yet you need all three to create a complete solution.

Defining IaaS

The simplest way to view IaaS is as a means of providing access to virtualized computer resources over an Internet connection. IaaS acts as one of three methods of sharing resources over the Internet, alongside SaaS and PaaS. AWS supports IaaS by providing access to virtualized hardware, software, servers, storage, and other infrastructure components. In short, you can use IaaS to replace every physical element in your computing setup except those required to establish and maintain Internet connectivity and those required to provide nonvirtualized services (such as printing). The advantages of IaaS are many, but here are the ones that most people consider essential:

>> The host handles tasks such as system maintenance, backup, and resiliency planning.

>> A client can gain immediate access to additional resources when needed and then doesn't need to worry about getting rid of them when the need has ended.

>> Detailed administrative tasks are handled by the host, but the client can manage overall administrative tasks, such as deciding how much capacity to use for a particular task.

>> Users have access to desktop virtualization, which means that their desktop appears on whatever device they happen to use at a given moment.

>> The use of policy-based services ensures that users must still adhere to company requirements when using computer resources.

>> All required updates (software and hardware) occur automatically and without any interaction required by the client.

WARNING

>> Keep in mind that there is no free lunch. AWS and other IaaS providers are interested in making a profit. They do so by investing in huge quantities of hardware, software, and management personnel to oversee it all. The benefits of scale help create profit, and many businesses simply can't create the setups they require for less money. However, you must consider the definite disadvantages of IaaS as well:

>> Billing can become complex because some services are billed at different rates and within different time frames. In addition, billing can include resource usage. The client must ensure that the amount on the bill actually matches

real-world usage; paying too much for services that the client didn't actually use can easily happen.

>> Systems-management monitoring becomes more difficult. The client loses control over the precise manner in which activities occur.

>> A lag often occurs between when a change in service is needed and when the host provides it, so the client can find that even though services are more flexible, they aren't as responsive.

>> Host downtime can affect a large group of people and prove difficult to fix, which means that a particular client may experience downtime at the worst possible time without any means to resolve it.

>> Building and testing custom applications can become more difficult. Many experts recommend using in-house equipment for application-development needs to ensure that the environment is both protected and responsive.

REMEMBER

IaaS service contracts vary a great deal between vendors. Even though this book focuses on AWS, you need to consider other offerings, including Windows Azure, Google Compute Engine, Rackspace Open Cloud, and IBM SmartCloud Enterprise. In some cases, you might actually find it useful to obtain services from multiple hosts to obtain the best service for a particular need.

Comparing IaaS to SaaS

SaaS is all about cloud-based applications. Products like online email and office suites are examples of cloud-based applications. A client typically accesses the application using a local application, such as a browser. The browser runs on local hardware, but the application runs on the host hardware. What a client sees is the application running in the browser as if it is working locally. In most cases, the application runs within a browser without any alteration to the local system. However, some applications do require the addition of plug-ins.

The difference between IaaS and SaaS is the level of service. When working with IaaS, a client typically requires detailed support that spans entire solutions. A SaaS solution may include only the application. However, it can also include the following:

>> Application runtimes

>> Data access

>> Middleware

>> Operating system support

>> Virtualization

>> Server access

>> Data storage

>> Networking

REMEMBER

SaaS typically keeps the host completely in control and doesn't offer any sort of monitoring. Even though the host keeps the application updated and ensures data security, the client company administrators typically can't access SaaS solutions in any meaningful way. (SaaS offers application usage, but not necessarily application configuration, and is therefore not as flexible as other alternatives.) In addition, the client company typically accepts the application as is, without any modifications or customizations. Using client-developed applications is out of the question in this scenario.

Comparing IaaS to PaaS

PaaS is more of a development solution than a production environment solution. A development team typically uses PaaS to create custom solutions or modify existing solutions. The development staff has full control over the application and can perform all development-related tasks, such as debugging and testing. As with the SaaS solution, the host normally maintains control over

>> Middleware

>> Operating system support

>> Virtualization

>> Server access

>> Data storage

>> Networking

In this case, however, the development staff can access the middleware to enhance application development without reinventing the wheel. Writing application code to make the application cloud-ready isn't necessary because the middleware already contains these features. The development team gains access to cloud-based application features that include the following:

>> Scalability

>> High availability

>> Multitenancy

>> SaaS enablement

REMEMBER

Administrators can also perform monitoring and management tasks within limits when working with a PaaS (depending on the contract the client has with the host). However, realize that PaaS is oriented toward development needs, so the developer takes precedence when it comes to performing some tasks that an administrator might normally perform. In addition, PaaS relates to development, not production setups, so the host may take care of all administration tasks locally.

Determining Why You Should Use AWS

Even though AWS has a lot to offer, you still need to consider how it answers your specific needs. This consideration goes beyond simply determining whether you really want to move to cloud-based services, but also takes into account other offerings that might serve your needs just as well (if not better). Even though this book is about AWS, you should compare AWS with other cloud services. You may choose to use AWS as part of your solution rather than as the only solution. Of course, this means knowing the areas in which AWS excels. The following sections address both of these possibilities: using cloud services other than AWS, or in addition to it.

Comparing AWS to other cloud services

You have many ways to compare cloud services. One of the ways in which companies commonly look at services is by the market share they have. A large market share tends to ensure that the cloud service will be around for a long time and that many people find its services both useful and functional. A recent InfoWorld article (http://www.infoworld.com/article/3065842/cloud-computing/beyond-aws-the-clouds-next-stage.html) points out that AWS currently corners 70 to 80 percent of the cloud market. In addition, AWS revenues keep increasing, which lets Amazon continue adding new features while maintaining existing features at peak efficiency.

TIP

The cloud services marketplace continues to change at a frantic pace, so you need to keep up-to-date on the various offerings that each provider supplies. In addition, you need to track pricing and other factors that affect your application development process. Your application development needs also change over time, which means that the services you use today may not meet your needs tomorrow. In short, don't assume that the choices you make are fixed.

REMEMBER

Large market share and capital to invest don't necessarily add up to a cloud service that fulfills your needs. You also need to know that the host can provide the products you need in a form that you can use. The AWS product list appears at http://aws.amazon.com/products/. It includes all the major IaaS, SaaS, and

PaaS categories. However, you should compare these products to the major AWS competitors:

>> Cisco Metapod (http://www.cisco.com/c/en/us/products/cloud-systems-management/metapod/index.html)

>> Google Cloud Platform (https://cloud.google.com/products/)

>> Joyent (https://www.joyent.com/)

>> Microsoft Azure (https://azure.microsoft.com/)

Of the competitors listed here, Google Cloud Platform comes closest to offering the same feature set found in AWS. However, in looking at the Google offerings, you should note the prominence of machine learning services that aren't found in AWS. On the other hand, AWS has more to offer in the way of the Internet of Things (IoT), applications, and mobile services.

Each of the vendors offering these services is different. For example, Joyent offers a simple setup that may appeal more strongly to an SMB that has only a few needs to address and no desire to become involved in a complex service. Microsoft, on the other hand, has strong SQL database-management support as well as the connection with the Windows platform that businesses may want to maintain. The point is that you must look at each of the vendors to determine who can best meet your needs (although, as previously stated, most people are voting with their dollars on AWS).

Defining target areas where AWS works best

In looking at the services that AWS provides, you can see that the emphasis is on enterprise productivity. For example, Google Cloud Platform offers four enhanced machine learning services that you could use for analysis purposes, but AWS offers only one. However, Google Cloud Platform can't match AWS when it comes to mobile service, which is an area that users most definitely want included for accessing applications. Unless your business is heavily involved in analysis tasks, the offerings that AWS provides are significantly better in many ways. Here are the service categories that AWS offers:

>> Compute

>> Storage and content delivery

>> Database

- » Networking

- » Analytics

- » Enterprise applications

- » Mobile services

- » IoT

- » Developer tools

- » Management tools

- » Security and identity

- » Application services

Considering the app types that AWS supports best

Theoretically, you could create just about any kind of application imaginable using AWS. The difference isn't in what tasks the application would execute or how the application would manage data — these issues are the same as when working at the desktop. What you need to consider is *where* the application would execute, which means understanding the capabilities of the underlying cloud environment in order to determine which applications that environment will support. You can divide AWS application types into these areas:

- » End-user applications that the user accesses directly using a browser.

- » End-user applications that currently execute within a browser but are augmented by background calls to AWS.

- » End-user applications that currently execute on the desktop but are augmented by background calls to AWS.

- » Management applications that interact directly with AWS.

- » Web-service applications that react to calls from a remote application.

- » Web-service applications that use a polled publish/subscribe model.

- » Web-service applications that use a push publish/subscribe model.

You can come up with other application types. This list gives you an idea of what's possible. The main point is that you still need to know something about the underlying environment. For example, if you want to create browser-based applications, you might rely on the Elastic Beanstalk service, which provides support for these default platforms:

>> Apache Tomcat for Java applications

>> Apache HTTP Server for PHP applications

>> Apache HTTP Server for Python applications

>> Nginx or Apache HTTP Server for Node.js applications

>> Passenger or Puma for Ruby applications

>> Microsoft IIS 7.5, 8.0, and 8.5 for .NET applications

>> Java SE

>> Docker

>> Go

REMEMBER

Consequently, the app types that AWS supports best is partly determined by the service that you use and which features you add to that service. However, just as you can extend Elastic Beanstalk to support other languages, you can also modify how the other services work as well. Extending a service necessarily means being able to run other app types. The bottom line is that you need to consider these issues:

>> Determining which service meets your app needs best directly out of the package.

>> Defining which service features you need to make the app run as well as, if not better than, the same app when run locally.

>> Expanding the service as needed to meet custom requirements.

>> Obtaining third-party package support as needed to allow data and other resources access.

>> Considering the need to modify application functionality to ensure full service in the cloud environment.

WARNING

Don't get the idea, however, that creating an app in the cloud is precisely the same as creating an app on your local system or within a browser environment. The cloud does present challenges (as described throughout the book). For example, when working with the cloud, you must consider latency issues that you might not need to consider when running the app in other environments. After all, you're still running the app across the Internet. You might also experience outages beyond your control (see the article at http://www.infoworld.com/article/3176098/cloud-computing/aws-outage-proves-one-cloud-isnt-enough.html for details on an 11-hour AWS outage that affected nearly half the Internet). If you have an app that is so critical that it can never go down, you may need to revisit the local data center or rely on multiple cloud products, which means coordinating the feature set of those products, thereby limiting your ability to leverage the flexibility offered by a specific cloud product.

Considering the AWS-Supported Platforms

If you haven't dealt with the cloud yet, you might be tempted to think of platforms as a specific combination of items. For example, when viewing your own local setup, you have a server that runs a specific operating system and has a specific set of hardware resources. The system has a specific Database Management System (DBMS) installed and relies on certain kinds of other software to provide end-user resources. The development platform is specific, too. You use a particular language with a predefined set of libraries to code application in just one way. The cloud doesn't work this way. When working with the cloud, you have an array of operating systems that can support any of a number of DBMSs and has access to a wide assortment of end-user resource products.

REMEMBER

Even the development environment is different. You can code at several different levels, as described in the "Considering the app types that AWS supports best" section, earlier in this chapter. In fact, when using the AWS Lambda service (https://aws.amazon.com/lambda/), you don't really consider platform or resources in the conventional sense at all. What you're most interested in is a process for obtaining a particular result given a certain bit of data regardless of the source or output. The environment no longer really matters; what does matter is the process and the result obtained from the process.

With all these caveats and differences in mind, the question becomes one of determining the best way to use particular services rather than what functionality you have available. The following sections give you a quick overview of how to obtain more information about AWS support for specific platform features, given a particular service.

Obtaining an overview of the supported platforms

AWS is all about the services. You can see these services divided into categories at https://aws.amazon.com/. A category exists for every need. In just looking at the broad assortment of categories shown in Figure 1-1, you could get overwhelmed quite quickly.

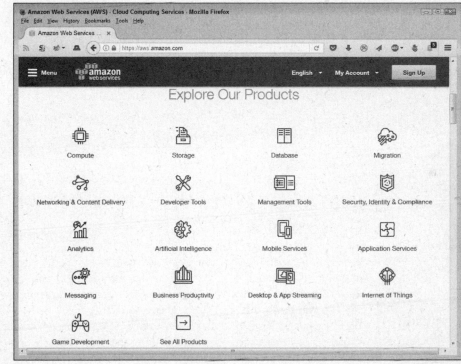

FIGURE 1-1: AWS Services break down into individual categories.

The problem becomes even more obvious when you open one of the categories. For example, Figure 1-2 shows the Compute category, which is the first place you should go to discover what you can access in the way of development platforms.

To perform most tasks, you create an EC2 virtual server. Drilling down into the EC2 virtual server information, you find a wealth of instance types from which to choose, a few of which fall into the free tier of services. The *instance types* define things like the number of CPUs, amount of memory, and type of storage supplied for your virtual server. You also need to consider the operating system, which means selecting between a Windows or Linux version, in this case.

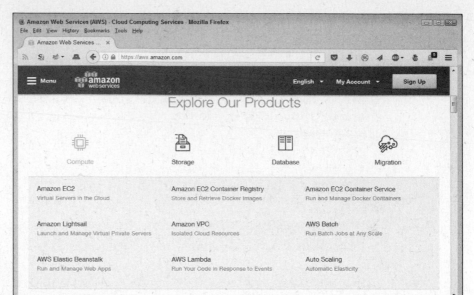

FIGURE 1-2:
Each category has a listing of services that it supports.

INSTANCE TYPES VERSUS PHYSICAL HARDWARE

An instance type differs from having real hardware in an important way. If you find that your real hardware isn't supporting a need, you have to buy more physical hardware. Likewise, when the rush is over, you need to get rid of excess hardware. Using a virtual server means that you can change the configuration as needed, including the operating system used. Instead of having to physically reconfigure a setup, you simply define new characteristics for the setup, and AWS takes care of the low-level details for you.

The trade-off can come in the form of cost. When reconfiguration becomes too easy and people find that they can access nearly infinite resources, they tend to waste resources, and applications become less robust and efficient (good for Amazon; bad for your organization). In addition, the ease of changing a configuration can lead to all sorts of design issues and even infighting in the various developer groups. The rest of the book deals with other issues that crop up when using AWS for development; just be aware for now that you can't always directly equate your localized or web-based development environment with the cloud-based development environment.

Choosing an appropriate platform for your needs

By now, you should have the idea that creating an appropriate platform isn't a matter of finding a set of AWS features to meet your app needs. What it comes down to is finding the set of features that helps you code

>> With the least effort

>> In the shortest time

>> For the least amount of money

The whole issue of cost can become significant with AWS because you quickly find yourself paying all sorts of hidden fees for things that you didn't know you needed or thought would be free. Although Chapters 2 and 3 do help with the cost considerations, this book doesn't provide the full treatment of the topic that you can find in *AWS For Admins For Dummies,* by John Paul Mueller (Wiley 2016). However, you do get enough information to make smart decisions about building a development environment and using that environment to create applications (which obviously is the purpose of this book).

The best way to find an appropriate platform for your development needs is to start slowly, using one of the services at a time and adding services only as you need them, rather than trying to build a complete development environment at the outset. If you attempt to create a complete development environment, you're almost certain to make serious mistakes with so many different services providing such a great amount of overlapping functionality. As previously mentioned, most developers start with an EC2 setup and possibly add the Lambda service to it to begin experimenting with AWS as a coding platform. AWS also provides access to the developer tools shown in Figure 1-3. The AWS Command Line Interface can prove extremely helpful in getting started with AWS because you get a feel for how things work in an interactive environment.

TIP

Use the free-tier services (as outlined in Chapters 2 and 3) as much as possible at the beginning to reduce the cost of experimentation. Only when you see an actual need to modify your configuration to use paid services should you make the change. Relying on this approach will give you a better feel as to how to make your setup efficient and what you can actually expect in the way of performance using less capable setups.

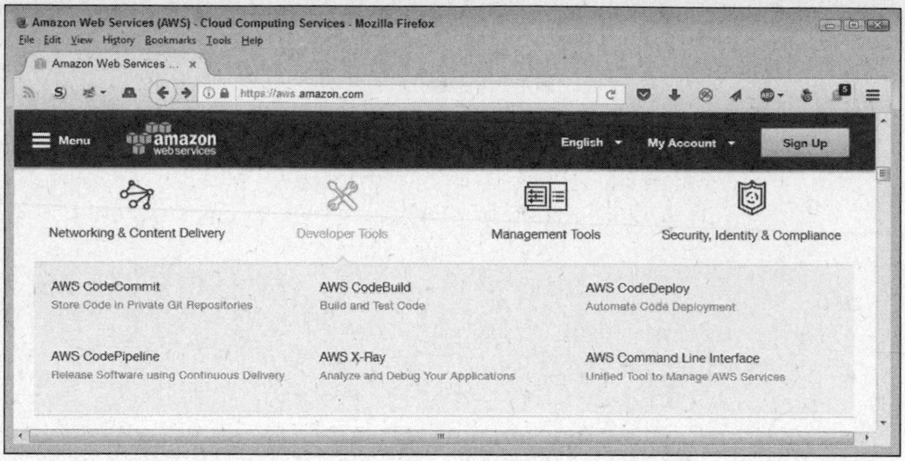

FIGURE 1-3:
Amazon provides
a wealth of
developer tools
to provide
development
support at a
variety of levels.

Chapter **2**

Obtaining Development Access to Amazon Web Services

As a developer, you need some knowledge of administration tasks on Amazon Web Services (AWS) before you can do much else. The reason is that you need to set up and configure some test scenarios to work with when performing development tasks. Obviously, you don't want to ruin a perfectly good production setup by using untested code. Discovering how AWS works is much easier if you have your own account and resources to work with. Of course, you don't want to have to pay for the learning time, which is why the first section of this chapter discusses the free services that AWS has to offer, and there are a lot of them. Unfortunately, free resources don't always remain free, and sometimes *free* is an illusion, so the chapter discusses these issues as well.

Development also means having some amount of hardware available for the task. In this case, you actually need several levels of hardware:

>> **User:** To even start working with your computer, you have basic user needs to meet. This chapter assumes that you have the hardware required to run the user environment for your system. Because you could end up simulating

more than one user, you may want to ensure that your system well exceeds the requirements for a single user, even when you plan to perform simulations through task switching (placing one user in hibernation while you act as another).

>> **Network:** You require a connection to the Internet and any local network resources needed to develop your application. This chapter doesn't cover any of these requirements. However, given that you plan to perform development tasks over the network, you may need to talk with your network administrator to ensure that you have proper rights and any additional hardware required to allow the bandwidth required to work with AWS.

>> **Development:** The programming language you choose will have certain hardware requirements, as will any developer add-ons you require. This chapter assumes that you know what these requirements are for your particular setup. You must plan this hardware in addition to any other hardware required for other purposes.

>> **AWS:** Interestingly enough, your AWS setup also requires hardware. This chapter discusses the hardware you typically want to have to ensure that AWS works properly. This hardware is in addition to the hardware you need to run your user, networking, and development environment.

To work as an AWS developer, you actually need two levels of AWS access. The first level of access provides an account that you use to set up and configure services such as Amazon Simple Storage Service (S3). The second level of access is your developer account, which includes obtaining a development key that you use to access AWS through code. This chapter helps you obtain both levels of access.

The final section of the chapter helps you test your setup. You perform the same tasks that you perform when developing an application, but a short version of them. In this case, you perform a quick S3 setup, test it, and then access it using scripted code. The idea is to ensure that you actually can access AWS as you work through the examples later in the book.

Discovering the Limits of Free Services

Amazon does provide the means for using many of its cloud services for free. In fact, you can see some of these services at http://aws.amazon.com/free/. However, as you look through the list of services, you see that some expire but others don't. In addition, some have limits and others don't. Those that do have limits don't have the same limits, so you need to watch usage carefully. It's really quite confusing. The following sections help clarify what Amazon actually means by saying some services are free.

Expiring services versus non-expiring services

Many of the AWS services you obtain through the free tier have expiration dates, and you need to consider this limitation when evaluating and possibly using the service to perform useful work. Figure 2-1 shows examples of services with an expiration date. Notice that you must begin paying for the service 12 months after you begin using it.

In some cases, the product itself doesn't have an expiration date, but the service on which it runs does. For example, when viewing the terms for using the free software, the software itself is indeed free. However, to run the software, you must have the required service, which does come with an expiration date (see Figure 2-2). In this case, the Amazon Mobile Analytics depend on Amazon S3 (listed near the bottom of the description). You have access to 100 million events per month free, but in order to export your event data, you need S3, which has an expiration date. Notice also that after you reach the 100 million events level, you must pay an additional amount for each additional million events, so free doesn't necessarily remain free.

You also have access to some products that are both free and have no expiration date. These nonexpiring offers still have limitations (and often caveats), but you don't have to worry about using those products within the limits for however long you want (or until Amazon changes the terms). Figure 2-3 shows an example of this kind of service. Notice that the service is free, doesn't expire, and doesn't depend on a service that expires. However, you must pay for both throughput and storage, so a cost is still involved.

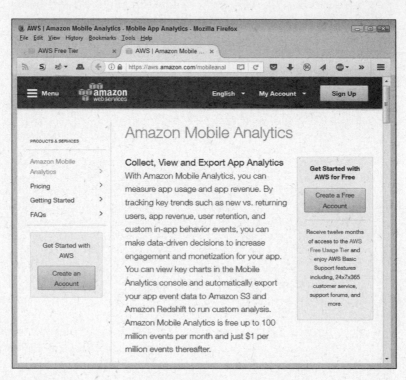

FIGURE 2-2:
Software may be free, but the service on which it runs might not be.

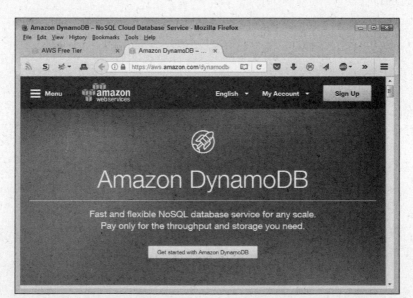

FIGURE 2-3:
A few services don't come with expiration dates.

REMEMBER

Knowing the terms under which you use a service is essential. The free period for services with an expiration date goes all too quickly, and you may suddenly find yourself paying for something that you thought remained free for a longer time frame. Given that Amazon can change the terms of usage at any time, you need to keep checking the terms of service for the services that you use. A service that lacks an expiration date today may have an expiration date tomorrow.

Considering the usage limits

Look again at Figures 2-1 through 2-3. Note that all these products have some sort of usage limit attached to them — even the free software — because of the software's reliance on an underlying service. (Some software relies on more than one service, so you must also consider this need.) For example, you can use Amazon Elastic Compute Cloud (EC2) for 750 hours per month as either a Linux or Windows setup. A 31-day month contains 744 hours, so you really don't have much leeway if you want to use the EC2 service continuously.

WARNING

The description then provides an example of usage. Amazon bases the usage terms on instances. Consequently, you have access to a single Linux or single Windows setup. If you wanted to work with both Linux and Windows, you would need two instances and could use them for only 15 days and 15 hours each month. In short, you need to exercise care in how you set up and configure the services to ensure that you don't exceed the usage limits.

The free, nonexpiring services also have limits. For example, when working with Amazon DynamoDB, you have access to 25GB of storage, 25 units of read capacity, and 25 units of write capacity (see Figure 2-4 for details). Theoretically, this is enough capacity to handle 200 million requests each month. However, whether you can actually use all that capacity depends on the size of the requests and how you interact with the service. You could easily run out of storage capacity long before you run out of request capacity when working with larger files, such as graphics. Again, you need to watch all the limits carefully or you could find yourself paying for a service that you thought was free.

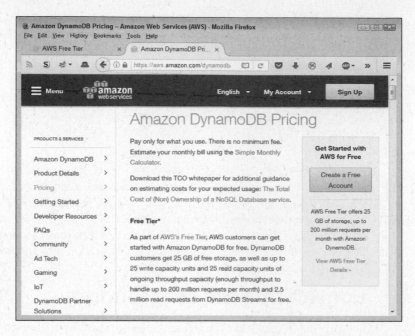

FIGURE 2-4:
Verify the free-tier usage details for a service before you commit to using it.

Considering the Hardware Requirements

No matter how many services AWS offers, you still require some amount of hardware to use the services. The amount of hardware you require when working with services in the cloud is minimal because the AWS hardware does all the heavy lifting. When working with services locally, you need additional hardware because AWS is no longer doing the heavy lifting for you. Therefore, you should consider different hardware requirements depending on where you host the AWS service. The following sections help you obtain additional information about working with both cloud and local services.

Hosting the services locally

Hidden in the AWS documentation is all sorts of useful information about various services. For example, AWS Storage Gateway (http://aws.amazon.com/documentation/storage-gateway/) will connect an on-premises *software appliance* (an application combined with just enough operating system capability to run on hardware or on a virtual machine) with cloud-based storage. In other words, you use the gateway to connect your application to the data storage it requires. It might seem as if running the gateway in the cloud would be a good idea because you wouldn't need to invest in additional hardware. However, when you look at the requirements shown in Figure 2-5, you see that the AWS Storage Gateway comes with specific hardware, instance, and storage requirements. (Only the hardware requirements appear in Figure 2-5.) The important thing to understand is that the cloud presents limits that you must consider during any planning stage.

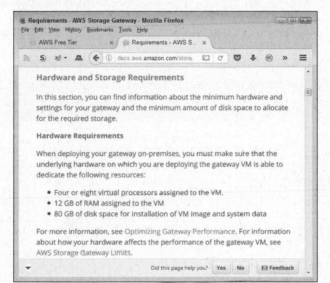

FIGURE 2-5: Using cloud-based services can come with limitations.

After you make certain that you can run your intended configuration, you can begin to consider the advantages and disadvantages of working in the cloud. For example, when hosting the service in the cloud, you get automatic scaling as needed, and Amazon performs many of the administrative tasks for you. Chapter 1 discusses many of the advantages of the cloud. However, for a realistic perspective, you must offset these advantages with awareness of the disadvantages, such as:

>> Potential for lower application speed

>> Need to maintain a reliable Internet connection

>> Loss of flexibility

>> Vendors going out of business

Even though basic hardware needs become less expensive, you do need to consider additional expenses in the form of redundancies. Most organizations find that the hardware costs of moving to the cloud are substantially less than maintaining a full IT department, which is why they make the move. However, you must make the move with the understanding that you have other matters to consider when you do.

Hosting the services in the cloud

When hosting services locally, you need to provide all the required infrastructure, which can get expensive. AWS does provide guidance on the minimum requirements for hosting a service locally. For example, Figure 2-5 shows the requirements for the AWS Storage Gateway.

TIP

A good rule of thumb when hosting services locally is to view any vendor-supplied requirements as minimums. If you don't plan to load the service heavily, these minimums usually work. However, when you click the Optimizing Gateway Performance link, the first suggestion you see is to add resources to your gateway, as shown in Figure 2-6. Planning for too much capacity is better than for not enough, but getting the configuration as close as possible to what you need will always help financially.

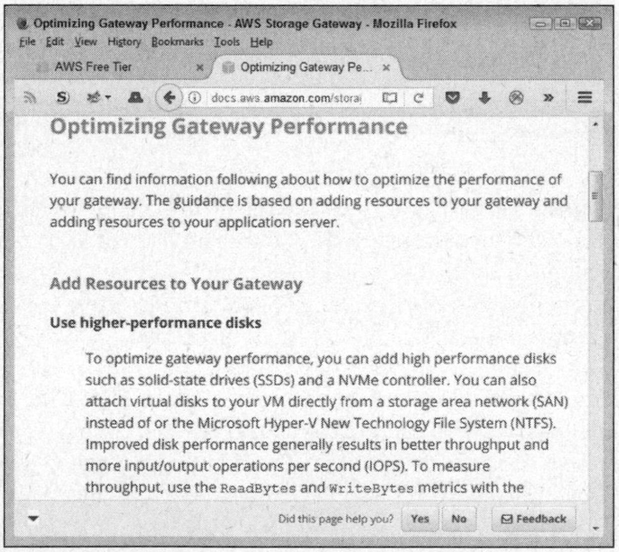

FIGURE 2-6:
Plan ahead for sufficient resources.

Not all the services will work locally, but you may be surprised to find that many do. The issue is one of defining precisely how you plan to use a given service and the trade-offs that you're willing to make. For example, when hosting a service locally, you may find it hard to provide the same level of connectivity that you could provide to third parties when hosting the same service in the cloud.

Defining a good development environment

After you know about the resources required for AWS and have accounted for the basics of your setup, you need to consider your development environment. The first issue you must consider is one of language. AWS doesn't care what IDE you use (although the choice of IDE determines which features you have available for remote access), but it does care about language. You must verify that AWS supports the language of your choice for the service you want to access. For example, Figure 2-7 shows the choices for Simple Queue Service (SQS).

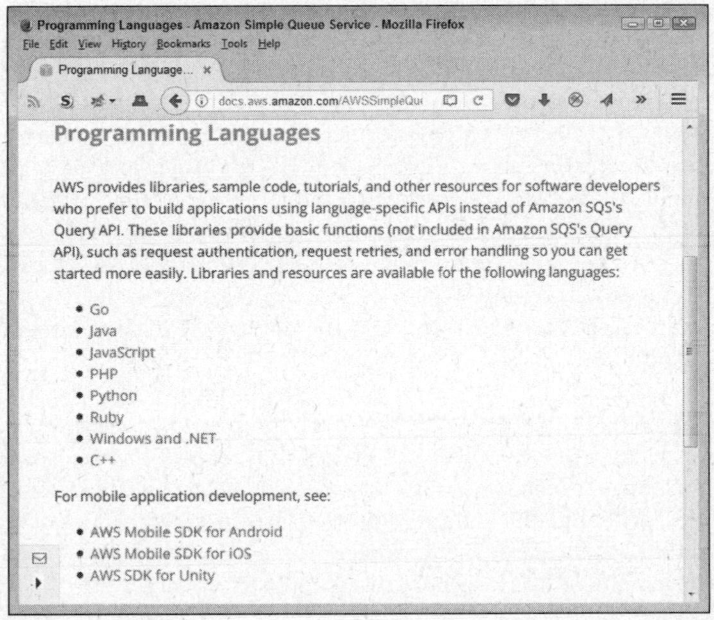

FIGURE 2-7:
Make certain that AWS provides support for the language you want to use.

You can create a deployment environment using EC2. The tutorial at http://docs.aws.amazon.com/cli/latest/userguide/tutorial-ec2-ubuntu.html describes how to perform this task. The main advantage of this approach is that you can theoretically develop AWS applications from anywhere because development no longer requires a local system with specific resources. However, this approach is most definitely not free, and it means that you must have a reliable Internet connection from wherever you want to perform development tasks — which is not a problem at work, but possibly an issue at home. The cloud-based development approach uses the AWS Command Line Interface (CLI), which is a tool you begin using in the "Installing the Command Line Interface Software" section of Chapter 5.

The main reason to use a localized development environment is that you retain access to local resources and the code libraries that your organization currently relies on to perform development tasks. This option also has an advantage in reliability because you don't rely on a remote connection to use it. If your Internet connection goes down, you can continue developing code (but testing isn't possible until the connection is restored). When using this option, you do need additional bandwidth — at least for testing purposes and permissions for the AWS access through the organization's firewall.

TIP

You aren't limited to just two options when working with AWS. For example, you could use a local development environment but place your code on S3. The use of cloud-based data storage means that you can have localized setups in several locations (so that you retain access to local resources) and still gain advantages of cloud-based development, such as having access to your code from any location where you have a development environment configured. The tutorial at `http://docs.aws.amazon.com/elasticbeanstalk/latest/dg/chapter-devenv.html` is also interesting because it tells you how to configure your development environment to use Elastic Beanstalk for project, source control, and repository use. As with a localized development environment, you still need required permissions for Internet access and enough bandwidth to handle the increase in data requests to make this option work well. In fact, the bandwidth requirements are higher than a local configuration, and the development environment must work with remote resources.

Choosing the correct development environment isn't easy, as described by articles such as the one at `https://blog.rackspace.com/the-case-for-using-aws-for-development-environments`. In many cases, the choice becomes one of personal preference and organizational requirements. For example, using a cloud-based development solution might not be an option when dealing with sensitive development tasks; security needs could trump other wants.

Getting Signed Up

The sign-up process lets you interact with AWS. To use AWS, you must have two levels of access:

>> **User:** The first level grants you user-level access to the various services. Even though this book doesn't provide you with an in-depth view of these services, knowing how to use them is a plus. AWS does provide tutorials to help you out, but you may also want to obtain *AWS For Admins For Dummies,* by John Paul Mueller (Wiley), for more detailed information on the services you can use for free to keep your learning curve costs to a minimum.

>> **Developer:** The second level, which you must obtain after getting user-level access, is developer access. Amazon wants to know who is using its service for a number of reasons, including billing, which means you need a developer ID to obtain the required programmatic access to services.

With these requirements in mind, the following sections help you get signed up so that you can start using AWS.

Obtaining an account

Before you can really do anything other than plan, you need an account. Discovering the wonders of AWS is a hands-on activity, so you really do want to work with it online. Consequently, this book assumes that you've gone through the free sign-up process described in the following steps:

1. **Navigate your browser to** http://aws.amazon.com/.

   The main Amazon Web Services page appears.

2. **Click Create a Free Account.**

   Unless you already signed into Amazon, you see a Sign In or Create an AWS Account dialog box like the one shown in Figure 2-8. If you already have an Amazon account and want that account associated with AWS, you can sign in using your Amazon account. Otherwise, you need to create a new account.

3. **Sign into an account or create a new one as required.**

   The Contact Information page appears, as shown in Figure 2-9. Notice that different pages exist for company and personal accounts.

4. **Supply the required company or personal contact information. Read and accept the customer agreement.**

5. **Click Create Account and Continue when you complete the form.**

   You see the Payment Information page, shown in Figure 2-10. Be aware that Amazon will bill you for any usage in excess of the free-tier level. Click View Full Offer Details if you have any questions about the level of support provided before you enter your credit or debit card information.

FIGURE 2-8:
Sign into or create an Amazon account.

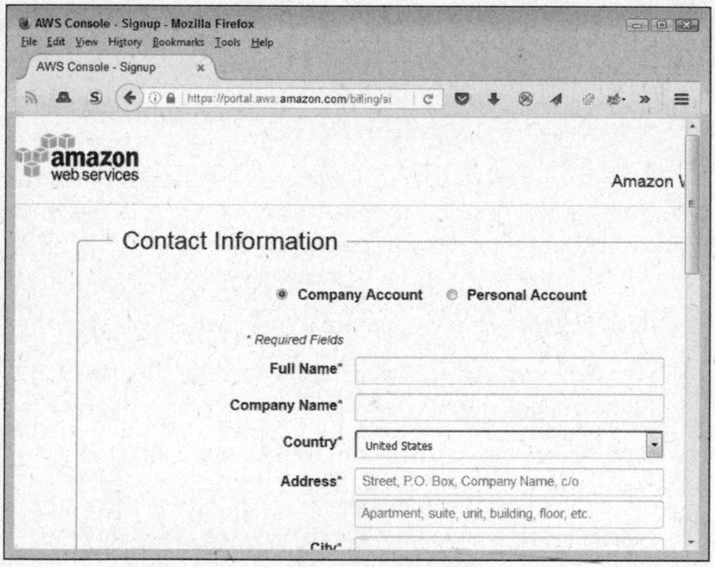

FIGURE 2-9:
Supply the required contact information for the kind of account you want.

BE SURE TO READ THE AWS CUSTOMER AGREEMENT!

Reading the customer agreement is essential because it contains items that you may not agree with. For example, Amazon states outright in section 3.2 that your data will remain private as long as law enforcement doesn't make a request to look at it. In addition, Amazon won't tell you about the disclosure of your information to the government should the government issue a gag order. These clauses are important because recent events have shed some interesting perspectives on these issues. For example, Apple refused to cooperate with the government in making iPhone data available by breaching iPhone security (see the article at https://www.washingtonpost.com/world/national-security/us-wants-apple-to-help-unlock-iphone-used-by-san-bernardino-shooter/2016/02/16/69b903ee-d4d9-11e5-9823-02b905009f99_story.html). Microsoft also has a pending lawsuit against the government with regard to electronic gag orders (see the article at http://www.nytimes.com/2016/04/15/technology/microsoft-sues-us-over-orders-barring-it-from-revealing-surveillance.html?_r=0). These issues are important, and you need to know what you're signing before you sign it, so be sure to read the agreement.

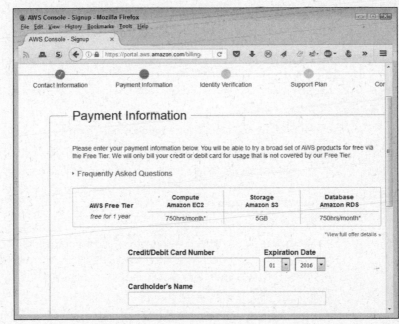

FIGURE 2-10: Provide a credit or debit card to use as payment.

6. **Provide the required credit or debit card information, supply the address information needed, and then click Continue.**

You see the Identify Verification page, shown in Figure 2-11. Amazon performs an automated call to verify your identity. You see a PIN provided onscreen. During the call, you say or type this PIN into your telephone keypad. The screen automatically changes as you perform each step of the identification process.

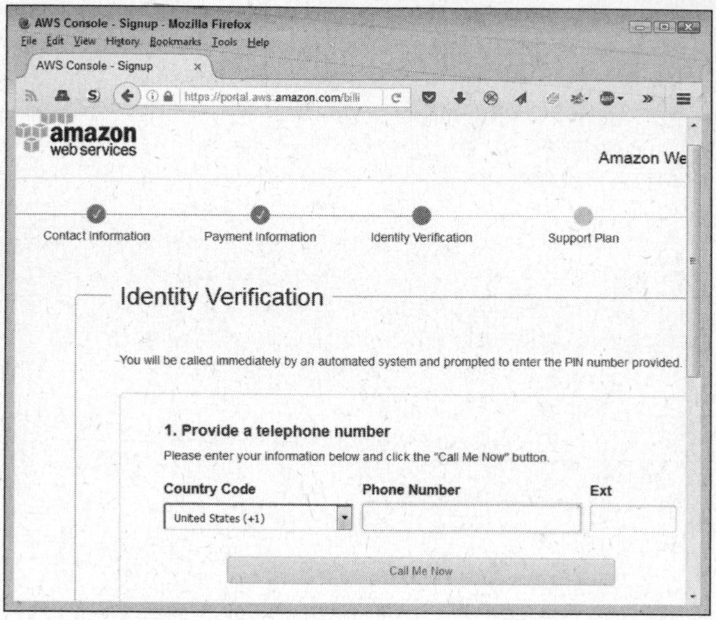

FIGURE 2-11: Supply the information needed to verify your identity.

7. **Click Continue to Select Your Support Plan.**

You see a listing of support plans, as shown in Figure 2-12. Only the Basic plan is included as part of the free tier. If you want to obtain additional support, you must pay a monthly fee for it. This is an example of one of the potential charges that you might pay for the free-tier service. You have the following support-plan options:

- **Basic:** Free support that Amazon offers as part of the free-tier support. Amazon doesn't offer any support through this option. You must instead rely on community support, which usually works fine for experimentation.

- **Developer:** Support that comes at $29/month at the time of this writing. A single developer (or other organizational representative) can contact the Support Center and expect a response within 12 to 24 hours. However, if you're serious about developing an application and anticipate using third-party products, you really need to consider the Business level.

- **Business:** Support that comes at $100/month at the time of this writing. A business user may contact the Support Center by phone and expect a one-hour response to urgent support problems as well as obtain help with third-party products.

- **Enterprise:** Support that comes at $15,000/month. This is the level of support provided for organizations that use AWS for mission-critical applications. The response time is only 15 minutes, and Amazon is willing to provide all sorts of technical help. Of course, the price is a tad on the steep side.

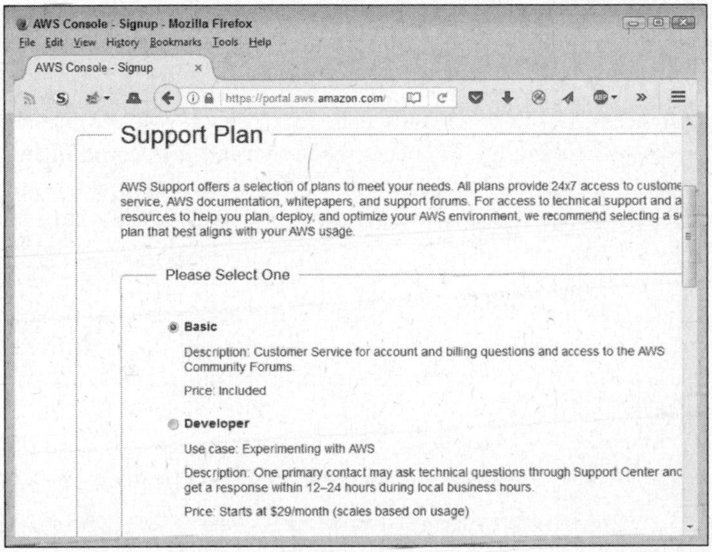

FIGURE 2-12: Select the level of support needed for your AWS use.

8. **Choose a support plan and click Continue.**

   Normally, you see a welcome page like the one shown in Figure 2-13. (However, you might also see a message saying that Amazon is setting up your account and will send you emails when your account is ready. Wait for the emails to arrive if you see these messages.) At this point, you can sign into the console and try a few tasks. The ten-minute tutorials are helpful in getting you started. The next section of the chapter gives you help getting started as well.

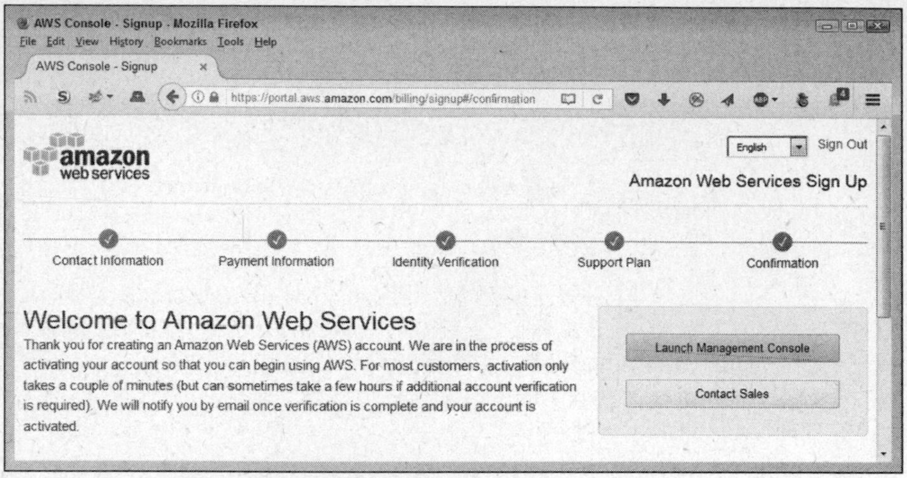

FIGURE 2-13: Start using AWS to perform useful tasks.

Getting access keys

You use access keys with API calls to allow the call to proceed. Without an access key, AWS rejects any requests made. Access keys come in two parts: public and secret. To safeguard your setup, the private key must remain private. During the creation process, you download both keys. Make sure you keep them in a safe place.

REMEMBER

The following steps help you create the access keys you need to work with the examples in the book. You can't use any of the coded examples without an access key. The access key found in the book's code is an example key. It won't return a usable result.

1. **Navigate your browser to** `https://console.aws.amazon.com/iam/`.

You see the Identity and Access Management (IAM) Console, shown in Figure 2-14.

2. **Click Groups in the Navigation pane.**

You see an option for creating a new group, as shown in Figure 2-15.

3. **Click Create New Group.**

AWS asks you to provide a group name.

4. **Type a group name (the book uses Developers) and click Next Step.**

AWS asks you to attach a policy to the group, as shown in Figure 2-16. Normally you choose a policy that provides just the level of access required by that group. For the purposes of this book, because you spend time exploring much of AWS, you choose a more encompassing policy. However, when working in a production environment, remember to use policies carefully.

FIGURE 2-14:
Use the IAM
Console to create
your access keys.

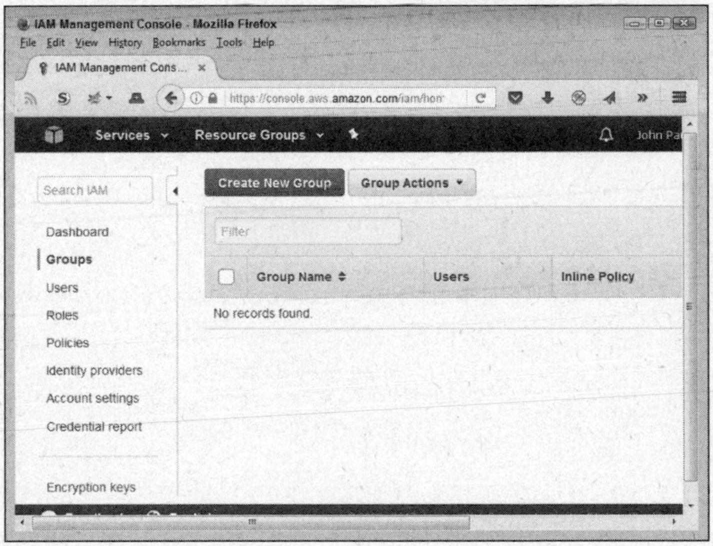

FIGURE 2-15:
The Groups tab
of the IAM
Console lets you
manage groups.

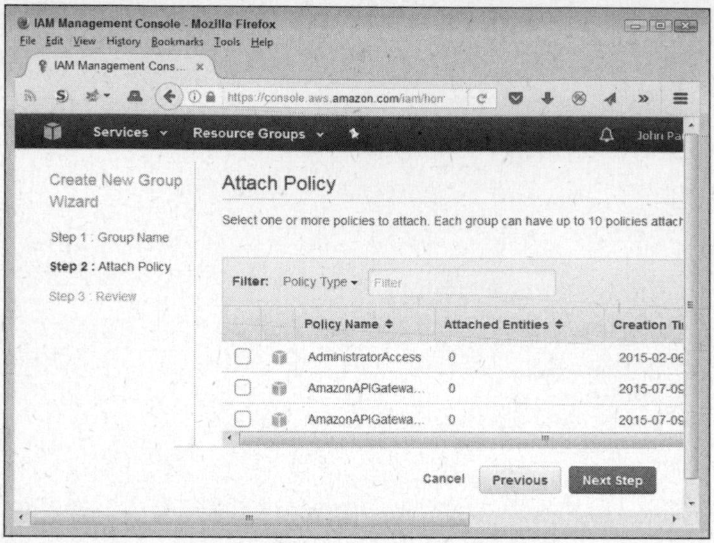

FIGURE 2-16:
Choose a policy for the group you create.

5. **Select AdministratorAccess and click Next Step.**

   You see a Review page where you can review the group's settings.

6. **Click Create Group.**

   The group is now ready for use. You see it in the Groups tab of the IAM Console. However, you still need to create a user account to obtain the required access keys.

7. **Select Users in the Navigation pane.**

   You see the Users tab of the IAM Console, shown in Figure 2-17.

8. **Click Add User.**

   AWS asks you to provide a username, as shown in Figure 2-18. Note that this page also provides the means for configuring the kind of user access.

9. **Type a username (the book uses John).**

   AWS lets you add more than one user at a time, as long as both users have the same requirements.

10. **Select both Access Type entries.**

    You require both access types to interact with the examples in the book.

11. **Configure the password settings for the user you want to create.**

    The default is to autogenerate a password and then require the user to change it during the next login. Because you want to create an account for yourself, you can save time by creating a custom password and deselecting the option that requires the user to change the password during the next login.

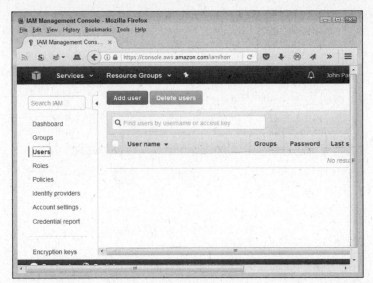

FIGURE 2-17:
The Users tab of
the IAM Console
lets you manage
users.

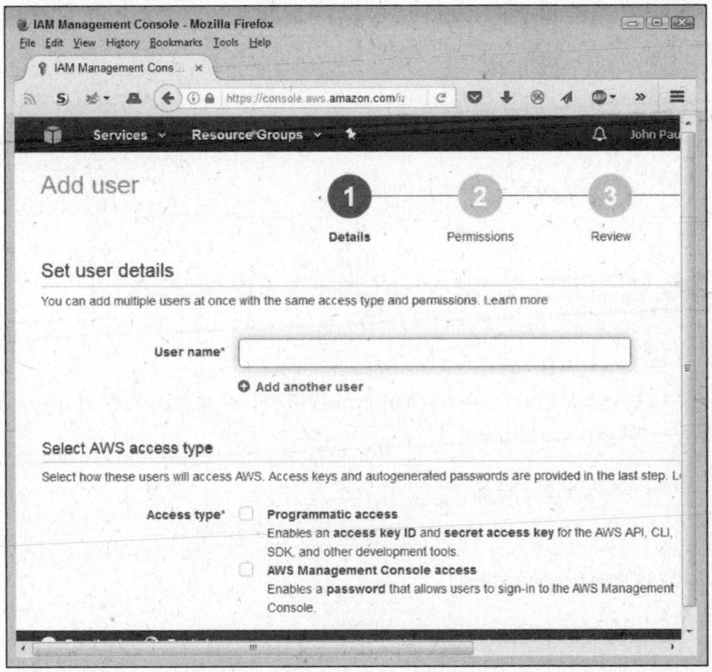

FIGURE 2-18:
Create a
username and
access type.

12. **Click Next: Permissions.**

AWS asks you to set permission for the user, as shown in Figure 2-19.

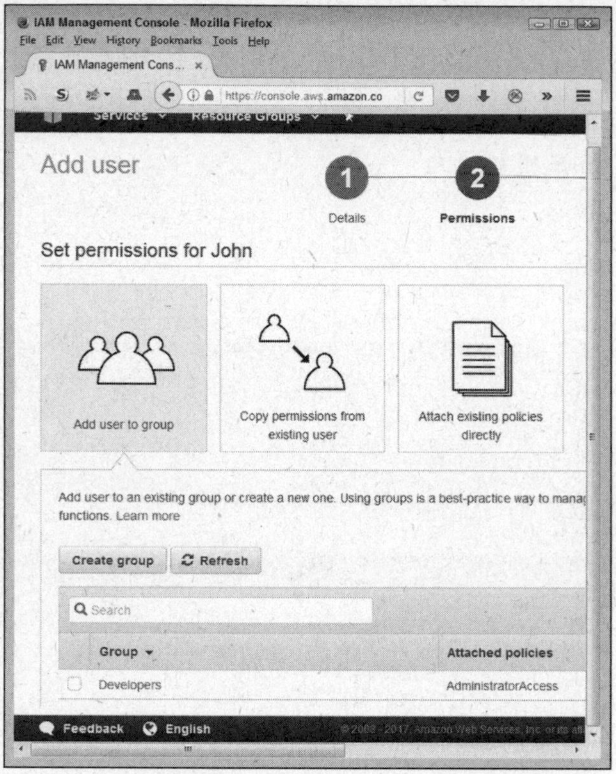

FIGURE 2-19:
Set the user
permissions.

13. **Choose Add User to Group and then select the Developers entry in the list of groups shown.**

14. **Click Next: Review.**

AWS shows you the configuration for your user.

15. **Click Create User.**

AWS generates the user and the user's access key.

16. **Click Download .CSV.**

Your browser downloads a .CSV file containing the public and secret keys for your user account. Keep these keys in a safe location.

You can create new access keys as needed by accessing the user's entry on the Users tab of the IAM Console and choosing the Security Credentials tab of the individual user's account. The Security Credentials tab contains a Create Access Key in the Access Keys area. Every time you create a new access key, you have the option of downloading a .CSV file containing the public and secret keys. To remove an existing key, click the X next to that key's entry on the Security Credentials tab.

Testing Your Setup

Now that you have a free account to use, you can give something a try. In this case, you create an online storage area, move a file to it, copy the file back to your hard drive, and then delete the file in the online storage. Moving data between local drives and the AWS cloud is one of the most common activities you perform, so this exercise is important, even if it seems a bit simplistic. The following steps help you through the process of working with files in the cloud:

1. **Click Sign in to the Console or choose My Account ⇨ AWS Management Console.**

    You see a sign-in page similar to the one shown in Figure 2-8, even if you just completed the sign-up process.

2. **Sign in to your account.**

    You see an AWS Services page like the one shown in Figure 2-20.

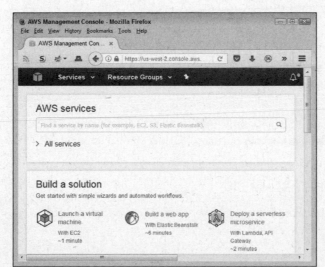

FIGURE 2-20: The console provides access to all the services you can use.

3. **Select S3 from the Services dropdown at the top of the page.**

   You see an introduction to the Sample Storage Service (S3) page. This page explains a little about S3. Make sure to read the text before you proceed.

   To use S3, you must first create a bucket. The bucket will hold the data that you transfer to AWS. In this case, you use the bucket to hold a file.

4. **Click Create Bucket.**

   You see the Create a Bucket dialog box, shown in Figure 2-21. The Bucket Name field contains the name that you want to give to your bucket. Choose a name that seems appropriate for the bucket's use. (See the bucket naming restrictions at http://docs.aws.amazon.com/AmazonS3/latest/dev/BucketRestrictions.html). The Region field tells where your bucket is physically stored. A local bucket will respond faster, but a bucket somewhere else in the world may provide additional resilience because it won't be as susceptible to local events, such as storms.

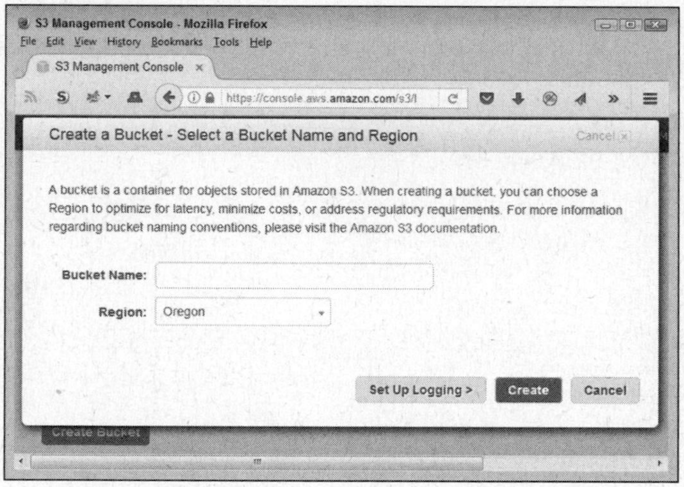

FIGURE 2-21: Define a name and region for your bucket.

5. **Type a bucket name (the example uses aws4d.test-bucket) and select a region (the example uses Oregon); then click Create.**

   You see a new page with a list of all your buckets, as shown in Figure 2-22. You can configure each bucket differently using the properties shown on the right side of the screen. For now, use the default properties to work with a file.

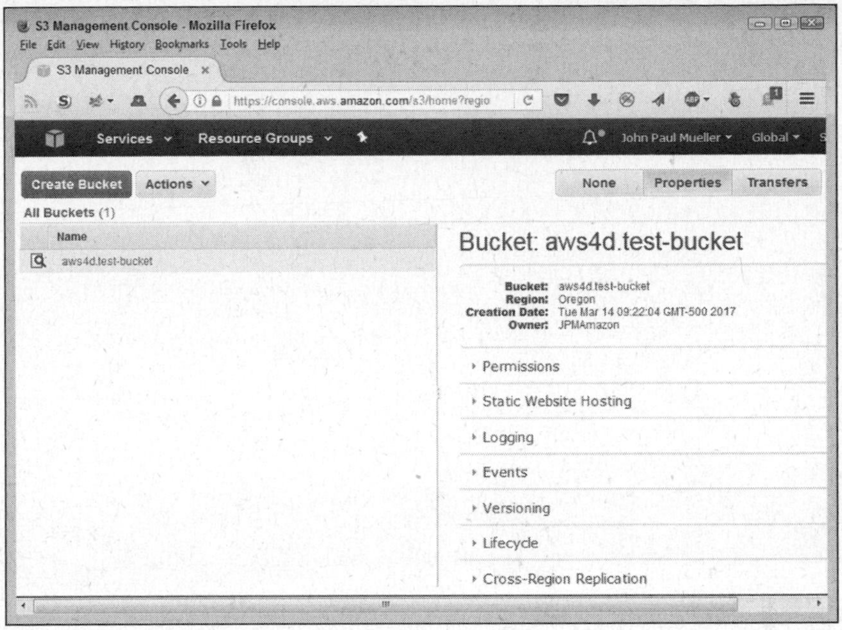

FIGURE 2-22:
S3 provides a
listing of the
buckets you
created.

6. **Click the bucket entry you just created.**

   You see a console for that bucket that tells you the bucket is empty.

7. **Click Upload.**

   You see an Upload – Select Files and Folders dialog box.

8. **Click Add Files.**

   You see a File Upload dialog box that will conform to the standard used for your platform.

9. **Select the file you want to upload (the example uses the outline for this book) and click Open.**

   The Upload – Select Files and Folders dialog box now contains a list of the files you plan to upload, as shown in Figure 2-23.

10. **Click Start Upload.**

    The file is added to your bucket, as shown in Figure 2-24.

11. **Select the box next to the file you uploaded.**

    Depending on the browser's capabilities, you can open the file for viewing or editing, or simply download it to your system.

12. **Choose Actions ⇨ Delete.**

    You see a dialog box asking whether you want to delete the file.

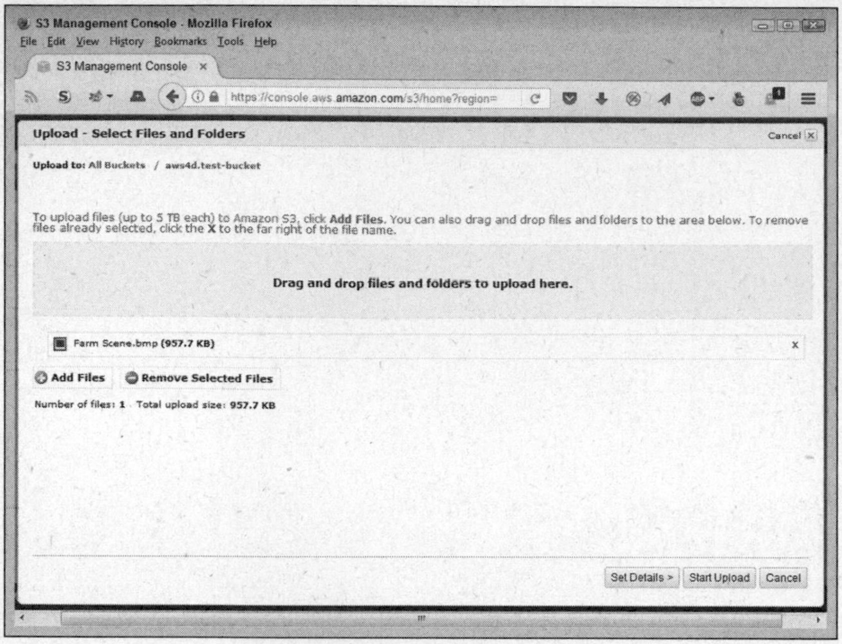

FIGURE 2-23:
You can see a list of the files you plan to upload to S3.

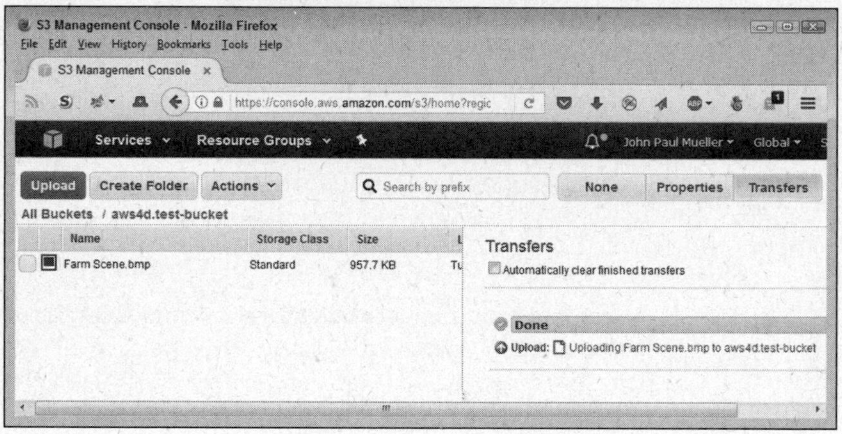

FIGURE 2-24:
The file now appears in your bucket.

13. **Click OK.**

S3 deletes the file. Your bucket is now empty again.

Congratulations! You have now used S3 to perform the first set of tasks for the book.

14. **Choose *<Your Name>* ⇨ Sign Out.**

AWS logs you out of the console. Logging out when you finish a session is always a good idea.

Chapter **3**

Choosing the Right Services

There seems to be a conspiracy to move developers to the cloud whether it makes sense to do so or not. Everywhere you read about development moving to the cloud, and the reasons for doing so seem dependent mainly on saving money. In some cases, you also read reasons that focus on saving time, ensuring remote access to application data, enhancing reliability, and a host of other issues, but the focus really is on saving money.

The problem is that if you don't choose services carefully, moving to the cloud may make your application more costly, less reliable, and less accessible, while at the same time costing you a lot more in the way of development time. Don't be fooled by the persuasive literature out there; moving to the cloud is always going to cost you in terms of development time. After all, you currently have a fully functional application, so moving that application to the cloud will cost you something. Even when looking at new development, you have an existing code base to use now, but the move will require you to build a new code base to use the cloud services. Part of the purpose of this chapter is to help you make good decisions regarding AWS, and the best way to do that is to emphasize what you can do free. Of course, you do eventually need to move to paid services, and this chapter considers that requirement as well.

Just because a service looks interesting and might be useful to your organization doesn't mean that it will work well with your application. AWS often provides more than one solution to meet a given need, and choosing the right solution will help you develop an application faster while achieving a better result. For example, you might need to choose between Simple Storage Service (S3), Elastic Block Storage (EBS), or Elastic File System (EFS), or use a combination of two or more of the services to make your application work right. The next section of this chapter addresses the requirement to match services to application need.

The final section of this chapter reviews security. Some developers mistakenly think that moving an application to the cloud reduces security needs because the cloud service will provide part of that security. However, the security you receive from the cloud service generally protects the cloud service, not your application, your infrastructure, or any required connectivity to the service. In fact, you might find that you need a lot more security when creating a cloud-based application, not less. Because developers are commonly held responsible for adding security into the application timeline, ensuring that you have enough time allotted in your schedule is essential. In addition, don't forget that you need to perform a lot more testing when moving to the cloud because now your setup is open to any hacker who decides it might be fun to break in.

Getting a Quick Overview of Free-Tier Services

Chapter 2 discusses specifics concerning the meaning of *free* when it comes to AWS. Some services are always free; some are free for a limited time frame. You must consider the limitations attached to all services, and some free items (such as software) are dependent on services that come with a price. With all these caveats in mind, the following sections discuss the various free services so that you know what tasks each free service performs.

REMEMBER

The goal is to understand which services are available for you to use to build applications. As you go through the service lists, you find that you have gaps in coverage that you must satisfy through custom programming or other third-party services. However, AWS has a lot to offer, so for now, just take the time needed to figure out how to use the existing services to meet your application needs. Note especially issues like limits on API requests, data storage, and bandwidth when reviewing the material.

Understanding the free services

In looking at the AWS pages, you may have noticed that they don't supply a single list of all the free services. What you get instead are various mixes of services that tell you something about the services but don't really help you understand what services are actually available. Table 3-1 lists the various services and tells you the vital statistics about each one so that you now have a single list of what you can get free.

TABLE 3-1 **Free AWS Service Summary**

Service Name	Description	Non-expiring	Limitations	In Beta
Amazon API Gateway	Allows you to roll your own API for use in applications generated by your own organization or any third party to whom you give access. Developers can create, publish, maintain, monitor, and secure APIs at any scale. The APIs can interact with web applications hosted by your organization or with Amazon services such as Amazon EC2 and AWS Lambda.	No	1 million API calls/month	No
Amazon AppStream	Delivers Windows applications to any device, including personal computers, tablets, and mobile phones. The application runs in the cloud, so the client platform need not run Windows to use the application. This service lets you integrate custom clients, subscriptions, identity, and storage solutions.	No	20 free hours/month	No
Amazon CloudFront	Defines a Content Delivery Network (CDN) used to send content from Amazon services to end users. This service supports dynamic, static, streaming, and interactive content.	No	50GB data transfer out; 2,000,000 HTTP and HTTPS requests	No
Amazon CloudWatch	Monitors the AWS cloud resources used by applications that you run on AWS. You can use this service to collect and track metrics, collect and monitor log files, set alarms, and automatically react to changes in your AWS resources. Essentially, this service enables you to track application activity through a variety of methods, such as log files.	Yes	10 Amazon Cloudwatch custom metrics; 10 alarms, 1,000,000 API requests; 5GB log data ingestion; 5GB log data archive; three dashboards with up to 50 metrics each/month	No

(continued)

TABLE 3-1 *(continued)*

Service Name	Description	Non-expiring	Limitations	In Beta
Amazon Cognito	Adds user sign-up and sign-in to web and mobile apps. It also allows user authentication using Facebook, Twitter, or Amazon, or a custom authentication solution. The resulting apps can make use of localized data storage when the device is offline, followed by data synchronization when the user reconnects.	Yes	50,000 Monthly Active Users (MAUs); 10GB cloud sync storage/month (12-month trial only); 1,000,000 sync operations/month (12-month trial only)	Yes
Amazon Data Pipeline	Transfers data between the various Amazon services as requested. For example, you can request to move data among services such as Amazon S3, Amazon RDS, Amazon DynamoDB, and Amazon Elastic MapReduce (EMR). This service also lets you transform the data so that the data appears in a form that the receiving service can accept. The focus of this service is on creating data transfer workloads.	No	Three low-frequency preconditions running on AWS/month; five low-frequency activities running on AWS/month	No
Amazon DynamoDB	Provides access to a NoSQL database service that supports both document and key-value store models. A NoSQL database is a high-speed nonrelational database model that specializes in ease of development, scalable performance, high availability, and resilience.	Yes	25GB storage; 25 units of read capacity; 25 units of write capacity	No
Amazon Elastic Transcoder	Converts (transcodes) media files from one format to another, normally to make the media play on devices such as mobile phones, tablets, and PCs.	Yes	20 minutes of Standard Definition (SD) transcoding or 10 minutes of High Definition (HD) transcoding	No
Amazon ElastiCache	Creates an in-memory data cache that improves application performance by transferring data from a long-term storage service, such as Amazon RDS, to memory. This service supports two open-source, in-memory caching engines: Memcached and Redis.	No	750 hours of Amazon ElastiCache cache/month	No

Service Name	Description	Non-expiring	Limitations	In Beta
Amazon Elasticsearch Service	Deploys the open source Elastisearch service, now simply called Elastic (https://www.elastic.co/), to the AWS cloud, where you can use it to perform both search and analysis tasks. Analysis tasks can include checking logs, monitoring applications, and performing clickstream analysis.	No	750 hours/month of a single instance; 10GB/month of optional Elastic Block Store (EBS) storage (magnetic or general purpose)	No
Amazon Mobile Analytics	Measures app usage and revenue, which lets you make data-driven decisions about app monetization and engagement in real time.	Yes	100,000,000 events/month	No
Amazon Relational Database Service (RDS)	Allows storage of data objects as part of a relational database. Amazon RDS currently supports six database engines: Amazon Aurora Oracle Microsoft SQL Server PostgreSQL MySQL MariaDB You can also use any combination of RDS General Purpose (SSD) or Magnetic storage.	No	750 hours of Amazon RDS single instance/month; 20GB of database storage; 10 million I/Os; 20GB of backup storage for automated database backups and DB Snapshots	No
Amazon Simple Email Service (SES)	Enables you to send transactional email, marketing messages, or other types of high-quality content as email messages. You can use this service to deliver messages to an Amazon S3 bucket, call custom code using an AWS Lambda function, or publish notifications to Amazon SNS.	Yes	62,000 outbound messages/month using Amazon SES from an Amazon EC2 instance directly or through AWS Elastic Beanstalk; 1,000 inbound messages/month	No
Amazon Simple Notification Service (SNS)	Creates a publication/subscription model for providing notifications to subscribers. You use this service to deliver messages. This service relies on the Amazon Simple Queue Service (SQS).	Yes	1,000,000 requests; 100,000 HTTP notifications; 1,000 email notifications	No

(continued)

TABLE 3-1 *(continued)*

Service Name	Description	Non-expiring	Limitations	In Beta
Amazon Simple Queue Service (SQS)	Provides a fully managed queuing service. Queuing lets you decouple cloud application components so that components need not run at the same time. This service is often used with Amazon Simple Notification Service (SNS).	Yes	1,000,000 requests	No
Amazon Simple Storage Service (S3)	Allows storage of data objects of any sort in the cloud. The three levels of storage enable you to perform short-term (Standard service), middle tier (Infrequent Access, IA), and long-term storage (Glacier). You can also configure data to automatically move between the various storage levels based on policies and uses.	No	5GB of Amazon S3 standard storage; 20,000 Get requests; 2,000 Put requests	No
Amazon Simple Workflow Service (SWF)	Enables developers to build, scale, and run applications that have parallel processes and sequential steps in the background.	Yes	1,000 Amazon SWF workflow executions; 10,000 activity tasks, signals, timers, and markers; 30,000 workflow days	No
AWS CodeCommit	Manages source using host secure and highly scalable private Git repositories. This storage technique works with any file type. You must supply the required Git tools.	Yes	5 active users/month; 50GB of storage/month; 10,000 Get requests/month	No
AWS CodePipeline	Creates a continuous application update delivery pipeline. You use this service to build, test, and deploy your code based on the release process models you define.	Yes	One active pipeline/month	No
AWS Device Farm	Performs mobile app testing against real phones and tablets that appear within the cloud. Using this service lets you test your app against a wider assortment of devices to ensure that customers won't encounter problems.	Yes	One-time trial of 250 device minutes	No

Service Name	Description	Non-expiring	Limitations	In Beta
AWS IoT	Allows connected devices to interact with cloud applications and other devices. Developers can also use this service to add AWS Lambda, Amazon Kinesis, Amazon S3, Amazon Machine Learning, Amazon DynamoDB, Amazon CloudWatch, AWS CloudTrail, and Amazon Elasticsearch Service support to applications.	No	250,000 messages (published or delivered)/month	Yes
AWS Key Management Service (KMS)	Manages keys used to encrypt data. The service lets you create and control keys using Hardware Security Modules (HSMs). You use this service with a number of other AWS services to provide a secure computing environment.	Yes	20,000 free requests/month	No
AWS Lambda	Runs custom application code without the need for provisioning or managing servers. You upload the code you want to run, and AWS Lambda does everything needed to run and scale your code with high availability.	Yes	1,000,000 free requests/month; 3.2 million seconds of compute time/month	No
Data Transfer	Transfers data between the various Amazon services automatically. For example, if you want to move data from EC2 to S3, you need to pay for the transfer.	No	15GB of bandwidth out, aggregated across all AWS services	No
Elastic Compute Cloud (EC2)	Provides access to a web service that offers resizable, cloud-based compute capacity. You use this service to access virtual server hosting.	No	750 hours of Windows or Linux platform support/month; 750 hours of an Elastic Load Balancer with 15GB data processing/month; 30GB of Amazon Elastic Block Storage; 500MB/month of Amazon EC2 Container Registry storage	No

REMEMBER

Consider some of the limitations within Table 3-1. For example, the AWS Device Farm service access doesn't expire. However, you get only a one-time free trial of 250 device minutes. This means that if you use five devices, you can test each of the devices for only 50 minutes before the free offer expires. You don't get a monthly allotment with this particular service, so carefully using the time you get is important.

When reviewing the terms of usage for various services, you need to read carefully and ask lots of questions. For example, the overview of Amazon AppStream tells you that you get 20 free hours per month, but that's where the description of what *free* means ends. The 20 free hours apply to the total of applications and devices you're using. For example, if you have four applications to run on five devices, you have only an hour of free usage per month, not 20 free hours as you might initially think.

WARNING

Some of the services will also seemingly appear out of nowhere when you get an invoice for the services you used. For example, AWS Data Transfer entries will appear anytime you need to transfer data from one service to another. These transfers occur in the background, so you may not even realize that they're happening (see `https://forums.aws.amazon.com/thread.jspa?threadID=78446` for an explanation of one such instance). The blog post at `https://blog.cloudability.com/aws-data-transfer-costs-what-they-are-and-how-to-minimize-them/` tells you how you can minimize these costs. In addition, the blog post helps you understand how the costs are tiered based on where the move takes place, such as between regions.

Working with the online labs

People learn differently. For some people, structured, hands-on activities beat reading or experimenting when it comes to learning something new. Even if hands-on activities aren't a first choice, having multiple learning-activity types tends to reinforce new skills and make them easier to retain. That's why an online lab, such as quikLABS (`https://run.qwiklabs.com/`), in which you can obtain structured, hands-on activities, can be so important to getting up to speed quickly. Figure 3-1 shows the quests page (explained shortly) for this site found at `https://run.qwiklabs.com/catalog`. Note the Developer - Associate entry designed to help you become an AWS Certified Developer.

quikLABS takes a game-like approach to learning. You go on quests to obtain specific new skills. Each time you complete a quest, you get a badge. In this way, the site offers positive feedback to make the learning process easier. You use real Amazon services rather than mockups during the learning phase, so what you learn in quikLABS applies directly to what you need to use AWS.

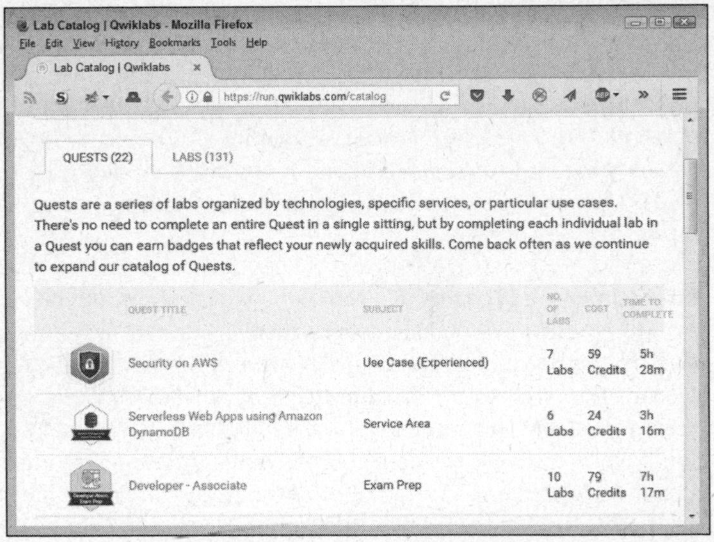

FIGURE 3-1:
quikLABS
provides you
with hands-on
activities that
help you learn
faster.

REMEMBER

As with most games, you need credits to buy services, and the credits cost money. As you can see in Figure 3-1, the Developer – Associate lab costs 79 credits and requires a total of seven hours and 17 minutes to complete. The pricing guide appears at `https://run.qwiklabs.com/payments/pricing`. Fortunately, you can try before you buy. Check out the free labs at `https://run.qwiklab.com/searches/lab?keywords=introduction`. The free labs will have Free in the Cost column. Many other labs on this page require just one credit, making them nearly free.

Choosing a free services path

The best way to start with AWS is to choose a service that you can use as a standalone service so that you have to deal with only a single service to start with. For example, the "Testing Your Setup" section of Chapter 2 describes how to work with S3. Because of how S3 works, you can use it as a standalone product. Later, you can use S3 with other products, but during the initial learning stage, S3 makes an excellent service to try. Think about it this way: You really need to discover how to use the tools that go with the services, and learning about the tools is a lot easier when you don't have to juggle so many services.

TIP

Part 2 of this book helps you get started with development tasks. Make sure you can interact with S3 at both the console and with API calls before you take the next step. Using this approach makes performing development tasks easier because you know both the configuration process and the methods used to access a single API.

The next step is to use a standalone service that can interact with a lot of other services and that you'll likely need to know about to perform tasks of any complexity level. For example, many AWS services rely on EC2, so it's a good idea to make EC2 the next step after you work with S3 for a while. S3 is relatively simple; EC2 is a step up in complexity and helps you see how AWS tools work in more detail. Chapter 6 gets you started with EC2 and helps you explore some of its more interesting features.

After you've spent enough time working with a single application and you understand how the AWS Console works better, you can move on to another service, such as Lambda (see Chapter 10). When working with Lambda, you must associate the function you create with another service, such as S3. At this point, you begin seeing how services interact. Because you've already spent time obtaining the skills required to use the console, you won't find juggling multiple services quite as hard as if you had jumped right into using Lambda. Each of the steps you take at the console is followed by API examples so that you develop the required skills in tandem.

REMEMBER

Some simpler services, such as Elastic Beanstalk (see Chapter 8), are free, but they don't appear in Table 3-1 (earlier in this chapter) because they include hidden costs. In this case, you don't pay for the service, but you do pay for the resources that the service uses. Elastic Beanstalk is always free, but the resources you store will always cost you something, so you need to keep these kinds of issues in mind as you work through the discovery phase of your AWS planning. Interestingly enough, Elastic Beanstalk is actually one of the easier services to use because you upload your application directly from the Integrated Development Environment (IDE), such as Visual Studio or Eclipse, used to build the application. As a developer, you need to be aware of when updates occur and how they affect your AWS setup.

Considering the eventual need for paid services

At some point, you need to consider the fact that you'll have to pay for the services you need to use AWS effectively. Yes, you can perform a considerable amount of careful testing before payment becomes necessary, but eventually you'll have to pay for something. This means planning for the services that you must pay for in advance so that you don't suddenly find yourself buried in debt during the discovery phase of your AWS adventure. Refer to Table 3-1, earlier in the chapter, to see which services expire after twelve months.

Amazon has a tendency not to tell you about any service costs; those costs just suddenly appear on your credit card statement. The following steps help prevent that scenario from happening:

1. **Choose My Account ⇨ My Billing Dashboard and log in to the system if necessary.**

   You see the Billing & Cost Management Dashboard, shown in Figure 3-2. (My personal information is blocked out of the figure, but you'll see your personal information.)

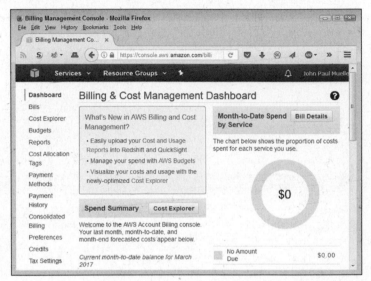

FIGURE 3-2: The Billing Management Console lets you manage settings for your AWS account.

2. **Click Preferences on the left side of the browser window.**

   You see a list of billing information preferences, as shown in Figure 3-3.

3. **Select Receive Billing Alerts and then click Save Preferences.**

   You see a message stating that AWS saved your preferences.

4. **Click Manage Billing Alerts.**

   Halfway down the page, you see the Alarm Summary section, shown in Figure 3-4.

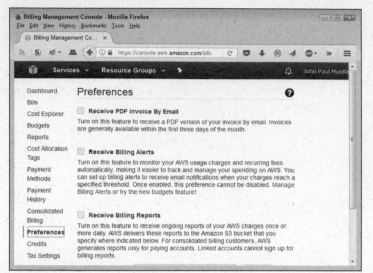

FIGURE 3-3:
Configure your billing preferences to ensure that Amazon talks to you about costs.

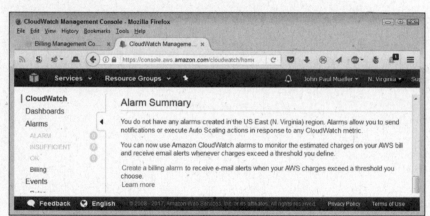

FIGURE 3-4:
Create an alarm to tell you about any charges.

5. **Choose Alarms\Billing on the left side of the display.**

   You see the Billing Alarms page, shown in Figure 3-5. Note the third paragraph, which tells you the number of free alarms and email notifications you receive each month. It's possible, though not likely, that you could get an alarm billing for the courtesy of a notification about getting billed for another service.

6. **Click Create Alarm.**

   You see the Create Alarm dialog box, shown in Figure 3-6. Use the fields in this dialog box to determine the level at which you get informed about charges and the email address used to inform you.

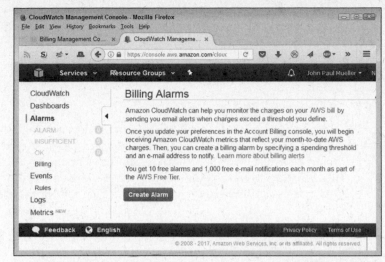

FIGURE 3-5:
Choose a metric
to monitor.

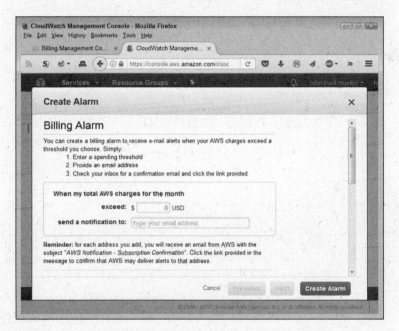

FIGURE 3-6:
Provide the
information
needed to create
the alarm.

7. **Enter an amount in the Exceed field.**

Entering a value of 0.01 ensures that you get alerts whenever Amazon adds a charge to your account. (You know about the charge after Amazon adds it, but knowing about the charge lets you make changes so that you don't keep accumulating additional charges.)

8. **Type an email address in the Send a Notification To field.**

The default display uses an email address. Click the Show Advanced option to obtain other notification options. For example, you can create a notification list, rather than send the alarm to just one person.

TIP

9. **Click Create Alarm.**

In most cases, you see the Confirm New Email Address dialog box, shown in Figure 3-7. The alarm isn't active until you confirm the email address, but you don't have to do so immediately. If you don't confirm the email address in 72 hours, Amazon cancels the alarm. During the testing phase for this book, the notification didn't appear immediately, so you need to be patient.

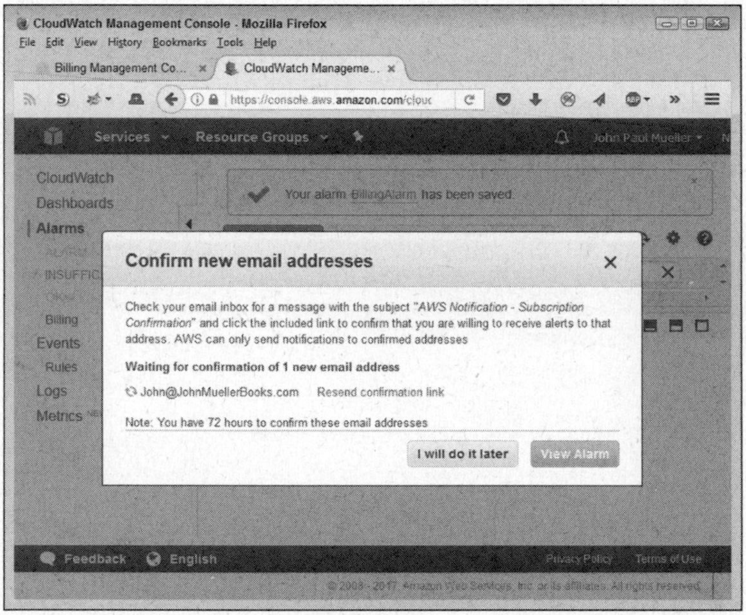

FIGURE 3-7:
Confirm the email address you want to use.

When you do confirm the email address, you see a page stating that the subscription is confirmed. It also provides you with the topic number for the subscription, and you see a link for unsubscribing to the notification when necessary.

After the email is confirmed, the dialog box shown in Figure 3-7 changes to show the change in status. You see a message that AWS is waiting for the confirmation of 0 new email addresses.

10. **Click View Alarm.**

Amazon begins notifying you whenever it charges your credit card for any amount exceeding the threshold you set. To verify that the alarm is set, choose Alarms\OK. You should see the alarm with a blank Config Status field (showing that you confirmed the alarm).

TIP

You must explicitly close your account when you finish using it. To close your account, choose My Account⇨Account Settings. Log in to the system, if necessary. At the bottom of the first page you see is a Close Account section. Click Close Account if you're certain that you're done using AWS. The same page has a Cancel Services section, in which you can cancel services you no longer need. This is a good option to use if you come to the end of the 12-month free-usage period and decide you want to continue working with services that don't have an expiration date.

Matching AWS Services to Your Application

Application development requires long-term planning. Even though you deliver a product in increasingly shorter intervals, the goal is to create an application that is flexible enough and reliable enough to deal with organizational needs long term. With this in mind, the following sections discuss some of the criteria you need to consider when matching AWS services to your application.

Working with services during the free period

Now that you understand what the services do, you need to start making choices about which services to try. Remember that you have only 12 months in which to make decisions about which services to use in your business. Twelve months may seem like a lot of time, but you'll find that it evaporates before your eyes as you try to juggle your day-to-day responsibilities, meetings, and other needs. In short, making a good decision on what to try during the limited time you have is essential. You may ultimately decide that AWS won't meet your needs at all (as unlikely as that might seem, given all that AWS has to offer).

TIP

Focusing on the important issues during the trial period is the key to making AWS work for you. When thinking about AWS, you must consider these issues:

>> **Cost:** Determine whether AWS will perform the task for less money.

>> **Speed:** Decide whether the speed penalty of using the cloud outweighs the benefits.

>> **Reliability:** Ascertain the risk of using the cloud versus keeping the task in house. (The cloud may actually prove more reliable.)

>> **Security:** Define the security requirements for your application and then decide whether the risk of using the cloud is acceptable.

>> **Privacy:** Specify the application's privacy requirements (especially the legal ones). Enduring a privacy breach when the data is housed on someone else's system can prove hard to manage and cause permanent damage to a company's reputation.

>> **Flexibility:** Consider whether the use of a cloud service will reduce flexibility to the point at which the application becomes unmanageable. In most cases, relying on the cloud reduces flexibility because the host reserves some configuration opportunities for in-house use only.

After you determine that using AWS poses acceptable risks and provides benefits to offset any negatives, you need to determine precisely which services to use. You may find that you can't support some services because of legal or speed requirements, even if you have a cost incentive for using those services. Work through the services one at a time before you begin experimenting; doing so will save time that you can use to better test the services that will meet your needs.

Interacting with services after the free period

The free period will end at some point. During the free period, you experiment with applications and could possibly deploy simple applications. However, after you're past this point, you need to consider how to continue interacting with AWS (or whether to try something else). The following list explores interaction needs from a variety of perspectives:

>> **Redundancy:** A huge problem with the cloud is that no one seems to realize that the cloud can fail. A recent news story serves to illustrate the point: `http://www.computerworld.com/article/3179761/cloud-computing/lessons-learn-from-the-recent-aws-s3-outage.html`. The S3 service was out for a number of hours in the US-EAST-1 region. The problem with this outage is that it didn't affect just S3 — it affected many other services, such as Dockerhub. In fact, the outage affected a huge swath of the Internet. If an outage like this can happen once, it can happen multiple times, and you need to plan for it by providing multiple data sources, some of which may not rely on the cloud at all.

>> **Compromises:** Every move comes with compromises of some sort. You may not feel as though you make compromises at first, but as the application grows into the various services, compromises begin to appear. During the application development stage, you need to determine what levels of services you require to ensure that the application continues to work as expected. Otherwise, you may get past the free period, have a lot invested in AWS, and only then figure out that users won't ever be happy with the compromises you need to make.

>> **Multiple provider options:** AWS and other online services often provide support for options that work across cloud providers. For example, you can support Docker apps across Amazon, Google, and Microsoft cloud services. Consequently, using Docker means that you could have a plan B in place that doesn't require you to jump through hoops when one of your cloud services has a failure.

Considering AWS Security Issues

The most secure computer in the world has no inputs whatsoever. Of course, this super-secure computer also has no real-world purpose because computers without inputs are useless. An individual-use computer, one without connections to any other computer, is the next most secure type. A computer whose connections exist only within a workgroup comes in next, and so on. The least secure computer is the one with outside connections. To use AWS, you must risk the security of your computer in a major way. Developers can quickly drive themselves crazy trying to keep these interconnected computers safe, but that's part of the job description. The following sections present some security issues that are specific to AWS.

WARNING

A single section of a book can't give you a complete security picture regarding the use of web services. In addition to the recommendations in the following sections, you must also follow best practices in securing the computer systems, the data they contain, your local network, and any third-party products you use. In addition, you must consider user training and the fact that users undoubtedly forget everything you tell them the second they leave the classroom, so diligent oversight is required. In short, the following sections present a small part of a much larger security picture.

Getting the Amazon view of security

Given that even the best efforts on the part of any vendor will likely provide only moderate security, the vendor should maintain a proactive stance on security.

Although Amazon spends a good deal of time trying to track and fix known security issues with its APIs, it also realizes that some vulnerabilities are likely to escape notice, which is where you come into play. Amazon has a stated policy of encouraging your input on any vulnerabilities you find, as described at `https://aws.amazon.com/security/vulnerability-reporting/`.

WARNING

Be sure to read Amazon's evaluation process. The process leaves room for Amazon to pass the blame for an issue onto a third party, or do nothing at all. Even though Amazon is proactive, you need to realize that you may still find vulnerabilities *that Amazon does nothing to fix.* As a result, security for AWS will always prove less than perfect, which means you also need to maintain a strong, proactive security stance and not depend on Amazon to do it all. The most important thing you can do when working with a cloud service vendor such as Amazon is to continue monitoring your own systems for any sign of unexpected activity.

Getting the expert view of security

As you work through your plan for using AWS to support your organization's IT needs, you need to read more than the Amazon view of issues such as security. Expecting Amazon to tell you about every potential security issue isn't unreasonable — it's just that Amazon requires proof before it deals with an issue. To get the full security story, you must rely on third-party experts, which means that you have to spend time locating this information online. (A visit to my blog at `http://blog.johnmuellerbooks.com` will help in this regard because I provide updates about issues, such as security, that relate to topics in my books).

A recent story serves to illustrate that Amazon is less than forthcoming about every security issue (see `http://www.bankinfosecurity.com/crypto-keys-stolen-from-amazon-cloud-a-8581/op-1`). In this case, white-hat hackers (security testers) have managed to hack into a third party's EC2 instance from another instance. After gaining access to the third-party instance, the researchers were able to steal the security keys for that instance. Amazon is unlikely to tell you about this sort of research, so you need discover it yourself.

REMEMBER

The problem with many of these stories is that the trade press tends to sensationalize them, making them appear worse than they really are. You need to balance what you know about your organization's setup, what Amazon has actually reported about known security issues, and what the trade press has published about suspected security issues when determining the security risks of using AWS as your cloud solution. As part of your planning process, you also need to consider what other cloud vendors provide in the way of security. The bottom line is that using the cloud will never be as secure as keeping your IT in house because more connections always spell more opportunities for someone to hack your setup.

Discovering the reality of Amazon security

The previous two sections discuss what Amazon is willing to admit when it comes to security and what researchers are trying to convince you is the actual state of security for AWS. These two opposing views are critical to your planning process, but you also need to consider real-world experiences as part of the mix. The security researchers at Worcester Polytechnic Institute created a condition under which AWS could fail. However, it hasn't actually failed in this way in the real world. The way in which AWS *has* actually failed is with its backup solutions.

The story at `http://arstechnica.com/security/2014/06/aws-console-breach-leads-to-demise-of-service-with-proven-backup-plan/` tells of a company that is no longer operational. It failed when someone compromised its EC2 instance. This isn't a contrived experiment; it actually happened, and the hackers involved did real damage. So this is the sort of story to give greater credence to when you plan your use of AWS.

Another story (see `http://gizmodo.com/security-hell-private-medical-data-of-over-1-5-million-1731548110`) relates how unexpected data dumps on AWS made third-party information available. In this case, the data included personal information garnered from police injury reports, drug tests, detailed doctor visit notes, and social security numbers. Given the implications of this data breach, the organizations involved could be liable for both criminal and civil charges. When working with AWS, you must temper the need to save money now with the need to spend more money later defending yourself against a lawsuit.

Employing AWS security best practices

Amazon provides you with a set of security best practices, and it's a good idea for you to read the associated white paper as part of your security-planning process. The white paper is at `https://aws.amazon.com/whitepapers/aws-security-best-practices/`. The information you get will help you understand how to configure your setup to maximize security from the Amazon perspective, but as the previous sections show, even a great configuration may not be enough to protect your data. Yes, you should ensure that your setup follows Amazon's best practices, but you also need to have plans in place for the inevitable data breach. This statement may seem negative, but when it comes to security, you must always assume the worst-case scenario and prepare strategies for handling it.

Using the IAM Policy Simulator to check access

Later chapters in the book will introduce you to a wealth of tools you can use as a developer to reduce your risk when working with AWS. (Accessing most of these tools will require that you log into your AWS account.) However, one of the more interesting tools you need to know about now is the IAM Policy Simulator (https://policysim.aws.amazon.com), which can tell you about the rights that a user, group, or role has to AWS resources. Knowing these rights can help you create better applications as well as lock down security so that users can rely on your applications to work, but within a safe environment. Figure 3-8 shows the initial IAM Policy Simulator display.

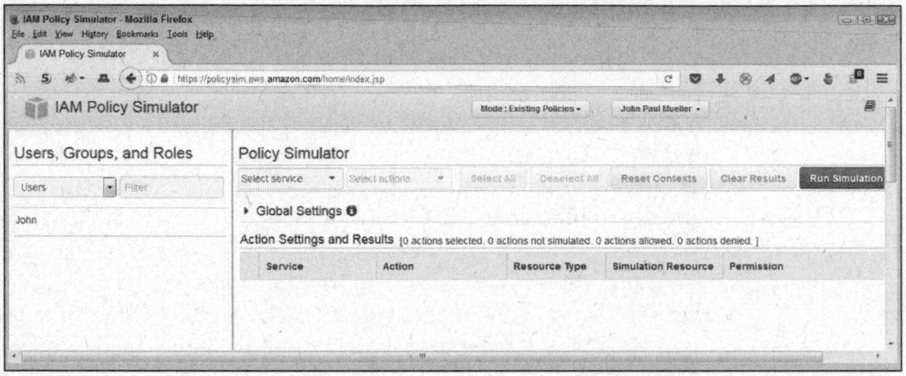

FIGURE 3-8:
Use the IAM Policy Simulator to discover how AWS security works.

To use this simulator, select a user, group, or role in the left pane. You can select one or more of the policies for that user, group, or role and even see the JavaScript Object Notation (JSON) code for that policy. For example, the AdministratorAccess policy looks like this:

```
{
    "Version": "2012-10-17",
    "Statement": [
        {
            "Effect": "Allow",
            "Action": "*",
            "Resource": "*"
        }
    ]
}
```

Essentially, this policy states that the user is allowed to perform any action using any resource. The Effect field can contain Allow or Deny to allow or deny an action. The Action field contains an asterisk (*) to show that all the actions come into play. Finally, the Resource field contains * to show that this policy affects every AWS resource. As the book progresses, you see a lot more JSON code, so don't worry too much about the particulars now.

To run a simulation against a particular user, group, role, or policy, you need to choose a service, such as Amazon Elastic File System. You can then select the actions you want to check or click Select All to select all the actions associated with the service. Click Run Simulation to complete the test. Figure 3-9 shows the results of running a simulation against the `AdministratorAccess` policy for every action of the Amazon Elastic File System.

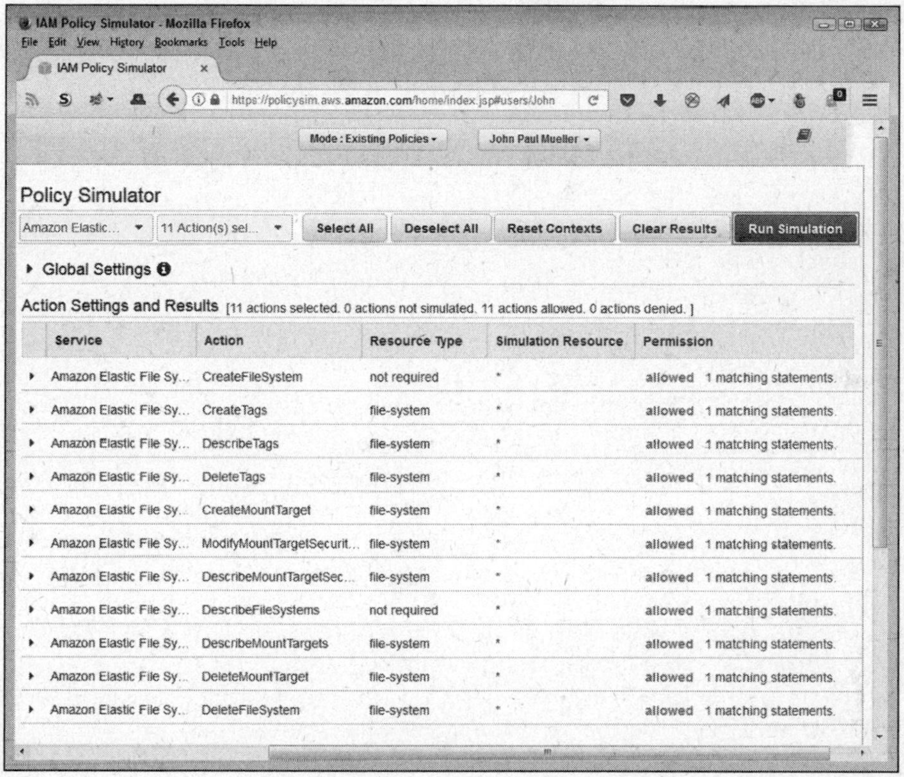

FIGURE 3-9: Administrators naturally have full access to every resource.

2

Starting the Development Process

Communicate with AWS.

Execute commands at the Command Line Interface (CLI).

Develop with Python.

Use browser-based methods.

Install and configure EC2.

Chapter **4**

Considering AWS Communication Strategies

ommunication is an essential part of application development. In fact, it has been an essential part of application development from the earliest days of computers. The use of client/server technology began in 1964 with OS/360 in which a remote job entry represented a request and the response was the output from the job. Today, communication takes place in all sorts of ways, and you need to know how to communicate with AWS to achieve results that your application can use to perform useful work. This chapter begins by looking at the major communication standards as they apply to AWS. You could easily fill a book or two with computer communication strategies in other environments.

AWS relies heavily on three communication strategies: REpresentational State Transfer (REST), eXtensible Markup Language (XML), and JavaScript Object Notation (JSON). In fact, you can see a short example of JSON used in the "Using the IAM Policy Simulator to check access" section of Chapter 3 with regard to security policies. You find these strategies used in the examples throughout the book. This chapter provides an overview of these three strategies in a way that helps prepare you to use them with the book's examples.

REMEMBER

This isn't a programming language book. The overviews give you some essential information about the three communication strategies, but you may find that you need additional information. Each of the strategy sections do provide links to online sources that you can use to learn more if you have no experience using the language. The remainder of the book doesn't necessarily assume that you have a strong understanding of the languages used, but you do need a familiarity with them to use the examples effectively.

Defining the Major Communication Standards

To interact with AWS in any meaningful way, you must communicate with it. Communication occurs at several levels, which include:

>> **Transport:** This is the underlying layer that actually transfers the data between parties.

>> **Discovery:** To interact with AWS, you need to know which methods are available. The discovery level allows you to use a common URL to request the list of available methods for a particular service in either XML or JSON as a list of hyperlinks.

>> **Request:** After you know which methods are available, you can make a request, and AWS provides a response.

You can easily break communication into more layers, but these layers represent the most basic and essential breakdown. Understanding these layers is enough to write robust applications using AWS. (As your applications become larger and more complex, and AWS adds more functionality, you may need to work with additional layers.) The following sections describe each of these layers noted in the preceding list.

Transporting the data

The first communication concern you must address is the matter of transport. AWS supports HTTP for nonsecure requests and HTTPS for secure requests for some services, including those in the following list:

>> Amazon Associates Web Service

>> Amazon CloudFront (HTTPS is required for the control API; currently only HTTP is accepted for the request API)

- » Amazon DevPay (HTTPS is required for the License Service)

- » Amazon Elastic Compute Cloud

- » Amazon Flexible Payments Service (HTTPS is required)

- » Amazon Fulfillment Web Service (HTTPS is required)

- » Amazon Mechanical Turk

- » Amazon SimpleDB

- » Amazon Simple Queue Service

- » Amazon Simple Storage Service

In most cases, using Secure Sockets Layer (SSL) in the form of HTTPS requests produces the best result because the information remains secure over the Internet. If the data you need isn't confidential in nature, you can sometimes achieve better application speed using HTTP instead. In some cases, you must use HTTP because the service doesn't support HTTPS, so be sure to check the service documentation before you make any assumptions.

TECHNICAL STUFF

Most developers know about both HTTP and HTTPS through desktop and browser application development. However, what you might not know is that AWS also supports Message Queuing Telemetry Transport (MQTT) (see the latest version information at http://docs.oasis-open.org/mqtt/mqtt/v3.1.1/mqtt-v3.1.1.html). This publish/subscribe messaging transport protocol addresses the needs of constrained devices, such as those used to perform the Internet of Things (IoT) and Machine-to-Machine (M2M) tasks. Even though this book doesn't address MQTT programming directly, you do need to know it exists. You can find more information about MQTT at http://mqtt.org/ and the AWS view of it at http://docs.aws.amazon.com/iot/latest/developerguide/what-is-aws-iot.html. AWS allows use of MQTT with a number of services, including

- » Amazon Simple Storage Service

- » Amazon DynamoDB

- » Amazon Kinesis

- » AWS Lambda

- » Amazon Simple Notification Service

- » Amazon Simple Queue Service

Obtaining an API method listing

Before you can do anything with AWS, you need to know which tasks (accessible using methods) are available. The API documentation can provide you with an overview of what you can do, but the actual list of available methods is flexible and varies by context. For example, you may not be able to perform certain tasks with some services because you lack a secure connection or you haven't configured the service to support the desired task.

One of the reasons that you want to use REST is that it doesn't map Create, Read, Update, and Delete (CRUD) requests directly to the HTTP as a protocol does (creating an unbreakable contract that you must modify every time you need to make a change). You make a request using a standard URL with a GET request and receive a list of hypermedia links to the actual method calls. The article on Hypermedia as the Engine of Application State (HATEOAS) describes how this process works in more detail.

TIP

Originally, REST relied on XML to provide the list of links to specific method calls, but using Hypermedia Access Language (HAL) (see `http://stateless.co/hal_specification.html` for details) enables you to use JSON instead, which is easier to understand. AWS currently relies on XML for any sort of API query because most developers seem to understand XML better. The examples in this book rely on XML because it's the native format for AWS. The article at `https://docs.aws.amazon.com/apigateway/api-reference/` provides details on the REST API.

TECHNICAL STUFF

At one time, AWS provided extensive support for the Simple Object Access Protocol (SOAP). In fact, you can still use SOAP to make requests, but only by using HTTPS (see articles such as the one at `https://aws.amazon.com/articles/1928` for details). In other cases, AWS no longer supports SOAP at all (see the article at `http://docs.aws.amazon.com/AWSEC2/latest/APIReference/using-soap-api.html` as an example of deprecation for the EC2 service). Consequently, even though you can theoretically use SOAP with AWS, this book doesn't discuss SOAP because REST is a better option.

Making a request

As you go through the examples in this book, you find that requests and responses follow the familiar patterns used with other web services. However, AWS is careful to ensure that you know that REST is merely the architecture and that API requests add something to REST; that is, they represent a different layer. In many cases, you see REST/query, which refers to REST used with an API call of some type.

REST AS AN ARCHITECTURAL STYLE

You come across many articles, white papers, books, and other documents that try to directly equate REST and SOAP. The two are different in a number of ways, even though there was initially a lot of confusion about these differences. REST is an architectural style, not a protocol like SOAP. Because REST is an architectural style, it isn't directly tied to any particular transport protocol, such as HTTP. You can use REST with any transport protocol for which there is a standardized URI scheme.

Even though you see many URI templates for accessing specific services in AWS in this book, REST doesn't support templates. Roy Fielding, the originator of REST, describes how REST is supposed to be hypermedia driven (go to http://roy.gbiv.com/untangled/2008/rest-apis-must-be-hypertext-driven). Of course, developers do need some means of putting code together quickly, so the URI templates end up being a shortcut that you can choose to use instead of requesting API information from AWS each time you make a call. The best way to view the whole concept of hypermedia driven is to envision REST in the context of a browser. Each time you visit a site, the browser grabs a list of the current content, including the hyperlinks, so you know where the site links now — not where it linked yesterday. Consequently, REST is dynamic and flexible; URL templates are static.

This book isn't about the purity of an implementation, nor does it bog you down with standards you really don't need to know to use AWS. As a result, you may see some sections that treat REST more like a Remote Procedure Call (RPC) than as pure REST. The goal of this book is to help you use the AWS APIs to access various services, which may mean bending some definitions to meet the AWS approach to defining them. Even so, Amazon does attempt to use the various technologies in the right way using the correct terminology. The discussion at http://stackoverflow.com/questions/19884295/soap-vs-rest-differences offers some interesting additional insights into REST misconceptions.

You must sign most REST requests you make to AWS. The "Getting access keys" section of Chapter 2 tells how to obtain the access keys you need to sign your request. The "Working with requests and responses" and "Overcoming those really annoying signature issues" sections of this chapter tell how to sign a request when using REST to make a request as part of a browser application. A signature contains more than just the access key, but you don't need to know the details just yet. All you need to know is that you must sign the request in most cases.

Some services, such as Simple Storage Service (S3), allow anonymous requests. To garner any significant amount of information, however, you must provide signed (authenticated) requests. Because anonymous requests are rare, this book doesn't cover them. However, the article at http://virtuallyhyper.com/2013/09/

`make-anonymous-amazon-s3-rest-request/` describes how to use such a request to fix a security problem with an S3 bucket.

REMEMBER

When making a request using the CLI or an SDK, the environment signs your request for you. Even though the request is still signed, you don't need to worry about performing the task manually. You can read more about signing particulars at `http://docs.aws.amazon.com/general/latest/gr/signing_aws_api_requests.html`.

Understanding How REST Works

Before you delve into the various SDKs that Amazon provides, trying to work with REST directly is a useful exercise because you gain insight into what the SDKs are doing under the cover. The following sections don't spend a lot of time looking at REST, but they do give you insight into how REST works, along with a good start-ing point and methods of overcoming some problems inherent in the AWS REST interface. Starting with Chapter 5, you work with other sorts of interfaces, such as CLI and the SDKs, that do a lot more of the work for you. Even so, going through these following sections and possibly experimenting with different requests will make a big difference in getting later sections to work easily.

Defining REST resources

When working with REST, you need to know about a few key issues. For example, you need to know about the HTTP methods. The tutorial at `https://www.tutorialspoint.com/restful/` gives you the details, but for the purposes of these examples, you work with the HTTP GET method exclusively. (You can find a host of REST tutorials online and should use one that matches your programming language of choice.)

Using AWS with REST requires that you also know a number of things about AWS. For example, you need to know the regions with which you want to interact. You can find a list of region names at `http://docs.aws.amazon.com/general/latest/gr/rande.html`. The examples in this section work with S3, which uses the endpoints found at `http://docs.aws.amazon.com/general/latest/gr/rande.html#s3_region`.

An endpoint, coupled with a bucket name, will get you started, but REST queries typically require a list of arguments separated by ampersands (&). To make even the simplest REST query with AWS, you must also know the values for three variables:

» **AWSAccessKeyId:** The public key that you obtained in Chapter 2. If you don't have an access key yet, you must obtain one before working through the exercises in this chapter.

» **Expires:** The time that the request expires. It must be an epoch time stamp value in seconds.

» **Signature:** A calculated value that includes a number of arguments. The Creating a signature section of the chapter provides additional information on this particular requirement.

Working with requests and responses

You can find all sorts of really complicated-looking examples of how to make a REST request in the Amazon documentation. After scratching your head for a while, you might be tempted to give up. However, all that you really need is a simple example to see what's going on. This section discusses the need to make a request in the simplest possible manner. It begins with a simple URL:

```
https://s3-us-west-2.amazonaws.com/<Bucket Name>/
?AWSAccessKeyId=<Public Key>&Expires=<Epoch Time>
&Signature=<Calculated Signature>
```

This request contains the location of the service, s3-us-west-2.amazonaws.com, which includes the region. If you use a different region, you need a different location. You must also supply the name of the bucket you create in Chapter 2. The book uses a bucket named aws4d.test-bucket, but because buckets must have unique names, your bucket name will differ.

The AWSAccessKeyId entry uses your public key, not the private (secret) key. The public key is the one you requested in the "Getting access keys" section of Chapter 2.

The Expires entry requires a little more explanation. Of course, most people have no idea how many seconds have elapsed since the start of the epoch, so you need a tool to calculate this value. You can find such a tool at https://www.epoch converter.com/. Figure 4-1 shows sample output from the tool.

Note that you can use Epoch & Unix Timestamp Conversion Tools to create future values, which is what you need for the Expires entry. The time you provide to AWS must occur in the future or you get an error stating that the time has already expired, as shown in Figure 4-2.

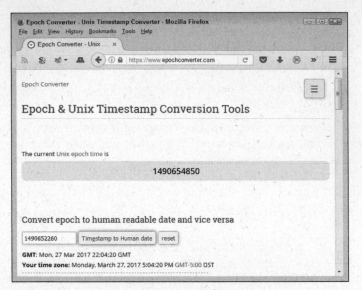

FIGURE 4-1:
The Epoch & Unix Timestamp Conversion Tools makes calculating time values easier.

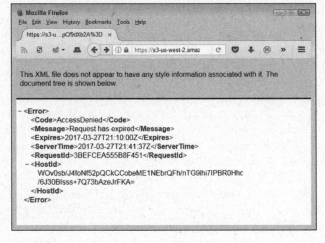

FIGURE 4-2:
Use the wrong time value and you get a request expired error message.

Another such site is the Timestamp Generator at `http://www.timestamp generator.com/`. This site is a better choice when you need to create the ISO 8601 time values required by some AWS calls.

The `Signature` provides the calculated signature. This particular calculation requires special care. The coding examples found at `http://docs.aws.amazon.com/general/latest/gr/signature-v4-examples.html` provide code snippets that you can use as a starting point for calculating the signature. However, they're just coding snippets. To actually make the code work with Java, for example, you must import at least two packages:

```
import javax.crypto.Mac;
import javax.crypto.spec.SecretKeySpec;
```

TECHNICAL STUFF

Depending on how you use the signature, you might also need to download and install the Apache Commons Codec package, found at https://commons.apache.org/proper/commons-codec/download_codec.cgi. This package provides access classes such as org.apache.commons.codec.binary.Base64. The point is, no matter which language you use, the code snippets that Amazon provides are only a starting point for performing the required calculation.

After you get the parts together for the basic S3 bucket request, you can plug the resulting URL into your browser. Figure 4-3 shows typical results for the bucket you created in the "Testing Your Setup" section of Chapter 2. It doesn't tell you much, but the output demonstrates that you have indeed made a connection, provided a usable request, and obtained a usable result in XML format.

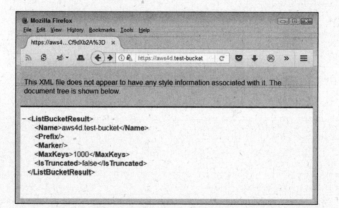

FIGURE 4-3:
The output from the URL call should provide you with information about your S3 bucket.

Overcoming those really annoying signature issues

It would be nice if everything worked precisely as planned when making your REST call to AWS. However, a number of issues can occur that result in an error message similar to the one shown in Figure 4-4. Note that the figure isn't complete. The key values are blocked to maintain the usability of the access keys.

The problem you see in Figure 4-4 can come from various sources. The first fix is to URL-encode the signature to ensure that special characters in the URL string don't confuse AWS. A tool you can use to overcome this problem is the URL Decoder/Encoder (http://meyerweb.com/eric/tools/dencoder/) shown in Figure 4-5. To use this tool, just paste the signature (not the entire URL) into the field and click Encode. The resulting signature doesn't contain any special characters, but rather uses URL encoding to prevent problems.

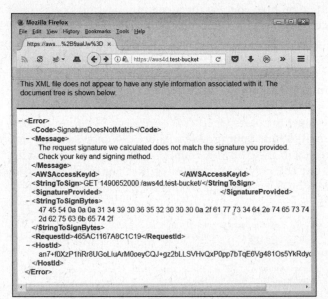

FIGURE 4-4:
Error messages can take various forms.

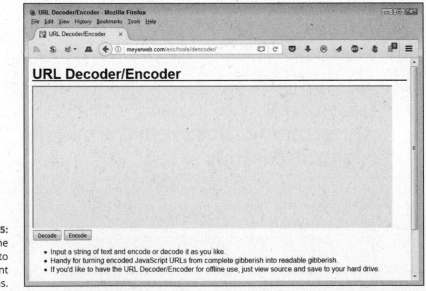

FIGURE 4-5:
URL-encode the signature to prevent problems.

Even if you use the Amazon-supplied code snippets, the signature calculation process can also go wrong. Look again at Figure 4-4, at the `StringToSign` and `StringToSignBytes` elements. These elements tell you what AWS was expecting when it checked the signature. Of course, it still doesn't give you a clue as to what value you should have provided for a signature. Fortunately, the Amazon Signature Tester (`https://aws.amazon.com/code/199`) can provide this information.

You download the Amazon Signature Tester to your hard drive. What you get is a README file and an HTML page that you load into your browser. Figure 4-6 shows how the bottom of this page appears. You want to work at the bottom of the page because it contains two fields that you need to supply: the `StringToSignBytes` element value and your secret key (which is left blank in the example figure).

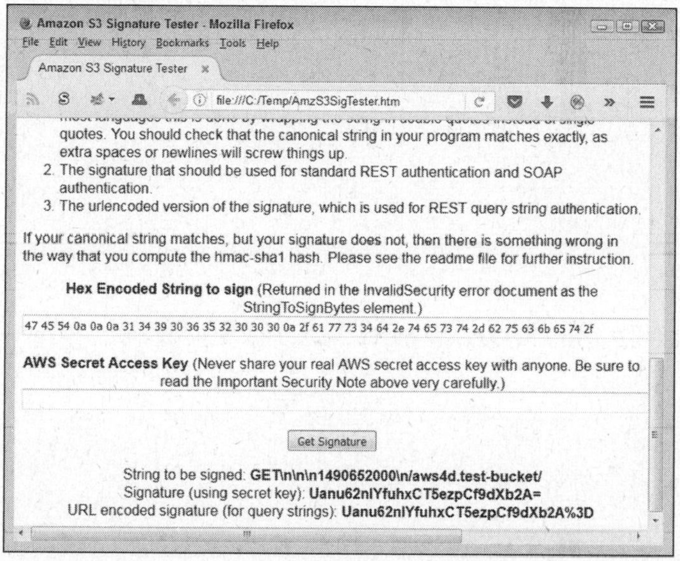

![Amazon S3 Signature Tester browser window showing instructions, the Hex Encoded String to sign field with value "47 45 54 0a 0a 0a 31 34 39 30 36 35 32 30 30 30 0a 2f 61 77 73 34 64 2e 74 65 73 74 2d 62 75 63 6b 65 74 2f", the AWS Secret Access Key field, a Get Signature button, and results: String to be signed: GET\n\n\n1490652000\n/aws4d.test-bucket/ Signature (using secret key): Uanu62nlYfuhxCT5ezpCf9dXb2A= URL encoded signature (for query strings): Uanu62nlYfuhxCT5ezpCf9dXb2A%3D]

FIGURE 4-6: The signature testing tool enables you to validate your signature code.

When you click Get Signature, you see the `StringToSign` element value as AWS sees it, the actual signature, and the URL-encoded signature. You use the URL encoded signature with your call to AWS. To validate this signature, simply replace the current value in the URL string with this new value. If the problem is in your signature code, the call should work as expected.

TIP

The reason you want to recheck the `StringToSign` element value is that AWS may see it differently than you do. For example, notice that in this case, there are three newline characters between `GET` and the `Expires` value of 1490652000. If your signature calculation code doesn't take this requirement into consideration, the signature will be wrong. You can find additional troubleshooting aids at `http://docs.aws.amazon.com/general/latest/gr/signature-v4-trouble shooting.html`.

IN THIS CHAPTER

» **Deciding on which platform to use**

» **Getting a copy of Python**

» **Interacting with the IAM Console**

» **Getting a copy of the CLI software**

» **Modifying S3 via CLI, Node.js, and Python**

Chapter **5**

Creating a Development Environment

WS supports a huge array of development options. From a platform perspective, you can use just about every major operating system with just about every major programming language and write your code using just about every major Integrated Development Environment (IDE). In fact, just from a platform perspective, AWS offers you a dizzying array of choices, so you need to choose carefully. A wrong choice doesn't mean instant failure, but it could mean a loss of time, increased use of resources, and some lost flexibility as well. Consequently, choosing the right platform and installing it to use AWS tools is important. This chapter can't possibly take you through every potential option. In fact, a single book couldn't accomplish the task. However, you do get a good overview of the options so that you can experiment on your own and make a good choice.

Besides traditional development, you can also interact with AWS in other ways. This chapter doesn't explore all the available methods, but it does introduce you to two methods that work well for developers. The first is the Command Line Interface (CLI) where you can experiment with AWS functionality without having to spend hours navigating the GUI. Using CLI also gives you a better sense of how AWS performs tasks in the background, which also makes writing code easy.

The second method is working with Node.js, which enables you to interact with JavaScript in a consistent manner. The techniques you discover using Node.js can help you create browser-based applications with greater ease. Often, you can struggle to see what's going on with the request/response cycle using code alone or working through CLI because both environments can provide unwanted processing. When working with a programming language, you use a Software Development Kit (SDK) or library that simultaneously makes performing tasks significantly easier (such as signing requests; see the "Overcoming those really annoying signature issues" section of Chapter 4) but also makes seeing what goes on harder because the SDKs tend to hide details. Using Node.js with JavaScript can make these details more apparent and significantly reduce your coding time when you discover just why some calls don't quite work as advertised.

The chapter ends with a programming example in Python. Although you may use a different programming language, Python can make illustrating how AWS works easier. All three of the examples (CLI, browser, and Python) at the end of the chapter focus on Simple Storage Service (S3) so that you can see how these three techniques for interacting with AWS compare.

Choosing a Platform

No "right" or "wrong" platform exists to use for AWS development; you should use the one that's best for your intended purpose, given your specific set of programming skills and the requirements of the application. The following sections discuss some of the many options you have in creating a development environment. These sections also tell you about the languages used for the examples in this book and reflect on why I chose these particular languages. You may choose other options for other reasons, and your choices aren't wrong.

Considering the AWS-supported options

To define a platform, you must consider a number of issues. The first consideration is the operating system. When working in the desktop environment, as most developers still do, you have the three basic options:

>> Linux

>> Mac OS/X

>> Windows

AWS provides support for all three of these operating systems in the form of both tools and SDKs. Depending on the specific version of Linux you use, you may have to compile your own tools, but the support is still available. Windows and Mac users have the comfort of knowing that AWS provides binaries that are easy to install and use.

Because both users and developers have become more mobile and demand to perform tasks anywhere, using any device, AWS also provides a level of support for mobile devices. These options currently help developers to work outside the office using a mobile device. However, the support you obtain in these environments can appear limited when compared to the desktop environments. For example, you might not be able to perform some tasks because of limits in the device environment or security concerns. Even so, AWS provides access to three major mobile operating system environments:

>> AWS Mobile SDK for Android

>> AWS Mobile SDK for iOS

>> AWS SDK for Unity

Deciding on an operating system is only the first step. The second step is to choose a programming language. The languages supported often depend on the service you want to use. Some services, such as S3, support a broader range of languages because Amazon expects developers to use them in a wider set of circumstances. However, the following list shows the language that AWS documents as being supported for most services:

>> Go

>> Java

>> JavaScript and Node.js

>> PHP

>> Python

>> Ruby

>> Windows and .NET

>> C++

TIP

You may not see your programming language of choice in this list. Fortunately, a third party may offer the support you need or the AWS documentation might not be complete. When in doubt, look for alternative sources of information for programming language support. For example, the article at https://aws.amazon.com/blogs/big-data/running-r-on-aws/ discusses how to use R with AWS, even though you don't see R listed as one of the supported languages. Given that this is an Amazon blog and not a third-party blog, you need to consider that the AWS documentation is simply outdated and Amazon will change it later.

This book doesn't present you with a preferred language for AWS development because a recommendation isn't possible without knowing your specific business circumstances. In fact, only you can answer the question of which operating systems, languages, and tools to use for your development project. However, you do need to consider these issues when making a choice:

>> **Characteristics:** The characteristics of the operating system, language, and tools you use to work with AWS determine the difficulty of creating applications that users find helpful. For example, even though .NET languages, like C#, have a steep learning curve, they also have a significant array of enterprise-level features and tools that make large enterprise projects easier. However, you might find that data analysis is much easier and faster with Python. If strong multiplatform support is a must, you might want to try Java instead. Developers who specialize in web applications might want to use JavaScript with Node.js. In short, there is no one perfect operating system, language, or toolset — just the combination that works best for you.

>> **Cost:** The choices you make for a platform also depend on cost. The relatively high speed of today's components has erased many of the issues that used to keep people devoted to a particular combination based on speed alone. You can create a platform using open source products that cost little or nothing today.

>> **Local ecosystem:** The skills possessed by the developers in your organization partly determine the platform you create. In addition, you must consider local resources and needs. For example, if your AWS application must interact with Office applications, using a .NET language on Windows might be your only choice, even if another language might actually do the job with a little less effort and at a lower cost. Changing the local ecosystem completely takes time, effort, and skills that your organization might not possess.

>> **Problem domain:** The goal of all applications is to manipulate data. All languages and tools can help you accomplish that task, but some are decidedly better than others at getting the job done. A large part of the process of determining platform characteristics is to determine how, when, where, and why you want to manipulate data. For example, R makes a much better data analysis language than C# does, but C# excels at interacting with other applications, such as Office.

Using JavaScript for browser examples

This book uses JavaScript alone wherever possible for browser examples. The use of JavaScript makes it possible to see precisely what you need to do and how you need to do it when creating web-based AWS applications. In addition, JavaScript is easy to change and instantly run again without the inconvenience of recompiling your application. It also runs on just about every platform out there, even if you choose (as unwieldy as it might be) to try to run code on your smartphone.

REMEMBER

Because a smartphone or tablet isn't a particularly good development environment, this book focuses on using JavaScript with browsers found on Windows, Linux, and Mac systems. The code isn't tested for the various AWS mobile platforms, but should still run as shown in the book. To use the examples, you must have a browser capable of running HTML5 and CSS3 code, along with the latest version of JavaScript.

Some examples will require the use of Node.js. The Node.js library is simply a set of tools that provides a runtime environment for JavaScript applications. The only purpose of using Node.js in this book is to reduce example complexity and make the steps required to interact with AWS clearer.

Using Python for local examples

Python is a good choice for experimenting with AWS because you get nearly instant feedback on the coding you perform with it, plus the language has only a small learning curve. In addition, as with JavaScript, Python is free, open source, and runs on every platform this book supports without any sort of code modification. Other languages also work for this purpose. For example, Java also runs on every platform, but you must use a compiler to work with it, and some developers have security concerns about working with Java.

REMEMBER

This book uses the Continuum Analytics Anaconda Python setup because it provides a notebook environment in which to run code. The notebook actually runs in a browser, so it's extremely flexible and doesn't require you to install a fancy Integrated Development Environment (IDE) to become productive. The Jupyter Notebook environment also supplies a place to display graphics and enables comprehensive commenting in an easily printed (report) format. You find the installation and basic usage instructions for working with Continuum Analytics Anaconda and Jupyter Notebook in "Obtaining and Installing Python," the next section in this chapter. However, you can also use pure Python and its tools to work with the code in this book. It won't be quite as convenient, but some people may prefer the ultimate in interactivity that the pure Python environment provides.

Obtaining and Installing Python

Before you can use Python for the examples in this book, you need a copy installed on your system. Even though you can find a number of Python distributions online, this book uses Continuum Analytics Anaconda version 4.3.1 because it's easy to use and provides a great working environment. The following sections help you obtain, install, and configure Anaconda for use with the examples in this book.

Obtaining Continuum Analytics Anaconda version 4.3.1

The basic Anaconda package is a free download that you obtain at `https://store.continuum.io/cshop/anaconda/`. Simply click Download Anaconda to obtain access to the free product. You do need to provide an email address to get a copy of Anaconda. After giving your email address, you go to another page, where you can choose your platform and the installer for that platform. Anaconda supports the following platforms:

» Windows 32-bit and 64-bit (the installer may offer you only the 64-bit or 32-bit version, depending on which version of Windows it detects)

» Linux 32-bit and 64-bit

» Mac OS X 64-bit

Because library support for Python 3.6 has become better than previous 3.*x* versions, you see both Python 3.*x* and 2.*x* equally supported on the Continuum Analytics site. This book uses Python 3.6 because the library support is now substantial and stable enough to support all the programming examples, and because Python 3.*x* represents the future direction of Python.

WARNING

The Miniconda installer can potentially save time by limiting the number of features you install. However, trying to figure out precisely which packages you do need is an error-prone and time-consuming process. In general, you want to perform a full installation to ensure that you have everything needed for your projects. Even a full install doesn't require much time or effort to download and install on most systems.

CHOOSING A PYTHON VERSION

This book uses the 3.6 version of Python for all the examples. The reason for this choice is that Python 3.6 provides access to a modern set of libraries that work well with AWS. You can also obtain a 2.7 version of Python. The libraries with this version aren't compatible with Python 3.6. In addition, Python 2.7 has some coding differences from the 3.6 version. Developers continue to update Python 2.7 because it offers access to libraries that data scientists commonly need for their work. Unfortunately, you can't use Python 2.7 with the examples in this book without modifying the code and changing the library selections. This book doesn't support Python 2.7.

The free product is all you need for this book. However, when you look on the site, you see that many other add-on products are available. These products can help you create robust applications. For example, when you add Accelerate to the mix, you obtain the capability to perform multicore and GPU-enabled operations. The use of these add-on products is outside the scope of this book, but the Anaconda site provides details on using them.

Installing Python on Linux

You use the command line to install Anaconda on Linux — you're given no graphical installation option. Before you can perform the install, you must download a copy of the Linux software from the Continuum Analytics site. You can find the required download information in the "Obtaining Continuum Analytics Anaconda" section, the preceding section in this chapter. The following procedure should work fine on any Linux system, whether you use the 32-bit or 64-bit version of Anaconda:

1. **Open a copy of Terminal.**

   The Terminal window appears.

2. **Change directories to the downloaded copy of Anaconda on your system.**

   The name of this file varies, but normally it appears as Anaconda3-4.3.1-Linux-x86.sh for 32-bit systems and Anaconda3-4.3.1-Linux-x86_64.sh for 64-bit systems. The version number is embedded as part of the filename. In this case, the filename refers to version 4.3.1, which is the version used for this book. If you use some other version, you may experience problems with the source code and need to make adjustments when working with it.

3. **Type** bash Anaconda3-4.3.1-Linux-x86.sh **(for the 32-bit version) or** bash Anaconda3-4.3.1-Linux-x86_64.sh **(for the 64-bit version) and press Enter.**

   An installation wizard starts that asks you to accept the licensing terms for using Anaconda.

4. **Read the licensing agreement and accept the terms using the method required for your version of Linux.**

   The wizard asks you to provide an installation location for Anaconda. The book assumes that you use the default location of ~/anaconda. If you choose some other location, you may have to modify some procedures later in the book to work with your setup.

5. **Provide an installation location (if necessary) and press Enter (or click Next).**

   The application extraction process begins. After the extraction is complete, you see a completion message.

6. **Add the installation path to your** PATH **statement using the method required for your version of Linux.**

You're ready to begin using Anaconda.

Installing Python on MacOS

The Mac OS X installation comes in only one form: 64-bit. Before you can perform the install, you must download a copy of the Mac software from the Continuum Analytics site. You can find the required download information in the "Obtaining Continuum Analytics Anaconda" section, earlier in this chapter.

The installation files come in two forms. The first depends on a graphical installer; the second relies on the command line. The command-line version works much like the Linux version described in "Installing Python on Linux," the preceding section of this chapter. The following steps help you install Anaconda 64-bit on a Mac system using the graphical installer:

1. **Locate the downloaded copy of Anaconda on your system.**

The name of this file varies, but normally it appears as Anaconda3–4.3.1–MacOSX–x86_64.pkg. The version number is embedded as part of the filename. In this case, the filename refers to version 4.3.1, which is the version used for this book. If you use some other version, you may experience problems with the source code and need to make adjustments when working with it.

2. **Double-click the installation file.**

An introduction dialog box appears.

3. **Click Continue.**

The wizard asks whether you want to review the Read Me materials. You can read these materials later. For now, you can safely skip the information.

4. **Click Continue.**

The wizard displays a licensing agreement. Be sure to read through the licensing agreement so that you know the terms of usage.

5. **Click I Agree if you agree to the licensing agreement.**

The wizard asks you to provide a destination for the installation. The destination controls whether the installation is for an individual user or a group.

WARNING

You may see an error message stating that you can't install Anaconda on the system. The error message occurs because of a bug in the installer and has nothing to do with your system. To get rid of the error message, choose the Install Only for Me option. You can't install Anaconda for a group of users on a Mac system.

6. **Click Continue.**

The installer displays a dialog box containing options for changing the installation type. Click Change Install Location if you want to modify where Anaconda is installed on your system. (The book assumes that you use the default path of ~/anaconda.) Click Customize if you want to modify how the installer works. For example, you can choose not to add Anaconda to your PATH statement. However, the book assumes that you have chosen the default install options, and no good reason exists to change them unless you have another copy of Python 3.6 installed somewhere else.

7. **Click Install.**

The installation begins. A progress bar tells you how the installation process is progressing. When the installation is complete, you see a completion dialog box.

8. **Click Continue.**

You're ready to begin using Anaconda.

Installing Python on Windows

Anaconda comes with a graphical installation application for Windows, so getting a good install means using a wizard, as you would for any other installation. Of course, you need a copy of the installation file before you begin, and you can find the required download information in the "Obtaining Continuum Analytics Anaconda" section, earlier in this chapter. The following procedure should work fine on any Windows system, whether you use the 32-bit or the 64-bit version of Anaconda:

1. **Locate the downloaded copy of Anaconda on your system.**

The name of this file varies, but normally it appears as Anaconda3-4.3.1-Windows-x86.exe for 32-bit systems and Anaconda3-4.3.1-Windows-x86_64.exe for 64-bit systems. The version number is embedded as part of the filename. In this case, the filename refers to version 4.3.1, which is the version used for this book. If you use some other version, you may experience problems with the source code and need to make adjustments when working with it.

2. **Double-click the installation file.**

(*Note:* You may see an Open File — Security Warning dialog box that asks whether you want to run this file. Click Run if you see this dialog box pop up.) You see an Anaconda 4.3.1 Setup dialog box similar to the one shown in Figure 5-1. The exact dialog box that you see depends on which version of the Anaconda installation program you download. If you have a 64-bit operating system, using the 64-bit version of Anaconda is always best so that you obtain the best possible performance. This first dialog box tells you whether you have the 64-bit version of the product.

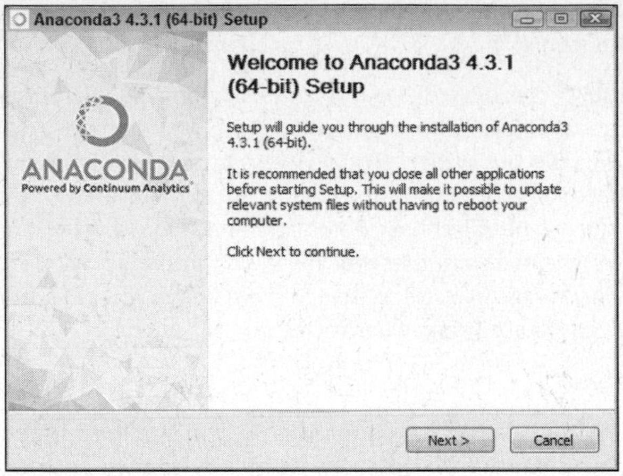

FIGURE 5-1:
The setup
process begins by
telling you
whether you have
the 64-bit version.

3. **Click Next.**

   The wizard displays a licensing agreement. Be sure to read through the licensing agreement so that you know the terms of usage.

4. **Click I Agree if you agree to the licensing agreement.**

   You're asked what sort of installation type to perform, as shown in Figure 5-2. In most cases, you want to install the product just for yourself. The exception is if you have multiple people using your system and they all need access to Anaconda.

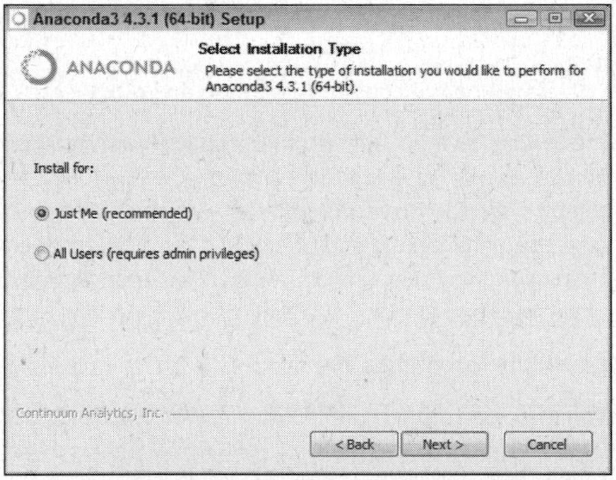

FIGURE 5-2:
Tell the wizard
how to install
Anaconda on
your system.

5. **Choose one of the installation types and then click Next.**

   The wizard asks where to install Anaconda on disk, as shown in Figure 5-3. The book assumes that you use the default location. If you choose some other location, you may have to modify some procedures later in the book to work with your setup.

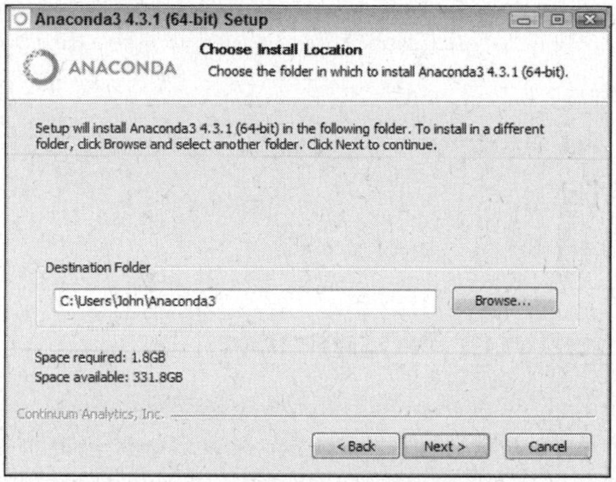

FIGURE 5-3:
Specify an installation location.

6. **Choose an installation location (if necessary) and then click Next.**

   You see the Advanced Installation Options, shown in Figure 5-4. These options are selected by default, and no good reason exists to change them in most cases. You might need to change them if Anaconda won't provide your default Python 3.6 setup. However, the book assumes that you've set up Anaconda using the default options.

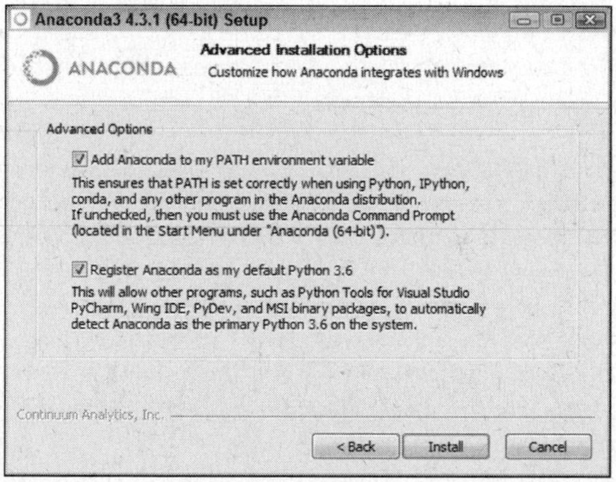

FIGURE 5-4:
Configure the advanced installation options.

7. **Change the advanced installation options (if necessary) and then click Install.**

   You see an Installing dialog box with a progress bar. The installation process can take a few minutes, so get yourself a cup of coffee and read the comics for a while. When the installation process is over, you see a Next button enabled.

8. **Click Next.**

   The wizard tells you that the installation is complete.

9. **Click Finish.**

   You're ready to begin using Anaconda.

Using Jupyter Notebook

To make working with the relatively complex code in this book easier, you use Jupyter Notebook. This interface lets you easily create Python notebook files that can contain any number of examples, each of which can run individually. The program runs in your browser, so which platform you use for development doesn't matter; as long as it has a browser, you should be okay.

A WORD ABOUT THE SCREENSHOTS

As you work your way through the book, you use an IDE of your choice to open the Python and Jupyter Notebook files containing the book's source code. Every screenshot that contains IDE-specific information relies on Anaconda because Anaconda runs on all three platforms supported by the book. The use of Anaconda doesn't imply that it's the best IDE or that the author is making any sort of recommendation for it; Anaconda simply works well as a demonstration product.

When you work with Anaconda, the name of the graphical (GUI) environment, Jupyter Notebook, is precisely the same across all three platforms, and you won't even see any significant difference in the presentation. (Jupyter Notebook is an evolution of IPython, so you may see online resources refer to IPython Notebook.) The differences that you do see are minor, and you should ignore them as you work through the book. With this in mind, the book does rely heavily on Windows 7 screenshots. When working on a Linux, Mac OS X, or other Windows version platform, you should expect to see some differences in presentation, but these differences shouldn't reduce your ability to work with the examples.

Starting Jupyter Notebook

Most platforms provide an icon to access Jupyter Notebook. Just click this icon to access Jupyter Notebook. For example, on a Windows system, you choose Start ⇨ All Programs ⇨ Anaconda 3 ⇨ Jupyter Notebook.

TIP

When working with the latest version of Anaconda, you see a message in the Jupyter Notebook Console that includes the URL you should use when connecting for the first time. The URL takes the form `http://localhost:8888/?token=long_series_of_numbers_and_letters` (where the token value is unique to your system). However, your browser generally opens for you automatically, so you won't have to enter this URL by hand.

WARNING

If you log out of Jupyter Notebook, you need the token value to log back in. Make sure to record the token somewhere safe in case you need it later. However, you generally won't need to supply a token when starting Anaconda locally. The local setup, which is the only one used in this book, automatically supplies the required token.

Figure 5-5 shows how the interface looks when viewed in a Firefox browser. The precise appearance on your system depends on the browser you use and the kind of platform you have installed.

If you have a platform that doesn't offer easy access through an icon, you can use these steps to access Jupyter Notebook:

1. **Open a Command Prompt or Terminal Window on your system.**

   The window opens so that you can type commands.

2. **Change directories to the `\Anaconda3\Scripts` directory on your machine.**

   Most systems let you use the CD command for this task.

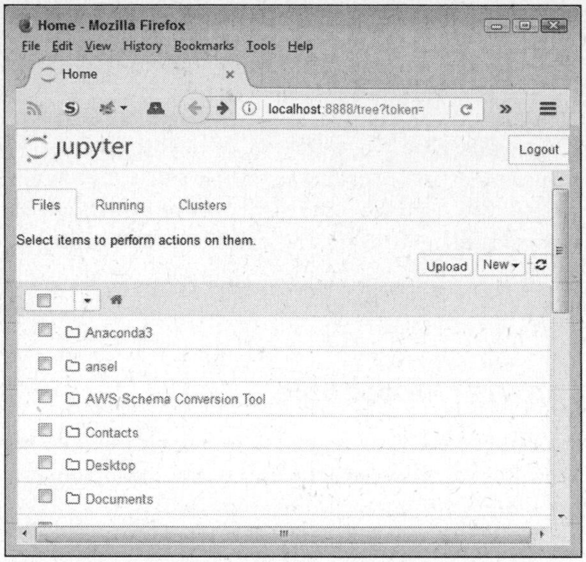

FIGURE 5-5:
Jupyter Notebook provides an easy method to create AWS examples.

3. **Type** python jupyter-notebook-script.py **and press Enter.**

   The Jupyter Notebook page opens in your browser. In general, you don't need to supply a token when starting Jupyter Notebook using this approach.

Stopping the Jupyter Notebook server

Make sure that you log out when you finish a session to ensure that your data is saved. Simply click the Logout in the upper-right corner of the window (as shown in Figure 5-5). If you later choose to log back in, you need the token provided by Anaconda during the initial login.

No matter how you start Jupyter Notebook (or just Notebook, as it appears in the remainder of the book), the system generally opens a command prompt or terminal window to host Jupyter Notebook. This window contains a server that makes the application work. After you close the browser window when a session is complete, select the server window and press Ctrl+C or Ctrl+Break to stop the server.

Defining the code repository

The code you create and use in this book will reside in a repository on your hard drive. Think of a *repository* as a kind of filing cabinet where you put your code. Notebook opens a drawer, takes out the folder, and shows the code to you. You can modify it, run individual examples within the folder, add new examples, and simply interact with your code in a natural manner. The following sections get you started with Notebook so that you can see how this whole repository concept works.

Defining the book's folder

It pays to organize your files so that you can access them easier later. This book keeps its files in the AWS4D4D (*AWS For Developers For Dummies*) folder. Use these steps within Notebook to create a new folder:

1. **(Optional) Navigate to the Documents folder on your system.**

Notebook generally displays the Documents folder in the initial list that it presents to you. If your platform uses a different default user folder to store documents, navigate to that folder instead. The purpose of storing the examples in your documents folder is to avoid potential security issues when running the code later.

2. **Choose New ⇨ Folder.**

Notebook creates a new folder named Untitled Folder, as shown in Figure 5-6. The file appears in alphanumeric order, so you may not initially see it. You must scroll down to the correct location.

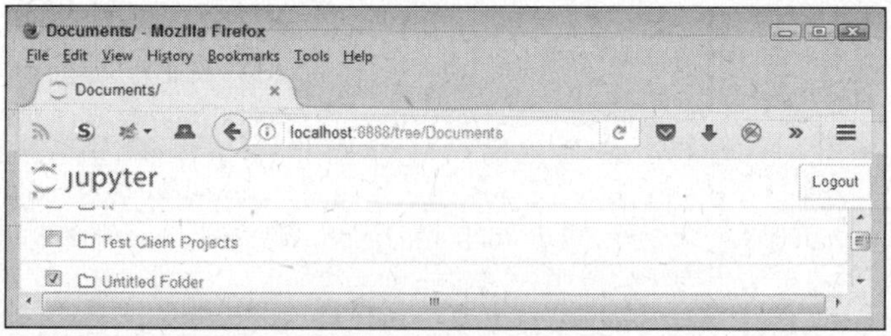

FIGURE 5-6:
New folders appear with a name of Untitled Folder.

3. **Select the box next to the Untitled Folder entry.**

4. **Click Rename at the top of the page.**

You see a Rename Directory dialog box like the one shown in Figure 5-7.

5. **Type AWS4D4D and click OK.**

Notebook changes the name of the folder for you.

6. **Click the new AWS4D4D entry in the list.**

Notebook changes the location to the AWS4D4D folder in which you perform tasks related to the exercises in this book.

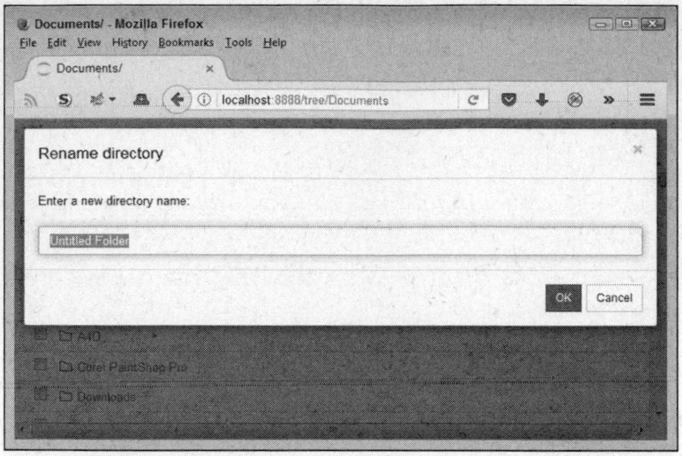

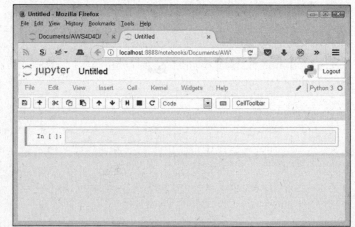

FIGURE 5-7:
Rename the folder so that you remember the kinds of entries it contains.

Creating a new notebook

Every new notebook is like a file folder. You can place individual examples within the file folder, just as you would sheets of paper into a physical file folder. Each example appears in a cell. You can put other sorts of things in the file folder, too, but you see how these things work as the book progresses. Use these steps to create a new notebook:

1. **Click New ➪ Python 3.**

A new tab opens in the browser with the new notebook, as shown in Figure 5-8. Notice that the notebook contains a cell and that Notebook has highlighted the cell so that you can begin typing code in it. The title of the notebook is Untitled right now. That's not a particularly helpful title, so you need to change it.

FIGURE 5-8:
A notebook contains cells that you use to hold code.

2. **Click Untitled on the page.**

   Notebook asks what you want to use as a new name, as shown in Figure 5-9.

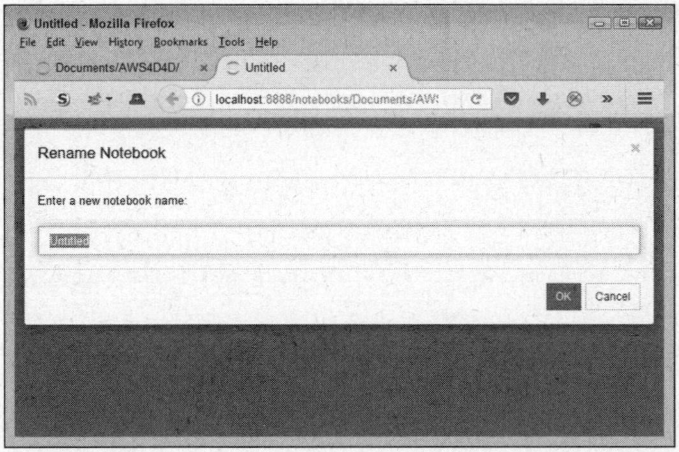

FIGURE 5-9:
Provide a new
name for your
notebook.

3. **Type** AWS4D4D; 05; Sample **and press Enter.**

   The new name tells you that this is a file for *AWS For Developers For Dummies,* Chapter 5, Sample.ipynb (the software automatically adds the correct file extension for you as needed). Using this naming convention lets you easily differentiate these files from other files in your repository.

Of course, the Sample notebook doesn't contain anything just yet. Place the cursor in the cell, type **print('Python is really cool!'),** and then click the Run button (the button with the right-pointing arrow on the toolbar). You see the output shown in Figure 5-10. The output is part of the same cell as the code (the code resides in a square box and the output resides outside that square box, but both are within the cell). However, Notebook visually separates the output from the code so that you can tell them apart. Notebook automatically creates a new cell for you. (The code for this section appears in the AWS4D4D; 05; Sample.ipynb file that is part of the downloadable source for this chapter as described in the Introduction.)

When you finish working with a notebook, shutting it down is important. To close a notebook, choose File ⇨ Close and Halt. You return to the Home page, where you can see that the notebook you just created is added to the list, as shown in Figure 5-11.

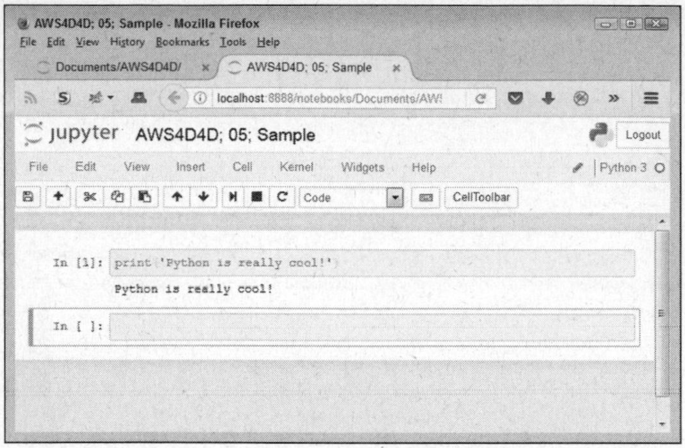

FIGURE 5-10:
Notebook uses cells to store your code.

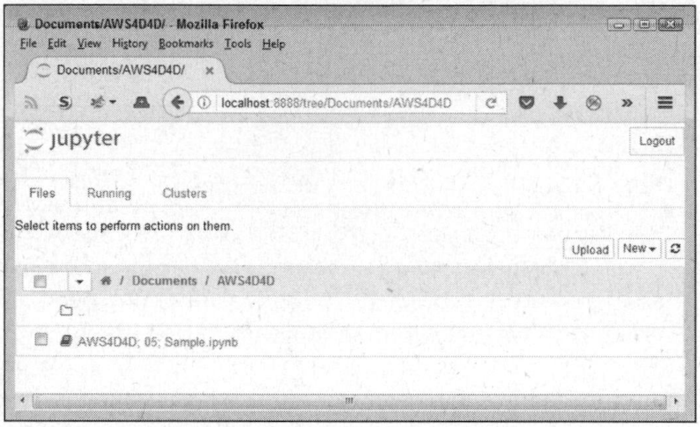

FIGURE 5-11
Any notebooks you create appear in the repository list.

Exporting a notebook

Creating notebooks and keeping them all to yourself isn't much fun. At some point, you want to share them with other people. To perform this task, you must export your notebook from the repository to a file. You can then send the file to someone else, who will import it into his or her repository.

The previous section shows how to create a notebook named AWS4D4D; 05; Sample. You can open this notebook by clicking its entry in the repository list. The file reopens so that you can see your code again. To export this code, choose File⇨Download As⇨Notebook (.ipynb). What you see next depends on your browser, but you generally see some sort of dialog box for saving the notebook as a file. Use the same method for saving the IPython Notebook file as you use for any other file you save using your browser.

Removing a notebook

Sometimes notebooks get outdated or you simply don't need to work with them any longer. Rather than allow your repository to get clogged with files you don't need, you can remove these unwanted notebooks from the list. Use these steps to remove the file:

1. **Select the box next to the AWS4D4D; 05; Sample.ipynb entry.**

2. **Click the trash can icon (Delete) at the top of the page.**

You see a Delete notebook warning message like the one shown in Figure 5-12.

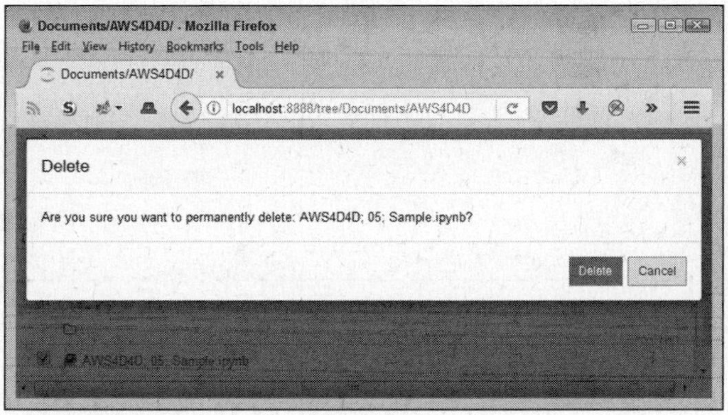

FIGURE 5-12: Notebook warns you before removing any files from the repository.

3. **Click Delete.**

The notebook file gets removed from the list.

Importing a notebook

To use the source code from this book, you must import the downloaded files into your repository. The source code comes in an archive file that you extract to a location on your hard drive. The archive contains a list of .ipynb (IPython Notebook) files containing the source code for this book (see the Introduction for details on downloading the source code). The following steps tell how to import these files into your repository:

1. **Click Upload at the top of the page.**

What you see depends on your browser. In most cases, you see some type of File Upload dialog box that provides access to the files on your hard drive.

2. **Navigate to the directory containing the files that you want to import into Notebook.**

3. **Highlight one or more files to import and click the Open (or other, similar) button to begin the upload process.**

   You see the file added to an upload list, as shown in Figure 5-13. The file isn't part of the repository yet — you've simply selected it for upload.

TIP

When you export a file, Notebook converts any special characters to a form that your system will accept with greater ease. The semicolons appear as %3B, and spaces appear as a + (plus sign). You must change these characters to their Notebook form to see the title as you expect it. Figure 5-13 shows the filename with this change in place.

4. **Click Upload.**

   Notebook places the file in the repository so that you can begin using it.

Working with the Identity and Access Management Console

Part of the reason you need to work with the Identity and Access Management (IAM) Console is to define your specific access to AWS and obtain your access keys as you did in the "Getting access keys" section of Chapter 2. However, that's really just the tip of the iceberg. In addition to creating access for yourself, you must often configure and test different levels of access to simulate the users your application supports. This means considering various security issues that you might not have to consider on your local network. The following sections help you through some of the details of working with IAM with regard to developing AWS applications. These sections won't make you a full-fledged administrator, but you gain the tools needed to develop robust applications.

Configuring root access

Even though the setup used for this book is experimental, you still don't want third parties to have access to it. In addition, if you maintain slack security for your test setup, any experiments you perform won't show real-world security conditions. The "Getting access keys" section of Chapter 2 shows how to obtain your developer keys after creating a basic account. When you navigate to the Identity and Access Management (IAM) Console at `https://console.aws.amazon.com/iam/`, you see there are still three steps to complete to configure basic security for your system, as shown in Figure 5-14. When you complete these steps using the techniques found in the following sections, you have a secure test platform that supports a single user, which is you. Obviously, you can add test users as needed later.

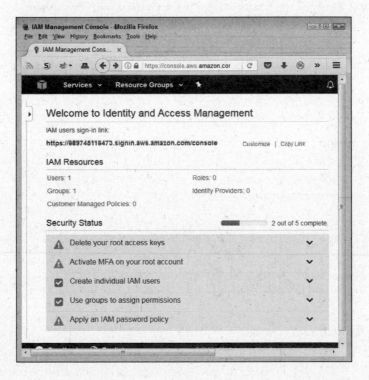

FIGURE 5-14: Complete the security configuration for your test setup.

Deleting the root access keys

Removing your root access keys makes it less likely that someone will gain access to your AWS setup and lock you out of it or corrupt your setup. The Amazon documentation provides a host of other reasons for this action, but from a developer perspective, when working on a test setup, these are the two main concerns. Using accounts with specific levels of access is important in maintaining security. The following steps help you delete your root access keys.

1. **Click Delete Your Root Access Keys in the IAM Management Console.**

You see a Manage Security Credentials button.

2. **Click Manage Security Credentials.**

Amazon tells you about the security credentials page for your AWS account.

3. **Click Continue to Security Credentials.**

You see the Your Security Credentials page, shown in Figure 5-15.

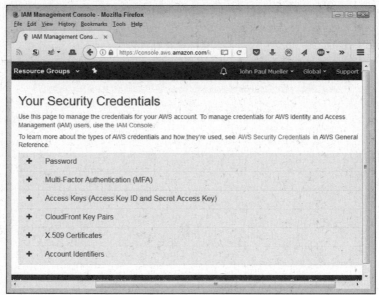

FIGURE 5-15: The Your Security Credentials page contains security information for root access to your account.

4. **Click Access Keys.**

You see a listing of access keys for your root access account. These keys are different from your user access account keys, which you save to a file in Chapter 2.

REMEMBER

Note the Create New Access Key button in this area. You can always create a new root access account key later if needed for a specific purpose. All you are doing now is removing the access so that no one can gain access to your root access account using programmatic means.

5. **Click Delete in the Actions column.**

   You see a warning message stating that you can't recreate the key later.

6. **Click Yes.**

   Amazon deletes the access key.

Using Multi-Factor Authentication (MFA)

MFA can be a complex issue with Amazon because you have a number of choices available to you. The summary presented at `https://aws.amazon.com/iam/details/mfa/` provides details on each of the options. Only three of these options work with your root access account, and only one of them is free at that level:

>> **Virtual MFA Device (free):** You use a smartphone or tablet device that adheres to the Time-Based One-Time Password (TOTP) algorithm standard (`https://tools.ietf.org/html/rfc6238`).

>> **Hardware Key Fob MFA Device (paid):** You obtain a special key fob from Amazon to identify yourself using a technique that's similar to that used by many financial institutions.

>> **Hardware Display Card MFA Device (paid):** You obtain a special credit card-like device from Amazon to identify yourself.

Each of these options has a different setup. You begin by clicking Activate MFA on Your Root Account in the display shown in Figure 5-14. Click Manage MFA next. You see a dialog box in which you choose the kind of MFA you want to use; then you follow the custom prompts to perform the required configuration.

Creating a password policy

A password policy helps ensure that anyone using the AWS services must use a password that hackers are less likely to break. Normally, administrators worry about password policies as part of the AWS configuration process. However, as a developer, you also need to be aware of these policies so that you can verify that they work with your application as part of the testing process. Unless you test against actual policies, your application may experience login problems or other security issues that you never envisioned during the testing process.

WARNING

Always assume that someone can break your security given enough time, resources, and desire to do so. Strong passwords, good security settings, reduced permissions, and so on all help give hackers a good reason to go bother someone else, but they never create a high enough barrier that a determined hacker won't break into your system. Consequently, in addition to all the best practices discussed in this chapter, you must employ monitoring to discover potential break-ins. In addition, conducting security audits and relying on third-party security firms are helpful to verify that the policies you have in place actually do work.

As part of creating your developer setup, configure the password policy to match the one used by your organization or the password policy you intend to use when the application goes live. The following steps tell you how to perform this task:

1. **Click Apply an IAM Password Policy in the IAM Management Console.**

You see the Manage Password Policy button.

2. **Click Manage Password Policy.**

You see the Password Policy page, shown in Figure 5-16.

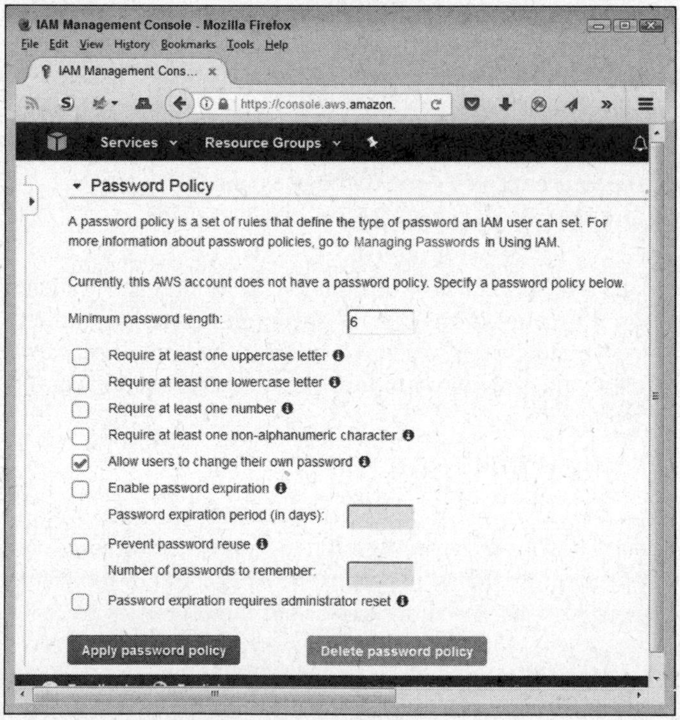

FIGURE 5-16:
Define a password policy that matches the one used by your organization.

3. **Check the entries that match the password policy for your organization.**

TIP

The black circle with a lowercase *i* icon provides you with additional information about each policy. To see the information, simply hover your mouse over the icon.

4. **Click Apply Password Policy.**

You see a message stating that AWS successfully updated the password policy.

Signing into a user account

Look again at Figure 5-14. Until now, you have used the root access login for your account, which can be a source of potential security problems when someone gains access to your system. To overcome this issue, you need to use the user access login instead. To accomplish this task, you use the link shown under the IAM Users Sign-in Link label, which is `https://889745118473.signin.aws.amazon.com/console` in Figure 5-14. The user level login URL for your site will differ from the one shown in the figure because you have a different account. Make sure to log out of the root access page before you log in to the user access page.

The user access login page looks like the one shown in Figure 5-17. However, the account number shown on your page differs from the one shown. To log into the user account, type your username and password in the fields supplied and then click Sign In. The page you see next looks similar to the one used for root access, except that you have access only to services and features specifically allowed by your user account.

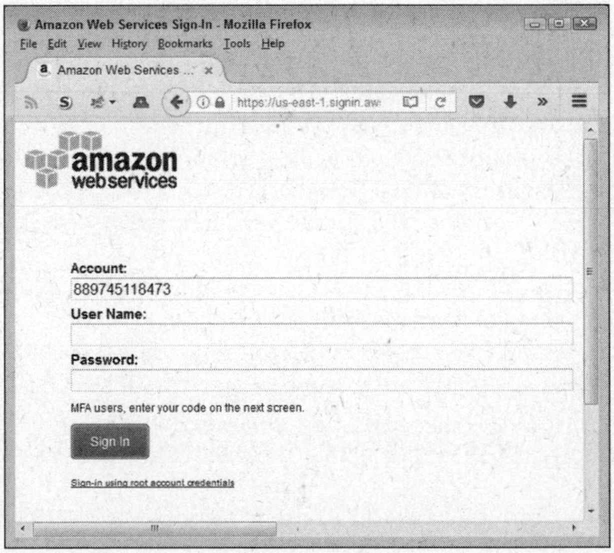

FIGURE 5-17:
Log in to your user account to perform development tasks.

Installing the Command Line Interface Software

CLI is an essential part of working with AWS, especially for a developer. You can use CLI to perform quick setups, determine whether specific calls worked as intended, obtain status information, and so on. There isn't anything new about CLI. After all, developers have used the command prompt or terminal window on desktop systems to perform various tasks for years. In fact, some developers create extensive batch file and script libraries to perform common tasks in the desktop environment. Using CLI with AWS is more of the same, despite the fact that you use it in a cloud environment. However, unlike the command prompt and terminal window, you don't have CLI installed on your system by default. With this in mind, the following sections help you get CLI installed and tested for use with the examples throughout the rest of the book.

Getting started with CLI

The AWS CLI software depends on Python. Consequently, in order to install CLI, you must first install Python using the techniques found in the "Obtaining and Installing Python" section of the chapter. The current version of CLI requires that you have one of the following:

>> Python 2.6.5 or above

>> Python 3.3 or above

The version of Python you installed for this book will work fine. Installing Anaconda also installs the pip utility that you use to perform various Python-specific tasks in the book. If you choose not to use Anaconda, you may need to install pip using the instructions found at https://pip.pypa.io/en/stable/installing/. However, you can check for pip by typing **pip --version** and pressing Enter at a command prompt or within a terminal window. If pip is present, you see the pip version number, location, and Python version number.

After you know that you have Python and pip installed, type **pip install --upgrade awscli** and press Enter to install CLI. The `install` command tells pip to install a package. The `--upgrade` option tells pip to upgrade any packages required to support CLI. The `awscli` keyword tells pip what to install, which is the AWS CLI. (Note that Amazon recommends using the `--user` option, which does install AWS CLI in a different folder, but also makes AWS CLI harder to access and use.)

After you press Enter, pip displays a series of messages telling you about the installation process. When the process completes, you return to the command prompt, as shown in Figure 5-18. At this point, CLI is ready for use.

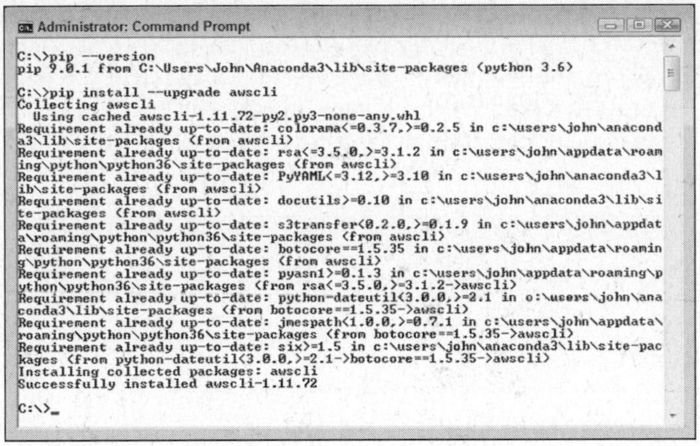

FIGURE 5-18:
You see
installation
messages as pip
does its work.

To verify that your installation works, type **aws --version** and press Enter. You see information about AWS CLI, as shown in Figure 5-19. Depending on your setup, you may also see a warning message about a lack of a file association for the .py file type, which you can ignore for this book.

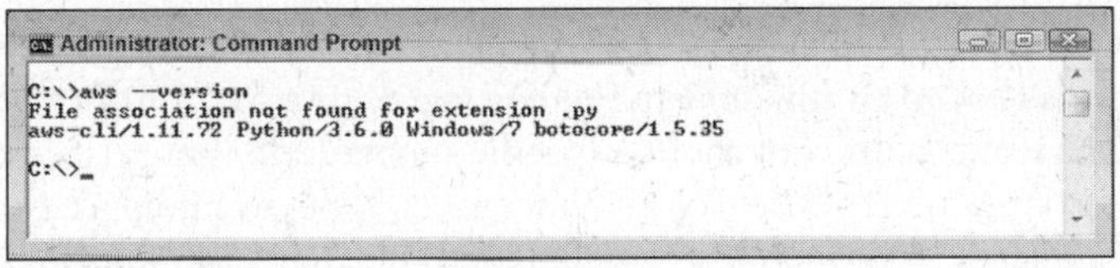

FIGURE 5-19:
Test your AWS CLI
setup by checking
its version
information.

Obtaining additional information and help

As with AWS, CLI is quite complex in its abilities. It has to be, given that you can access every AWS service using it. Consequently, this chapter and those that follow give you an overview of what you can do, rather than a precise description of everything possible. It would take a book, or even two, devoted to that topic to describe everything CLI can do.

Because of CLI's complexity, you need to know how to obtain help when you need it to perform specific tasks. The first place to look is on the AWS site at https:// aws.amazon.com/cli/. This site provides you with access to tools such as a CLI reference and access to the community forum. The community forum is especially important because you can use it to obtain answers to questions that no one else has thought to ask about and those special situations where it looks like there is a glitch in CLI's behavior (and it often turns out that there really is one). The AWS site also provides you with usage examples and other useful information for working with CLI.

The second place to look is AWS itself. Type **aws help** at the command line and press Enter. You see the first page of a multipage help screen, like the one shown in Figure 5-20. Notice the -- More -- entry at the bottom. This entry tells you there is more information to see. Press the spacebar to see it.

The aws help command can provide you with a lot of information. For example, if you want to find out about a specific service, add that service name to the end of the command. To discover more about S3, type **aws help s3** and press Enter. You see a list of additional S3 command options. Say that you want to discover more about configuring S3. In this case, you type **aws help s3-config** and press Enter. The S3 overview help provides you with this more detailed help topic, so you can drill down as you need more information to perform specific tasks.

Configuring S3 Using CLI

After you have CLI installed on your system using the instructions found in the previous section of this chapter, you can begin using it to perform useful tasks. For a developer, that means being able to perform configuration, check status, and do other sorts of low-level tasks with the various AWS services. The following sections look at how you can use CLI to perform essential tasks with S3. Going through these exercises helps you better understand how S3 works, in addition to allowing you to perform development-required tasks.

Creating the aws utility configuration file

To use the aws utility to perform tasks using AWS CLI, you must create a configuration file. The configuration file contains a number of pieces of information, including both your public and secret keys (see the "Getting access keys" section of Chapter 2 for details). The following steps help you perform this configuration task:

1. **Open a command prompt or terminal window.**

2. **Type** aws configure **and press Enter.**

You see a prompt asking for your public key, as shown in Figure 5-21. (None of the screenshots in this section actually show the keys, which have been blanked out for security reasons.)

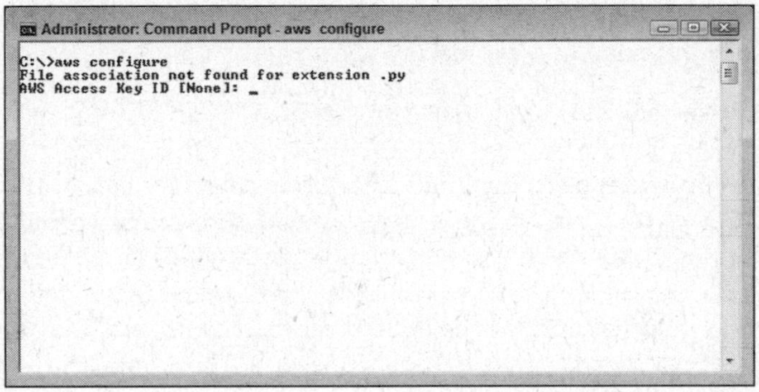

FIGURE 5-21:
Provide the public key that you obtained from AWS.

```
C:\>aws configure
File association not found for extension .py
AWS Access Key ID [None]: _
```

3. **Type your public key string and press Enter.**

In most cases, you can copy and paste your key directly from the .csv file used to store it. The method you use depends on your operating system. For example, when working at the Windows command prompt, you right-click and choose Paste from the context menu. You see a prompt asking for your private key.

4. **Type your private (secret) key string and press Enter.**

You see a prompt asking for the default region used to access data. The region you provide, such as us-west-2, should match the region you use when interacting with AWS from the consoles. A list of regions appears at http://docs.aws.amazon.com/AmazonRDS/latest/UserGuide/Concepts.RegionsAndAvailabilityZones.html. The examples in this book rely on us-west-2; however, the use of this particular region won't affect the results you see when working with a different region.

5. **Type the region information and press Enter.**

The configuration routine asks for an output format. Choose one of the following options (the book relies on `table` output for the sake of clarity; aws uses `json` by default):

- `json`: The default format outputs the data using the JavaScript Object Notation (JSON) technique, which relies on name/value pairs. An advantage of this format is that it works well for direct input with some languages, such as Python. You can see a basic JSON tutorial at `https://www.w3schools.com/js/js_json_intro.asp`.

- `text`: Outputs the data using simple text. The advantage of this approach is that no formatting is involved, so you can easily modify it to meet any need. However, the output can be a little hard to read.

- `table`: Outputs the data using table-formatted text. The advantage of this approach is that the output is easily read directly at the command line.

6. **Type the output format and press Enter.**

You return to the command prompt.

TECHNICAL STUFF

The configuration command creates two new files for you. Both of these files appear in the `.aws` folder on your system. The precise location depends on the operating system you use. For example, on a Windows system, you generally find the files in the `C:\Users\<UserName>\.aws` folder. After you complete this task, the `config` file contains the region you want to use and the output format. However, you can add other entries as needed. The `credentials` file contains your public and private keys.

Obtaining S3 information

To ensure that your aws utility works as expected, you need to try a test access of AWS. Type **aws s3 ls** and press Enter. You begin with the aws utility, followed by the name of the service you want to access, which is `s3`. The `ls` command lists the content of an S3 object. Because you haven't provided a specific location in S3, what you see as output is a listing of the S3 buckets you've created, as shown in Figure 5-22. Note that the output contains the execution date and time. The bucket name will match the name you provided, rather than the name shown in the figure.

You can try uploading a file to your bucket. To perform this task, you use the copy or `cp` command. The `cp` command requires that you provide a source location and a destination location. The source and destination can be a local folder or S3 bucket. Although you wouldn't use this technique to perform a local copy, you can copy from a local folder to an S3 bucket, from an S3 bucket to a local folder, or between S3 buckets. For example, to copy a file named `colorblk.gif` from a local folder named win to the S3 bucket, you would type something like `aws s3 cp "c:\win\colorblk.gif" s3://aws4d.test-bucket/colorblk.gif` and press Enter. You must provide a source and destination that match your setup. To ensure that the file is actually uploaded, you use the `ls` command again, but this time you add the bucket name. Figure 5-23 shows the result of a successful copy and listing.

```
Administrator: Command Prompt

C:\>aws s3 ls
File association not found for extension .py
2017-03-14 09:22:04 aws4d.test-bucket

C:\>_
```

```
Administrator: Command Prompt

C:\>aws s3 cp "c:\win\colorblk.gif" s3://aws4d.test-bucket/colorblk.gif
File association not found for extension .py
upload: win\colorblk.gif to s3://aws4d.test-bucket/colorblk.gif

C:\>aws s3 ls aws4d.test-bucket
File association not found for extension .py
2017-04-06 11:03:55        1715 colorblk.gif

C:\>_
```

Configuring S3 Using Node.js

One method for interacting with S3 that works essentially the same way across all platforms, even mobile ones, is to rely on a browser. When coupled with HTML5, CSS3, and JavaScript, a browser provides a powerful method for interacting with AWS. Using best practices ensures that your browser application remains secure, provides a robust and reliable application environment, and allows users to perform required tasks anywhere using any device. Given that most users expect this level of flexibility today, knowing how to make a browser environment work properly is important.

REMEMBER

You actually have multiple ways to make your browser interact with AWS using JavaScript, and you can find them at https://aws.amazon.com/javascript/. This book uses the Node.js approach because it's the easiest, requires no additional downloads except Node.js, and presents how to work with JavaScript in the clearest manner. The following sections get you started using Node.js with S3.

Installing Node.js

Node.js is a development environment and library of routines and helps automate development tasks. Most web developers rely heavily on automation because they simply don't have time to reinvent the wheel with every project (and no strong need to do so; in fact, it's counterproductive). Using Node.js not only reduces the time and complexity of writing applications but also makes interactions with them more consistent. It's a lightweight, efficient library based on Chrome's V8 JavaScript engine.

TIP

To get your copy of Node.js, navigate to the Node.js site at https://nodejs.org/en/download/ and download a version that matches your platform. You may find that your setup works better when the copy you download also matches your browser. If you're using a 32-bit browser, get 32-bit Node.js. In addition, get a binary version rather than source code if at all possible to reduce the amount of work you need to do.

After you have the file on your machine, open the file and follow the prompts presented by the wizard to complete the installation. Avoid installing Node.js in a path with a space it in — spaces tend to cause problems when working in certain environments, so avoiding them works best. The examples in this book assume that you have used an installation directory of C:\nodejs\.

Configuring Node.js

Before you can use Node.js, you need to configure it to interact with AWS. The following steps get you started:

1. **Open a Node.js Command Prompt.**

   A Node.js command prompt window appears. The Node.js Command Prompt appears with the other Node.js icons. For example, when working with Windows, you choose Start ➪ All Programs ➪ Node.js ➪ Node.js Command Prompt.

2. **Change directories to your Node.js directory.**

   For example, if you used the recommended installation folder for Windows, you'd type **CD \nodejs** and press Enter.

3. **Type** npm init **and press Enter.**

   The Node.js Package Manager (npm) utility helps you configure your Node.js installation. The init command takes you through the process of creating a package.json file. Creating the package.json file prevents some errors during the AWS library installation, but you don't really do anything with it in this book.

4. **Press Enter after each of the questions presented by the wizard.**

   Eventually you see a summary of the entries. The npm utility will ask whether the entries are OK.

5. **Type** y **(for yes) and press Enter.**

The npm utility creates the package.json file.

6. **Type** npm install aws-sdk **and press Enter.**

The npm utility installs the AWS SDK as a package (essentially a kind of library). You may see a message stating, WARN nodejs@1.0.0 No repository field. It's safe to ignore the error message. Node.js is now configured for use.

Dealing with credentials

As with any other access to your AWS account, you must provide security credentials to make a call. You may see all sorts of convoluted ways to perform this task. However, the easiest way to get the job done is to let CLI do it for you. The steps in the "Creating the aws utility configuration file" section, earlier in this chapter, create required configuration files that Node.js can use as well.

Dealing with Cross Origin Resource Sharing (CORS)

Modern browsers prevent you from accessing resources on another domain within a script because doing so can cause significant security issues. A hacker could modify a script to download a virus or other unwanted content without the user's permission or knowledge. However, given the way in which users interact with the Internet today, being able to access resources, such as files, from another domain is not only useful, it's required. Using CORS enables people to share resources in a secure way. This book doesn't detail precisely how this process happens, but you can read about it at https://developer.mozilla.org/en-US/docs/Web/HTTP/Access_control_CORS.

As with any other resource on another domain, you must make your S3 bucket available to JavaScript before you can do anything with it. AWS doesn't enable CORS support by default because Amazon has no way of knowing how you want to share resources. Consequently, you must enable CORS support for your S3 bucket by writing a CORS configuration, which, oddly enough, requires use of XML. The following steps tell you how to configure S3 to enable CORS:

1. **Sign in to AWS using your user account.**

2. **Navigate to the S3 Console at** https://console.aws.amazon.com/s3.

You see the S3 bucket created in the "Testing Your Setup" section of Chapter 2. If not, you need to recreate the bucket, because browser-based operations are bucket specific.

3. **Click the link for your S3 bucket.**

   AWS presents the bucket details, as shown in Figure 5-24. (The bucket details will differ from those shown in the figure.)

FIGURE 5-24: Open your bucket to enable CORS on it.

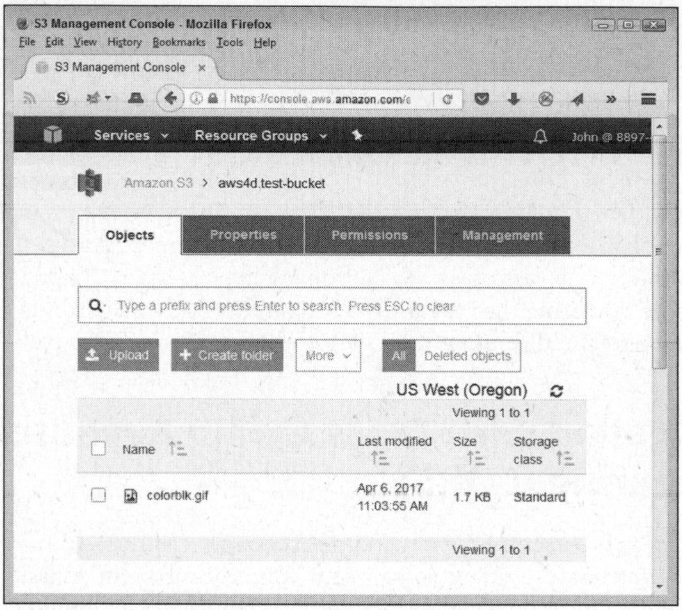

4. **Open the Permissions tab.**

   Note the options for managing bucket security shown in Figure 5-25, including CORS configuration. Enabling CORS does allow a browser access to the S3 resources, but a user must still authenticate to gain any privileges, and those privileges appear as part of a bucket policy.

5. **Click CORS Configuration.**

   You see the sample CORS configuration, shown in Figure 5-26. Note that the ARN for the bucket appears as part of the information near the top. The sample policy provides access to everyone using the `GET` method, but only for the purpose of authorization. Without any other headers defined, CORS is effectively disabled. You find a list of common headers at `http://docs.aws.amazon.com/AmazonS3/latest/API/RESTCommonRequestHeaders.html`.

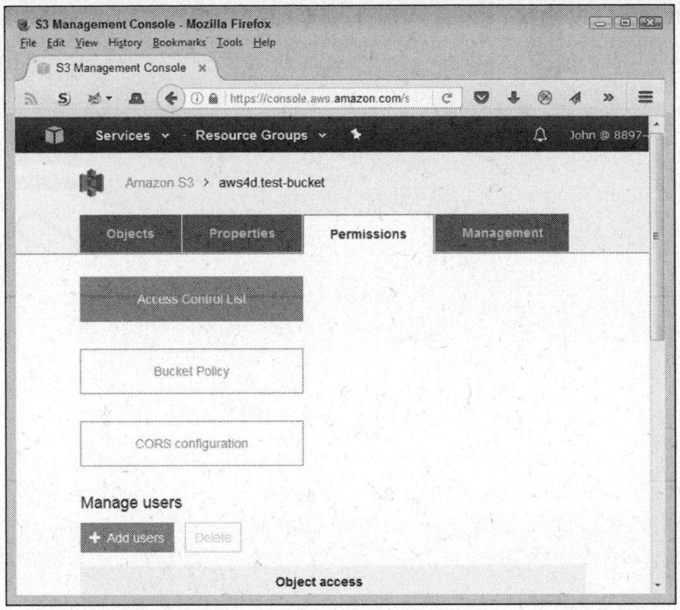

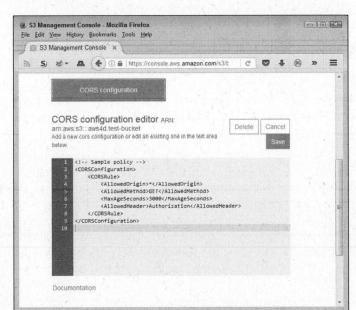

FIGURE 5-25:
Bucket security
relies on more
than just CORS.

FIGURE 5-26:
The default CORS
configuration
doesn't provide
any useful access.

6. **Modify the sample CORS configuration entry to look like the following code:**

```
<CORSConfiguration>
    <CORSRule>
        <AllowedOrigin>*</AllowedOrigin>
        <AllowedMethod>GET</AllowedMethod>
        <AllowedMethod>POST</AllowedMethod>
        <AllowedMethod>PUT</AllowedMethod>
        <AllowedMethod>DELETE</AllowedMethod>
        <AllowedHeader>*</AllowedHeader>
    </CORSRule>
</CORSConfiguration>
```

The changes allow the browser to make REST calls to obtain information, upload new files, and delete existing files, among other things, using the GET, POST, PUT, and DELETE REST methods. However, before any of this can happen, the user must still have permission to perform the tasks.

7. **Click Save.**

AWS enables CORS using the policy you put in place.

Making a call

After completing the work required to make Node.js interact with AWS, you can finally use it to do something interesting. The following steps show how to interact with AWS using Node.js. Of course, you use Node.js quite often as the book progresses.

1. **Type** var AWS = require('aws-sdk'); **and press Enter.**

Note the ending semicolon for the command. This command loads the aws-sdk library that you installed in the "Configuring Node.js" section of the chapter. If you see an error, go through the steps in that section again to ensure that you have a good install. You also need to ensure that you have configured your security credentials before proceeding.

2. **Type** s3 = new AWS.S3(); **and press Enter.**

You can specify certain arguments for this call, but accepting the defaults works best. This command provides you with access to the S3 service commands. The output from this command shows all sorts of information about the S3 service and your interaction with it. For example, you find your public access key in the list of items. You also find information about service settings and the endpoints used to access it.

3. **Type the following code, precisely as shown, pressing Enter at the end of each line:**

```
s3.listBuckets(function(err, data) {
    if (err) {
        console.log("Error", err);
    } else {
        console.log("Bucket List", data.Buckets);
    }
});
```

4. **Press Enter an additional time.**

   You see a long list of output that details precisely how Node.js makes the call. For example, you discover the handshaking used to create the initial connection. However, the final two lines tell you what you need to know:

```
Bucket List [ { Name: 'aws4d.test-bucket',
    CreationDate: 2017-03-14T14:22:04.000Z } ]
```

Experimenting at the Node.js prompt is interesting and helpful when you're trying something new, but it isn't permanent. You can create a file that contains all the commands you just typed and save it on disk. In fact, you can find this file as List Buckets.js in the downloadable source code for this chapter (the book's Introduction tells you how to find it). To run this file, copy it to your \nodejs folder, open a command prompt, and then type **node ListBuckets** and press Enter. Don't include the file extension. Figure 5-27 shows sample output from this command.

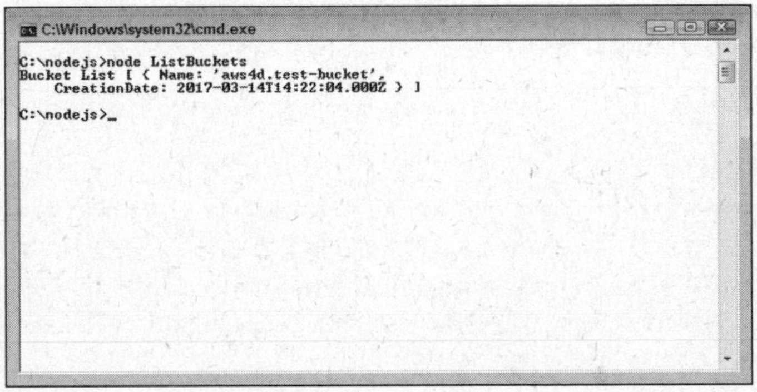

C:\nodejs>node ListBuckets
Bucket List [{ Name: 'aws4d.test-bucket',
    CreationDate: 2017-03-14T14:22:04.000Z }]

C:\nodejs>_

FIGURE 5-27:
The JavaScript commands you create can appear within a file.

Configuring S3 Using a Desktop Application

Even though many people consider the desktop dead, it still represents the most powerful and flexible method of interacting with AWS services. Using desktop applications also enable you to create environments in which local resources and cloud resources interact seamlessly under a level of control that isn't possible using other approaches. In addition, the desktop environment often provides the developer with access to unique resources and leverages a developer's full grasp of various programming languages. With this in mind, this section of the chapter demonstrates how to create an application that interacts with S3 using a desktop application written using Python.

Installing boto

Python uses a library named boto to interact with AWS. As with all Python libraries, it's easy to install if you have the pip utility installed. Anaconda comes with pip, so you shouldn't have to do anything special to perform the installation. To install boto, open a command prompt or terminal window, type **pip install boto3** (don't type the comma), and press Enter. The installation should go quickly. After a few installation lines, you should see a success message. You can read more about boto at https://aws.amazon.com/sdk-for-python/.

Listing S3 buckets

The process for getting the bucket list in Python is quite short. (You can access this example code in the AWS4D4D; 05; ListBuckets.ipynb file for this chapter in the downloadable source, as explained in the Introduction.) First, you need to access the boto library using this code:

```
from boto.s3.connection import S3Connection
```

Now that you have library access, create a connection to the library using this code:

```
conn = S3Connection('AccessKey', 'PrivateKey')
```

Make sure to provide your public access key as the first argument and your private access key as the second argument. The connection, conn, gives you access to all the S3 information. The following code retrieves a list of all your buckets and displays their names onscreen:

```
buckets = conn.get_all_buckets()
for bucket in buckets:
    print(bucket.name)
```

Chapter **6**

Creating a Virtual Server Using EC2

Most developers who create major Amazon Web Services (AWS) applications interact with Elastic Compute Cloud (EC2) at some point because EC2 enables you to move the computing environment to the cloud. Even though working with a local server might be easier for the developer, users demand "anywhere" access to applications using any device. Consequently, your cloud-based application must remain accessible to a range of devices, from smartphones to desktop PCs, and from any location imaginable (as well as a few locations you might not consider). A local server setup can't provide this sort of environment; you really do need to move to the cloud. The first section of this chapter considers the issue of availability, among many other EC2 development-related issues.

As a developer, you need several methods for configuring EC2. This chapter considers two of them: the console and the Command Line Interface (CLI). You have other options as well, such as writing an application to perform the task, but these two options represent the best way to get started. In general, you use the console when performing an administrator-level initial configuration and CLI when performing tweaks to observe application performance under various conditions. However, both options provide full EC2 access.

AWS provides you with several storage options. Chapter 5 discusses access to Simple Storage Service (S3), which is great for short-term storage or for storing objects of various kinds. However, many developers are more acquainted with block storage of the type provided by Elastic Block Store (EBS). In this case, you have access to a directory-like structure that provides a familiar way to interact with data. You can combine EBS with Glacier to create a long-term, archived storage solution.

When you create an EC2 instance, you can access various kinds of storage after performing the required configuration. Two common storage types are instance stores, which provide temporary block storage that doesn't survive instance stops, and image stores, which offer longer-term storage. Each kind of storage has a place in your development strategy, and the last part of the chapter explains how.

Getting to Know the Elastic Compute Cloud (EC2)

Consider the meaning of *elastic* in many of the AWS service names. When you see the word *elastic*, you should think of the ability to stretch and contract. All the AWS documentation alludes to this fact, but it often makes the whole process sound quite complicated when it really isn't. Just think about a computer that can stretch when you need more resources and contract when you don't. With AWS, you pay only for the services you actually use, so this capability to stretch and contract is important because it means that your organization can spend less money and still end up with just the right amount of services needed.

REMEMBER

Even though some members of your organization might fixate on the issue of money, the real value behind the term *elastic* is time. Keeping your own equipment right sized is time consuming, especially when you need to downsize. Using EC2 means that you can add or remove computing capacity in just a few minutes, rather than weeks or months. Because new requirements tend to change quickly today, the capability to right-size your capacity in minutes is crucial, especially if you really do want that pay raise.

Understanding basic EC2 configuration

From a developer perspective, the elastic nature of EC2 enables you to translate your development environment into something that you could only simulate in the past — a test environment in which you can consider the trade-offs presented by various configurations. Having an elastic environment means that you can actually test your application under various conditions so that you can make configuration recommendations based on real-world knowledge. In addition, you can simulate failure conditions and thereby build a troubleshooting notebook before you release an application to production. Just as you do with your local server, you have choices to make when building an EC2 *instance* (a single session used to perform one or more related tasks). The instance can have these characteristics:

>> **Operating system:** Linux or Windows.

>> **Instance size:** You can size the instance to provide a small number of services or to act as a cluster of computers for huge computing tasks (and everything in between). In fact, you can create optimized instances for tasks that require more resources in the following areas:

- CPU

- Memory

- Storage

- GPU

As the tasks that you assign to an instance change, so can the instance configuration. You can adjust just the memory allocation for an instance or provide more storage when needed. Most developers don't worry too much about how much things cost, but that situation changes as you move to the cloud. Your test system will require an investment, so knowing your options could reduce operating costs and make you look better in the boss's eyes. Here are the pricing models available with EC2:

>> **On Demand:** You pay for what you use.

>> **Reserved Instance:** Provides a significantly reduced price in return for a one-time payment based on what you think you might need in the way of service.

>> **Spot Instance:** Lets you name the price you want to pay, with the price affecting the level of service you receive.

WARNING

Autoscaling is an EC2 feature that you use to ensure that your instance automatically changes configuration as the load on it changes. Although it represents a great solution for administrators on production systems, it could pose problems for developers in the test environment because you can't be sure about the characteristics of your test setup. In general, you want to avoid using autoscaling on test systems so that you can maintain firmer control over test conditions.

CONSIDERING WHAT AUTOSCALING DOES

Rather than require someone to manage EC2 constantly, you can allow the instance to make some changes as needed based on the requirements you specify. The metrics you define determine the number and type of instances that EC2 runs. The metrics include standards, such as CPU utilization level, but you can also define custom metrics as needed. A potential problem with autoscaling is that Amazon charges the organization for the services it uses, which can mean an unexpectedly large bill. Every EC2 feature comes with pros and cons that you must balance when deciding on how to configure your setup.

Defining the security setup

AWS also provides distinct security features. Developers are usually well acquainted with most of these features from a programming perspective. The use of these security features becomes more detailed as the book progresses. However, here is a summary of the security features used with EC2:

>> **Virtual Private Cloud (VPC):** Separates every instance running on the physical server from every other instance. Theoretically, no one can access someone else's instance (even though it can happen in the real world (see https://rhinosecuritylabs.com/2016/02/aws-security-vulnerabilities-and-the-attackers-perspective/ for details on how hackers have broken into EC2 instances in the past).

>> **Network Access Control Lists (ACLs) (Optional):** Acts as a firewall to control both incoming and outgoing requests at the subnet level.

>> **Identity and Access Management (IAM) Users and Permissions:** Controls the level of access granted to individual users and user groups. You can both allow and deny access to specific resources managed by EC2.

>> **Security Groups:** Acts as a firewall to control both incoming and outgoing requests at the instance level. Each instance can have up to five security groups, each of which can have different permissions. This security feature provides finer-grained control over access than Network ACLs, but you must also maintain it for each instance, rather than for the virtual machine as a whole.

>> **Hardware Security Device:** Relies on a hardware-based security device that you install to control security between your on-premises network and the AWS cloud.

WARNING

No amount of security will thwart a determined intruder. Anyone who wants to gain access to your server will find a way to do it no matter how high you build the walls. In addition to great security, you must monitor the system and, by assuming that someone will break in, deal with the intruder as quickly as possible. Providing security keeps the less skilled intruder at bay as well as helps keep essentially honest people honest, but skilled intruders will always find a way in. The severity of these breaches varies, but it can actually cause businesses to fail, as in the case of Code Spaces (see `http://arstechnica.com/security/2014/06/aws-console-breach-leads-to-demise-of-service-with-proven-backup-plan/` for details). A number of security researchers warn that AWS is prone to security lapses (see `http://www.crn.com/news/security/300073621/security-researcher-warns-amazon-web-services-security-prone-to-dangerous-lapses.htm` for details). However, don't assume that other cloud services provide better security. Anytime you use external services, you take significant risks as well.

PROBLEMS WITH AUTOSCALING

When you read the AWS documentation and get to the part about autoscaling, it sounds as if you won't ever need to worry about the load on your servers. In fact, although the text in the documentation is correct, it has some gaps. For example, the documentation doesn't really address issues like response time and latency. As you scale your AWS configuration up to meet additional demand, you may also find that response time and latency create a problem. The video at `https://www.youtube.com/watch?v=Nswo-4ZIXkI` is helpful in explaining this issue, but the essence of any scaling scenario is that having more virtual machines means more communication taking place between machines, which slows things down. Think about it this way: When a meeting takes place at work, having more people usually means that the meeting goes slower and you accomplish less because you have more lines of communication to consider.

The problems of autoscaling are made worse in two ways. The first is that working in the cloud tends to be slower than using physical hardware because of the communication distances and the number of layers involved. The second problem is that autoscaling tends to increase the problem of having too many machines in the communication loop. If you manually scale your setup, you may decide to create a single instance with considerably greater capacity than the initial instance you created. Autoscaling would create a whole bunch of instances of that initial, smaller instance to do the same thing. Automation isn't always the correct way to handle scaling issues, so you need to consider this requirement as part of your EC2 configuration.

Using the standard storage options

A final consideration is the use of storage. Each instance comes with a specific amount of storage based on the kind of instance you create. If the instance storage doesn't provide the functionality or capacity you need, you can also add Elastic Block Store (EBS) support. The main advantage of using EBS, besides capacity and flexibility, is the capability to define a specific level of storage performance to ensure that your application runs as expected.

Working with Elastic Block Store (EBS) Volumes

The "Testing Your Setup" section of Chapter 2 is your first exposure to S3, and you might be tempted to think that S3 can provide what you need for a test server. However, the most important piece of information to know about S3 now is that it isn't a file system and doesn't act like a hard drive. EBS is more like the hard drives you have in your physical file server. As the name states, EBS is block storage, same as any other hard drive is, except that you access it in the cloud. You format the drive, just as you would a drive in your physical server, and you can mount it to an EC2 instance. The main point is that EBS makes your EC2 instance work and act more like a physical server, so it provides the kind of storage that most developers know. The following sections describe EBS in detail.

Knowing the EBS volume types

Just as there isn't only one kind of hard drive, so there isn't one kind of EBS volume. Amazon currently provides access to both Solid-State Drive (SSD) and Hard Disk Drive (HDD) volumes. SSD provides high-speed access, and HDD provides lower-cost access of a more traditional hard drive. Amazon further subdivides the two technologies into two types each (listed in order of speed):

>> **EBS Provisioned IOPS SSD:** Provides high-speed data access that you commonly need for data-intensive applications that rely on moderately sized databases.

>> **EBS General Purpose SSD:** Creates a medium-high-speed environment for low-latency applications. Amazon suggests this kind of volume for your boot drive. However, whether you actually need this amount of speed for your setup depends on the kinds of applications you plan to run.

>> **Throughput Optimized HDD:** Defines a high-speed hard drive environment, which can't compete with even a standard SSD. However, this volume type will work with most common applications, and Amazon suggests using it for big data or data-warehouse applications. This is probably the best option to choose when money is an issue and you don't really need the performance that SSD provides.

>> **Cold HDD:** Provides the lowest-speed option that Amazon supports. You use this volume type for data you access less often than data you place on the other volume types (think data you use once a week, rather than once every day). This isn't an archive option; it's more like a low-speed option for items you don't need constantly, such as a picture database.

REMEMBER

As you move toward higher-speed products, you also pay a higher price. For example, at the time of writing, a Cold HDD volume costs only $0.025/GB/month, but an EBS Provisioned SSD volume costs $0.125/GB/month. You can find price and speed comparison details at `http://aws.amazon.com/ebs/details/#piops`. The table provided contains some interesting statistics. For example, all the volume types top out at 16TB and support a maximum throughput per instance of 800MB/s.

Creating an EBS volume

To use EC2 effectively for development, you must create an EBS volume first. The EBS volume is part of the instance configuration process described later, in the "Discovering Images and Instances" section of this chapter. The two easiest methods for creating an EBS volume are the console and CLI. However, you can also write a custom application to perform the task (assuming that you perform this task often enough to make the effort worthwhile).

REMEMBER

In the "Signing into a user account" section of Chapter 5, you sign into your user account for the first time. When performing configuration tasks, such as config-uring EBS, make sure to rely on your user account rather than your root account to perform the task. The following sections assume that you use your user account. However, they should also work using the root account.

Using the console

By far the easiest method for creating an EBS volume is the console. The following steps describe how to create a simple volume that you can use with EC2 for the procedures in this book. However, you can use these same steps for creating vol-umes with other characteristics later.

1. **Sign into AWS by using your user account.**

2. **Navigate to the EC2 Console at** `https://console.aws.amazon.com/ec2/.`

    You see the page shown in Figure 6-1. Notice the Navigation pane on the left, which contains options for performing various EC2-related tasks. The Resources area of the main pane tells you the statistics for your EC2 setup, which currently includes just the one security group that you see how to create in the "Getting access keys" section of Chapter 2.

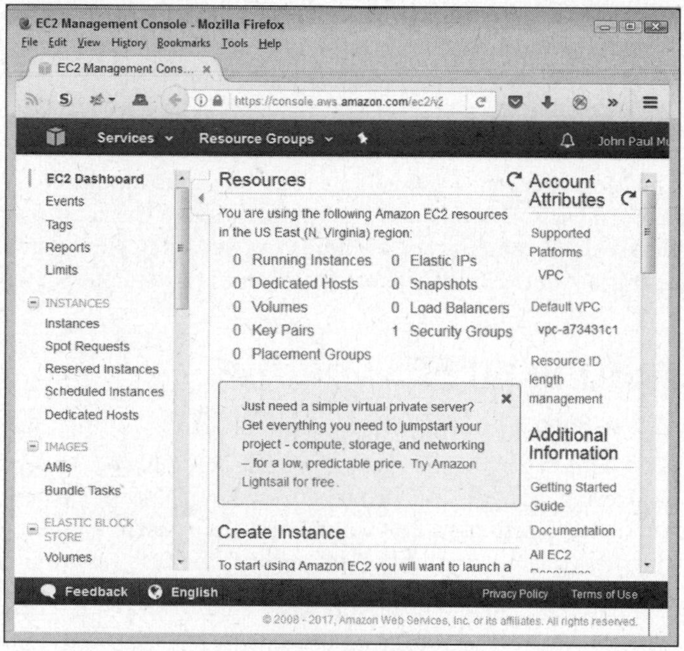

FIGURE 6-1:
The EC2 Console tells you all about your current EC2 configuration.

3. **Choose an EC2 setup region from the Region drop-down list at the top of the page.**

    The example uses the Oregon region.

4. **Select Elastic Block Store ➪ Volumes in the Navigation pane.**

    The EC2 Console shows that you don't currently have any volumes defined.

5. **Click Create Volume.**

    You see the Create Volume dialog box, shown in Figure 6-2.

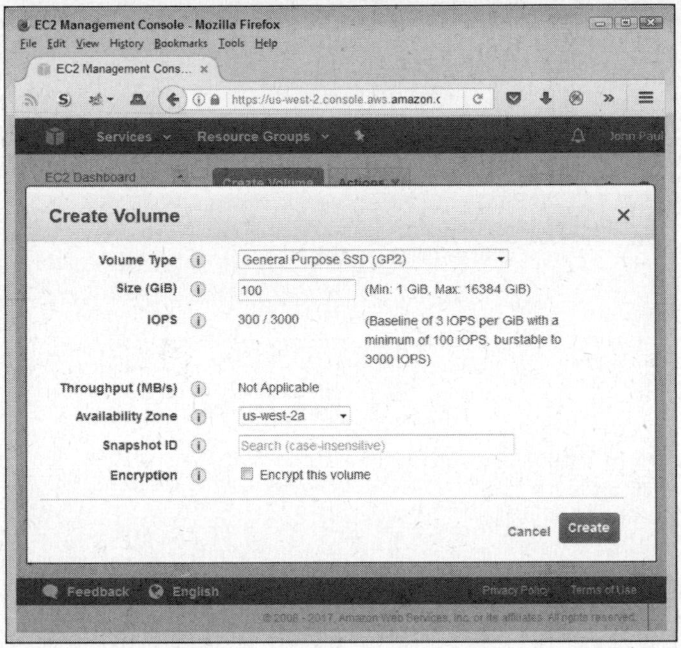

FIGURE 6-2:
The Create Volume dialog box contains settings for defining a new EBS volume.

Notice that you can choose a volume type and size, but not the Input/output Operations Per Second (IOPS) or the throughput, which are available only with certain volume types. The Availability Zone field contains the location of the storage, which must match your EC2 setup. The Snapshot ID field contains the name of an S3 storage location to use for incremental backups of your EBS data. You can also choose to encrypt sensitive data, but doing so places some limits on how you can use EBS. For example, you can't use encryption with all EC2 instance types. The discussion at `http://docs.aws.amazon.com/ AWSEC2/latest/UserGuide/EBSEncryption.html` provides additional information about encryption.

This book uses the default EBS volume settings, but in a real developer environment, you select settings that match the production environment in which the application will operate. Unlike a local setup, cloud-based development lets you recreate the production environment precisely, which provides significant advantages during the development process. Using the same environment during development and testing helps ensure that you see any cloud-induced errors, as well as discover any potential performance issues.

TIP

6. **Click Create.**

AWS creates a new volume for you and displays statistics about it, as shown in Figure 6-3. Note that the State field on the Description tab says Available. You can't make changes to the volume until AWS makes it available.

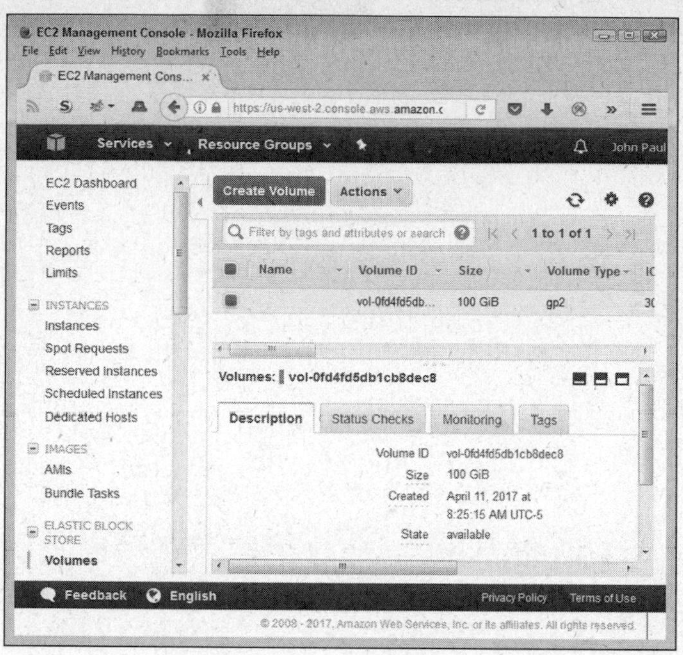

FIGURE 6-3:
A new volume displays all pertinent statistics, such as the size and state.

The new volume lacks any sort of backup. The next step configures a snapshot that AWS uses to perform incremental backups of the EBS data, reducing the risk of lost data.

7. **Choose Actions ⇨ Create Snapshot.**

You see the Create Snapshot dialog box, shown in Figure 6-4. Notice that AWS fills in the Volume field for you and determines the need for encryption based on the volume settings.

8. **Type** EBS.Backup **in the Name field, type** Test Backup **in the Description field, and then click Create.**

You see a dialog box telling you that AWS has started the snapshot.

9. **Click Close.**

The volume is ready to use.

When you finish this example, you can delete the volume you created by selecting its entry in the list and choosing Actions ⇨ Delete Volume. You automatically create the required EBS volume required for your EC2 setup in the "Creating an instance" section, later in this chapter. However, in a real-world setup, you can attach this volume to any EC2 instance or detach it when it's no longer needed.

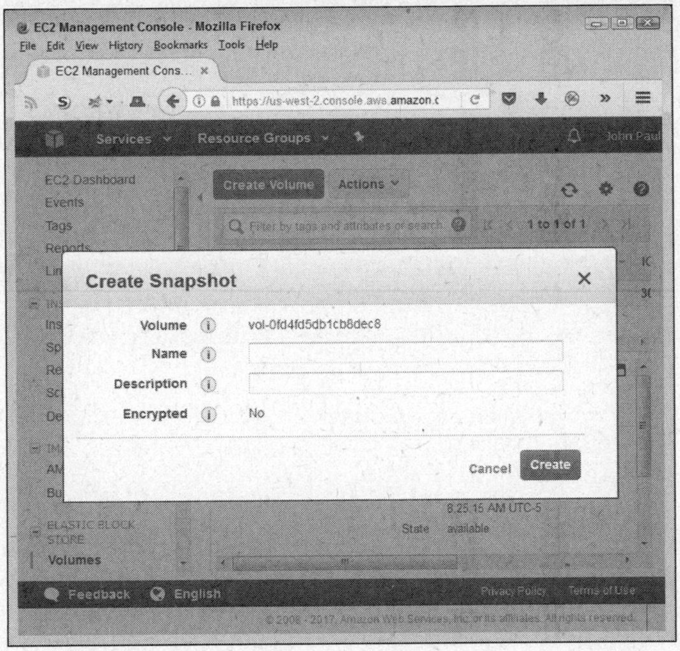

<figure>
FIGURE 6-4:
Define an S3 connection to use for your EBS volume backup.
</figure>

Using CLI

Working with CLI means that you can automate tasks using a variety of methods, such as batch files. However, even if your goal isn't automation, using CLI means that you can perform tasks using fewer steps. The trade-off is that the potential for error is higher and you must also know the minimum commands required to perform tasks. The following steps repeat the process discussed in the previous section but use CLI. The steps assume that you have already downloaded and configured CLI for use by employing the instructions found in the "Installing the Command Line Interface Software" section of Chapter 5.

1. **Open a command prompt or terminal window that allows access to the aws utility.**

2. **Type** aws ec2 create-volume --availability-zone us-west-2a --size 100 --volume-type gp2 **and press Enter.**

The book uses the us-west-2a, US West (Oregon) availability zone. However, you can use any availability zone required for your setup. You must provide a size. In looking at Figure 6-2, you see that the default size is 100GiB. Also important is to specify the volume type, which is GP2, as shown in the figure. You see the volume creation information, shown in Figure 6-5. Note the VolumeId field near the bottom. This value is important for many other tasks, so you need to keep track of it.

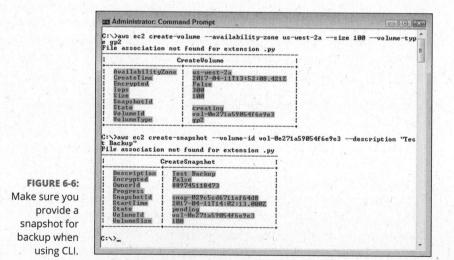

FIGURE 6-5:
CLI shows the
characteristics
of the volume you
created.

As with the volume you created in the GUI, you don't have a snapshot in place for backup. The next step performs this task.

3. **Type** aws ec2 create-snapshot --volume-id vol-0e271a59054f6e9e3 --description "Test Backup" **and press Enter.**

    You must replace the --volume-id argument with the actual VolumeId value from your setup, as shown in Figure 6-5. The VolumeId for your setup is unique, so you can't type the VolumeId shown in the book. CLI creates a snapshot of the EBS volume. This part of the example points to one of the problems with using CLI. No command-line switch exists for naming the snapshot, so you must accept whatever name AWS provides. The limitation means using names like snap-029c5cd6711ef64d8, which are much harder to read and type than EBS.Backup. Figure 6-6 shows the output of this command.

FIGURE 6-6:
Make sure you
provide a
snapshot for
backup when
using CLI.

Using CLI means typing just two commands in three steps instead of the nine steps required if you use the console. The time savings can become substantial, especially when you need to set up a number of development configurations. When you finish this example, you can delete the volume you created by typing **aws ec2 delete-volume --volume-id vol-0e271a59054f6e9e3** and pressing Enter. As before, you must replace the `--volume-id` argument with the actual VolumeId value from your setup.

Discovering Images and Instances

An *Amazon Machine Image (AMI)* is a kind of blueprint. You tell AWS to use an AMI to build an instance. As with blueprints, AWS can use a single AMI to build as many instances as needed for a particular purpose. Every instance created with the AMI is precisely the same from the developer's perspective. AMI is one of the EC2 features that enable you to autoscale. Amazon uses the AMI to create more instances as needed so that your application continues to run no matter how many people may want to access it.

REMEMBER

You don't have to create an AMI; Amazon provides several default AMIs that you can use. However, if you want to create a custom environment to use with EC2, you need to create your own AMI. As a developer, you likely want to use custom AMIs, as needed, that the organization's administrators define. The reason to use a custom setup is to ensure that your development environment matches the production environment in which the application will operate. Consequently, as a developer, you seldom need to create an AMI; you either use one of the default AMIs or a custom AMI that your organization already uses. This book assumes that you use one of the default AMIs. The following sections show the easiest method for creating an instance using one of Amazon's AMIs.

DEFINING A CUSTOM AMI

Theoretically, if you're a consultant and you must configure your system to match a client's system, you may need to create your own custom AMI (relying on the customer's AMI is a better scenario because you don't have to worry about configuration issues getting in the way of a functional application). Before you can use an AMI, you must first create and configure it as described at http://docs.aws.amazon.com/AWSEC2/latest/UserGuide/AMIs.html. In addition, you must register the AMI with AWS. After you've registered it, you can tell AWS to create (launch) instances based on the AMI. A user or application connects to an instance in order to use it, and a developer can configure an instance to meet particular requirements. You can copy your AMI between regions to help improve overall application speed if you want. To stop using an AMI, you deregister it.

Generating security keys

To access your EC2 instance securely, you need to generate security keys. These keys enable you to be verified as the person logging on to the EC2 instance. The following steps help you create a key pair that you need when creating your instance in the next section:

1. **Select Network & Security ⇨ Key Pairs in the Navigation pane.**

AWS tells you that you don't have any key pairs defined.

2. **Click Create Key Pair.**

You see a Create Key Pair dialog box that asks for a key pair name.

3. **Type** MyKeyPair **in the Key Pair Name field and click Create.**

You see a download dialog box for the browser that you use. Be sure to save a copy of the key pair as a Privacy-Enhanced Mail (.pem) file. The article at http://fileformats.archiveteam.org/wiki/PEM tells more about this particular file format.

4. **Save the** .pem **file to disk.**

The Key Pairs page now shows a key pair named MyKeyPair with all the pertinent information.

Creating an instance

The process for creating an EC2 instance can become quite complex. You can manually create key pairs used to log in to the instance, for example, or create a special security group to help maintain EC2 security. In addition, you can use a custom AMI to configure your instance. The problem is that all these extra steps make what should be a relatively simple process for experimentation purposes quite difficult. The following steps show the easiest, fastest method for creating an EC2 instance. However, keep in mind that you can do a lot more with EC2 set-ups than described in this chapter. This procedure assumes that you have already logged in and selected the same region used for your EBS volume.

1. **Select Instances ⇨ Instances in the Navigation pane.**

AWS tells you that you don't have any EC2 instances running.

2. **Click Launch Instance.**

You see a series of AMI entries, as shown in Figure 6-7. Amazon owns all these AMIs. You can also choose to use your own AMI or obtain access to an AMI through the AWS Marketplace or Community.

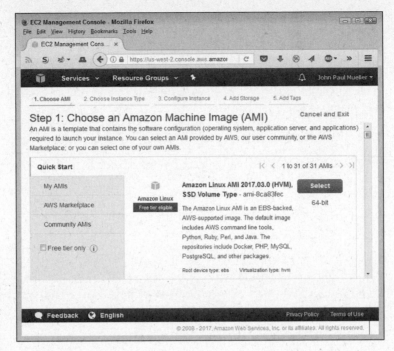

TIP

Note that the first AMI is marked as Free Tier Eligible. Unless you want to pay for using EC2, you must select one of the Free Tier Eligible entries, which include Amazon Linux, Red Hat Linux, SUSE Linux, Ubuntu Linux, and Windows Server (all in various versions). To ensure that you don't accidentally choose a paid option, select the Free Tier Only check box on the left side of the page.

3. **Click Select next to the Amazon Linux AMI 2017 entry.**

You see a listing of instance types, as shown in Figure 6-8. One of the instance types is marked Free Tier Eligible. You must choose this option unless you want to pay for your EC2 instance.

REMEMBER

Choosing to configure the instance details or change storage requirements will create a new instance type. The new instance type won't be free-tier eligible. You can view the various configuration options available, but click Cancel instead of creating the instance if you want to continue working with AWS free of charge.

4. **Select the instance type that you want to create and then click Review and Launch.**

You see the Step 7: Review Instance Launch page, shown in Figure 6-9. The figure shows the Security Groups section. When you create your instance, Amazon warns you that anyone can access it. Given that you probably want to work with EC2 privately, you must modify the security group settings to reduce the risk of prying eyes.

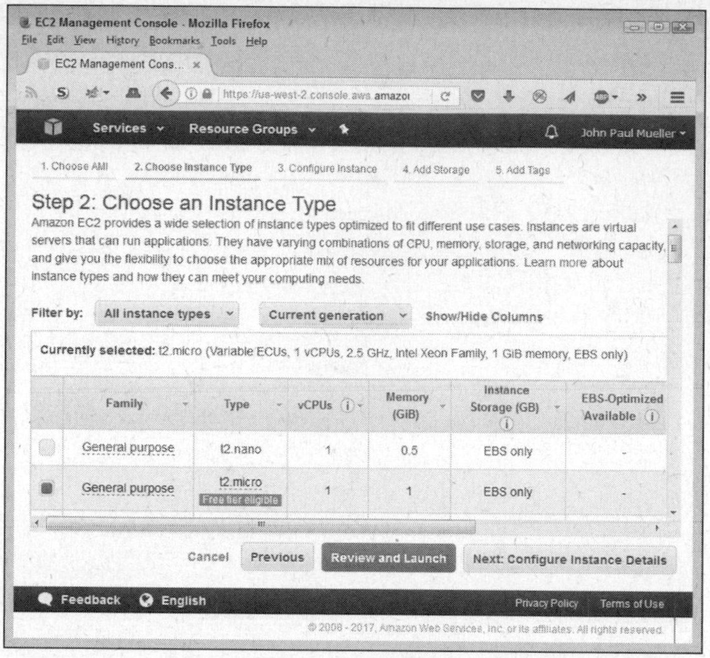

FIGURE 6-8:
Choose the kind of instance you want to create.

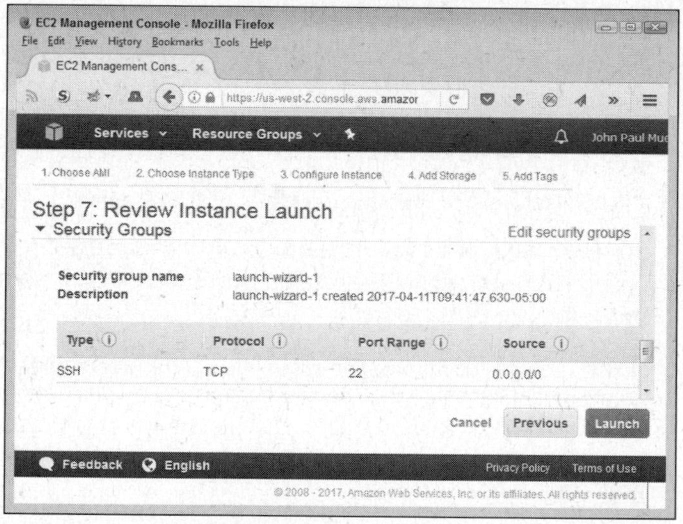

FIGURE 6-9:
Review the instance configuration before you launch it.

5. **Click Edit Security Groups.**

   You see the Step 6: Configure Security Group page, shown in Figure 6-10.

6. **Type** Default-Launch **in the Security Group Name field.**

   Use a group name that's both short and meaningful to avoid potential confusion later.

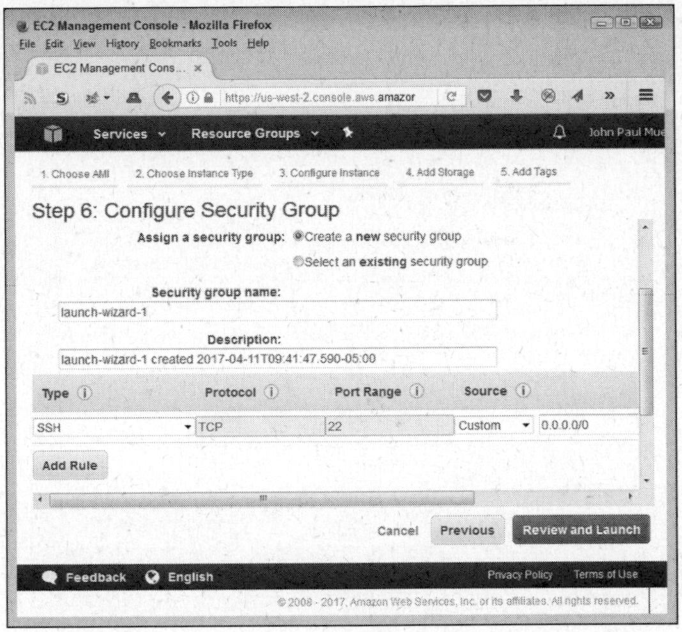

FIGURE 6-10:
Create a new, more secure security group for your EC2 setup.

7. **(Optional) Type a group description in the Description field.**

8. **Choose All Traffic in the Type field.**

   Using this option gives you maximum EC2 access. However, in a real-world setup, you limit the Type field entries to just the protocols you actually plan to use. For example, if you don't plan to use Secure Shell (SSH) to interact with EC2, don't include it in the list of allowed protocols.

9. **Choose My IP in the Source field.**

   By limiting the access to just your IP, you reduce the likelihood that anyone will access the EC2 setup. However, intruders can find all sorts of ways around this precaution, such as by using IP spoofing (see `http://searchsecurity.techtarget.com/definition/IP-spoofing` for more details about this technique).

10. **Click Add Rule.**

    AWS adds the rule to the list. Click the *X* next to the new rule that AWS automatically generates in some cases to remove it; you don't need it.

11. **Click Review and Launch.**

    The EC2 Management Console takes you back to the Step 7: Review Instance Launch page, shown previously in Figure 6-9.

12. **Click Launch.**

    You see a Select an Existing Key Pair or Create a New Key Pair dialog box, as shown in Figure 6-11.

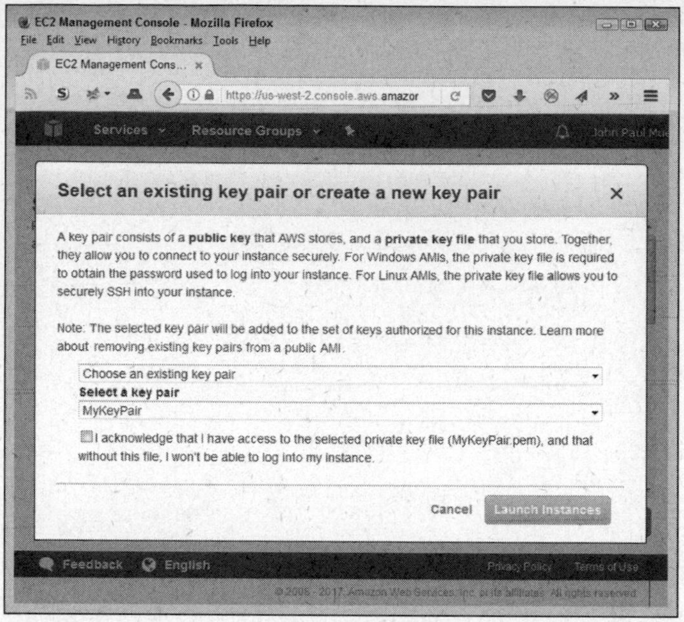

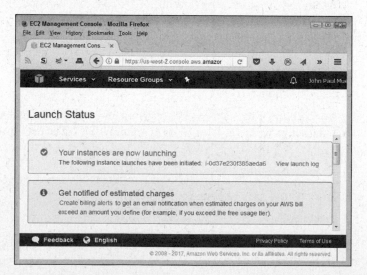

FIGURE 6-11:
Choose the key pair that you want to use.

13. **Select Choose an Existing Key Pair in the first field.**

14. **Select MyKeyPair in the second field.**

15. **Select the check box to acknowledge that you have access to the private key and then click Launch Instances.**

    AWS starts your EC2 instance. A dialog box provides additional information about your instance, as shown in Figure 6-12. Note the link for your instance in the Your Instances Are Now Launching box.

FIGURE 6-12:
Amazon provides additional information about your instance while you wait for it to start.

16. Click the link for your instance.

You see the running instance information, as shown in Figure 6-13.

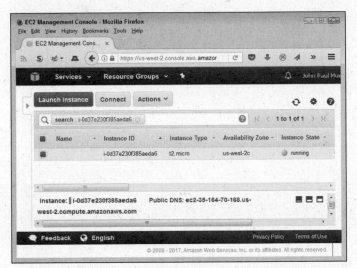

FIGURE 6-13:
Verify that your instance is running before you attempt to connect to it.

Connecting to the instance

You have all sorts of options for connecting to your instance. For example, Windows users have the option of using PuTTY (see `http://www.chiark.greenend.org.uk/~sgtatham/putty/` for details). However, the easiest method for connecting to your instance is to use the Connect button found on the Instances page, shown in Figure 6-13. Unfortunately, to use this option, your browser must support Java and you must have Java enabled. Because of security concerns, some browsers no longer support Java or create significant hurdles to using Java. If you have Java configured to start only with permission, you must provide the required permission when asked. If you truly don't want to work with Java, you can find additional, platform-specific options at `https://docs.aws.amazon.com/AWSEC2/latest/UserGuide/AccessingInstances.html`.

After you click Connect, you see two options for connecting to your instance, as shown in Figure 6-14. Using a Standalone SSH Client means installing a product such as PuTTY on your system. If you want the simple method, select the second option, A Java SSH Client Directly from My Browser (Java required; newer versions of Firefox don't provide this support unless you use the Extended Support Release, ESR, found at `https://www.mozilla.org/en-US/firefox/organizations/`).

You must supply the location of the key pair file on your hard drive in the Private Key Path field. After you supply this information, click Launch SSH Client. If this is the first time you use this feature, some warning messages appear and then the client installs on your system. After initialization, you see an SSH client similar to the one shown in Figure 6-15, and you can interact with your EC2 setup through this client.

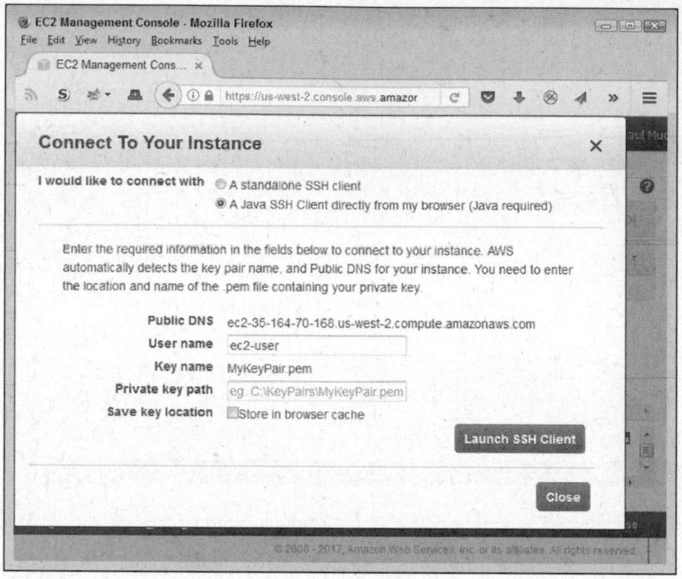

FIGURE 6-14:
Using a Java client is the easiest connection method.

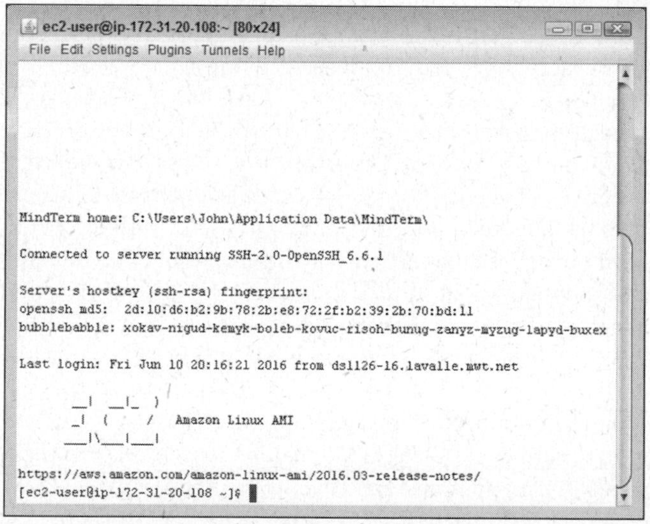

FIGURE 6-15:
After you connect, you can begin working with your EC2 instance.

To prove to yourself that you really have connected to EC2, start a copy of Python by typing **Python** at the prompt and pressing Enter. A copy of Python starts and displays its version number. To exit Python, type **quit()** and press Enter. Type **exit** and press Enter to end the EC2 session. Choose File ⇨ Close to close the SSH client terminal.

3

Performing Basic Development Tasks

Chapter **7**

Understanding AWS Input/Output

Previous chapters of the book take you through creating a developer setup, performing essential Amazon Web Services (AWS) configuration tasks, and ensuring that you can actually contact AWS to perform useful work. You also see how to use command-line interface (CLI), browser-based, and desktop-based methods to perform these tasks, in addition to working with the AWS console. Of course, these are all good starting points for a developer, but developers need to know a lot more about how input and output works when dealing with an application programming interface (API), which is what you're really dealing with when working with AWS. Other people see services, but what you really need to see are black boxes where a given input provides a specific output.

AWS typically performs tasks using two specific data formats: JavaScript Object Notation (JSON) and eXtensible Markup Language (XML). This chapter doesn't provide you with a primer on these two formats, but it does offer some references you can use to update your skills as needed. The chapter also gives you the AWS view of these formats — an understanding of how you can expect AWS to use JSON and XML to make structured input and output possible. For example, when creating a security policy, you describe the policy using JSON. To perform Create, Read, Update, and Delete (CRUD) operations that involve security in your applications, you need to know the grammar that AWS uses for this task.

Part of any organization's input/output are custom APIs. After all, you have your own business processes to consider as part of any development solution. AWS provides the means for including custom APIs using the Amazon API Gateway. This chapter gives you a good starting point for working with the Amazon API Gateway by explaining basic functionality, defining what is meant by models and templates, and then demonstrating several ways to interact with the Amazon API Gateway (console, CLI, and use of application code). Discovering how to use the Amazon API Gateway is an essential part of working with AWS fully to meet specific application requirements.

Considering the Input/Output Options

While you work with the console applications, perform some simple requests using REST, and interact with AWS using other basic means, you might notice that AWS relies heavily on JSON. In fact, you might notice that XML is completely absent. It's absent because JSON is the default option for both application input and output. However, you do have other options when working with AWS; you simply need to make the requests using the appropriate means. The most common alternative input and output is XML. However, you can also use appropriately formatted plain-text requests. This chapter considers what you need to do to work with XML, but the same approach works when using other data-formatting strategies.

When working with AWS, you must consider the services that you want to use. In some cases, your only viable input/output option is JSON. For example, the message thread at https://forums.aws.amazon.com/thread.jspa?messageID=690027 discusses the use of non-JSON data with a Lambda function. According to the various inputs, it's currently impossible to do this (although an AWS developer did say that the development team added this sort of input as a backlog item). The point is that you do have significant limits when working with non-JSON data while interacting with AWS.

Fortunately, you can overcome some of the data-format issues by using a mapping template as described in the "Mapping templates" section, later in this chapter. Essentially, a mapping template enables you to map the incoming data type to the data type needed by the backend. You need one template for each kind of data format you support. For example, an application might support three types: text/plain, application/json, and application/xml, each of which would require a separate template.

Mapping templates can resolve both input and output data needs. However, it pays to be cautious in your expectations of how well the mapping will work.

For example, the message thread discussion at `https://forums.aws.amazon.com/message.jspa?messageID=651944` talks about some issues in getting XML input and output to work properly. AWS is a complex setup that has grown quickly and is experiencing some growing pains. Fortunately, the development staff seems to be willing to listen to bug reports and requests for needed upgrades.

Working with JSON

At one time, AWS relied heavily on XML to perform tasks. However, today you find that AWS relies almost exclusively on JSON to perform tasks. In fact, more than a few developers have complained that not everyone has moved to XML yet, and the AWS developers do plan to add some XML functionality back into the API. The reasons for using JSON instead of XML are many, but here are the most commonly cited:

>> **Shorter:** JSON requires less code than XML to convey the same information.

>> **Quicker:** Smaller data exchanges mean that you spend less time reading and writing data.

>> **Support of Arrays:** XML doesn't support arrays, which is a major problem in today's data environment.

>> **Object output:** Parsing JSON automatically produces an object that requires less manipulation to process.

>> **Clearer:** The chance of misinterpreting a JSON data stream is lower than with XML.

This book assumes that you have enough JSON knowledge to understand the example code. Of course, that's quite an assumption. You may have only passing knowledge of JSON, or no knowledge at all. The best way to get started with JSON is to rely on tutorials, such as the following:

>> **W3Schools.com:** `https://www.w3schools.com/js/js_json_intro.asp`

>> **TutorialsPoint:** `https://www.tutorialspoint.com/json/`

>> **w3resource:** `http://www.w3resource.com/JSON/introduction.php`

TIP

You can also take an online course at places like Lynda, at `https://www.lynda.com/JSON-training-tutorials/1551-0.html`. When working with a specific language, knowing how that language interacts with JSON is also helpful. For example, you can find a tutorial about JSON interactivity with Python at `https://code.tutsplus.com/tutorials/how-to-work-with-json-data-using-python--cms-25758`.

Working with XML

Sometimes technology moves at an astounding pace, leaving many people behind. It's a problem because the old code and old data doesn't go away — it's still there, and people still need to use it. That's the problem with XML. Looking at message threads like the one at https://forums.aws.amazon.com/message.jspa?messageID=651944 tells you that many developers have problems working with an AWS fixated on JSON because they still have to deal with XML, sometimes in ways that make converting the data to JSON impossible. Keeping the need to support XML in mind, a few of the examples in this book help demonstrate the required techniques. However, moving your data to JSON format as quickly as possible will reduce the work required to use AWS.

WARNING

AWS doesn't support the use of XML with some services. For example, as pointed out by the message thread at https://forums.aws.amazon.com/thread.jspa?threadID=221346, you can't use XML as input to Lambda. In this case, you must use JSON. The AWS development team representative promised to place XML support on the backlist of items to add to Lambda, but other message threads, like the one at http://stackoverflow.com/questions/37194999/aws-api-gateway-accept-xml-request, show that Amazon still hasn't added this support. You need to ensure that the service you want to access will support XML input before writing an application that will never work.

This book assumes that you know enough about XML to understand the various examples that rely on it. Most developers know a little more about XML than JSON because XML has been around a lot longer. However, some developers haven't been exposed to XML, so you need to know where to find additional information. The best tutorials are at

>> **W3Schools:** https://www.w3schools.com/xml/

>> **TutorialsPoint:** https://www.tutorialspoint.com/xml/

>> **XMLFiles.com:** http://www.xmlfiles.com/xml/

TIP

You may need some other method than tutorials to understand XML fully. Sites such as Lynda (https://www.lynda.com/XML-training-tutorials/334-0.html) provide you with online, hands-on courses. In fact, Lynda offers an array of courses that cover all the XML disciplines. Seeing how XML works with your language of choice is also important. After you have the basics down, you might want to try tutorials that provide language-specific interaction, such as the Python-specific XML tutorial at https://wiki.python.org/moin/Tutorials%20on%20XML%20processing%20with%20Python.

Working with Amazon API Gateway

The API Gateway provides the means to interact with Amazon using a number of methodologies. It consists of resources and methods. A *resource* is an object providing one or more operations that you interact with using appropriate HTTP verbs, including GET, POST, and DELETE. Combining a resource path with a specific operation on that resource creates a *method*. API users can call methods to obtain controlled access to resources and receive a response. To maintain control, you define mappings between the method and the back end. The following sections help you better understand how the API Gateway creates a controlled resource-access environment.

Defining the uses for the API Gateway

Viewing the API Gateway as an integration strategy is essential. You use it in the following ways to provide access to code on your AWS setup:

» **Control service:** Relies on REST to provide access to various AWS services. For example, you can use it for access to the Lambda service functions you create (see Chapter 10). This feature also enables access to specific services, such as Amazon DynamoDB, Amazon S3, and Amazon Kinesis. This form of API Gateway access offers the following access methods:

- REST API requests and responses

- Console

- CLI

- SDK (for supported platforms and languages)

» **Execution service:** Offers deployed API access to back-end functionality. You use standard HTTP protocols or a language-specific SDK to perform this task.

REMEMBER

As with any other form of web service, the API Gateway enables you to secure access to the back end. You can use IAM roles and policies or API Gateway custom authorizers to perform this task. Of the two, using IAM is generally the easiest and fastest method, and using a custom authorizer provides better flexibility. Most developers will find that using the IAM approach works best, and you should use it as your first choice.

Defining the security requirements

The "Signing into a user account" section of Chapter 5 tells you how to sign in to your user account rather than rely on the root account. A user account is important to ensure that you keep your AWS configuration safe. However, a user account designed for a developer isn't the best account for a client application to use. When creating a production application, you need to create other users and other groups by using the techniques shown in Chapter 2. In fact, the best idea is to use the same users and groups as found in your production environment, which you can likely obtain from an administrator.

AWS assigns security based on policies. A *managed policy* is one that AWS supplies. Any custom policy you create is an *inline policy.* Both policy types rely on JSON-formatted entries, such as the one shown here for the `AmazonAPIGatewayAdministrator` managed policy:

```
{
  "Version": "2012-10-17",
  "Statement": [
    {
      "Effect": "Allow",
      "Action": [
        "apigateway:*"
      ],
      "Resource": "arn:aws:apigateway:*::/*"
    }
  ]
}
```

The policy depends on a statement that defines the effect the policy has on specific actions for a given resource. Even though the code might look daunting, it makes sense if you take it apart and look at each element individually.

The hardest part of creating a policy is to define the Amazon Resource Name (ARN). In this case, the ARN refers to AWS and the API Gateway service found in AWS. You can further refine specific resources. The resource at http://docs.aws. amazon.com/general/latest/gr/aws-arns-and-namespaces.html tells you more about ARNs and furnishes you with everything needed to create an ARN. In addition, you often find the ARN listed for a resource when you view that resource's information, as shown in Figure 7-1.

REMEMBER

You must have your security setup in place before you try to create your API Gateway. Part of the configuration process requests this information, so you need to consider security before you create an API. (Adding more security later means going back through the configuration process.) Of course, this workflow makes sense because you don't want to create an API that anyone can access until you get around to completing the security requirements.

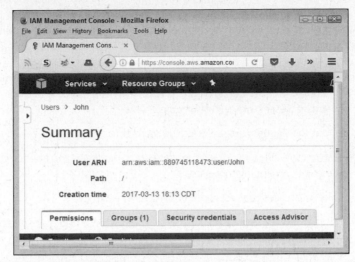

FIGURE 7-1:
AWS often supplies the ARNs you need in the console displays.

Understanding models

Before anyone can interact with a resource, describing the data format used by that resource is vital. A *model* describes the data format of the request or response body. You need a model to create a strongly typed SDK for an API and use it to

>> Validate the data

>> Generate a mapping template

TIP

Creating a model will save you a lot of time and reduce the likelihood that your API will experience reliability and security issues. However, Amazon doesn't require you to create a model to generate a mapping template, so the use of a model is optional.

Mapping templates

The front end you create may not match the back end used to obtain a response. To get the front end to talk with the back end, you must create a *mapping template* between the two. The map transforms the request body into a form that the back end understands, and the response body into a form that the front end understands, using a script that is formatted in the Apache Velocity Template Language (VTL) (http://velocity.apache.org/engine/devel/vtl-reference.html). The idea is to get the client talking with the web service.

A mapping template follows a precise pattern of communication. Every time a client interacts with your API, the following set of steps occurs:

1. Client makes request to Method Request object. The Method request object ensures that the client request contains all required data in the correct form and addresses any security requirements.

2. Method Request object sends the request to the Integration Request object.

3. Integration Request maps the request format to the form required by the API using the mapping template.

4. API processes requests and formulates a response.

5. Integration Response object accepts the response and maps the response to the form required by the client using the mapping template.

6. Method Response receives the response from the Integration response. The Method Response can react to the response in various ways and format the response for the client as needed.

7. Client receives the response from Method Response.

Creating an API Gateway using the console

In this section, you create a simple API by using one of the Amazon examples. The idea is to help you get started using APIs with a minimum of fuss so that you can see the API workflow. Later examples will help you create custom APIs so that you can see all the ways in which you can modify API behavior. The following steps get you started.

1. **Sign into AWS by using your user account.**

2. **Navigate to the API Gateway Console at** `https://console.aws.amazon.com/apigateway/`.

   AWS displays a welcome message and displays a Get Started button (unless you created an API Gateway previously).

3. **Choose an API Gateway setup region from the Region drop-down list at the top of the page.**

   The example uses the Oregon region.

4. **Click Get Started.**

   AWS displays a message about creating an example API. The example produces a Pet Store API using Swagger (`http://swagger.io/`), which is a popular application for producing APIs. You can create your APIs by using Swagger and import them directly into AWS.

5. **Click OK.**

You see the display shown in Figure 7-2. Notice that you can

- Create a new API using just the console functionality.

- Import a new API that you created using Swagger.

- Run the example API to see how API Gateway works.

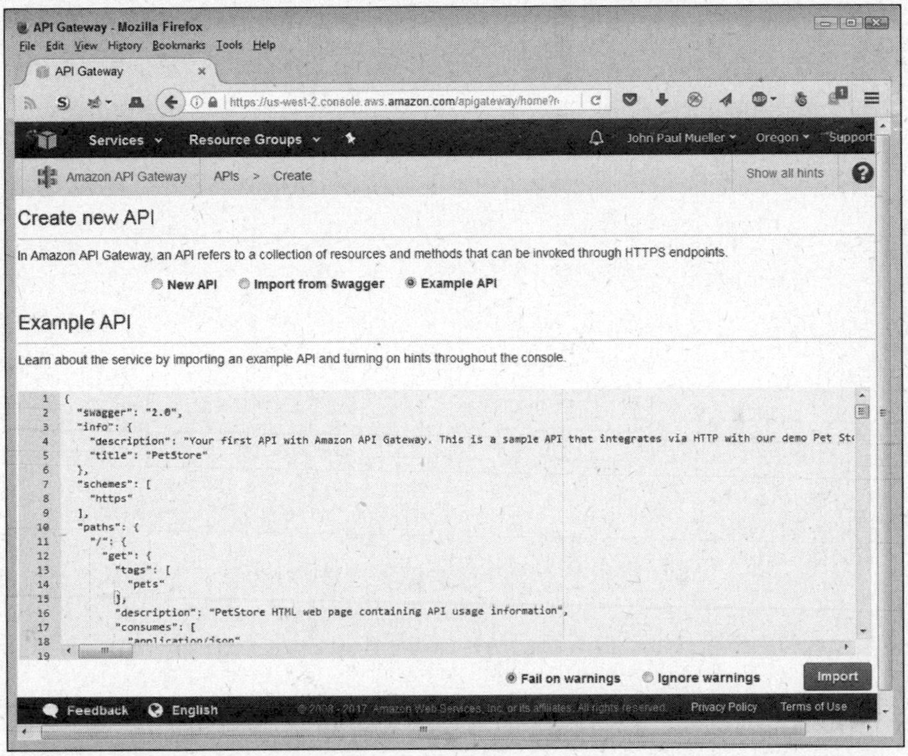

FIGURE 7-2:
You have a number of options for creating a new API on AWS.

This example uses the third option, Example API. You can see the JSON code used to create the example API below the three options. The options regarding warnings help you ensure that the API you import will actually work with Amazon. In most cases, you want to enable Fail On Warnings to ensure that you don't import an invalid API description.

6. **Choose Example API; choose Fail on Warnings; then click Import.**

You see the Resources view, shown in Figure 7-3. The Navigation pane on the left shows you the kinds of information that is available. In the middle is a hierarchical view of the API. The right pane shows a detail view of the selected resource. The API is only imported at this point. You can perform all sorts of additional tasks, such as creating new methods and resources. You can also view the details of a particular element, such as a method.

7. **Click POST in the Resource Tree.**

   You see the POST method execution, shown in Figure 7-4. Note that the conversation begins with the client and follows the process mentioned in the "Mapping templates" section, earlier in this chapter. Each of the little bull's-eye dots is a hint. You can click them to get additional information about that element. You can also click the major headings, such as Method Request, to learn more about that element and configure it as part of working with the API. To test the API, you click TEST (with the lightning bolt) in the Client element, as described in the next step.

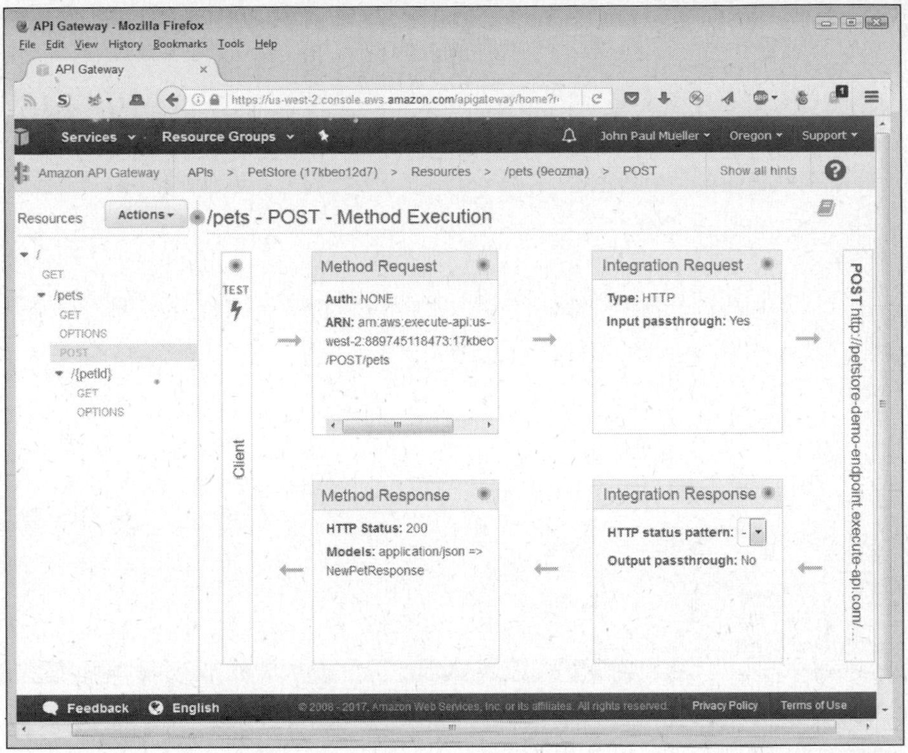

FIGURE 7-4:
Detail views show
how various
Resource Tree
elements work.

8. Click TEST in the Client element.

You see the display shown in Figure 7-5. This page shows all the potential elements required to make a test as well as which ones you actually require. For example, you don't need any headers, stage variables, or client certificates. (A number of other potential inputs don't appear in the figure.) However, this example does require a Request Body entry to work properly.

9. Type the following code in the Request Body field:

```
{"type": "cat", "price": 50.00}
```

The JSON request asks for a pet of type cat at a price of $50.00.

10. Click Test.

You see output similar to that shown in Figure 7-6. Note that you see the default headers with a status of 200 (showing a successful request). The response body contains the original request and a message value of success. The response headers show the kind of information you can expect from this kind of request. Finally, you see a series of log entries that tell you precisely how the request and response process proceeded. Now that you know the API works, you can deploy it.

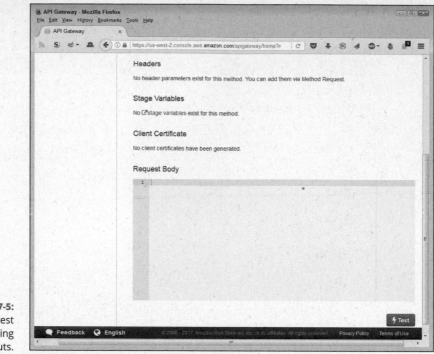

FIGURE 7-5:
Performing a test means providing required inputs.

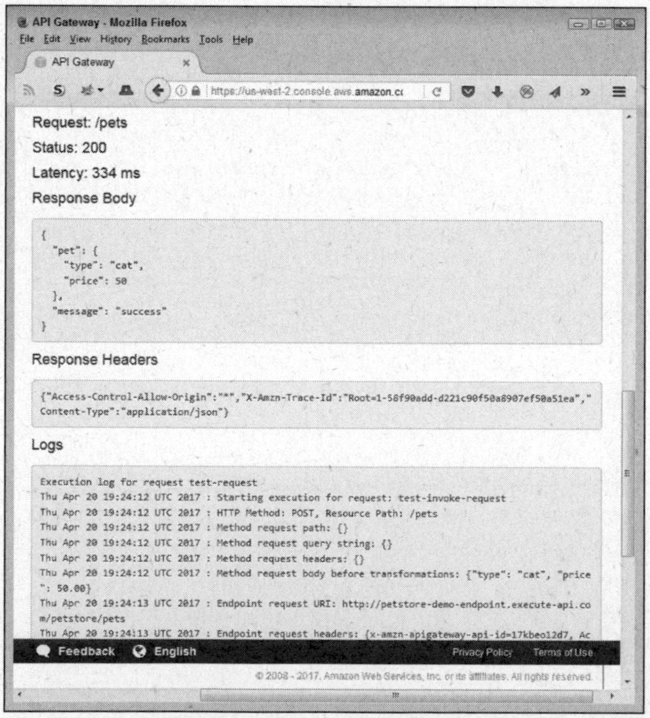

FIGURE 7-6:
The testing process helps you visualize how the API will work.

11. **Select the forward slash (/) entry in the Resource Tree.**

To deploy an API, you must select the root node of the Resource Tree.

12. **Choose Actions ⇨ Deploy API.**

You see a Deploy API dialog box like the one shown in Figure 7-7. You must describe the level of deployment so that everyone working on the project will know the API's status.

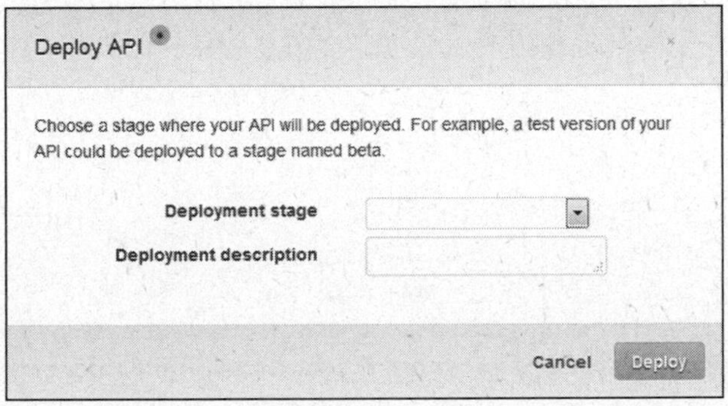

Deploy API

Choose a stage where your API will be deployed. For example, a test version of your API could be deployed to a stage named beta.

Deployment stage

Deployment description

Cancel   Deploy

13. **Choose [New Stage] in the Deployment Stage field.**

14. **Type** TestDeploy **in the State Name field.**

You may optionally include a stage and deployment description, but they aren't required for the example.

15. **Click Deploy.**

You see the detail information about the deployment, as shown in Figure 7-8. The information for your deployment will vary from the information shown in the figure. Note especially the Invoke URL field near the top. The example is now ready to work with.

It's time to see whether the API actually works. Open a new browser window. Using the Invoke URL field entry as a starting point, add a question mark and then a name/value pair, like the one shown here: `https://17kbeo12d7.execute-api.us-west-2.amazonaws.com/TestDeploy/pets/?type=cat`. In this case, you ask for all the cat entries. Figure 7-9 shows example output from this call.

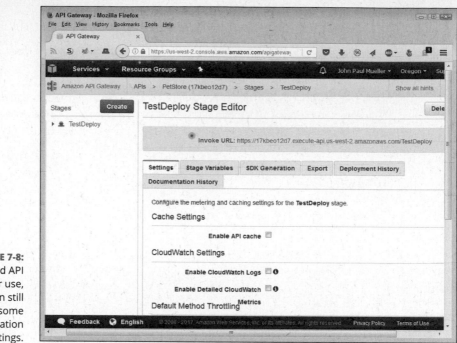

FIGURE 7-8:
The deployed API is ready for use, but you can still change some configuration settings.

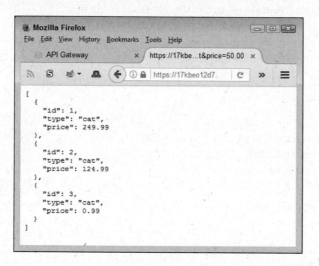

FIGURE 7-9:
Use the GET method to ask for all the cat entries.

You can also see a specific entry. All you need is the ID value added to the URL to see a specific entry, as shown here: `https://17kbeo12d7.execute-api.us-west-2.amazonaws.com/TestDeploy/pets/2`. The output appears in Figure 7-10. Look again at the Resource Tree in Figure 7-4, earlier in the chapter. The path includes /pets, followed by /{petId}. When you use this new URL, you use that additional path rather than provide a GET input argument (which you do when adding the ? after /pets).

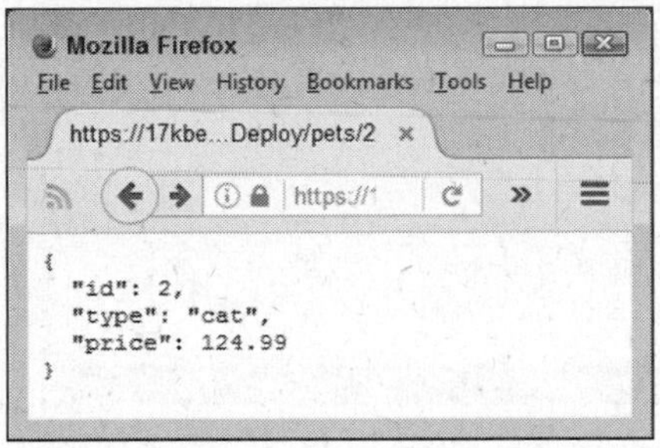

FIGURE 7-10:
Provide an ID to obtain a specific entry.

> To test the POST method easily, you need a third-party product such as Postman (https://www.getpostman.com/). When using the POST method, you use JSON code just as you did when testing the POST method during the client test earlier in this section.
>
> TIP

Accessing an API Gateway using the CLI

You can certainly create an API using CLI, but using the GUI to create the API is probably a lot easier when working with AWS. However, you might still want to access the API through CLI to see how it works in this environment (and make things easier for yourself when you create applications).

A common thread when working with API Gateway CLI commands is the need for a REST API ID and a resource ID. Fortunately, these two pieces of information are easy to find as long as you know where to look. Select the / entry in the Resource Tree. You see the information shown in Figure 7-11.

At the top of the page, you see the following:

```
APIs > PetStore (17kbeo12d7) > Resources > / (4al7ycfwb6)
```

The 17kbeo12d7 entry is the value you supply to the --rest-api-id argument when making calls. You need this value to make most of the calls. The 4al7ycfwb6 entry is the value you supply to the --resource-id argument when requested. This second value sees use only with specific calls.

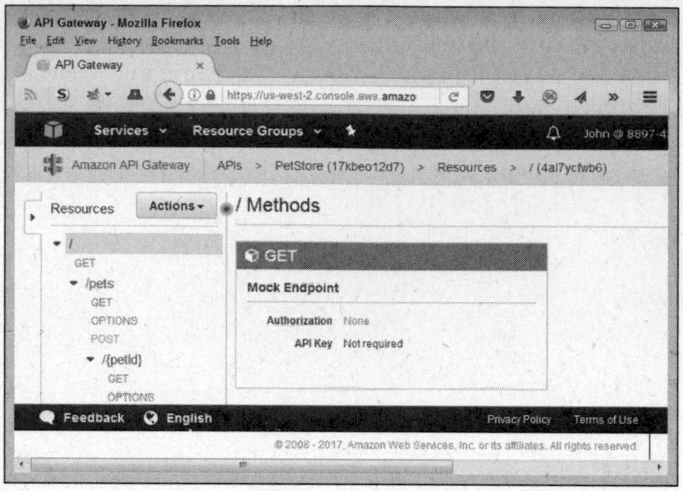

FIGURE 7-11:
Obtain the REST API ID and resource ID values.

The various CLI calls for API Gateway appear at http://docs.aws.amazon.com/cli/latest/reference/apigateway/, and as you can see, there are many of them. This section looks at two of these calls because they provide different kinds of output. Some calls output text, which you can display directly in the command prompt or terminal window; others output HTML or some other format that doesn't display well at the command prompt. To see one of the former commands in action, type **aws apigateway get-rest-api --rest-api-id 17kbeo12d7** and press Enter. Remember to replace the --rest-api-id argument with the value for your example API. Figure 7-12 shows typical output.

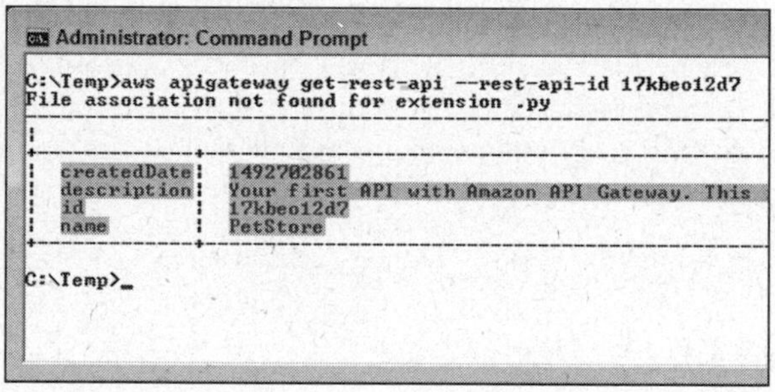

FIGURE 7-12:
Obtain information about the example API.

This output looks fine in the command window. However, if you want to obtain information about an existing method resource, you need some means to display HTML as output. To create the HTML output, type **aws apigateway**

get-method --rest-api-id 17kbe012d7 --resource-id 4al7ycfwb6 --http-method GET > Output.html and press Enter. You must replace both the **--rest-api-id** and **--resource-id** entries with values from your example API. In addition, the redirection used for this example is for Windows. Make sure that you redirect the output using the redirection for your platform. After you execute the command, load the resulting file in your browser. Figure 7-13 shows typical output.

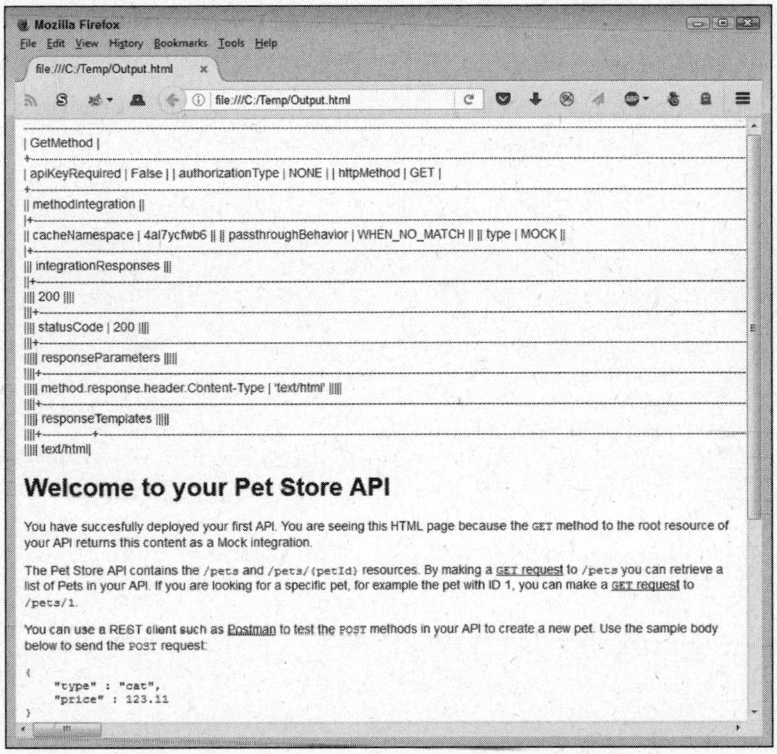

FIGURE 7-13:
Display HTML
output in your
browser.

IN THIS CHAPTER

» **Understanding the Elastic Beanstalk (EB) feature set**

» **Creating and deploying an EB application**

» **Performing application updates**

» **Deleting old applications**

» **Monitoring your application**

Chapter **8**

Developing Web Apps Using Elastic Beanstalk

A t one time, developers created desktop applications to harness the power and flexibility that desktop systems can provide. In many situations, developers still need this power and flexibility, but more and more application development occurs on the web. The reasons for this change are many, but they all come down to convenience. Users want to use applications that can run on any device, anywhere, and in the same way.

To make this device mobility happen, developers use web applications that run in a browser or a browser-like environment, which is where Elastic Beanstalk (EB) comes into play. Using EB enables developers to create applications that run anywhere on any device, yet don't suffer from problems of reliability and scalability that can occur when using a company-owned host. In addition, using EB makes the development process significantly faster because the developer need not worry about anything other than the code used to manipulate organizational data. The first section of this chapter explores how EB makes moving applications to the cloud easier for everyone involved.

Developers don't normally need to deploy applications in the production environment, but you do need to deploy them in the test environment, so this chapter shows how to install an EB application. You work with simple code in this chapter, but the process of installing the application is the same no matter the complexity of the underlying application. The chapter looks at multiple deployment methods because you can't necessarily rely on any single method. You also see how to deal with application configuration issues that affect how your application works and who can access it. In addition, this chapter discusses the requirements for making updates and getting rid of applications after you finish using them.

REMEMBER

The deployment, update, and retirement tasks are an essential part of using EB, even if you plan to keep the application private to your organization. Developers need to understand these tasks as part of discovering how to create efficient designs. The more efficient the design, the less likely administrators and users are to encounter problems that will require fixes later.

Whether your application is public or private, you probably want to monitor it, especially when fine-tuning it during the development process. This chapter shows how to use native EB functionality to perform the task. By using the EB monitoring features, you can integrate all your application activities using a single interface and ensure tight integration between the monitoring software and the application.

Considering Elastic Beanstalk (EB) Features

EB enables you to easily upload, configure, and manage applications of all sorts. An application isn't useful unless people can access it with ease and make it perform whatever tasks it's designed to perform in the most seamless manner possible. Achieving these goals requires the hosting platform to support various programming methodologies on a variety of platforms so that developers can use the tools most suited to a particular need. When working with AWS, you can currently create web applications (in the easiest-to-access form available) using these languages (with more to follow):

>> Java

>> .NET

>> PHP

>> Node.js

>> Python

» Ruby

» Go

» Docker

The applications run in managed containers for the language you choose. A *managed container* is one in which the host manages application resources and ensures that the application can't easily crash the system. The container acts as a shield between the application you're working with and every other application that the system hosts.

EB supports a number of platforms. The platform you choose for your development setup should match the platform for your organization. When a given platform lacks language support, development and administration must decide on an appropriate mix for the cloud, which often has different requirements than a local setup. Matching the language (to meet developer needs) with a platform (to meet administrator needs) on a host can prove difficult, but EB is up to the task because it provides support for these web application platforms:

» Apache

» Nginx

» Passenger

» IIS

EB is designed to simplify application deployment and management in a way that allows a developer more time to code. The three cornerstones of EB application support are the following:

» **Deployment:** Getting the application onto the server so that someone can use it.

» **Management:** Configuring the application as people find problems using it.

» **Scaling:** Providing a good application experience for everyone by ensuring that the application runs fast, reliably, and without any security issues.

As part of this whole picture, EB also relies on application health monitoring through Amazon CloudWatch. The Amazon CloudWatch service helps you determine when application health issues require the host to make changes in the application environment, such as by using autoscaling to make sure that the application has enough resources to run properly.

Deploying an EB Application

Before you can use your EB application, you must *deploy* it (make it accessible) on a server. Deployment involves the following steps:

1. Creating an application entry.

2. Uploading the application to Amazon. You perform this step as part of creating the application entry.

3. Configuring the application so that it runs as anticipated, which is also part of creating the application entry on the first pass, but you can also change the configuration later.

4. Configuring the application environment so that it has access to required resources. You perform the initial setup while creating the application entry, but you make configuration changes later based on the results of the monitoring that you perform.

5. Testing the application to determine whether it works as anticipated.

WARNING

EB comes with no additional charge; however, you must pay for any resources that your application uses. Be sure to keep this fact in mind as you work through the chapter. The examples don't require much in the way of resources, but you do need to pay for them, which means that you may need permission to install the applications before you proceed. The chapter structure is such that you can simply follow along with the text if desired. The following sections describe how to deploy an EB application.

Creating the application entry

Before you do anything else, you need to define an application entry in order to run an application using EB. The application entry acts as a sort of container for holding the application. AWS provides a number of methods for creating application entries. The following sections describe each of these methods and explain the reasoning for using each approach in specific situations.

Using the console

The console approach to creating an application entry offers the greatest level of support, which makes creating basic, one-time application entries easy. However, using the console isn't necessarily the fastest approach. Also, you can't script it, and finding some of the details can be difficult. The following steps describe how to create the application entry using the console approach:

1. **Sign in to AWS using your user account.**

2. **Navigate to the Elastic Beanstalk Console at** `https://console.aws.amazon.com/elasticbeanstalk`.

   You see a Welcome page that contains interesting information about Elastic Beanstalk and provides links to additional information and sample applications. In the upper-right corner, you see Create New Application.

   At the bottom of the page, you see the Select a Platform list box, shown in Figure 8-1. This list box lets you create a test setup that requires only a single click. However, the default options include configuring your environment to use both load balancing and autoscaling. Consequently, when you try to complete the setup, you see an error message stating that the application can't start until you upgrade your EC2 configuration. The upgrade will cost you money, and you don't actually require the additional functionality for the purposes of this book.

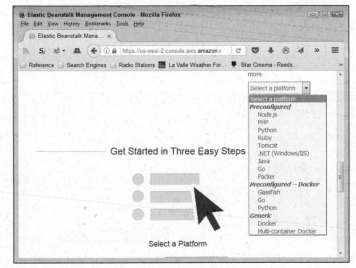

FIGURE 8-1:
Avoid using the one-click, Select a Platform option whenever possible.

3. **Click Create New Application.**

   You see the Application Information page, shown in Figure 8-2. You need to provide an application name (identity) and, optionally, describe it.

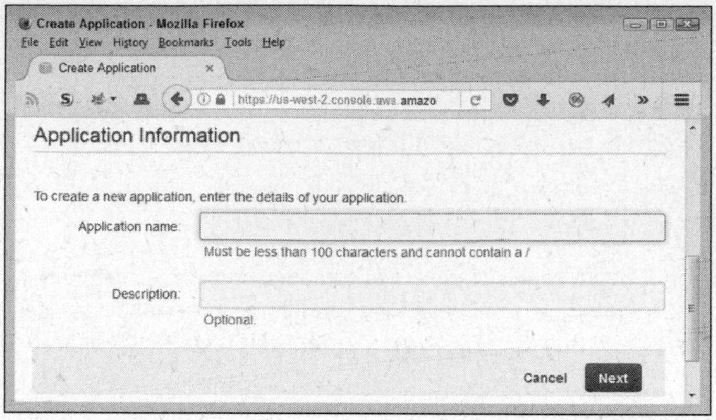

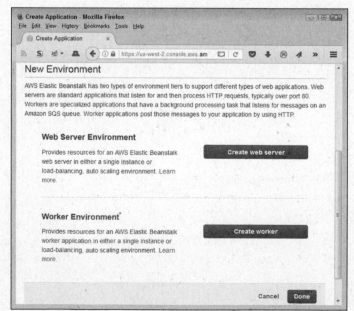

FIGURE 8-2:
Identify your
application and
describe it.

4. **Type** TestApp **in the Application Name field, type** A test application. **in the Description field, and then click Next.**

   You see the New Environment page, shown in Figure 8-3. EB provides two default environments:

   - **Web Server Environment:** Lets you run web applications using any of the languages that support web development.

   - **Worker Environment:** Creates a background application that you can call on in a variety of ways. Background applications don't provide user interfaces, so you normally use this option to create support for another application.

FIGURE 8-3:
Choose an
application
environment.

5. **Click Create Web Server.**

EB asks you to configure the environment type, as shown in Figure 8-4. The Preconfigured Configuration field contains a listing of languages that you can use. The Environment Type field defines how to run the application: single instance or using both load balancing and autoscaling.

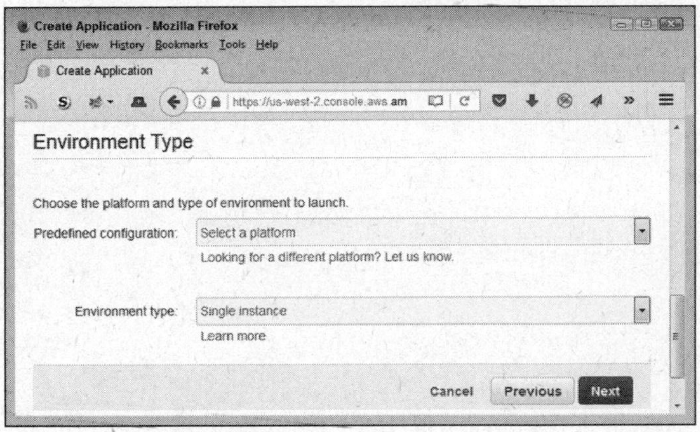

FIGURE 8-4:
Define the
application
environment
type.

6. **Choose PHP in the Preconfigured Configuration field, choose Single Instance in the Environment Type field, and then click Next.**

You see options for an application source, as shown in Figure 8-5. Normally you upload your own application or rely on an application defined as part of a Sample Storage Service (S3) setup. However, because this is an example, the next step will ask you to use a sample application. Working with sample applications makes experimenting easier because you know that nothing is wrong with the application code to cause a failure.

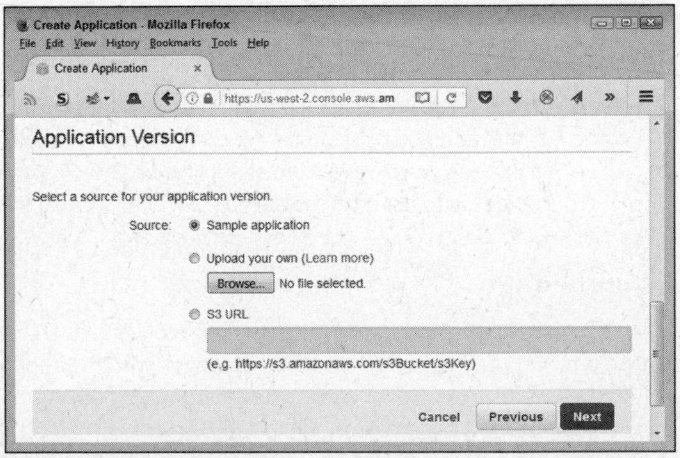

FIGURE 8-5:
Specify the
source of the
application code.

7. **Select the Sample Application option and click Next.**

EB displays the Environment Information page, shown in Figure 8-6. You must create a unique environment name for your application.

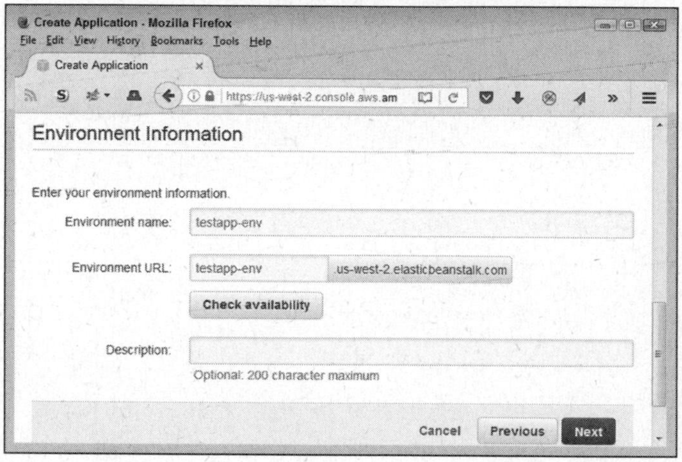

FIGURE 8-6:
Provide a name for the application environment.

8. **Type** MyCompany-TestEnv **in the Environment Name field.**

Note that EB automatically provides an Environment URL field value for you. In most cases, you want to keep that URL to ensure that the URL will work properly. The Environment URL field automatically provides the location of your EC2 instances to run the web application, so normally you won't need to change this value, either.

9. **Click Check Availability.**

The square around the Environment URL field changes to green if the check is successful. Otherwise, you need to provide a different Environment Name field entry.

10. **Type** A test environment. **in the Description field and then click Next.**

EB asks about the use of additional resources, as shown in Figure 8-7. Remember that additional resources generally incur fees, so keep these options blank when working with a test application. The RDS DB option creates a link to a database to use with the application. The VPC option creates a Virtual Private Cloud (VPC) to run the application.

11. **Click Next.**

At this point, you need to define the configuration details, shown in Figure 8-8. The options you use depend on how you want to run the application. However, the steps tell you how to maintain a free setup. Using other Instance Type field settings could incur costs.

FIGURE 8-7:
Avoid using additional resources unless you actually need them.

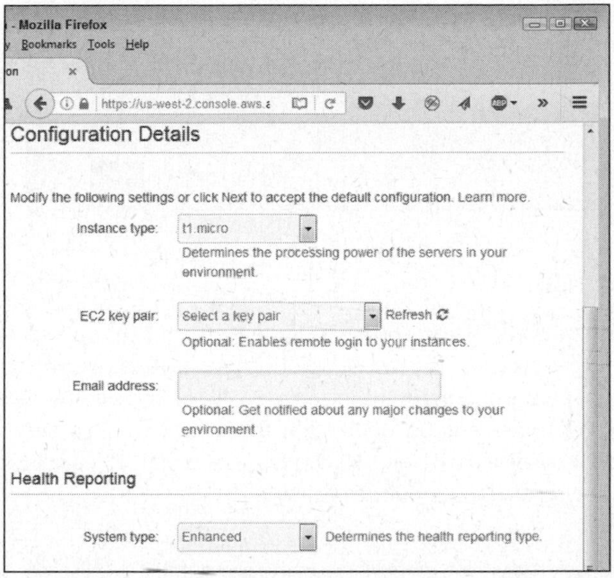

FIGURE 8-8:
Specify the instance environment for running the application.

12. Choose t2.micro in the Instance Type field and the key pair (defined in the "Generating security keys" section of Chapter 6) that you want to use.

13. (Optional) Type your email address in the Email Address field.

14. Choose Basic in the System Type field (Health Reporting section) and then click Next.

EB asks whether you want to define Environment Tags. These are key value pairs used to help configure your application. The sample application doesn't require any tags.

15. Click Next.

You see the Environment Tags page, shown in Figure 8-9. This page can become important to developers who need to configure environment tags as part of an application setup. The tags use name value pairs, just as you use when configuring your environment variables in any localized operating system. This example doesn't require any tags, but you should keep them in mind.

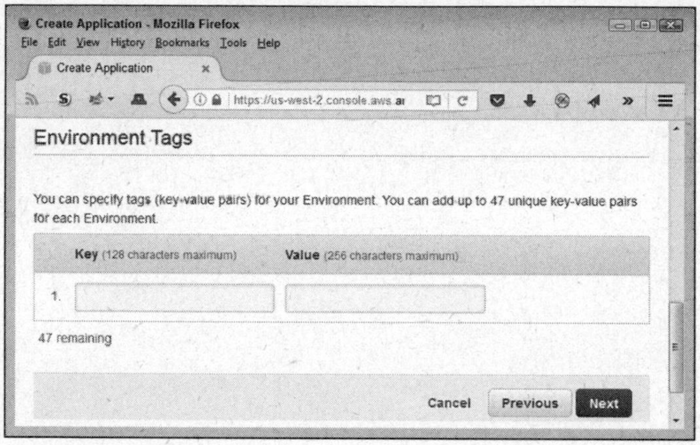

FIGURE 8-9:
Define any
environment tags
needed to
support your
application.

16. **Click Next.**

The Permissions page, shown in Figure 8-10, contains options for creating or using permissions. The test setup doesn't contain any permissions, so you won't see any options in the Instance Profile or Service Role fields. If you had already defined another application, these fields would allow you to reuse those existing permissions. EB creates a set of default permissions for you, which you can later modify as needed.

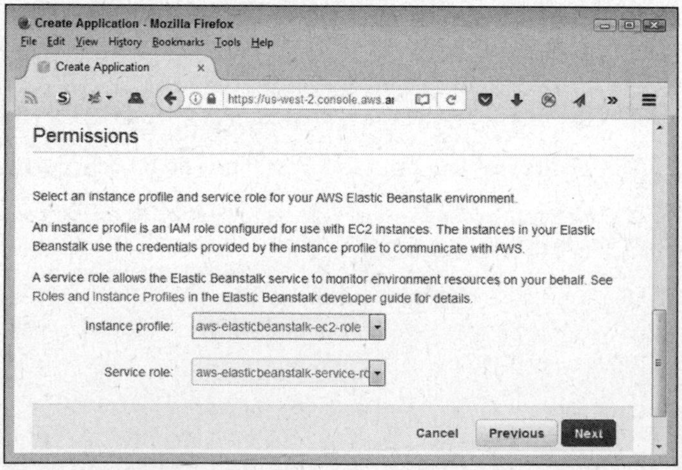

FIGURE 8-10:
The Permissions
page lets you
reuse permis-
sions as needed.

17. Click Next.

You see a Review page that contains all the settings made so far in the procedure. Check the settings to ensure that you made the entries correctly.

18. Click Launch.

You see EB launching your application, as shown in Figure 8-11. Be patient: This process can require several minutes to complete.

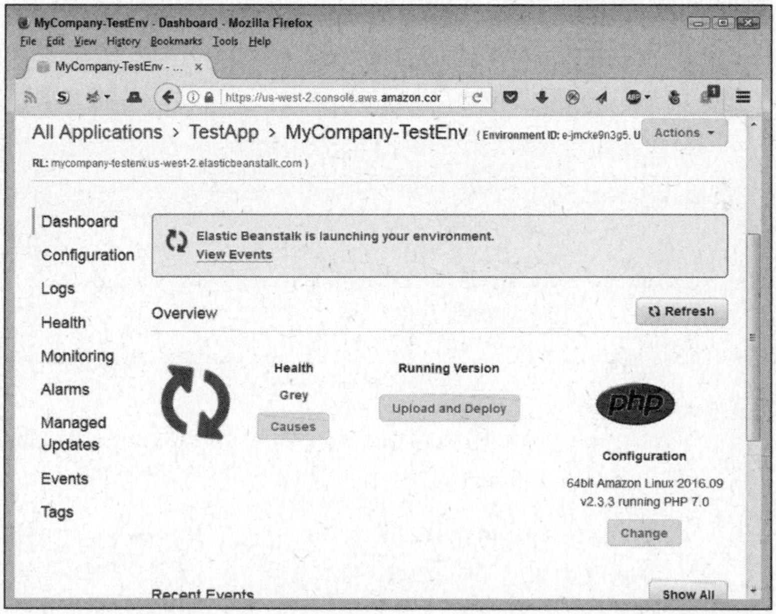

FIGURE 8-11: Wait for the application to deploy.

TIP

You can find some sample applications at http://docs.aws.amazon.com/elasticbeanstalk/latest/dg/RelatedResources.html. Just download the application and then use it as part of following the exercises in this section and the sections that follow. (The "Installing Node.js" section of Chapter 5 discusses how to obtain a copy of Node.js and install it on your system when needed. However, you don't need it for the example in this chapter.) The sample applications cover a number of the languages and platforms, but not all of them. If you download an application and install it using the techniques found in this chapter, you must also pay for resources that the application requires to run.

Installing EB CLI

The "Installing the Command Line Interface Software" section of Chapter 5 discusses how to install the basic AWS CLI software. In fact, you use this version to interact with S3 in that chapter in the "Configuring S3 Using the CLI" section. In order to work with EB, you need an EB version of CLI. To obtain the needed software, open a command prompt or terminal window, type **pip install --upgrade awsebcli**, and press Enter. You see a relatively long list of messages followed by a success message.

To test your setup, type **eb --help** and press Enter. Figure 8-12 shows the help screen you see after a successful installation.

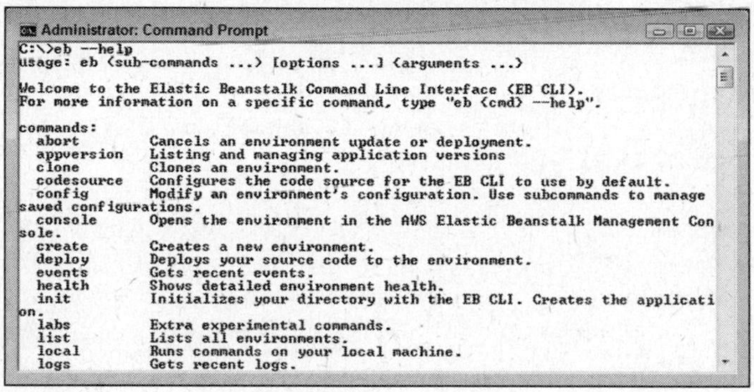

FIGURE 8-12:
Check your eb CLI installation to ensure success.

Before you can use eb to perform useful work, you must initialize it. The following steps get you started.

1. **Type** eb init **and press Enter.**

   The wizard asks you to select a region.

2. **Type the number corresponding to the region you want to use and press Enter.**

   The book uses us-west-2 (Oregon), which is selection 3. You need to choose the number corresponding to the region you select earlier in the chapter. If you followed the process in the "Using the console" section, earlier in this chapter, you see TestApp listed as one of the application choices, as shown in Figure 8-13. The remaining steps assume that you did create the application and are choosing TestApp as your application. Creating a second application will incur costs, so use the existing application if possible.

3. **Type an application number and press Enter.**

   The eb utility continues the configuration process. Unless you have source control setup, the process ends here. Otherwise, you need to follow the steps required to configure your particular kind of source control.

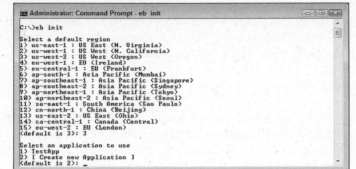

FIGURE 8-13:
Choose an
existing applica-
tion or create a
new one.

Using the EB CLI

After you install and configure eb CLI, you can perform all the same tasks with it as you do by using the console. The difference for a developer, of course, is that you can now script your tasks. For example, to see a list of all EB environments, you type **eb list** and press Enter. The output shows the environment you created in the "Using the console" section of the chapter.

REMEMBER

You can start with a simple command and then refine it. If you want to know what refinements are available, add the --help argument after a command. For example, eb list --help shows the optional arguments for the list command.

Using eb isn't limited to the AWS console or the command line, either. For example, when you type eb open and press Enter, you see the EB sites opened in a browser. If you want to see a specific site, you need to add the environment name, such as MyCompany-TestEnv, to the command. You can find a list of eb CLI commands at http://docs.aws.amazon.com/elasticbeanstalk/latest/dg/eb3-cmd-commands.html.

Performing tasks programmatically

Another way to perform tasks is by using programming languages such as Python. What you need is access to an AWS SDK for the language. In the case of Python, you use boto. (You can access this example code in the AWS4D4D; 08; EB Check.ipynb file for this chapter in the downloadable source code provided for this book; see details in the Introduction.) The code begins by importing the required library and then creating a client to use it.

```
import boto3
client = boto3.client('elasticbeanstalk')
```

After you gain access to EB, you can perform the same sorts of tasks that you can at the console or by using CLI. For example, the following code lists all of the applications available to you, unless you specify a particular application:

```
client.describe_applications()
```

The output is comprehensive, telling you all about the application so that you can perform additional tasks. In addition to the application name, you also discover details such as when you created the application and any description you supplied with it. You can find a list of available methods at https://boto3.readthedocs.io/en/latest/reference/services/elasticbeanstalk.html.

Testing the application deployment

After you complete the steps in the "Using the console" section of the chapter, you have an application running. Look again at Figure 8-11 to see the URL field entry near the top of the page. (It's in really small print, so you might have to look hard to see it.) Click this link to see your application running. The sample PHP application displays the page shown in Figure 8-14.

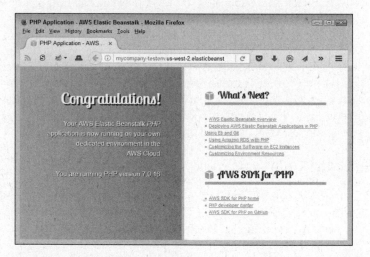

FIGURE 8-14: The deployed application works like any other web application.

Setting application security

Any code you deploy using EB becomes immediately public at the URL provided in the URL field unless you change the security rules. This means that you really do need to verify that the page is safe to display before you deploy it. However, you can also make the page private by following these steps:

1. **Choose Services ⇨ EC2 from the menu at the top of the page.**

   You see the EC2 Dashboard page.

2. **Choose Network & Security ⇨ Security Groups from the Navigation pane.**

   EC2 displays a list of security groups, as shown in Figure 8-15. The selected security group in the figure is the one used with EB. If you followed the procedure in the "Creating the application entry" section, earlier in this chapter, you should see a security group with a similar name.

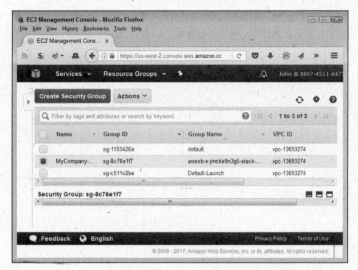

FIGURE 8-15: The EC2 security groups contain the security group used to configure EB.

3. **Select the security group entry for EB configuration and choose Actions ⇨ Edit Inbound Rules.**

   EC2 displays the Edit Inbound Rules dialog box, shown in Figure 8-16. You can change any configuration option for the security group that will modify the way in which incoming requests work. For example, you can change the HTTP type to HTTPS to create secure access to the page. However, in this case, you can use a simpler method to secure access to the page in a reasonable way: Simply disallow access from sources other than your system.

4. **Choose My IP in the Source field for both HTTP and SSH access of the security group.**

   EC2 modifies the rules as expected.

REMEMBER

   To make this setup work, you must also provide access to the website to the instance security group. Otherwise, when you attempt to perform updates, the updates will fail.

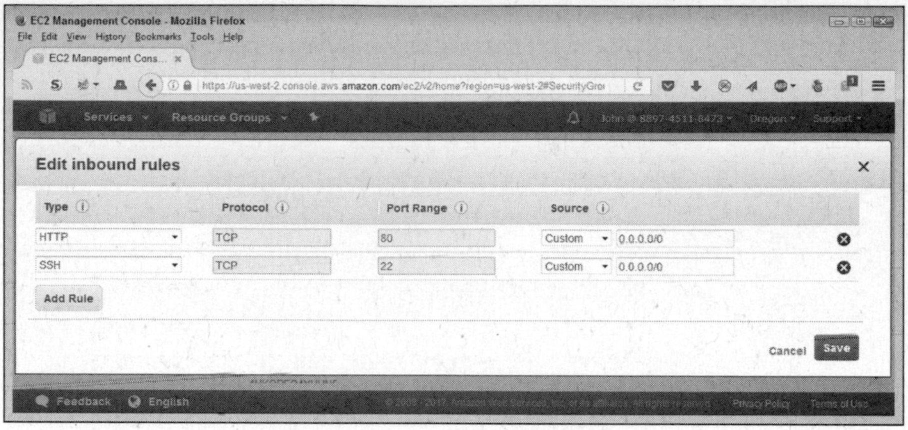

FIGURE 8-16:
Modify the rules to ensure that access remains restricted.

5. **Click Add Rule.**

   You see a new rule added to the list.

6. **Choose All Traffic in the Type field and All in the Protocol field.**

   These two settings provide complete access to the security group.

7. **Choose Custom in the Source field and type** sg **in the text field after it.**

   You see a listing of security groups for your server as shown in Figure 8-17. A source can consist of a Classless Inter-Domain Routing (CIDR) address, IP address, or security group ID. Typing sg tells EC2 that you want to use a security group. Note that one of the security groups in the list specifically mentions the AWSEBSecurityGroup, which is the security group that you want to use.

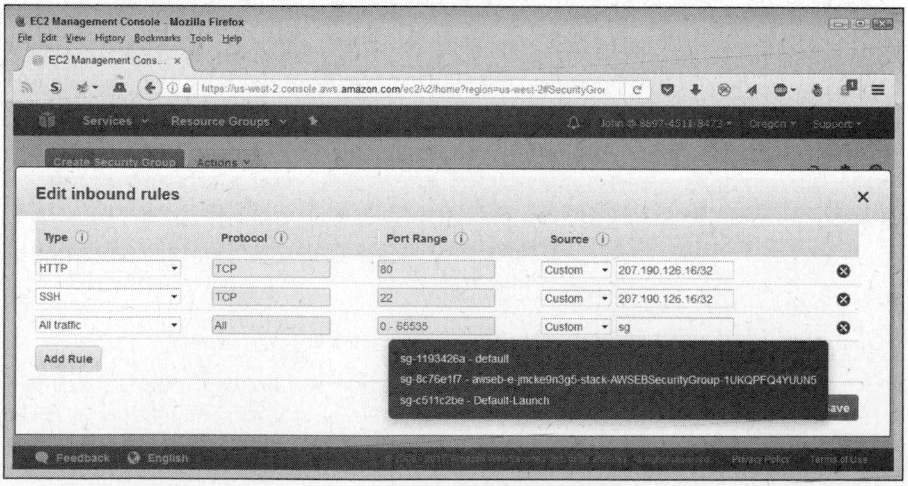

FIGURE 8-17:
Choose an existing security group to allow instance access to your EB setup.

8. **Click the security group for the website instance in the list.**

   The security group appears in the Source field.

9. **Click Save.**

   The inbound security rules now prevent access to the site by any entity other than the website instance or you.

REMEMBER

The IP address supplied when you choose My IP in the Source field uses the IP address of your current location. If other people use the same router (and therefore the same IP address), they also have access to the website. Consequently, setting the inbound rules does help provide security, but only a certain level of security. In addition, the IP address can change when you reset the router and then reconnect to the Internet provider. Consequently, you may find that you lose access to the test site you've created because of the change in IP address. If you suddenly find that you have lost access, verify that your IP address hasn't changed.

Configuring the application

You can modify the application EB application configuration as needed. You initially set all these configuration options during the creation process, but getting the settings correct at the outset isn't always possible. Simply select the Configuration entry in the EB Navigation pane and you see the listing of application configuration entries, as shown in Figure 8-18.

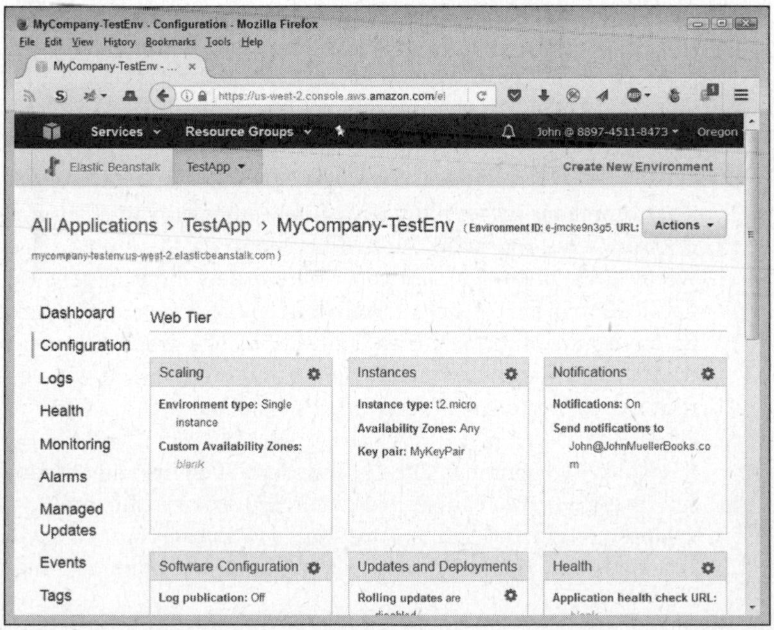

FIGURE 8-18:
Using the configuration entries to change how your application runs.

To change a configuration option, click the button next to the heading, such as Scaling, that you want to modify. You see a new page that contains the configuration options. After you make the configuration changes, click Apply to make them active or click Cancel when you make a mistake.

Working with application environments

The application environments appear on the initial EB environments page, shown in Figure 8-19. An application can have multiple environments so that you can test it under multiple conditions. The capability to use multiple environments enables you to perform extensive testing to find the correct environment — the one that serves application users the best for the lowest possible cost.

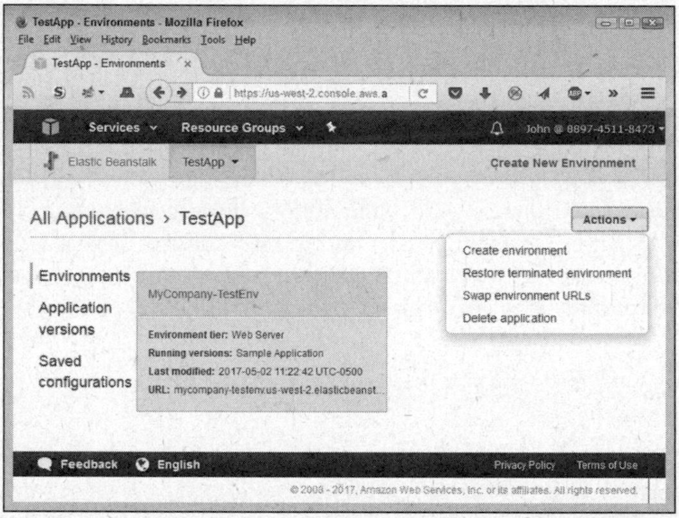

FIGURE 8-19: Application environments control how your application runs.

The commands for working with a new environment or interacting with multiple environments appear in the Actions menu on this initial page in the GUI. When working on this page, you can create a new environment (and use an existing application in it), restore a terminated environment, swap the URLs used to access an environment, or delete an application. The graphic shows you some essential basics about the environments. For example, when you see a green box, you know that the environment is operating as expected without fault.

TIP

Swapping environment URLs is an essential environment management technique for developers. You can test a new configuration without telling anyone about it by swapping the active URL for one that isn't in use. The users will see the new environment, but not really know that the new environment is in place. The feedback you receive in this case is unbiased. Yes, the user can see that something has changed, but because the change isn't broadcast, the feedback reflects actual changes in functionality rather than biased input that's affected by knowledge of the change.

To interact with the environment in a meaningful way, you must click its entry on this main page. The Actions menu on the environment's page contains options for loading a configuration, saving a configuration, swapping the URLs used to access environments, cloning an environment (producing an exact copy), rebuilding an environment, and terminating an environment. The point is that these options all deal with a specific environment rather than environments as a whole.

TIP

This is one case in which using EB CLI is definitely faster than working with the GUI because you don't spend nearly so much time trying to figure out where to execute a command. You can find a list of environment management commands for EB CLI at http://docs.aws.amazon.com/elasticbeanstalk/latest/dg/eb-cli3-getting-started.html. For example, to obtain the status of all your environments, type **eb status** and press Enter at the command prompt. You see the output shown in Figure 8-20. The textual output is actually easier to interact with, especially if you happen to be color-blind. You can obtain additional information using the eb status --verbose command. If you manage a large number of environments, use the --region argument to limit the number of outputs.

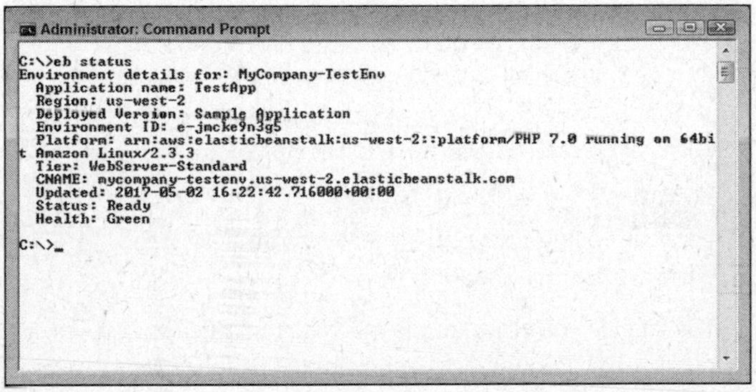

FIGURE 8-20:
Using the command line is definitely faster than the GUI when working with environments.

```
Administrator: Command Prompt

C:\>eb status
Environment details for: MyCompany-TestEnv
    Application name: TestApp
    Region: us-west-2
    Deployed Version: Sample Application
    Environment ID: e-jmcke9n3g5
    Platform: arn:aws:elasticbeanstalk:us-west-2::platform/PHP 7.0 running on 64bi
t Amazon Linux/2.3.3
    Tier: WebServer-Standard
    CNAME: mycompany-testenv.us-west-2.elasticbeanstalk.com
    Updated: 2017-05-02 16:22:42.716000+00:00
    Status: Ready
    Health: Green

C:\>_
```

Updating an EB Application

Applications don't exist in a vacuum: organizational and other requirements change, environments evolve, user needs change, and so on. As the application functionality and operation changes, so must the application configuration and setup. The environmental needs change as well. In other words, you must perform an EB update to keep the application current so that users can continue using it.

The following sections describe the kinds of changes you need to consider during an update.

Getting the sample code and making a change

You're extremely unlikely to upload just one version of your application. An application actually has a life cycle, and change is simply part of the process. Making changes using the sample application means getting the current code and then doing something with it. The following steps help you get a copy of the current application and perform a small change on it. (You can access the modified version of the example code in the php-v2 folder for this chapter in the downloadable source code provided with this book, as explained in the Introduction.)

1. **Download the** php-v1.zip **file found at** http://docs.aws.amazon.com/elasticbeanstalk/latest/dg/RelatedResources.html.

2. **Expand the archive into its own folder (directory) on your hard drive.**

   You see a number of application files, including index.php. The index.php file contains the code used to display the web page shown previously in Figure 8-14. Modifying the code changes how the web page appears.

3. **Open the** index.php **file using any text editor.**

   The text editor must output pure text files without any formatting. For example, Notepad on Windows systems, gedit on Linux systems, and TextEdit on Mac systems are all examples of pure text editors. On the other hand, Microsoft Word, LibreOffice, and FreeOffice are all examples of editors that you can't use to make modifications to PHP files.

4. **Locate the line that reads** <h1>Congratulations!</h1> **and replace it with** <h1>Hello There!</h1>.

   The change you've just made modifies the greeting you see. It's a small change, but it serves to demonstrate how modifications typically work.

5. **Save the file.**

   The modified file is now ready to upload to Amazon.

Uploading the modified application

To see any coding changes you make, you must upload the changes to AWS. It doesn't matter how complex the application becomes: At some point, you use the same process to upload changed files. The following steps describe how to perform this task:

1. **Place the files for your application into an archive.**

   The normal archive format is a `.zip` file.

2. **Open the application dashboard by clicking its entry in the initial EB page.**

   You see options for working with the application, as shown in Figure 8-21.

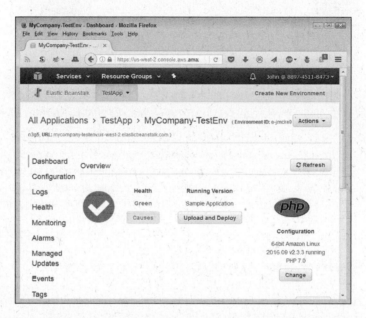

FIGURE 8-21:
The application dashboard lets you perform application-related tasks.

3. **Click Upload and Deploy.**

   You see an Upload and Deploy dialog box like the one shown in Figure 8-22.

4. **Click Browse.**

   You see a File Upload window consistent with your platform and browser.

5. **Select the file containing the modified application code and click Open.**

   EB displays the filename next to the Browse button.

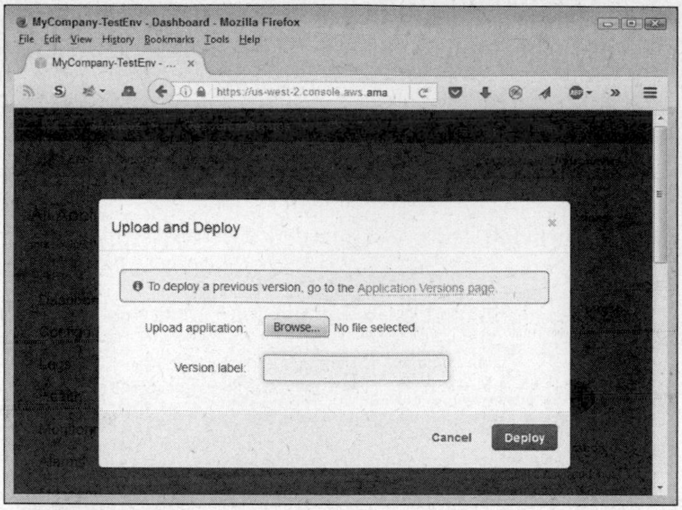

FIGURE 8-22:
Use the Upload and Deploy dlalog box to upload new application versions.

6. **Type** Changed-Greeting **in the Version Label field and then click Deploy.**

    EB displays messages telling you that it's updating the environment. Be patient; this process can take a few minutes to complete. At some point, the application indictor turns green again (and you see the check mark icon), which means that you can test the application using the same procedure described in the "Testing the application deployment" section, earlier in this chapter. What you should see is a change in greeting from "Congratulations!" to "Hello There!"

Switching application versions

You now have two application versions uploaded to the EC2 instance. In some cases, you may have to switch between application versions. Perhaps a fix in a new version really didn't work out, so you need to go to an older, more stable, version. The following steps describe how to switch between versions:

1. **Click Upload and Deploy.**

    Look again at Figure 8-22. Notice the Application Versions Page link. This page contains a listing of all the versions available for use.

2. **Click the Application Versions Page link.**

    You see the Application Versions page, shown in Figure 8-23. The last field of the table shows where each version is deployed. In this case, Changed-Greeting is deployed, but Sample Application isn't.

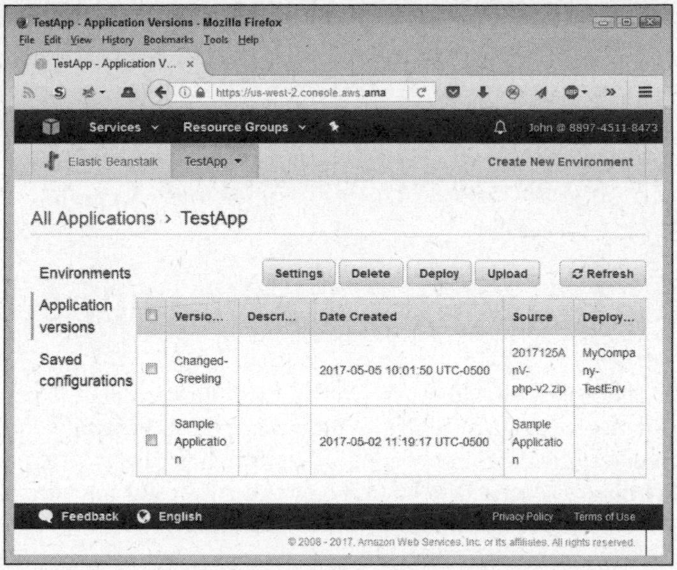

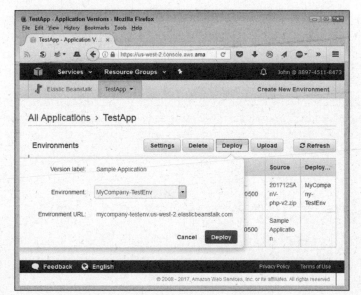

FIGURE 8-23:
The example now has two available versions.

3. Check the Sample Application version and click Deploy.

EB displays the deployment options, shown in Figure 8-24. The fields contain the same environment settings as before. You don't want to change these settings unless you want to create a new environment.

FIGURE 8-24:
You specify deployment options as part of making an update available.

4. **Click Deploy.**

   EB displays messages telling you that it's updating the environment. At some point, the application indictor turns green again, which means that you can test the application using the same procedure found in the "Testing the application deployment" section, earlier in this chapter.

Removing Unneeded Applications

EB applications get old just as any other application does. Software becomes outdated to the point at which additional updates become counterproductive and expensive; creating a new application becomes easier. When an application gets old enough, you need to shut it down in a graceful manner and remove it after training users to use whatever new application you have in place.

WARNING

Transitions from one application to another are one of the most difficult development tasks. Foreseeing everything that can go wrong is difficult, plus transitions add layers of complexity that developers may not understand. This chapter can't provide you with everything needed to perform a transition, but it does show you the mechanics of removing an EB application you no longer need. However, before you remove the application, make sure that you have the transition process well planned and have backup processes in place for when things go wrong.

To remove an application from an instance, you select its entry in the Application Versions page (refer to Figure 8-23) and click Delete. However, before you delete an application, be sure to have another version of the application deployed to the instance, or site users may suddenly find that they can't access your site.

To delete an entire application, including all the versions, select the Environments page, shown previously in Figure 8-19. Choose Actions➪Delete Application to remove the entire application. Removing the application doesn't remove the EC2 instance.

Monitoring Your Application Using Amazon CloudWatch

Monitoring lets you determine whether the application environment is sufficient for your application. For example, you may decide that you require a different instance type because of the amount of traffic. To monitor your application, choose the Monitoring option in the Navigation pane. EB displays the information shown in Figure 8-25.

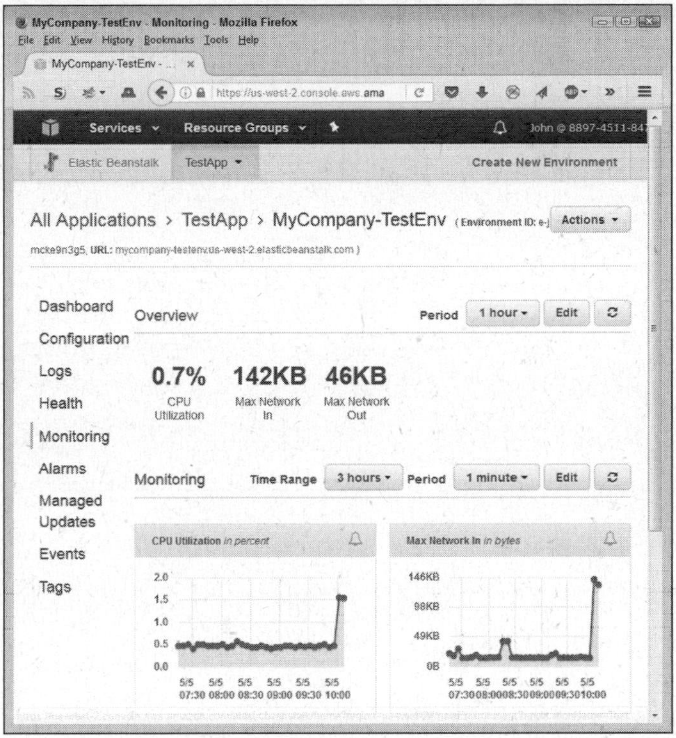

FIGURE 8-25:
Monitor your application to determine when it requires environment changes.

As shown in Figure 8-25, the test application uses hardly any of the resources provided to it, so you don't need to make any changes. Of course, this is an expected outcome given that you're the only one with access to the application. The line graphs below the text output show graphically how many resources your application uses. You can also change the monitoring criteria for longer monitoring sessions (to show generalized trends over a 24-hour period, for example).

Each of the graphs in Figure 8-25 has a button associated with it. When you click the button, you see a page for creating an alarm, as shown in Figure 8-26. Each alarm entry must have a unique name. You then provide a monitoring period, metric-specific thresholds, and notification information. When you complete the form, click Add. You can see the alarms you set for your EB application by choosing Alarms in the Navigation pane. When an alarm occurs, a message about it comes to you through the notification method (such as an email message) that you selected.

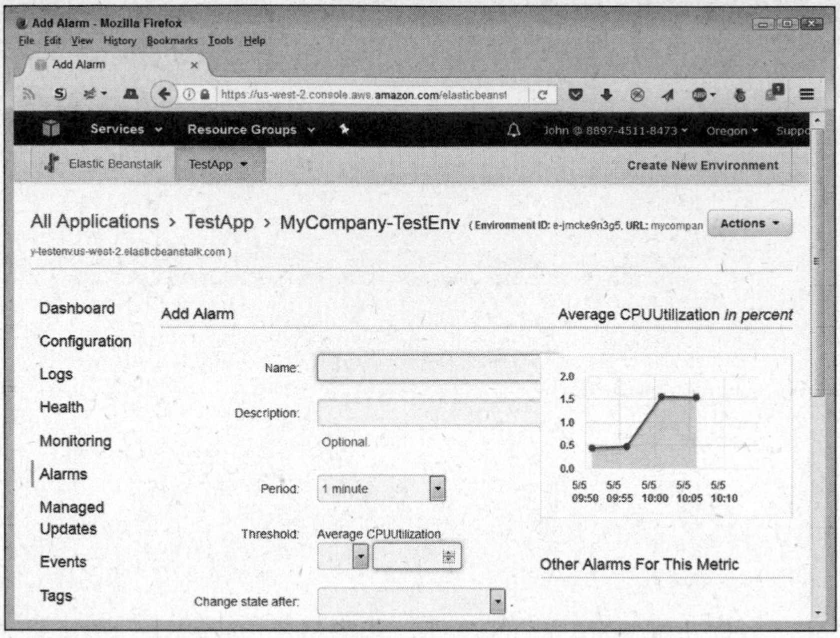

FIGURE 8-26: Set alarms as needed to prevent failures because of lack of resources.

Chapter 9

Developing Batch Processes and Scripts

The chapters up to this point in the book rely on performing tasks one at a time using a variety of methods that include the console GUIs, Command Line Interface (CLI), and specially designed applications. That is, you perform tasks one at a time without any chance of automating the task. That's the best approach while you're discovering how the various services work. However, after you know how the services work and need to perform tasks quickly, you're ready to add automation.

You can automate AWS tasks using two techniques: batch processing (requesting that AWS perform a series of related tasks on a schedule) and scripting (writing code to perform unrelated tasks at any desired time). This chapter begins by reviewing the options you have for performing both levels of automated processing.

Most developers use automation to perform tasks, so you might already have tools that you like using. The next three sections of the chapter discuss methods of performing both batch processing and scripting using traditional methods. Your specific method might not appear in the chapter, but the basic techniques for performing localized batch and script processing remain essentially the same.

It doesn't take long for popular environments such as AWS that have enough complexity to attract custom tool development. The final section of the chapter helps you work with aws-shell, a custom tool developed by Amazon developers to make working with AWS services considerably easier. Because aws-shell is custom built to work with AWS, it includes many automation features that your favorite tool doesn't have. This final section helps you understand the benefits of using aws-shell but doesn't seek to move you from your favorite tool to something that might seem unfamiliar or less useful.

Considering the Batch-Processing and Script Options

Batch processing and scripting both have the same essential focus: to automate tasks. To be productive, developers need some way to automate tasks, which allows a focus on unique development needs. However, batch processing and scripting go about the automation process in different ways, and they each have a different place in the developer's toolbox. The following sections discuss differences between batch processing and scripting, and help you understand the role of each. In addition, you consider the options available for accomplishing each automation type.

Defining the difference between batch processing and scripting

Batch processing and scripting have different purposes when it comes to working with AWS (or any other cloud-based application strategy for that matter). Here's a basic summary of the differences between the two:

>> **Batch processing:** Uses a data focus to manage data directly either online or offline. The purpose of batch processing is to manipulate the data in some way to make it easier to process. For example, updating the data with the latest numbers requires a batch process. You can also use batch processing for data shaping. Removing redundant records or filling in missing data also works well as a batch process. The point is that batch processing focuses on data manipulation using repetitive methodologies.

REMEMBER

Batch processing does have some specific characteristics. Developers often associate batch processes with highly variable usage patterns that have significant usage peaks. For example, end-of-the-month data processing falls into this category. The batch process is the same each month, but the pattern can vary significantly depending on the amount of data to process and any special requirements (such as the addition of year-end processing). A batch-processing scenario can also require a complex setup using multiple AWS services to keep track of jobs, provide job status updates, track job performance, and automate fault tolerance by automatically resubmitting failed jobs.

» **Scripting:** Uses a task focus to accomplish goals that may not directly change data. For example, measuring application efficiency or adding new application modules both work as scripted tasks. Most scripts run in real time, but you can also schedule scripts to run later. Scripts tend to provide greater flexibility than batch processes, but scripts also require more work to create. Scripts offer a task-specific approach to perform both application and data manipulation using flexible methodologies.

REMEMBER

Scripting solutions tend to handle uncertainty better than batch solutions. When performing a batch task, you know that certain data will require manipulation at given times to meet specific goals. A scripting scenario may handle uncertain data at unusual intervals to meet goals based on conditions, some of which are unforeseen. For example, you don't create new users every day, and the data and requirements for adding a user changes over time; consequently, adding users is a task that you handle better using scripts.

» **Overlapping and Combining:** As with everything, no absolute rule exists saying that you must use a particular approach for a particular need. For example, it's perfectly acceptable to perform ad hoc monitoring using a batch process or data manipulation using scripting approaches. Often, the best approach is the one that you're most familiar with and that allows you to perform the task most quickly. In addition, you must consider the availability of tools and the costs involved in automating the task. You may also find that you need to combine scripting and batch processing, creating another type of overlap between the two. For example, you might create a script that calls on a batch file and then schedule that script to run at a particular time each day.

Understanding the batch-processing options

You have access to a wide assortment of batch-processing options when working with AWS. In fact, so many options are available that covering them all in a single book chapter isn't possible. This book is written with the developer in mind, so the following sections address batch-processing options that involve various levels of complexity and flexibility. For example, using AWS Batch is simple, but it may lack some of the flexibility you need to address specific needs.

DEFINING THE CLOUD DIFFERENCE

Many developers are used to working with clusters or other localized batch methods. The cloud provides an entirely different kind of environment, and you need a completely different sort of batch-processing approach to work with the cloud. For starters, clusters tend to provide specific features to address particular workload needs. The cloud environment is far more generic. A cloud solution handles multiple workload scenarios with equal ease.

When working locally, you have to deal with hardware that has specific capacity and availability. The cloud changes all that. When working with AWS, you can add as much capacity as you need and the added hardware is instantly available. In addition, you have considerable flexibility in configuring that hardware in specific ways. However, when working in the cloud, you must also consider price. All that added capacity, flexibility, and availability comes at a cost.

A cluster environment usually relies on policies and priorities to allocate resources. The cloud environment has no such limitations. In addition, when working in the cloud, every group can have an individualized environment, which means that the whole idea of allocating fixed resources according to a policy no longer works. The controlling factor becomes one of benefit. The payback for a particular batch process must exceed the cost of performing the batch processing using whatever means the group in question requires. The policy is replaced with a cost/benefit analysis to determine effectiveness of a particular strategy.

Using AWS Batch

AWS Batch (https://aws.amazon.com/batch/) is possibly the simplest cloud-based batch-processing solution that you'll find. It's also easy to set up, and you don't pay for anything but the resources that the service uses. As with most AWS services, you have access to an API for interacting with AWS Batch (http://docs.aws.amazon.com/batch/latest/APIReference/Welcome.html), so you can easily add batch processing directly to your application. According to the article at https://venturebeat.com/2016/12/01/aws-launches-batch-processing-service-in-preview/, Amazon introduced AWS Batch in response to similar services offered by other cloud-based vendors.

AWS Batch may sound like a perfect solution, but you need to know that the simplicity and ease of setup come at the cost of flexibility. For example, if you need to integrate local data or work with other cloud-based solutions, AWS Batch won't do the job unless you're willing to perform a lot of custom development. The kludge you create to glue things together will be fragile, which means that you also need to consider the reliability of the result. AWS Batch is a good solution, but you need to think about its limitations before delving into it.

Extending AWS Batch with Docker (https://www.docker.com/) is possible. Of course, this still means creating a custom solution of sorts, but Docker provides great support for creating a wealth of application types. According to http://docs.aws.amazon.com/batch/latest/userguide/Batch_GetStarted.html, you can simply submit your Docker image to AWS Batch instead of creating a batch job as normal. The article at https://aws.amazon.com/blogs/compute/creating-a-simple-fetch-and-run-aws-batch-job/ gives you the information needed to build a basic fetch-and-run job. You can use this information to begin creating more complicated batch-job scenarios.

Using Amazon EC2 Spot

Many developers will find that using a simple solution such as AWS Batch won't work, but that doesn't mean you can't rely on AWS to create a batch-processing solution. The article at https://aws.amazon.com/blogs/compute/cost-effective-batch-processing-with-amazon-ec2-spot/ describes how you can couple various AWS services together to create a batch-processing solution that's both robust and flexible. The problem is that now you're looking at a significant amount of complexity because the solution in question relies on a number of services:

>> **EC2:** Provides processing power.

>> **S3:** Individual buckets hold incoming and outgoing data.

>> **Lambda:** Triggers event processing when new data arrives in the incoming bucket.

>> **SQS:** Holds the job-processing queue.

>> **DynamoDB:** Contains status information about the various jobs and allows for job updates.

>> **EFS:** Provides file system-type storage for EC2.

Depending on how you configure the setup, the number of services can increase. Yes, this is a complete solution based exclusively on AWS, but to obtain the flexibility and scalability that most businesses need, you also have to consider the complexity and the potential fragility of the setup.

Creating a batch process using CLI

One of the ways you can use to reduce the complexity of creating a purely AWS approach to batch processing is to rely on CLI scripts. The article and resources at https://github.com/danilop/SampleBatchProcessing provide one such approach to the problem. As with most flexible solutions, this one relies on a number of AWS services to get the job done. However, by scripting the setup, you make creating new configurations as needed easier.

Understanding the scripting options

As with batch processing, too many script solutions exist to discuss in a single chapter. In fact, if anything, you have more scripting choices when working with AWS than you have batch solutions. The script solutions also tend to vary more in approach, functionality, and flexibility.

Scripts can also execute automatically based on events. Chapter 10 discusses one such option using Lambda. The following sections provide an overview of common scripting options to meet generalized scripting scenarios. You need to do your homework and view the wide variety of options before making a final choice. These sections help make you aware of the potential solutions so that you can wade through the vast number of options with greater ease.

Working with SDKs

Most people associate scripting with simple languages. However, today developers often create script-like applications using languages capable of complex tasks such as Java and Python. With this in mind, the first place a developer should look for scripting solutions is at the SDKs that Amazon provides at `https://aws.amazon.com/code`. The page includes SDKs for many major languages, and you use the SDKs to simplify development tasks that can include scripting various configuration tasks.

TIP

Note that this same page includes a variety of example applications based on the SDKs. Many of these examples actually show how to implement scripting solutions. For example, the Simple E-mail Service (SES) scripts found at `https://docs.aws.amazon.com/ses/latest/DeveloperGuide/Welcome.html` fall into the scripting category because they really aren't end-user applications. Another such example appears at `https://aws.amazon.com/code/4026240853893296`. This example shows how to bootstrap applications using AWS CloudFormation. The point is that you can use your favorite language to create needed AWS scripts.

Using AWS OpsWorks

AWS OpsWorks (`https://aws.amazon.com/opsworks/`) is a Chef-based (`https://www.chef.io/solutions/infrastructure-automation/`) application configuration management system that performs essential tasks automatically. The interesting thing about this setup is that if you know how to write Chef scripts (`https://docs.chef.io/resource_script.html`), you can use the same knowledge to automate AWS actions (see the article at `http://docs.aws.amazon.com/opsworks/latest/userguide/cookbooks-101-basics-commands.html`).

SCRIPTING AND THE DEVELOPMENT ENVIRONMENT

You can use scripting to answer more than just application-development needs. A script need not end up as an end-user application. For example, to save money during development, you can use scripts to turn AWS instances off during nonuse times, such as the weekend (assuming that you're not one of those developers who lives in the office). The idea is to have AWS services that are used solely for development tasks running only when you're performing development work. Turning the services on and off by hand would be time consuming and error prone, so scripting provides a great alternative.

You can also use scripts to control the development environment. Chapter 8 discusses how you can create multiple Elastic Beanstalk (EB) environments to test numerous application conditions using the same URL. When your EB setup becomes relatively complex, you need some means to ensure that everything gets switched around so that your end user sees a pure environment. Scripting provides a great answer: Simply execute a script to move between setups as needed.

TIP

One of the benefits of relying on a product such as Chef is that it works across multiple environments (`https://www.chef.io/solutions/cloud-management/`). This means that you can use Chef scripts to integrate multiple cloud solutions and help them work together to achieve specific goals. Chef currently works with these cloud-based environments:

>> Amazon AWS

>> Google Compute Engine

>> HP Cloud

>> IBM Smartcloud

>> Microsoft Azure

>> OpenStack

>> Rackspace

>> VMWare

Relying on the EC2 Run Command

The EC2 Run command (`https://aws.amazon.com/ec2/run-command/`) gives you the means to run scripts from a remote location. As with some other AWS solutions, this one is free except for the resources used to complete any requested tasks. This is an AWS-only solution, which means that you can run commands anywhere across AWS (including across multiple EC2 instances), but you can't use the scripts to perform tasks on other cloud-based environments or on your local system. As a result, the potential for integration of task environments is limited. The article at https://www.infoq.com/news/2016/07/aws-multi-cloud-scripting offers some additional insights about this solution.

Depending on third-party solutions

Many third-party solutions out there promise to make scheduling tasks easier and provide a level of automation similar to that found in scripting. For example, ParkMyCloud (http://www.parkmycloud.com/) makes it easy to schedule a wide range of tasks that you might normally script using custom code. The blog posts at http://www.parkmycloud.com/blog/ obviously try to convince you that you can't live without this solution, but they also offer good food for thought even if you choose not to use ParkMyCloud.

Using a third-party solution may save time and effort scripting, but it also gives you ideas for creating scripts that will truly make you productive. The point is that you need to choose options that help save money so that your development budget isn't wasted on resources you don't actually use. Unlike a local development environment, a cloud environment offers options such as turning off running instances. By optimizing your development environment, you keep costs under control and may find that developing in the cloud is actually less expensive and more efficient than using local resources.

Performing Batch Processing Locally

Localized batch processing uses the built-in capabilities of systems owned by an organization. You can use batch processing for a variety of tasks. Larger businesses will naturally want to use cloud-based batch processing for common needs, partly because their IT departments are large and complex. However, a smaller business could use localized batch processing for all needs depending on what those needs are. Something as simple as Task Scheduler (https://msdn.microsoft.com/library/windows/desktop/aa383614.aspx) on Windows can enable you to perform tasks and a schedule on AWS. Interestingly enough, many localized task-scheduling applications include programmable access through APIs, so you can turn even a rudimentary capability into something better suited to meet needs in the cloud. Here are some issues to consider for localized batch processing:

>> **Management:** Many organizations want to reduce software management requirements and localized batch processing does need local talent to

maintain. However, offsetting the need for additional human resources is the capability to maintain firm control over the batch process.

» **Integration:** Cloud-based batch processing may not work well with local batch-processing needs. Where you need to integrate local and cloud resources, using a localized batch-processing strategy may work better.

» **Reliability:** There is a misperception that cloud-based means extreme reliability. However, AWS can and does go offline. The stories at `https://www.geekwire.com/2017/amazon-explains-massive-aws-outage-says-employee-error-took-servers-offline-promises-changes/` and `https://www.theregister.co.uk/2017/03/01/aws_s3_outage/` tell you how bad things can get. In this case, AWS didn't even tell anyone it was down, so no one could know there was even a need to recover. A localized batch-processing solution can prove to be every bit as reliable as a cloud-based solution. The difference is the kinds of issues that will affect the two solution types. A localized solution is more susceptible to local events, such as outages due to weather. Cloud-based solutions are more susceptible to global events or to human error (because far more humans are involved, more potential failure points exist).

» **Security:** Using local batch processing is generally more secure than using cloud-based batch processing because you can exercise tighter control over when and how the batches execute. The more sensitive the data you manage using batch processes, the more careful you need to be with regard to security.

» **Speed:** No matter how you look at it, unless your data resides with just a single cloud provider in just one location and you have no need to integrate local data, local batch processing is going to be faster than a cloud-based solution. Given that developers are constantly fighting time (in that users want everything fast, and then faster still), speed is a major concern when considering the use of localized batch-processing techniques.

Developing Scripts

Creating scripts often means working with the CLI to determine how to create the required commands. This development process involves playing with AWS to ensure you understand what is going on at a low level. Fortunately, the CLI does provide some functionality to make it easier to perform tasks and develop scripts resulting from your efforts faster.

» **Client-side filtering:** Trying to process every result, even if you may eventually need them, consumes a lot of local resources. You can fine-tune the results you actually use on the client side by adding the `--query` command line switch. To use this switch, you must make your request using the JSON Matching Expression Path (JMESPath, which is pronounced James Path) language described at `http://jmespath.org/`. The article at `http://opensourceconnections.com/blog/2015/07/27/advanced-aws-cli-jmespath-query/` provides some interesting examples of how to use JMESPath with AWS.

» **Command completion:** When working with Linux systems, you can enable command completion. This feature enables you to press Tab to complete a command rather than type the entire command from scratch. You can discover more about command completion at `http://docs.aws.amazon.com/cli/latest/userguide/cli-command-completion.html`.

» **Multiple profiles:** The `aws` utility `config` file (found in the user's `.aws` folder) can contain multiple profiles, each of which can contain different IAM user role settings. These profiles appear in a `[profile name]` block where you replace `name` with the name of the profile. Using multiple profiles also lets you perform tasks using the appropriate credentials. Modify the `aws` utility `credentials` file to add other credentials to the list. Each credential pair (private and public key) appears in a separate `[name]` block. To switch between roles, you add the `--profile name` command-line switch to your command.

» **Server-side filtering:** By default, AWS serves up a list of 1,000 for various requests. Moving that data across the network slows your script to a crawl. The `--filter` command-line switch supplied with many commands enables you to reduce the number of results coming from the server to the client, thereby improving overall scripting speed.

» **Service configuration defaults:** The `aws` utility `config` file can contain default settings for the various services. The use of default settings makes it possible to type shorter commands and ensures that you execute the commands consistently. Each default setup appears with the service name, an equals sign, and the settings. For example, here is a default S3 setup:

```
s3 =
   max_concurrent_requests = 100
   max_queue_size = 10000
```

» **Text output:** Often you need to have text-only output to pass to another command in a pipe. In this case, you use the `--output text` command-line switch to remove the extra characters that often cause problems with textual output.

» **Waiting:** Some script commands require quite a bit of time to execute, and you can't proceed to the next step until they complete. In this case, you can add the `wait` argument to the command to tell the CLI that you want to wait for the command to complete before proceeding. The wait argument always appears after the service name, such as `aws ec2 wait`.

Using Scripts Locally

Some developers get caught up with all kinds of fancy scripting schemes when a simple solution will do just fine. In many cases, all you really need is the scripting capabilities provided by your local platform. The main reasons to use this approach are simplicity and speed.

The command processor for platforms such as Windows will repeat any series of aws utility commands as a script. All you really need to do is record the commands you commonly use in a text file with an appropriate extension, such as `.bat`. Depending on the platform capabilities, you may have access to complex flow control functionality as well, but even the most basic command processor supports limited flow control.

Using an ad hoc scripting approach like this is also fast because you can put the script together in minutes. You won't want to create a complex script this way, but a simple series of steps will work fine. The idea is to keep the task small and approachable.

After you get past basic needs, however, a command-processor approach won't work. You still have access to options such as Anaconda. The notebooks you can create by using Python code in Anaconda can become extremely complicated. Performing any task from your system that you could perform from a cloud-based solution is possible; however, you must consider the following issues when using this approach:

>> **Availability:** The script you create is available only on your system (or network). Consequently, if someone else needs the script, you must send it separately because you lack a centralized repository of scripts that anyone in your organization can use.

>> **Security:** Keeping scripts local does tend to ensure that only people who have a need to access the script can actually access it. In addition, you can more easily control when and how someone uses the script.

>> **Speed:** Because localized scripts drag every piece of data across the network, you incur a speed penalty using them. However, using techniques such as filtering can mitigate this issue, and you might actually find that your scripts execute faster when you must couple the AWS output with information from local sources.

Interacting with aws-shell

Trying to remember every aws utility command, even with the availability of help, is tough. In fact, it's downright impossible. So you can spend hours with the online documentation and type endless experimental commands, or you can get some type of help. The aws-shell utility works with the aws utility to provide an interactive CLI experience. You use it to make working with aws easier. The following sections discuss how you can use aws-shell to make your script and batch-process experience better.

Considering aws-shell features

The aws-shell utility (https://aws.amazon.com/about-aws/whats-new/2015/12/aws-shell-accelerates-productivity-for-aws-cli-users/) comes with a host of interesting features. The interactivity alone makes it worth using, but you also get these additions as part of the package (make sure to also check out the blog that is available from within the preceding article link):

>> **Auto-completion:** As you type commands, you see a list of available options to complete the next step. For example, after you type aws, you see a list of services that you can add as the next step in the command process.

>> **Auto-suggestion:** If the shell recognizes a pattern to the values you type, it gives you a completed command. Pressing Tab automatically enters the remaining text.

>> **Command history:** Even though most command-prompt and terminal-window implementations retain a command history, the information is available for only the current session. The aws-shell utility stores this information in a file for later use.

>> **Dot (.) commands:** The aws-shell gives you access to additional aws-shell–specific commands through the dot (.) prompt. Here are a few examples:

- **.edit:** Provides the means for saving the commands you type as part of a shell script.

- **.profile:** Modifies the profile used to execute commands so that you don't have to include the --profile argument every time you type a command.

- **.cd:** Changes the directory to the specified location on disk.

>> **Fuzzy searches:** You may not remember an argument or other command component precisely. Typing a value that appears as part of the actual argument displays a list of suggestions that you can use in place of that part you remember.

>> **Inline documentation:** Help is always available as part of the shell. As you type values, the shell automatically displays help for that value so that you can be sure you're typing the right information.

>> **Server-side auto-complete:** Typing a command component that requires a server-side value, such as an ARN, usually requires a lookup on your part. When using aws-shell, the shell performs the lookup for you and displays a list of acceptable values.

>> **Shell command access:** If you need to access the underlying operating system commands, type an exclamation mark (!) before the command. For example, type **! dir** and press Enter to obtain a directory listing on a Windows system.

>> **Shorthand auto-complete:** You can use shorthand notation to define a specific longer sequence of commonly used commands. Typing the shorthand form is the same as typing the full sequence.

>> **Toolbar options:** The status bar shows a list of function keys that you can press to obtain specific functionality from aws-shell. For example, you can turn fuzzy searches on or off as needed.

Getting aws-shell

Because you have Anaconda installed on your system, you also have an appropriate version of Python installed, and you can use the pip utility to perform the task. To install aws-shell, open a command prompt or terminal window, type **pip install --upgrade aws-shell**, and press Enter. You see a series of installation messages as pip performs the installation process, as shown in Figure 9-1.

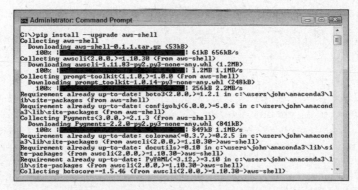

FIGURE 9-1:
Perform the installation of the aws-shell using pip.

To test your installation, type **aws-shell** and press Enter. You see the initial display, shown in Figure 9-2. Note that the status bar shows the function keys you can press to enable or disable specific `aws-shell` features. At this point, you might want to get a cup of coffee because the documentation must download; waiting for a few minutes for this process to complete makes using `aws-shell` easier.

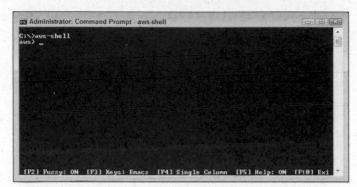

FIGURE 9-2:
Start aws-shell for an initial test.

Performing simple tasks

Most previous commands found in this book begin with aws or some other CLI command. Note the prompt in Figure 9-2. Every command you type assumes that you have preceded it with aws. Consequently, if you want to perform a task using Elastic Beanstalk, you type **elas** to display a list of commands. It's then possible to press the down-arrow key to select one of these commands as shown in Figure 9-3.

FIGURE 9-3:
Use the down-arrow key to select a command.

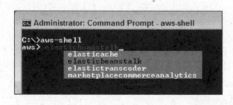

Press the spacebar to continue the command. You now see a list of commands that you can type, along with help information, as shown in Figure 9-4. Note that the help information is actually getting in the way in this case. You can turn it off by pressing F5. (Unfortunately, pressing F5 right at this moment will cause the command to terminate, but you can start it again without a problem.)

The service name appears in red letters. Type **des** after the space. You see a listing of possible commands, as shown in Figure 9-5. As before, you press the down-arrow key to select a particular command. For this example, select `describe-environments`. When you select a particular command, the text turns turquoise.

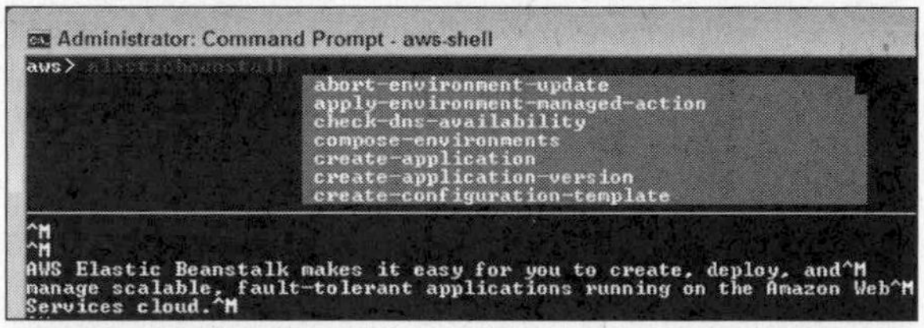

FIGURE 9-4:
The aws-shell
utility provides
you with all the
information
needed to create
useful commands
quickly.

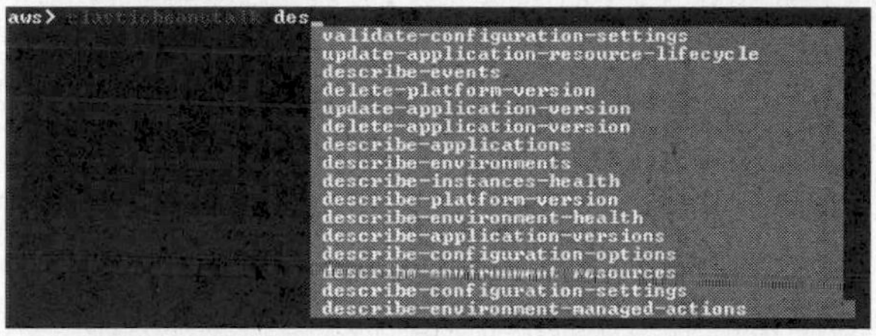

FIGURE 9-5:
Choose a
command to
execute.

The default setup for aws for this book is to output information in tabular form. Type -- to display a list of options for this command, as shown in Figure 9-6. Use the down-arrow key to select --output. Note that the options appear in dark green. The help screen also tells you what to type next. In this case, you type a string that contains the format you want to use for the output.

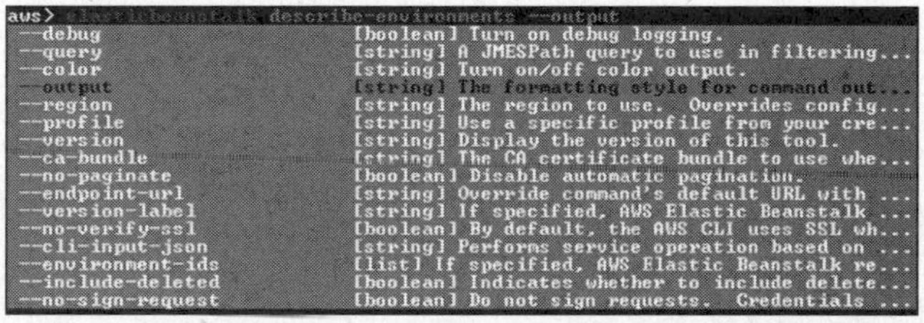

FIGURE 9-6:
Select options to
modify command
execution.

Press the spacebar to select the command. This time, you don't see any help information; you must know that text is one of the options. Type **text** and press Enter. You see the command output, as shown in Figure 9-7.

FIGURE 9-7:
After the
command
executes, you see
the output just as
you would when
using aws.

Of course, you can just as easily see the output in JSON format. Press the up-arrow key and you see the command repeated. Press Backspace to remove text and type **json**. Press Enter. Figure 9-8 shows the new output. This technique relies on using the command history. Interestingly enough, even after you stop and restart aws-shell, you have access to this command simply by using the command history.

FIGURE 9-8: Using the history feature makes modifying commands easy.

The display has gotten messy at this point. You can clean it up on most platforms using the clear screen (cls) command. Of course, this means accessing the under-lying command processor. Type **!cls** and press Enter. If your system supports the cls command, you see the screen cleared.

Obtaining help

One of the commands that you don't see listed when you work with aws-shell is help. The command is still there, but you have to remember that it is available. For example, to see the help associated with the ec2 service, type **ec2 help** and press Enter. You see output similar to that shown in Figure 9-9. The aws-shell utility automatically uses any paging utility available on your platform to display one page of help information at a time.

Editing your commands

One of the handiest features of aws-shell is the capability to save your commands in permanent form. After you experiment for a while and know you have the right set of commands in place, it's time to create a script or batch file. To perform this task, type **.edit** and press Enter. What you see is the text file editor for your particular platform with the history of the commands you have typed, as shown in Figure 9-10.

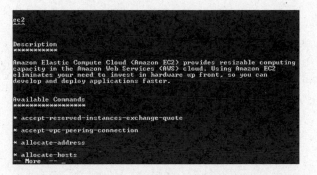

FIGURE 9-9:
The aws-shell
utility provides
full access to
aws help.

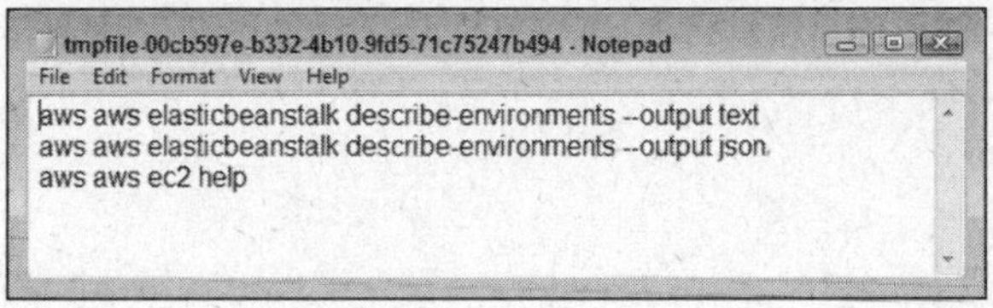

FIGURE 9-10:
Commands you
type appear
in the text file
that you save
as a script.

Note that the file lacks the `!cls` command that you type in the "Performing simple tasks" section, earlier in this chapter. The only commands you see are those that you actually type for aws. You can edit this file and then save it as needed. For example, when working with Windows, you can save the file with a `.bat` file extension and repeat the commands as a script.

TIP

Of course, if you want to use aws-shell as a means for creating scripts, you really do need to clear the history before each session. No command exists for performing this task now. Consequently, you must delete the `history` file found in the `\.aws\shell` folder of your system. This folder also contains an `awsshellrc` file that you can use to change the default settings for your aws-shell setup.

IN THIS CHAPTER

» **Defining the Lambda feature set**

» **Working with Lambda at the console**

» **Building a basic Lambda application**

» **Adding Simple Queue Services (SQS) support**

Chapter **10**

Responding to Events with Lambda

Amazon designed AWS Lambda to let you build and run applications in the cloud. The applications you create depend on Node.js (https://nodejs. org/), a JavaScript environment that you used in Chapter 5 to interact with S3. You can create AWS scripts with Node.js on your local system and then upload them to Lambda to execute within the cloud environment. You typically use Lambda to perform tasks in these situations:

» As a response to an event triggered by a service or application

» As part of a direct call from a mobile application or web page

REMEMBER

Lambda doesn't cost you anything. However, Amazon does charge you for each request that your code makes, the time that your code runs, and any nonfree services that your code depends on to perform useful work. In some cases, you may find that a given service doesn't actually cost anything. For example, you could use S3 with Lambda at the free-tier level to perform experimentation and pay only for the code requests and running time. The examples in this chapter don't require that you actually run any code — you simply set up the application to run should you desire to do so, but the setup itself doesn't incur any cost.

The first several sections of the chapter focus on discovering and configuring Lambda, and creating a simple application for it. However, the real power of Lambda comes from pairing it with a number of services. For example, you discover in Chapter 9 that Lambda is part of a strategy for performing batch processing on AWS. The last section of this chapter looks at using Lambda with SQS to perform multiservice tasks.

Considering the Lambda Features

Before you can actually work with Lambda, you need to know more about it. Saying that Lambda is a code-execution environment is a bit simplistic; Lambda provides more functionality because it helps you do things like respond to events. However, starting with the concept of a serverless code-execution environment, one that you don't have to manage, is a good beginning. The following sections fill in the details of the Lambda feature set. Even though this information appears as an overview, you really need to know it when working through the examples that follow in this chapter.

Working with a server

Most applications today rely on a specific server environment. In a production scenario, an administrator creates a server environment, either physical or virtual, configures it, and then provides any required resources a developer may need. The developer then places an application created and tested on a test server of precisely the same characteristics on the server. After some testing, the administrator comes back and performs additional configuration, such as setting up accounts for users. Other people may get involved as well. For example, a DBA may set up a database environment for the application, and a web designer may create a mobile interface for it. The point is that a lot of people get involved in the process of getting this application ready for use, and they remain involved as the application evolves. The time and money spent to maintain the application is relatively large. However, the application environment you create provides a number of important features that you must consider before moving to a serverless environment:

>> The server is completely under the organization's control, so the organization chooses every feature about the server.

>> The application environment tends to run faster than even the best cloud server can provide (much less a serverless environment, in which you have no control over the server configuration).

>> Any data managed by the application remains with the organization, so the organization can reduce the potential for data breaches and can better adhere to any legal requirements for the data.

>> Adding more features to the server tends to cost less after the organization pays for the initial outlay.

>> A third party can't limit the organization's choice of support and other software to use with the application, nor can it suddenly choose to stop supporting certain software functionality (thereby forcing an unexpected application upgrade).

>> Security tends to be less of a concern when using a localized server as long as the organization adheres to best practices.

Working in a serverless environment

Using a localized server does have some significant benefits, but building, developing, and maintaining servers is incredibly expensive because of the staffing requirements and the need to buy licenses for the various pieces of software. (You can mitigate software costs by using lower-cost open source products, but the open source products may not do everything you need or may provide the same services in a less efficient environment.) However, organizations have more than just cost concerns to consider when it comes to servers. Users want applications that are flexible and work anywhere today. With this in mind, here are some reasons that you may want to consider a serverless environment for your application:

>> **Environment duplication:** For a developer, the capability to precisely duplicate the production environment as a test environment is essential. Otherwise, usage, performance, and even some coding issues will remain unresolved until the application actually goes into production. Using a serverless environment enables you to create as many copies of the production environment as needed because all you consider is environment settings — not hardware, software, or anything else for that matter.

>> **Improved development team efficiency:** Reducing the number of people involved in a process generally increases efficiency because you have fewer lines of communication and fewer human failure points as well. In addition, the developer needs to worry only about writing great code — not whether the server will function as expected.

>> **Low learning curve:** Working with Lambda doesn't require that you learn any new programming languages. In fact, you can continue to use the third-party libraries that you like, even if those libraries rely on native code. Lambda

provides an execution environment, not an actual coding environment. You use a Lambda function (explained in the "Creating a Basic Lambda Application" section, later in this chapter) to define the specifics of how your application runs.

TIP

Lambda does provide a number of prebuilt function templates for common tasks, and you may find that you can use one of these templates instead of building your own. It pays to become familiar with the prebuilt templates because using them can save you considerable time and effort. You just need to tell Lambda to use a particular template with your service resources.

>> **Lower hardware and administration cost:** You don't have hardware costs because Amazon provides the hardware, and the administration costs are theoretically zero as well. However, you do pay for the service and need to consider the trade-off between the cost of the hardware, administration, and services.

>> **Automatic scaling:** You can bring on additional hardware immediately without any startup time or costs. However, automatic scaling can be a two-edged sword for the developer because it can serve to hide both speed and resource-usage issues. In general, you want to configure your setup for the expected usage level and then test using automatic scaling later.

>> **Increased reliability:** Because Amazon can provide additional systems immediately, a failure at Amazon usually doesn't spell a failure for your application. What you get is akin to having multiple sets of redundant failover systems.

WARNING

Many of Amazon's services come with hidden assumptions that can cause problems. For example, with Lambda, Amazon fully expects that you use other Amazon services as well. A Lambda app can react to an event such as a file being dropped into an S3 bucket by a user, but it can't react to an event on your own system. The user may drop a file onto a folder on your server, but that event doesn't create an event that Lambda can see. What you really get with Lambda is an incredible level of flexibility with significantly reduced costs as long as you want to use the services that Amazon provides with it. In the long run, you may actually find that Lambda locks you into using Amazon services that don't really meet your needs, so be sure to think about the ramifications of the choices you make during the experimentation stage.

Starting the Lambda Console

The Lambda Console provides you with one way in which to interact with Lambda (you can also use CLI and programmatic methods). It gives you a method for telling Lambda what to do with the code you upload. Using the Lambda Console takes what could be a complex task and makes it considerably easier so that you can focus on what you need to do, rather than on the code-execution details. Lambda automatically addresses many of the mundane server setup and configuration tasks for you. With this time savings in mind, use these steps to open a copy of the Lambda Console:

1. **Sign into AWS using your user account.**

2. **Navigate to the Lambda Console at** `https://console.aws.amazon.com/lambda`.

   You see a Welcome page that contains interesting information about Lambda and what it can do for you. However, you don't see the actual console at this point.

3. **Click Get Started Now.**

   You see the Select Blueprint page, shown in Figure 10-1. The initial examples in this chapter rely on the blueprints so that you can see how you can quickly prototype a potential solution. Prototyping lets you create ad hoc solutions quickly. As your need for flexibility and functionality increases, you can move to the API. Developers use both the blueprints and the API as needed.

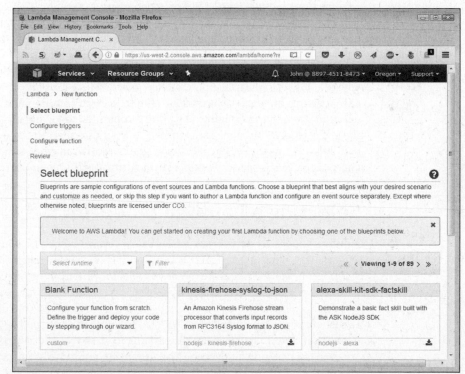

FIGURE 10-1: Access the Lambda functionality through blueprints to make tasks easy.

Creating a Basic Lambda Application

The previous section discusses the Lambda Console and shows how to start it. Of course, just starting the console doesn't accomplish much. To make Lambda useful, you need to upload code and then tell Lambda how to interact with it. To make things easier, one Lambda programming technique relies on the concept of a blueprint, which works much as the name implies. It provides a basic structure for creating the function that houses the code you want to execute. The following sections describe how to create a Lambda application using a blueprint and interact with the application in various ways (including deleting the function when you finish with it).

REMEMBER

Creating, configuring, and deleting a function won't cost you anything. However, if you actually test your function and view metrics that it produces, you may end up with a charge on your credit card. Be sure to keep the requirement to pay for code-execution resources in mind when going through the following sections. If you configured your AWS account as described in the "Considering the eventual need for paid services" section of Chapter 3, you should receive an email telling you about any charges accrued as the result of performing the procedures in the following section.

Selecting a Lambda blueprint

Lambda supports events from a number of Amazon-specific sources such as S3, DynamoDB, Kinesis, SNS, and CloudWatch. This chapter relies on S3 as an event source, but the techniques it demonstrates work with any Amazon service that produces events that Lambda can monitor.

When working with blueprints, you need to know in advance the requirements for using that blueprint. For example, Figure 10-2 shows the blueprint used in this chapter, s3-get-object-python. The blueprint name tells you a little about the blueprint, but the description adds to it. However, the important information appears at the bottom of the box. In this case, you see that the blueprint uses Python 2.7 and S3. Every blueprint includes these features, so you know what resources the blueprint requires before you use it.

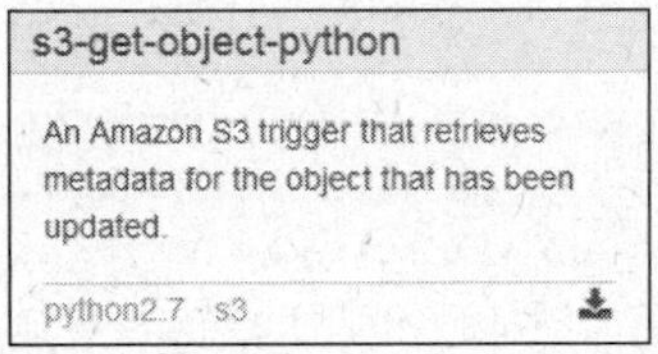

FIGURE 10-2: Determine the requirements for using a blueprint at the outset.

s3-get-object-python

An Amazon S3 trigger that retrieves metadata for the object that has been updated.

python2.7 · s3

A WORD ABOUT PRODUCT VERSIONS

An interesting detail about the use of Python 2.7.x is that it isn't the most current version of Python available. Many people have moved to Python 3.4.x (see the downloads page at https://www.python.org/downloads/ for details). In fact, you can find versions as high as 3.6.1 used for applications now, so you may question the wisdom of using an older version of Python for your Lambda code.

Given that the copy of Anaconda used for this book relies on Python 3.6.1, you may need to perform a separate Python 2.7.x version download to work with Lambda when you choose to use the default Python 2.7.x settings. There is also an option to use Python 3.6.1, but you must select it separately; see the "Configuring a function" section for details. This downloaded version will reside in its own folder, and you can access it as a separate development environment.

Python is unique in that some groups use the 2.7.x version and other groups use the 3.4.x and higher version. Developers, data scientists, and others who perform data-analysis tasks mainly use the 2.7.x version of Python because of its stronger library support (although this support need is changing), so Amazon has wisely chosen to concentrate on that version. (Eventually, all development tasks will move to the 3.x version of the product.) Using the 2.7.x version means that you're better able to work with other people who perform data-analysis tasks. In addition, if Amazon used the 3.x version instead, you might find locating real-world application examples difficult. The Python 2.7.x code does have compatibility issues with Python 3.x, so if you choose to use Python 3.x anyway, you also need to update the Amazon code.

You may find that Amazon uses odd versions of other languages and products as well. In some cases, the choice of language or product version has to do with updating the Amazon code, but in other cases, you may find that the older version has advantages, such as library support (as is the case with Python). Be sure to look at the versions of products when supplied because you need to use the right version to get good results when working with Lambda.

TIP

Amazon provides a number of blueprints, and finding the one you need can be time consuming. Adding a condition to the Filter field or choosing a programming language from the Language field reduces the search time. For example, to locate all the S3-specific blueprints, type S3 in the Filter field. Likewise, to locate all the Python 2.7 blueprints, choose Python 2.7 in the Languages field.

REMEMBER

Amazon licenses most of the blueprints under the Creative Commons Zero (CC0) rules (see `https://creativecommons.org/publicdomain/zero/1.0/` for details). This means that Amazon has given up all copyright to the work, and you don't need to worry about getting permission to use the blueprint as part of anything you do. However, the operative word in the Amazon wording on the blueprint page is *most*, which means that you need to verify the copyright for every blueprint you use to ensure that no hidden requirements exist that oblige you to get a license.

Configuring a function

Using the Lambda Console and a blueprint means that the function-creation process is less about coding and more about configuration. You need to tell Lambda which blueprint to use, but the blueprint contains the code needed to perform the task. In addition, you tell Lambda which resources to use, but again, it's a matter of configuration and not actual coding. The only time that you might need to perform any significant coding is when a blueprint comes close to doing what you want to do but doesn't quite meet expectations.

The example that follows uses the S3 bucket that you see how to create in the "Testing Your Setup" section of Chapter 2. However, you can use any bucket desired. The bucket simply holds objects that you want to process, so it's a matter of choosing the right bucket to perform the required work. The blueprint used in this section, s3-get-object-python, simply reports the metadata from the objects dropped into the bucket. Follow these steps to generate a message every time someone adds a file to your S3 bucket:

1. **Click s3-get-object-python.**

You see the Configure Event Sources page, shown in Figure 10-3.

TIP

Even though the blueprint automatically chooses event-source information for you, you can still control the event source in detail. For example, you can change the Event Source Type field to choose a service other than S3, such as Kinesis, S3, CloudWatch, or DynamoDB. To see the list of other services, click the S3 icon. A drop-down list appears that contains the other services that you can interact with when using this blueprint. The blueprint shows that information from the selected service flows to Lambda in this particular case.

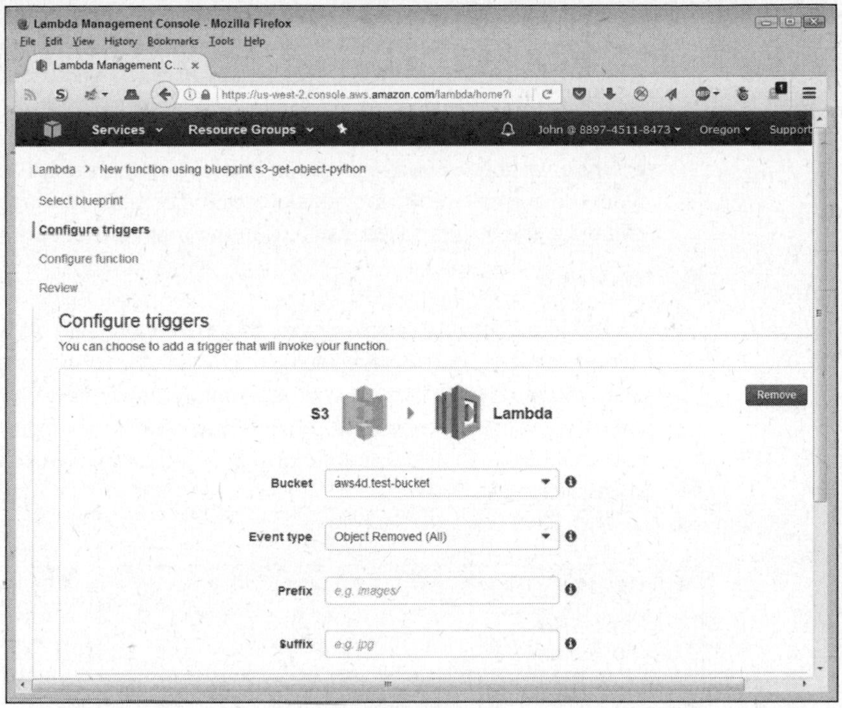

FIGURE 10-3:
Define the
event source you
want to use.

2. **Select an object source in the Bucket field.**

   The example assumes that you want to use the bucket that Chapter 2 tells you how to create. However, any bucket you can access that receives objects regularly will work fine for this example. AWS simply chooses the first S3 bucket, so configuring this field is essential.

3. **Choose the Object Created (All) option in the Event Type field.**

   S3 supports three event types:

   - Object Created (All)
   - Object Removed (All)
   - Reduced Redundancy Lost Object

   Within these three main event types are subevents that better control the information that Lambda sends to the script. For example, when working with Object Created, you can choose from one of the following:

   - Put
   - Post
   - Copy
   - Complete Multipart Upload

Even though Lambda receives all the events, you use the entries in the Prefix and Suffix fields to filter the events so that you react only to the important events. For example, you can choose to include a folder path or part of a filename as a prefix to control events based on location or name. Adding a file extension as the suffix means that Lambda will process only files of a specific type. The example provides simple processing in that it reacts to any item created in the bucket, so it doesn't use either the Prefix or Suffix fields.

4. **Click Next.**

   You see the Configure Function page, shown in Figure 10-4. As with the Configure Event Sources page, it pays to check out the Runtime field. In this case, you can choose from a number of options, everything from Python 2.7 to Java 8. You can even choose Python 3.6. Even when the blueprint description tells you that it supports a specific language, you often have a choice of other languages to use as well.

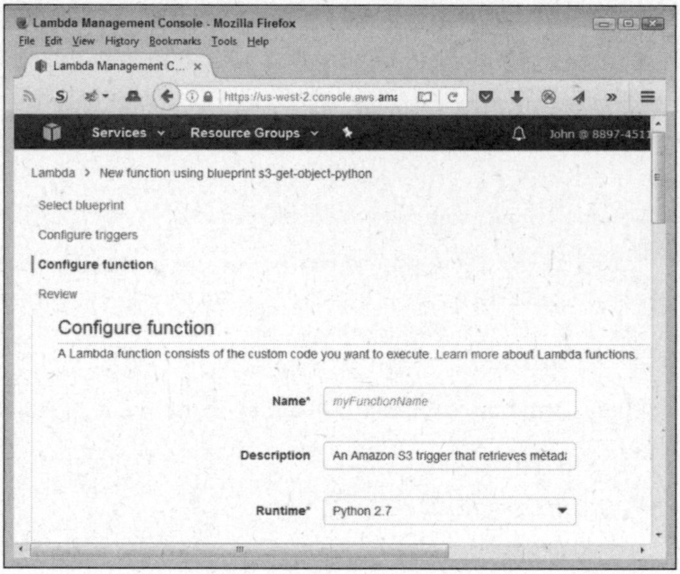

FIGURE 10-4:
Name and describe your function.

5. **Type** MyFunction **in the Name field.**

   Normally, you provide a more descriptive function name, but this name will do for the example and make it easier to locate the function later when you want to remove it.

6. **Scroll down to the next section of the page.**

   You see the code used to implement the function, as shown in Figure 10-5. As a developer, you can choose to use the existing function, edit the code inline to modify function processing, upload a new function in the form of a `.zip` file, or obtain a function file from Amazon S3. The point is that a blueprint provides a starting place for developers but doesn't lock you into any particular implementation. For now, the example assumes that you have chosen to use the default implementation.

FIGURE 10-5: Changing the function code is as easy as editing it in place if desired.

REMEMBER

Notice that the Python code contains a function (specified by the `def` keyword) named `lambda_handler`. This function handles (processes) the information that S3 passes to it. Every language you use has a particular method for defining functions; Python uses this method. As part of configuring the Lambda function, you need to know the name of the handler function.

7. **Scroll down to the next section of the page.**

You see two sections: the Lambda Function Handler and Role section and the Advanced Settings section, as shown in Figure 10-6. The blueprint automatically defines the Handler field for you. Note that it contains the name `lambda_handler` as the handler name. When you use custom code, you must provide the name of the function that handles the code in this section.

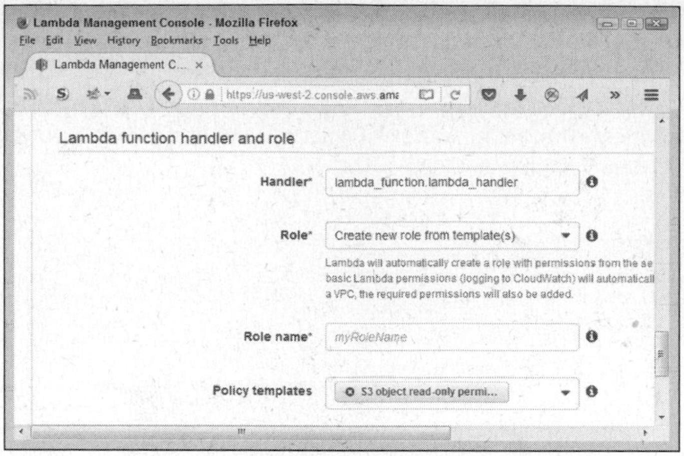

FIGURE 10-6:
Define the execution specifics of the Lambda function.

The first part of the entry, `lambda_function`, is the name of the file that contains the handler function. As with the function name, the blueprint automatically provides the appropriate name for you. However, if you upload a file containing the code, you must provide the filename (without extension) as the first entry. Consequently, `lambda_function.lambda_handler` provides the name of the file and associated handler function. The filename is separated from the handler function name by a period.

8. **Choose Create New Role from Templates in the Role field.**

   You must tell AWS what rights to use when executing the lambda code. The environment provides several default roles, or you can create a custom role to use instead. The example uses a default role.

   When you choose Create a Custom Role, AWS opens a new page containing the role definition, as shown in Figure 10-7. AWS fills in the details for you. However, you can click View Policy Document to see precisely what rights you're granting to the lambda function.

   If you have an existing role you want to use, you select Choose an Existing Role in the Role field. The page changes to include an Existing Role field that you can use to choose the existing role. This option becomes available only when you have already defined a role in the past.

9. **Type** S3ToLambda **in the Role Name field.**

   You must provide a name for your role, even when using a template.

10. **Select S3 Object Read-only Permissions in the Policy Templates field.**

   The policies define how Lambda interacts with the service. You must choose a policy that reflects this need. There is only one default S3 template — one that allows read-only access to objects, which is the safest option.

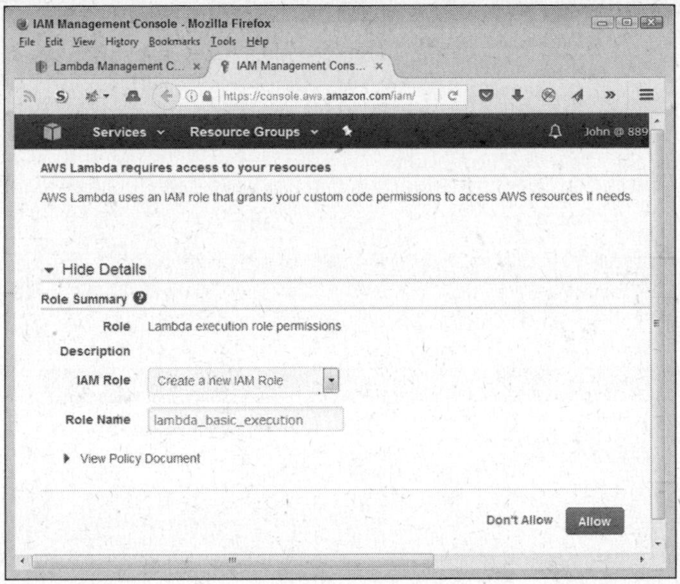

FIGURE 10-7:
Define the
execution
specifics of the
lambda function.

11. **Click Next.**

The Review page, shown in Figure 10-8, shows the settings for this function.

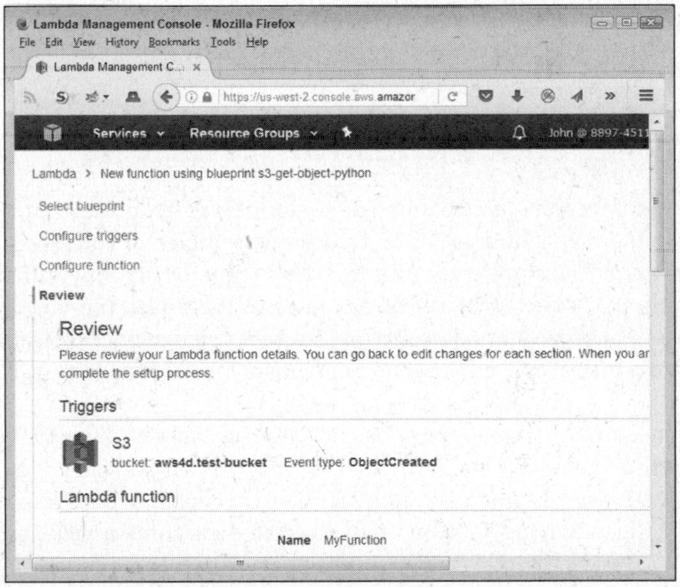

FIGURE 10-8:
Verify that the
function settings
are correct.

12. Click Create Function.

If you chose not to enable the function, the function exists but doesn't do anything. You aren't incurring any costs at this point. AWS displays the page shown in Figure 10-9. Note the Test button in the upper-left corner. Clicking this button tests the function but also causes the function to incur costs.

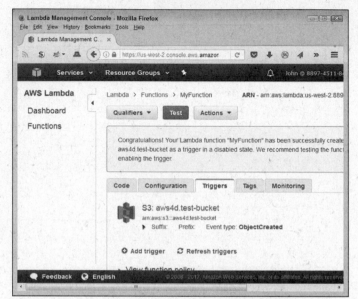

FIGURE 10-9: The function is ready to use.

Using ensembles for functions

Sometimes you can accomplish some incredibly interesting tasks without performing any coding at all by creating ensembles of functions available as blueprints. For example, you can use the s3-get-object blueprint to retrieve objects from an S3 bucket of specific types and then pass the object onto DynamoDB, where another Lambda function, such as microservice-http-endpoint, passes it onto a microservice that your company owns for further processing.

You can even double up on blueprints. The same DynamoDB content can trigger another Lambda function, such as `simple-mobile-backend`, to send alerts to mobile users about new content. You can achieve all these tasks without any significant coding. All you really need to do is think a little outside the box as to how you can employ the blueprints that Amazon provides and combine them in interesting ways.

Most of the Amazon blueprints are used for other purposes online. For example, you can see how to modify the s3-get-object-python blueprint to accommodate a product named Logentries (https://logentries.com/) at https://logentries.com/doc/s3-ingestion-with-lambda/. Another product, Logsene (https://sematext.com/logsene/), also uses the blueprint as a starting point (see details at https://github.com/sematext/logsene-aws-lambda-s3). For an example of a combined-service use, check out the article at https://micropyramid.com/blog/using-aws-lambda-with-s3-and-dynamodb/, which is about using S3 with DynamoDB. These blueprints get real-world use by third-party companies that use the blueprint as a starting point to do something a lot more detailed and interesting.

Creating the test setup

Before you can test your new function, you need to upload a file to the bucket you create in Chapter 2. This means opening the S3 Management Console, selecting the bucket, and uploading a file to it just as you do in Chapter 2. The example assumes that you've named this file HappyFace.jpg.

WARNING

Filenames are case sensitive. Consequently, if you name your file happyface.jpg and try to access it from the test code as HappyFace.jpg, the output will tell you that the code can't access the file. At first, you may think that you have a permissions problem because of the error message you receive from Amazon. However, verifying the capitalization of the filenames you use during the testing process can save you a lot of time and frustration.

Testing the function

Every Lambda handler function receives two pieces of information: an event and its context. The event and context can include any sort of data, but to make things simple during testing, the test functionality relies on *strings*, that is, text that appears within double quotation marks ("). The text is bundled within a pair of curly brackets ({}) so that the test function receives information just as it normally would. The following steps show how to test your new Lambda function:

1. **Click Test.**

   AWS displays the default testing template, which is Hello World. You need to select the testing template for S3 or the test will fail.

2. **Choose S3 Put in the Sample Event Template field.**

   You see the Input Test Event page, shown in Figure 10-10. To make this template function correctly, you make three small code changes, as the next steps explain.

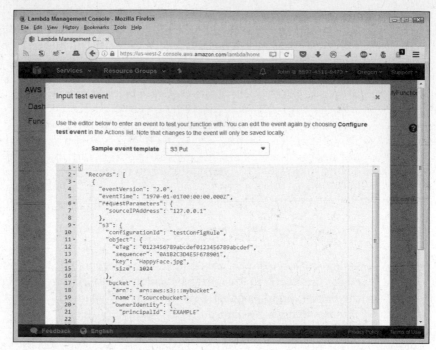

FIGURE 10-10:
The test code
data to the
function.

3. **Change the** "key" **entry as shown here:**

```
"key": "HappyFace.jpg"
```

4. **Change the** "arn" **entry to match the arn for your bucket.**

The Amazon Resource Name (ARN) tells AWS where to find the bucket. The ARN for your S3 bucket will differ from the ARN I use here. However, your ARN entry will look something like this:

```
"arn": "arn:aws:s3:::aws4d.test-bucket",
```

WARNING

Make sure to create the ARN correctly. The number of colons between various elements is essential. The best way to avoid problems is to copy the ARN from a screen location that you know is correct and paste it into your code. Otherwise, you can spend hours trying to find the one missing or extra colon in your code.

5. **Change the** "name" **field to match the name of your bucket.**

In this case, you provide only the bucket name. It should look something like this:

```
"name": "aws4d.test-bucket",
```

6. **Change the** `"principleId"` **field to match the name of the file owner.**

You can verify this name by clicking the file entry in S3. Use the value that appears in the Owner field on the Overview tab for the file in question.

7. **Click Save.**

AWS saves the test code for you and returns you to the test page shown in Figure 10-10.

At this point, you can click Test again. In most cases, Amazon won't charge you anything because your S3 resource usage will remain within the limits of the free tier. However, by executing the test code, you can incur a small cost. Figure 10-11 shows an example of the output you see. The output correctly shows that the content type for HappyFace.jpg is `"image/jpeg"`.

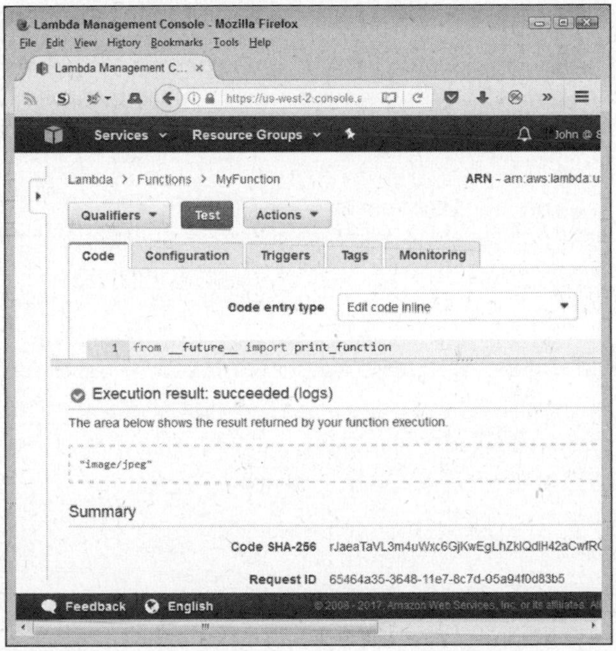

FIGURE 10-11:
The test output correctly identifies the content type.

There are actually two output sections. Figure 10-11 shows the returned value. The test also prints a value, as shown in Figure 10-12. This information appears below the return value and tells you more about the test. For example, you see that the test lasted 312.86 ms and that Amazon billed you for 400 ms worth of resource time. More important, this output differentiates between a returned value and a printed value (as described in more detail later in the chapter, in the "Modifying the function code" section.

FIGURE 10-12:
Tests can output
both a return
value and printed
values.

START RequestId: 65464a35-3648-11e7-8c7d-05a94f0d83b5 Version: $LATEST
CONTENT TYPE: image/jpeg
END RequestId: 65464a35-3648-11e7-8c7d-05a94f0d83b5
REPORT RequestId: 65464a35-3648-11e7-8c7d-05a94f0d83b5 Duration: 312.86 ms   Billed Duration: 400 ms

Fixing test function errors

If you make a mistake and the test fails, you can change the test conditions by choosing Actions ⇨ Configure Test Event. You see the test event information, shown in Figure 10-10, where you can make changes to your setup. Perform any required changes and click Save to replace the previous results.

Checking the function metrics

In addition to various levels of testing, you can also view the metrics for your function by clicking the Monitoring tab. Figure 10-13 shows typical metrics for Lambda functions. In this case, you see how many times events have triggered the function, the duration of each call, and the number of errors that the functions have experienced.

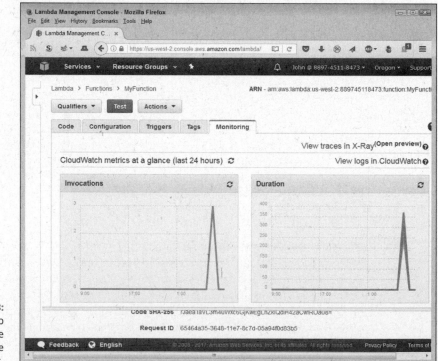

FIGURE 10-13:
Metrics can help
you determine
how well the
function works.

Modifying the function code

The default `lambda_handler()` code gives you a good starting point, but you may decide to modify it to meet specific needs. In fact, if you look at the code, it already has one suggested addition (the book shows a reformatted version of the AWS code due to the length of some of the AWS code lines):

```python
def lambda_handler(event, context):
    #print("Received event: " +
    #    json.dumps(event, indent=2))

    # Get the object from the event and show
    # its content type
    bucket = event['Records'][0]['s3']['bucket']['name']
    key = urllib.unquote_plus(
        event['Records'][0]['s3']['object']['key'].
        encode('utf8'))
    try:
        response = s3.get_object(Bucket=bucket, Key=key)
        print("CONTENT TYPE: " + response['ContentType'])
        return response['ContentType']
    except Exception as e:
        print(e)
        print('Error getting object {} from bucket {}. ' +
            'Make sure they exist and your bucket is in' +
            ' the same region as this function.'.
            format(key, bucket))
        raise e
```

The first line prints the event information received as part of the S3 Put test event. The `json.dumps()` method creates human-readable output with white space to make it easier to understand the event values. Remove the comments from the initial `print()` function so that it now appears as

```python
print("Received event: " +
    json.dumps(event, indent=2))
```

Click Save and Test to save the code change. The output changes to show the additional `print()` output, which shows the information the function receives as input:

```
START RequestId: 91ad569c-364c-11e7-a6b1-db58dabe4ac3
    Version: $LATEST
Received event: {
```

```
  "Records": [
    {
      "eventVersion": "2.0",
      "eventTime": "1970-01-01T00:00:00.000Z",
      "requestParameters": {
        "sourceIPAddress": "127.0.0.1"
      },
      "s3": {
        "configurationId": "testConfigRule",
        "object": {
          "eTag": "0123456789abcdef0123456789abcdef",
          "key": "HappyFace.jpg",
          "sequencer": "0A1B2C3D4E5F678901",
          "size": 1024
        },
        "bucket": {
          "ownerIdentity": {
            "principalId": "Your ID Here"
          },
          "name": "aws4d.test-bucket",
          "arn": "arn:aws:s3:::aws4d.test-bucket"
        },
        "s3SchemaVersion": "1.0"
      },
      "responseElements": {
        "x-amz-id-2":
            "EXAMPLE123/5678abcdefghijklambdaisawesome/
            mnopqrstuvwxyzABCDEFGH",
        "x-amz-request-id": "EXAMPLE123456789"
      },
      "awsRegion": "us-east-1",
      "eventName": "ObjectCreated:Put",
      "userIdentity": {
        "principalId": "EXAMPLE"
      },
      "eventSource": "aws:s3"
    }
  ]
}
CONTENT TYPE: image/jpeg
END RequestId: 91ad569c-364c-11e7-a6b1-db58dabe4ac3
REPORT RequestId: 91ad569c-364c-11e7-a6b1-db58dabe4ac3
    Duration: 241.10 ms    Billed Duration: 300 ms
```

The point is that you can begin with a simple function but then move toward additional complexity, eventually building a complex function to perform required tasks. Starting with the blueprint, as shown in this section, doesn't mean that the code must remain simple. All you're really doing is creating a useful starting point from which to build the code you need.

TIP

Note the `print()` call that displays `response['ContentType']`. You have access to a wealth of information from the bucket, as described at `http://boto3.readthedocs.io/en/latest/reference/services/s3.html#S3.Client.get_object`. Of course, you can use calls other than `s3.get_object()` to obtain other sorts of information.

Deleting the function

You don't want to keep a function around any longer than necessary because each function invocation costs money. One way to keep costs down is to disable the function by clicking the Enabled link for the function in the Event Sources tab and choosing Disable when you see the configuration dialog box. The function will continue to perform its task as long as just one of the event sources remains enabled, so you must disable all event sources to stop the function from responding to events.

At some point, you simply won't need the function, and keeping it around is a recipe for unexpected costs. To delete a function, choose Actions ⇨ Delete Function. AWS will ask whether you're sure that you want to delete the function. Click Delete to remove the function and all its configuration information.

Interacting with Simple Queue Services (SQS)

The Simple Queue Service (SQS) acts as a place where you can temporarily send messages. Depending on how you configure your setup, one service can drop messages into the queue and another can pick them up for processing. The result is an asynchronous method of detail with messages of various sorts. The use of queues lets you even out peaks and valleys in data requests so that you can use services more efficiently. The following sections get you started with SQS.

Creating a queue using the console

Before you can do much with SQS, you need a queue. It's possible to create a queue using the console, CLI, or programmatically. This section uses the console to create the queue simply to allow you to see how the console appears. Later sections look at SQL using both CLI and Python programming techniques. The following steps help you create the queue.

1. **Sign into AWS using your user account.**

2. **Navigate to the SQS Console at** https://aws.amazon.com/sqs/.

   You see a Welcome page that contains interesting information about SQS and what it can do for you. However, you don't see the actual console at this point.

3. **Click Get Started with Amazon SQS for Free.**

   You see a second helpful page of SQS information.

4. **Click Get Started Now.**

   You finally see a Create New Queue page, as shown in Figure 10-14. You can create a standard queue or a First In/First Out (FIFO) queue. The two queue types are quite different, and you need to exercise care in choosing one over the other. The FIFO queue is the best option when working in a transactional environment in which you require precise message control. The standard queue serves most development needs.

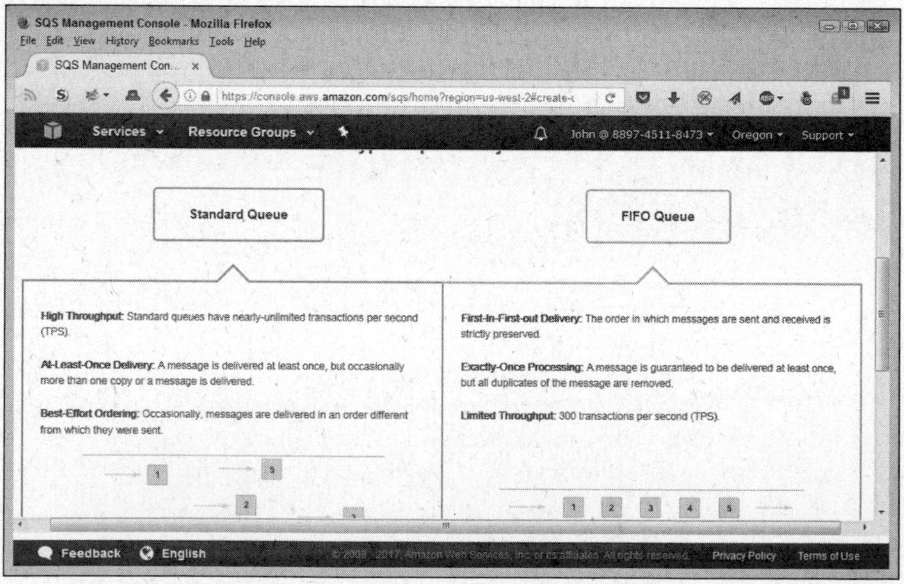

FIGURE 10-14: Choose between a standard and FIFO queue based on application requirements.

5. **Type** TestQueue **in the Queue Name field.**

Every queue you own must have a unique name.

6. **Verify that the value in the Region field is correct.**

You should normally use the same region you use for your EC2 and S3 setups. If the region value is incorrect, choose a new value from the region drop-down list at the top, right side of the page.

7. **Choose Standard Queue and then click Quick-Create Queue.**

You see the SQS Console, shown in Figure 10-15. The console starts with the new queue selected so that you can see queue details. The console shows that the queue currently has no messages available and no messages being processed.

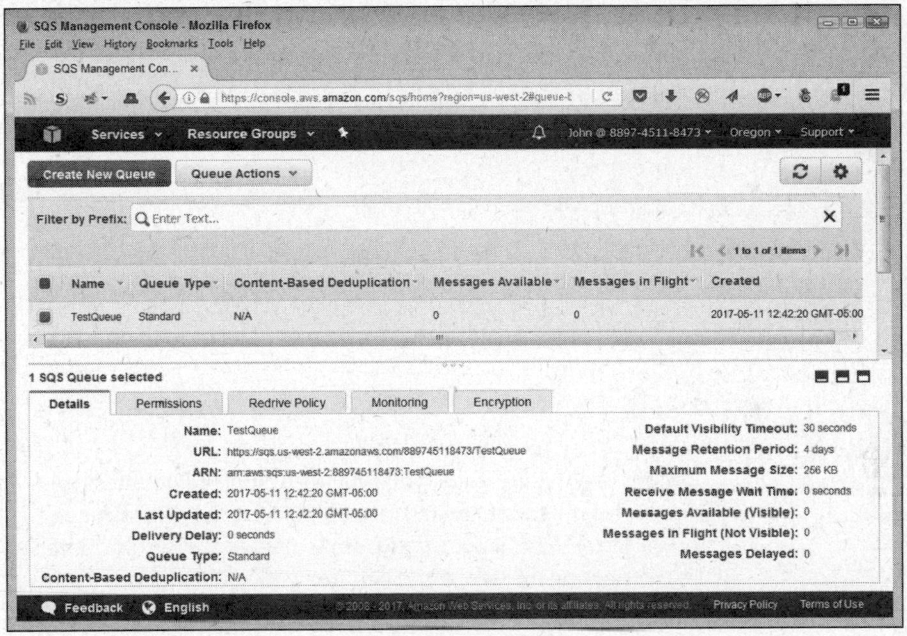

FIGURE 10-15:
The SQS Console shows the queues you have in place and their status.

TIP

You also have an option to configure the queue before you use it. In this case, you click Configure Queue instead. This option lets you change the default parameters, such as the maximum message size and the number of days that the queue retains messages. In most cases, the default parameters work fine for test setups used by developers.

Working with the CLI to configure SQS

You can use the CLI to perform every task you can think of that you normally perform in the console, including creating queues. Look carefully at Figure 10-15 to see a URL field for TestQueue. The URL field is essential because it provides the key for accessing the queue you create. To test queue access, try creating a message by typing **aws sqs send-message --queue-url https://sqs.us-west-2.amazonaws. com/889745118473/TestQueue --message-body "Hello There!"** and pressing Enter. To make this command work, you must replace the --queue-url value with the URL for your queue. You see the output shown in Figure 10-16. If you update the console display at this point, you see that the queue now has one message in it.

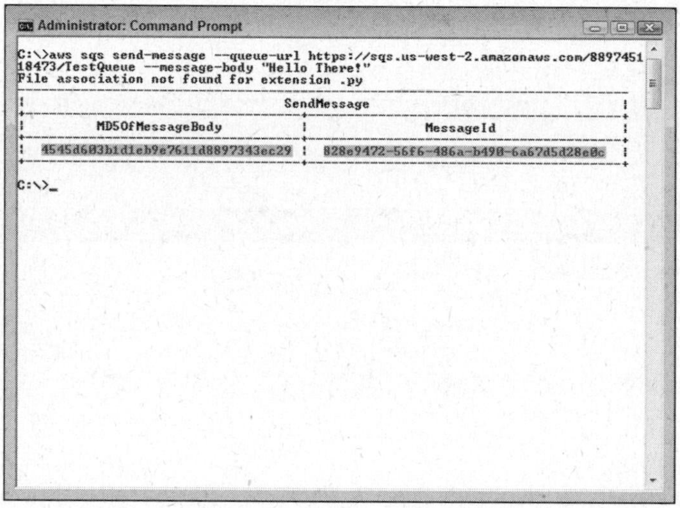

FIGURE 10-16: The CLI command sends a message to the queue.

To retrieve the message, you type **aws sqs receive-message --queue-url https:// sqs.us-west-2.amazonaws.com/889745118473/TestQueue --output text** and press Enter. The use of text output makes the output smaller and easier to see. Remember again to use the URL for your queue and not the one in the book. The output appears in Figure 10-17. Note the long series of seemingly incoherent letters and numbers at the end of the output, starting with AQEB. This long string is the receipt handle, which you need to delete the message.

Viewing the message doesn't remove it from the queue. To remove the message, you must actually delete it. To delete a message, you need the receipt handle, shown in Figure 10-17. For example, to delete the message in the example, you enter **aws sqs delete-message --queue-url https://sqs.us-west-2.amazonaws. com/889745118473/TestQueue --receipt-handle AQEBrFMb1m9xlPFSf0PHYop+ o+Bh3/q3cl6CwxLY4+OOWsu1qcsevjqiSKiOKz5w85TLBUp2+2t76pzHMxMo6pV ABwJODtWy6dzbh5k/qBxLQrodzOjZJIhZModKLnH8GftiTSqC0msgZg59R3K**

W6E3J2G52oBn7JvC8BOAnoFU8PKIty/2YeargA/2ur6RmvqSgXZUCSeYiv86FfaKy fEbB3AJ4+nTNe5MA+Fzx2ykBxojL1LDJHsbHsgyxBej9+R6qmerzSyzFQtswHU0S bNMjWnFdiVn9uZ0SA3wSoJwCKiC9JV2jMd2W9uAXELNpc9QiTQtm89Nb77PF4 qTnqAhDb1+3zV65PzqWkIIQ2LRvWDDwo+IL2ssL8ThW0ePlAJ5drgDo6U8V9Zil aWq1KCn+BA== and press Enter. Using the console definitely makes some tasks harder, but you can copy the receipt handle directly from the screen and then paste it back as necessary.

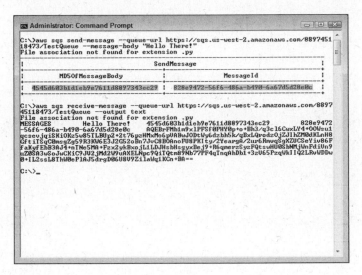

Writing a program in Python

Python and boto3 makes working with SQS significantly easier than working with the CLI. You use the following code to create a new message. (You can access this example code in the AWS4D4D; 10; SQS Check.ipynb file for this chapter in the downloadable source, as explained in the Introduction.)

```python
import boto3

sqs = boto3.client('sqs')

response = sqs.send_message(
    QueueUrl = "https://sqs.us-west-2.amazonaws.com" +
    "/889745118473/TestQueue",
    MessageBody = "Hello There!")
print(response)
```

The output contains `'HTTPStatusCode': 200` when you successfully create a new message. The idea is the same as using the CLI. However, the implementation is a little shorter. Using Python also makes obtaining just the content you need easier. The following code retrieves the message from the queue:

```
msg = sqs.receive_message(
    QueueUrl = "https://sqs.us-west-2.amazonaws.com" +
    "/889745118473/TestQueue")
print(msg['Messages'][0]['Body'])
```

The output shows only the message body in this case, which consists of `"Hello There!"`. A single message response is a `dict` that can contain multiple messages, so you access each message as an individual `list` item. Within the message are attributes, such as `Body`, that you use to access individual data members.

Deleting a message is much easier than working with the CLI. The following code shows you how.

```
sqs.delete_message(
    QueueUrl = "https://sqs.us-west-2.amazonaws.com" +
    "/889745118473/TestQueue",
    ReceiptHandle = msg['Messages'][0]['ReceiptHandle'])
```

The output shows the response metadata. The important entry is `'HTTPStatus Code': 200`, which tells you that the deletion occurred as intended.

Using Lambda to create entries

The previous section of the chapter should give you an idea of how you might like SQS and S3 using Lambda. Look again at the "Modifying the function code" section, earlier in the chapter. You now have the ability to change how that code works so that it uses the queue you just created to contain the information about the file. Here's an updated version of the code in that section with the changes marked in bold type, but this code will send a message to SQS in addition to performing the print tasks:

```
from __future__ import print_function

import json
import urllib
import boto3

print('Loading function')
```

```
s3 = boto3.client('s3')
sqs = boto3.client('sqs')


def lambda_handler(event, context):
    #print("Received event: " +
    #    json.dumps(event, indent=2))


    # Get the object from the event and show
    # its content type
    bucket = event['Records'][0]['s3']['bucket']['name']
    key = urllib.unquote_plus(
        event['Records'][0]['s3']['object']['key'].
        encode('utf8'))
    try:
        response = s3.get_object(Bucket=bucket, Key=key)
        print("CONTENT TYPE: " + response['ContentType'])
        sqs_resp = sqs.send_message(
            QueueUrl =
            "https://sqs.us-west-2.amazonaws.com" +
            "/889745118473/TestQueue",
            MessageBody =
            "CONTENT TYPE: " + response['ContentType'])
        print(sqs_resp)
        return response['ContentType']
    except Exception as e:
        print(e)
        print('Error getting object {} from bucket {}. ' +
            'Make sure they exist and your bucket is in' +
            ' the same region as this function.'.
            format(key, bucket))
        raise e
```

Note that you must add the SQS client outside the lambda_handler() function. The code in the lambda_handler() function looks almost precisely the same as the code used in the Python example. Working through your code additions using Python reduces the time and effort in making Lambda interoperability work. The printed output will look the same as when you execute the code in Anaconda.

Unfortunately, the code won't run right now because unlike your Anaconda installation, the Lambda function doesn't have permission. To add the required permission, select the Permissions tab for the queue in the SQS Console. As shown in Figure 10-18, the queue currently lacks a permission statement, which means that only the queue owner can access the queue.

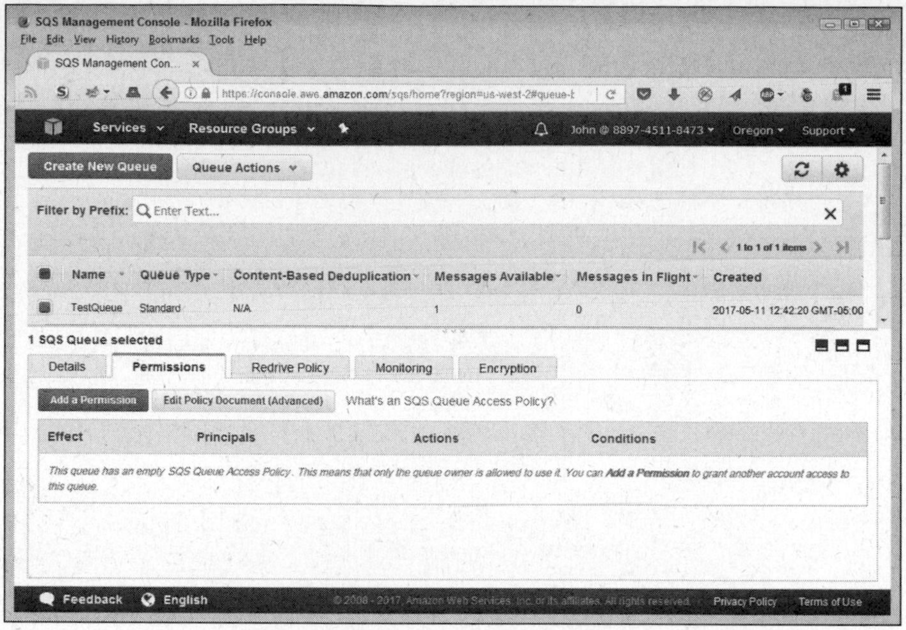

FIGURE 10-18:
Lambda must
have permission
to access the
queue.

Click Add a Permission to add a new permission statement to the queue. You see
the Add a Permission to TestQueue dialog box, shown in Figure 10-19.

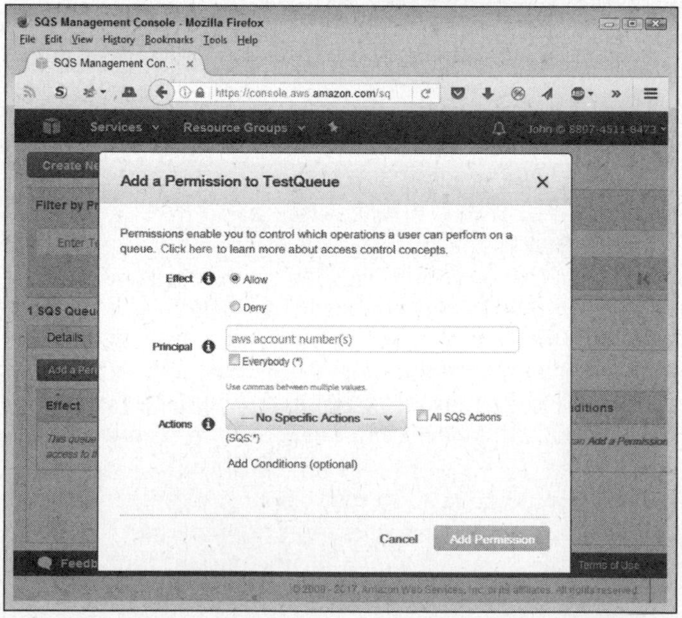

FIGURE 10-19:
Lambda must
have permission
to access the
queue.

Given that you want everyone to have access to the queue to add, retrieve, and possibly delete messages, select Everybody. In the Actions field, select Send Message, ReceiveMessage, and DeleteMessage. You really don't want to give everyone any of the other permissions. Click Add Permission, and you see the new permission shown in Figure 10-20.

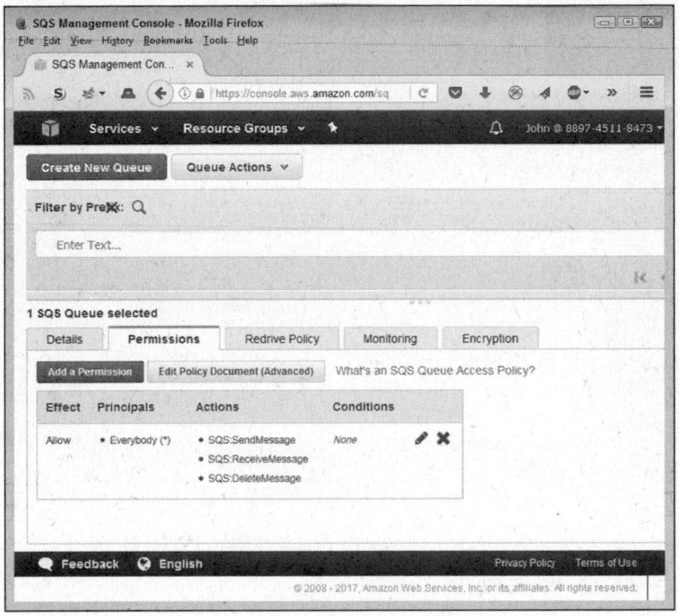

FIGURE 10-20: Everyone now has the required message permissions.

At this point, you can click Test in the Lambda Console to test the new code. The code should succeed as it did before. The only difference is that the printed output now contains the content from the SQS client `print()` statement.

However, you need to verify that everything worked as it should by going back to the SQS Console. Select TestQueue and choose Queue Actions ⇨ View/Delete Messages. You see the View/Delete Messages in Test Queue dialog box, shown in Figure 10-21.

Click Start Polling for Messages. You see the single message, with the correct content, as shown in Figure 10-22. If desired, you can select this message and click Delete Messages to remove it. AWS will ask whether you're sure before making the deletion.

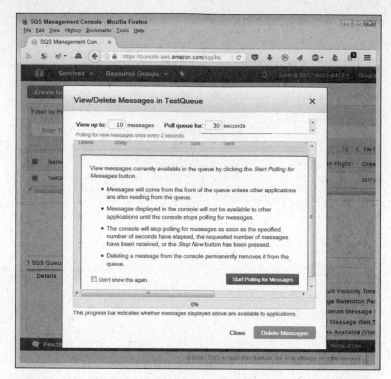

FIGURE 10-21:
Use the SQS
Console features
to view the
messages.

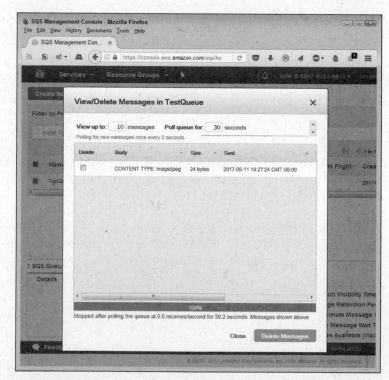

FIGURE 10-22:
SQS lets you
review the
messages from
Lambda.

4
Interacting with Databases

Install and configure the Relational Database Service (RDS).

Work with MySQL.

Modify option groups, events, and parameter groups.

Upload and download data.

Interact with NoSQL databases using DynamoDB.

Chapter **11**

Getting Basic DBMS Using RDS

B usiness thrives on data — lots of data — most of it in extremely complex forms. It isn't a recent phenomenon either. Some of the most persuasive arguments for creating computers in the first place focused on the need to manage data efficiently. So you shouldn't be surprised to find that AWS supports the Relational Database Service (RDS) and that it provides robust support for complex data setups. In fact, you can likely use the same DBMS in the cloud that you use on your local servers. The major difference between the two, of course, is that cloud-based data storage offers greater convenience while the private network data storage tends to offer better security. Obviously, there are a great many other differences, which this chapter covers.

RDS is complex enough that you likely have team members who do nothing but perform management tasks. However, just about every developer spends at least a little time working with RDS in a management capacity, so this chapter also discusses techniques that you can use to manage RDS. Administrators tend to use the management console exclusively to perform management tasks, but developers also use the Command Line Interface (CLI) and custom application code, so this chapter discusses all three options. In most cases, even developers perform initial management tasks using the management console simply because the task is complex and the management console makes things easier.

This chapter doesn't introduce you to the inner workings of RDS so that you can create complex DBMS configurations. For one thing, simply too many options are available to do the topic justice in just one chapter, or even in an entire book. However, you do need a simple database to use to work with the example code in the chapter, so you do find out how to get started creating your own DBMS using RDS. Of course, this leads into creating an application that uses the sample database.

The final section of the chapter discusses load balancing and scaling from a developer perspective. An administrator might worry about getting maximum speed using the fewest resources, but a developer must consider the need to match a test server to a production server well enough to perform credible application testing. The difference in perspective is important, so this chapter focuses on the developer view of things. Of course, you also get the basics of working with load balancing and scaling.

Considering the Relational Database Service (RDS) Features

The main purpose of a relational database is to organize and manage consistent pieces of data using tables that relate to each other through key fields. For example, an employee table may have a relation to a telephone number table connected through the employee ID. Because an employee can have multiple telephone numbers, each single entry in the employee table can have multiple connections to the telephone number table. Although this is a gross simplification of Relational Database Management Systems (RDBMS), it serves a purpose for this chapter.

To perform management tasks correctly, you must have a reliable Database Management System (DBMS) built upon a specific engine. The database engine you choose determines the characteristics and flexibility of the management environment. In addition, the database engine can also affect how well the RDBMS scales when you increase load, data size, or other factors. Also important is to have the means to create a copy of your database using both *replication* (the copying of individual data elements) and *cloning* (the copying of the entire database). The following sections describe how RDS helps you achieve all these goals.

Choosing a database engine

AWS RDS supports a number of database engines. Of course, supporting a single RDBMS might at first seem to do the trick because they all essentially do the same thing. However, you must consider a number of factors when choosing a database engine. These factors include (in order of importance):

>> The RDBMS currently used for most of your existing projects

>> Coding needs, such as the capability to execute scripts in specific ways

>> Interoperability needs, especially when working with other organizations

>> Automation needs, such as the capability to execute scripts in response to events or at a specific time

>> Security concerns that may override other needs for data storage

>> Data storage size or type requirements

>> Management requirements

REMEMBER

For developers, the overwhelming first priority in choosing an RDBMS is using the same database that the organization uses to ensure a smooth transition from the test to the production environment. An exception to this rule occurs when the organization plans to consolidate RDBMS products and is therefore moving to a new product to meet specific needs. Given that the number of RDBMS engines available today is huge, RDS is unlikely to ever support them all. As of this writing, RDS supports six database engines, each of which has characteristics in its favor, as explained in the following list:

>> **Amazon Aurora:** This product is essentially a MySQL clone. If you like MySQL, you probably like Amazon Aurora as well. However, according to a number of sites, Amazon has managed to make Aurora faster, more scalable, and inclusive of a number of interesting additional features. Of course, you pay a higher price for Amazon Aurora as well, so if you don't need the extra features, using MySQL is probably a better choice. The articles at http://2ndwatch.com/blog/deeper-look-aws-aurora/ and http://izoratti.blogspot.com/2014/11/it-does-not-matter-if-aurora-performs.html provide a more detailed comparison of Amazon Aurora to MySQL.

>> **MariaDB:** This is another MySQL clone, but it also has a significant number of additional features that you can read about at https://mariadb.com/kb/en/mariadb/mariadb-vs-mysql-features/. You need to consider a few major differences when choosing this product. For one thing, MariaDB is pure open source, which means that it uses a single license that is easier to manage than MySQL. However, because of the licensing, enterprise customers deal with equivalent open source implementations in MariaDB (such as thread pool), instead of the original MySQL implementations, which can result

in compatibility issues. MariaDB is also currently locked at the MySQL 5.5 level, so you may not have access to the latest MySQL features needed to make your application work.

>> **MySQL:** This product isn't quite as old as some of the other RDBMS offerings that Amazon supports, but it does serve as the standard to which other products are judged. The problem with being the leader is that everyone takes pot shots at you and tries to unsettle your customers, which is precisely what is happening to MySQL. You can read about some of the pros and cons of choosing MySQL at `http://www.myhostsupport.com/index.php?/News/NewsItem/View/58` and `https://www.smartfile.com/blog/the-pros-and-cons-of-mysql/`. The fact is that MySQL sets the standard, so it likely provides the most stable and reliable platform that you can choose when these issues are the main concern.

>> **Oracle:** This product has been around for years, so it has a long history of providing great support and significant flexibility. What sets Oracle apart from a few other products, such as MySQL and SQL Server, is that Linux administrators and developers tend to prefer it. As with MySQL, Oracle is a standard setter that everyone likes to compare with other products, even when those comparisons aren't a good match. Unlike other products in this list, viewing Oracle Cloud as a separate product from the enterprise setup is essential; the two products aren't completely compatible and have differing feature sets. You can find some pros and cons of using Oracle Cloud at `http://www.socialerp.com/oracle-private-cloud.php`.

>> **PostgreSQL:** This is a combination product in that most people view it as an open source version of Oracle but also go to great lengths to compare it with MySQL. Developers like PostgreSQL because it provides a significant number of features that MySQL tends not to support. In addition, the transition for developers from Oracle or SQL Server is relatively easy because PostgreSQL tends to follow their lead. However, MySQL tends to provide better ease of use and is somewhat faster than PostgreSQL. You can find some interesting pros and cons about this product at `http://www.anchor.com.au/hosting/dedicated/mysql_vs_postgres` and `https://www.digitalocean.com/community/tutorials/sqlite-vs-mysql-vs-postgresql-a-comparison-of-relational-database-management-systems`.

>> **SQL Server:** This product provides essential RDBMS functionality with a considerable number of add-ons. The important thing to remember about SQL Server is that Microsoft created it for Windows, and everything about this product reflects that beginning. In general, administrators find that working with SQL Server is relatively easy unless they need to use a broad range of those add-ons. Developers like SQL Server because it integrates well with the Microsoft language products. You can read pros and cons about this product

at http://www.infoworld.com/article/3013601/application-development/new-features-in-sql-server-2016.html, http://www.theregister.co.uk/2013/05/28/sql_server_2012_second_look/, and http://www.sqlserverf1.com/pros-and-cons-of-running-sql-server-on-premise-vs-azure-cloud/.

REMEMBER

Even with this short overview of the various choices, you can see the need to research your RDS choice completely before committing to a particular option. In some cases, you may need to configure a dummy setup and perform tests to see which option works best for your particular application. After you begin to fill the RDBMS with real-world data, moving to another database engine is usually an expensive, error-prone, and time-consuming task. The smart developer takes additional time to make a good choice at the outset, rather than discover that a particular choice is a mistake after the application moves into the development (or, worse yet, production) stages.

Understanding the need to scale efficiently

The capability of your application to scale depends on its access to resources. AWS provides consistent access to its resources by using autoscaling, which is a combination of automation and scaling. Monitors generate events that tell services when an application requires additional resources, such as servers, to maintain a constant level of output so that the user doesn't see any difference between a light and a heavy load. Even though the real-world performance of autoscaling may not provide precisely this level of consistency (see the "Problems with autoscaling" sidebar in Chapter 6 for details), the automation does work well enough so that most users won't complain from an AWS perspective.

REMEMBER

A problem with RDS, or any other database service for that matter, is that resources include data. No matter what you do, throwing additional resources at data management issues will only go so far. At some point, the sheer weight of the data becomes an encumbrance. Searching through several million records to find the one record you need takes time, no matter how many servers you allow and how much memory you provide. With this time factor in mind, you need to consider these issues when working with AWS to create an application that scales well when large amounts of data are involved:

>> **Use the right RDBMS:** Amazon makes a number of database managers available, as described in the preceding section of this chapter, "Choosing a database engine." Even though your first inclination is to use the database engine that you use most commonly in your organization now, speed considerations may trump consistency in this case. If you want your application to scale well, you may need to choose an RDBMS that provides optimal speed in a cloud environment.

>> **Organize the data using best practices:** This book doesn't address DBMS-specific concerns, such as the use of normalization. The use of best practices gives you a good starting point to ensure that your application scales well. A best practice comes into play when experimentation shows that it usually has good results.

>> **Experiment to find good RDBMS optimizations:** Knowledge resources usually focus on the general case because no one can possibly know about your specific needs. However, trade-offs occur when you use various general organizational and optimization techniques, and you need to consider the price of each trade-off when compared to application speed and the application's capability to scale well under load. In some cases, relying on a best practice that works well in general may not produce the desired result in your specific case.

>> **Play with AWS to determine whether additional resources will help:** AWS may really be able to help you overcome some speed and scaling issues by allowing you access to resources that you wouldn't normally have. The AWS documentation offers some clues as to when allocating additional resources (and spending more to do it) will yield a desired result. Unfortunately, the only way to verify that using additional AWS resources will provide acceptable gain for the price paid is to experiment and monitor the results of testing carefully.

Defining data replication

Data replication is often associated with data availability. When a failure occurs, RDS uses the replica instead so that users don't see much, if any, reduction in application speed. Amazon recommends that you place your replica in a different availability zone from your main database to ensure that the replica also addresses regional issues, such as a natural disaster. When a failure occurs because of a tornado or other natural disaster in one area, the replica in a region that has good conditions can take over until RDS makes repairs to the main database.

REMEMBER

From a development perspective, you generally won't see any difference in coding an application when using data replication. The data replication occurs in the background and the failover support is invisible outside Amazon. What you do need to do is perform setups to create the data replication and to monitor it once you have it configured. If your application is for administrators, you definitely need to code these features into your application. However, from a data access perspective, no difference exists, so user-level applications require no special code.

Amazon relies on SQL Server Mirroring to provide data replication when you choose SQL Server as your RDBMS. For replication, you can also choose to use Multi-AZ (http://docs.aws.amazon.com/AmazonRDS/latest/UserGuide/Concepts. MultiAZ.html) when using any of these RDBMSs:

>> MariaDB

>> MySQL

>> Oracle

>> PostgreSQL

Another use of data replication is as a means to help data scale better when working with large datasets or a large number of users. A *Read Replica* has a copy of the data in the main database, but you can't change it. Applications connect to the Read Replica version of the data, rather than the main copy, to reduce the load on the main database when performing read-only tasks such as queries and data analysis. This feature is available only to MySQL, MariaDB, and PostgreSQL RDBMS users. The main advantage is that your application gains a considerable scaling feature. The main disadvantage is that Read Replica updates occur asynchronously, which means that the read-only data may contain old information at times. You can read more about this feature at `http://docs.aws.amazon.com/AmazonRDS/latest/UserGuide/USER_ReadRepl.html`.

Cloning your database

Replication is data-based copying of data. You ask AWS to create a copy of your data, but not necessarily the entire database. Cloning focuses on copying the entire database, including the data. AWS supports cloning by using *database snapshots,* a sort of picture of the database at a specific instant in time. Database snapshots get used in multiple scenarios:

>> **Backup:** Restoring a snapshot helps a failed RDS instance recover to a known state.

>> **Testing:** Placing a snapshot on a test system provides real-world data that a developer or other party uses to test applications or processes.

>> **Cloning:** Copying a snapshot from one RDS instance to another creates a clone of the source RDS instance.

Creating the snapshot means telling AWS where to copy the database and providing credentials for encrypted databases. You can create a database snapshot in a number of ways:

>> Manually by using the RDS Management Console

>> Automatically by scheduling the snapshot using the RDS Management Console

>> Programmatically by using the RDS API

When you use automation to create the snapshot, AWS automatically deletes the snapshot at the end of its retention period, when you disable automated database snapshots for an RDS instance, or when you delete an RDS instance. You can keep manually generated database snapshots for as long as needed.

WARNING

Copying a database snapshot from one region to another incurs data transfer charges in addition to any charges that you incur creating the snapshot or using other service features. You should consider the cost of performing this task in advance because the charges can quickly mount for a large database (see `http://aws.amazon.com/rds/pricing/` for pricing details). In addition, Amazon places limitations on copying database snapshots from certain sources. For example, you can't copy a database snapshot to or from the AWS GovCloud (US) region (see `http://docs.aws.amazon.com/AmazonRDS/latest/UserGuide/USER_Copy Snapshot.html` for details).

Managing RDS

Developers, DevOps, Administrators, and DBAs all work with DBMS in different ways to perform different tasks. Developers often view management as a series of setup, testing, and tweaking operations because these kinds of management follow the application development cycle. Consequently, developers tend to work with management tools differently from everyone else. When working with RDS, you have three essential methods for performing management tasks:

>> **Management console:** Perform the initial DBMS setup and the complex tweaks needed to ensure maximum security, reliability, and speed.

>> **CLI:** Script repetitive short tasks that don't rely on significant amounts of output and perform one off operations, such as status checks.

>> **Custom code:** Define complex repetitive tasks that require considerable effort when using the console and obtain unique output presentations based on business logic.

You may find that you use each of these methods for other purposes or that there is some overlap between them. The point is that each method is important and has a particular place in your toolbox. With this in mind, the following sections show how to perform various RDS management tasks using each of the common methods.

Accessing the RDS Management Console

As with every other part of AWS, you can use a special management console to work with RDS. The RDS Management Console enables you to choose an RDBMS, create a database, add tables and other objects to the database, and make the database accessible to an application. You also use the RDS Management Console to perform administrative tasks, such as to configure security. Use the following steps to access the RDS Management Console:

1. **Sign into AWS by using your user account.**

2. **Navigate to the RDS Management Console at** `https://console.aws.amazon.com/rds`.

   You see a Welcome page that contains interesting information about RDS and what it can do for you, as shown in Figure 11-1. However, you don't see the actual console at this point. Notice the Navigation pane at the left. You can click the left-pointing arrow to hide it as needed. Many of the RDS Dashboard options are the same as those used by EC2, which is no surprise, given that you use EC2 to support the database.

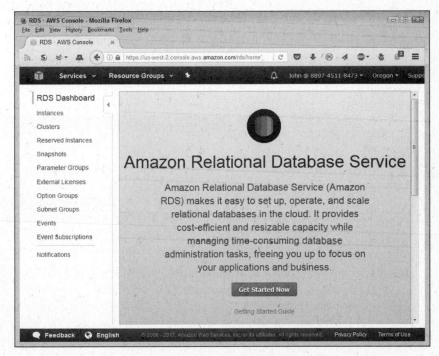

FIGURE 11-1: Getting started with the Amazon Relational Database Service (RDS).

3. **Click Get Started Now.**

You see the Select Engine page, shown in Figure 11-2. Notice that you can select a major vendor and then a specific version of that vendor's product. For example, the screenshot shows three versions of SQL Server (others are available).

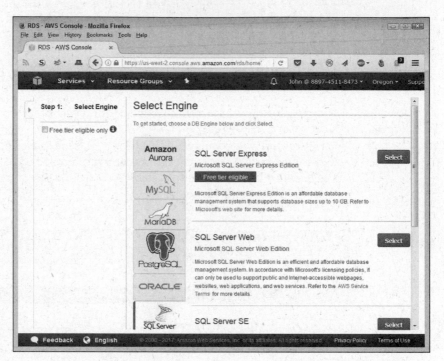

FIGURE 11-2:
Choose a vendor and then a specific vendor product.

The examples in this chapter rely on MySQL because you can also download a free local copy from https://www.mysql.com/downloads/. The MySQL Community Edition is free, and you can obtain trial versions of the other editions. Most vendors do provide a free version of their product for testing and learning purposes. In addition, MySQL works on most of the platforms that readers of this book will use.

TIP

Select Free Tier Eligible Only if you want to select only a free-tier database. You still see the other options, but the Select button is grayed out so that you won't inadvertently select a paid option. Using free options can save you money on software, but developers must also choose an option that works with the database the organization uses. Otherwise, you encounter potential problems when moving your application from testing to production.

4. Click Select next to the MySQL Community Edition entry.

You see the Specify DB Details page, shown in Figure 11-3. Notice that the Navigation page specifies that this DBMS is free-tier eligible. The right pane contains all the details about the DBMS instance.

FIGURE 11-3: Specify the details used to create the database instance.

5. Select the Only Show Options that are Eligible for RDS Free Tier.

Choosing this option helps ensure that you don't choose features that will require payment later.

6. Choose MySQL 5.6.27 in the DB Engine Version field.

REMEMBER

The DB Engine Version field doesn't automatically select the most current version. It appears to select the most commonly used version instead. In addition, the drop-down list doesn't display the versions in order. Make sure that you look through the entire list for the version you need before assuming that AWS might not make it available.

7. Choose db.t2.micro in the DB Instance Class field.

To retain free-tier compatibility, you must choose this particular class. It pays to review the free-tier requirements found at https://aws.amazon.com/rds/free/. This informational page provides details about free-tier usage, such as the instance type, the kinds of database product you can choose, memory requirements, and so on.

WARNING

Because the free-tier requirements can change at any time, you must review the free-tier materials before making choices about the database you want to work with. You may need to modify the selections used in this chapter to ensure that you maintain free-tier support and don't incur any expenses.

8. **Ensure the Multi-AZ Deployment field displays a value of No.**

When using the free-tier options, AWS greys this field out and automatically selects No for you. A Multi-Availability Zone (Multi-AZ) configuration makes your setup more reliable and faster by creating duplicate databases in multiple zones. The "Defining data replication" section, earlier in this chapter, describes the concept in more detail. The discussion at https://aws.amazon.com/rds/details/multi-az/ provides additional details specifically regarding Multi-AZ.

9. **Choose General Purpose (SSD) in the Storage Type field and type 20 in the Allocated Storage field.**

When working with MySQL Community Edition, you must allocate at least 5GB of storage. However, the free tier allows you to allocate up to 20GB, which is the maximum amount that the MySQL Community Edition can use. To get the maximum performance from your experimental setup, you want to allocate as much memory as you can.

TIP

Depending on the DBMS you choose, the wizard may warn you that choosing less than 100GB of storage can cause your application to run slowly when working with high throughput loads. This warning isn't a concern when creating an experimental setup, such as the one defined for this chapter. However, you do need to keep the storage recommendations in mind when creating a production setup.

10. **Type MyDatabase in the DB Instance Identifier field.**

The instance identifier provides the means for uniquely identifying the database for access purposes. Usually you choose a name that is descriptive of the database's purpose and is easy for everyone to remember.

11. **Type a username in the Master Username field.**

The master user is the administrator who manages the database and will receive full access to it. A specific person should have the responsibility, rather than assign it to a group (where responsibility for issues can shift between people). When working as a sole developer on a project, you should type your username in this field to keep things easy. When working in a group setting, make sure you get the correct username and password from the group leader or administrator.

12. **Type a password in the Master Password field, repeat it in the Confirm Password field, and then click Next Step.**

You see the Configure Advanced Settings page, shown in Figure 11-4. This page lets you choose the VPC security group used to identify incoming requests (before they arrive at the DBMS); the authentication directory used to authenticate database users who rely on Windows Authentication; the networking options used to access the DBMS (such as the port number); the backup plan; the monitoring plan; and the maintenance plan. You do need to set the VPC security group to ensure that you can access the database. However, the remaining defaults will work for the examples in this chapter.

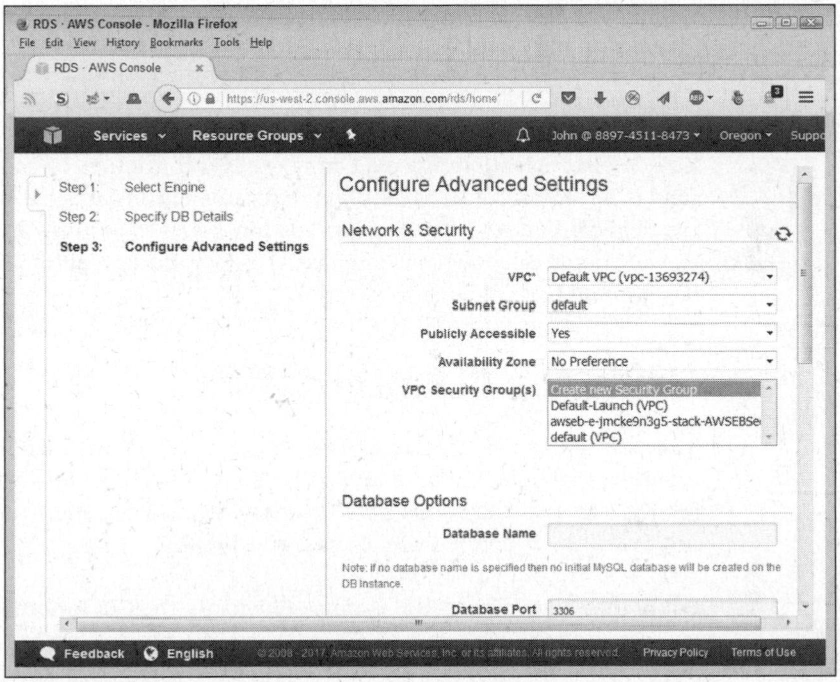

FIGURE 11-4:
Define the connectivity, backup, monitoring, and maintenance details.

13. **Choose the Default-Launch security group created as part of defining the EC2 setup.**

Depending on the DBMS you choose, you may find other database options that you can set. For example, MySQL lets you provide the name of an initial database. It pays to go through the settings carefully to ensure that you make maximum use of wizard functionality.

14. **Type** FirstDatabase **in the Database Name field and then click Launch DB Instance.**

AWS starts the instance creation process.

15. **Click View Your DB Instances.**

You see the RDS Management Console, as shown in Figure 11-5.

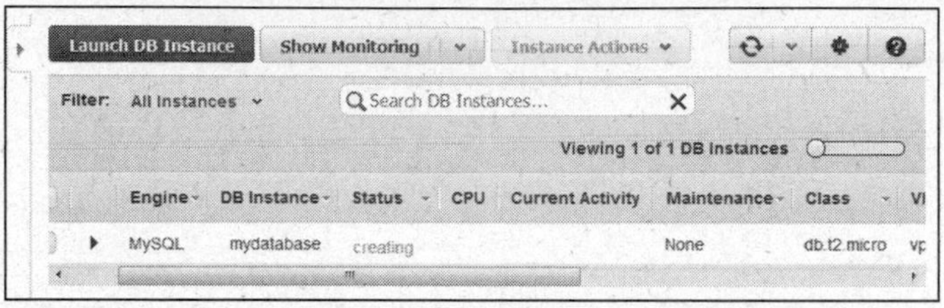

FIGURE 11-5:
Creating your first database provides access to the RDS Management Console.

REMEMBER

The database creation process can take several minutes to complete. The Status field (refer to Figure 11-6) tells you the status of the database. As long as the Status field continues to say Creating, you must wait to perform any additional tasks. However, you can download and install any products required to access the database (if you haven't done so already).

Using the CLI alternative

This section of the chapter shows how to interact with RDS using the CLI. It assumes that you created a MySQL database by using the steps in the previous section and that the Status field for that database currently reads Available (and not Creating). If not, it's time for a coffee break.

Using the CLI to access RDS is much like using the CLI for other tasks. You begin each command with `aws rds`. The command reference appears at `http://docs.amazonaws.cn/cli/latest/reference/rds/index.html`. Some of the information you can obtain using this approach is quite interesting. For example, you might wonder about potential updates for the current version of the database engine you're using. To test what information you get with the example, type **aws rds describe-db-engine-versions --engine mysql --engine-version 5.6.27** and press Enter. You see the output shown in Figure 11-6.

The output shows that you have a number of potential upgrades available, but none of them is an automatic upgrade — you'd need to apply each specifically. Three of these upgrades represent a major version upgrade, which means heavy research on the part of the developer before making the upgrade. Yes, you need to research every upgrade, but minor upgrades tend to provide less in the way of new features.

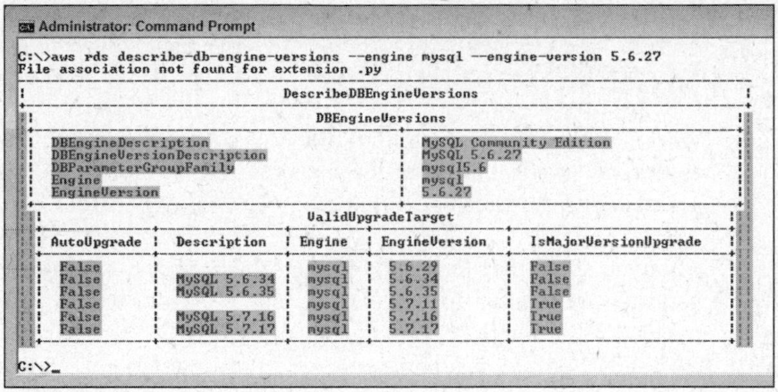

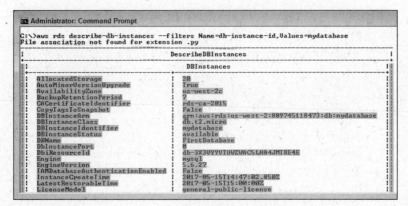

FIGURE 11-6:
Use the CLI to obtain useful information about the database engine or to manage it.

A few of the CLI commands are unclear. For example, when you want to discover more about a particular instance, you use the `describe-db-instances` command. However, if you have a number of instances defined, you need to further identify specifically which attribute by using the `--filters` argument as described at `http://docs.amazonaws.cn/cli/latest/reference/rds/describe-db-instances.html`. A filter can rely on the `DBInstanceIdentifier` or `DBCluster Identifier` values. To make this command work, you must define which kind of identifier you're supplying and the one or more values associated with that identifier. In the case of the example, you type **aws rds describe-db-instances --filters Name=db-instance-id,Values=mydatabase** and press Enter to obtain information about the database created for this chapter. Note how the information appears in the command. The `aws` utility can be quite picky about the format in this case. The output appears in Figure 11-7.

FIGURE 11-7:
Some commands require some special formatting and input.

Performing management tasks programmatically

Working with RDS programmatically works better when you interact with it at the command line first. Most of the concepts are the same between the two environments, but most developers find that working with the CLI is faster.

REMEMBER

After you do move from the CLI to a programming environment, make certain that you use the correct documentation. For example, when working with Python, make sure to use the boto3 documentation at http://boto3.readthedocs.io/ en/latest/reference/services/rds.html, not the boto documentation. In this case, the two environments are completely incompatible, and code written for one is guaranteed not to run in the other. (You can access the example code for this chapter in the AWS4D4D; 11; RDS.ipynb file in the downloadable source, as explained in the Introduction.) To start, you must create an RDS client:

```
import boto3
client = boto3.client('rds')
```

To determine the update versions for the current product version, you rely on the describe_db_engine_versions() function. The input arguments are the same as at the command line, but to obtain the information, you drill down into the output, as shown here:

```
for target in client.describe_db_engine_versions(
    Engine='mysql', EngineVersion='5.6.27') \
    ['DBEngineVersions'][0]['ValidUpgradeTarget']:
        print(target['EngineVersion'])
```

The output for this example is the same as when working with the CLI. Of course, the Python code removes all extraneous information:

```
5.6.29
5.6.34
5.6.35
5.7.11
5.7.16
5.7.17
```

Using Python lets you filter the output in a number of ways. For example, you might find just those updates that don't require a major upgrade.

Getting the instance information is also similar to working with the CLI. Here is the Python code used for this task:

```
client.describe_db_instances(
    DBInstanceIdentifier='mydatabase')['DBInstances'][0]
```

This is the simplified version, but it obtains only the information for a single instance, as shown here (some information isn't shown to save book space):

```
{'AllocatedStorage': 20,
 'AutoMinorVersionUpgrade': True,
 'AvailabilityZone': 'us-west-2c',
 'BackupRetentionPeriod': 7,
 'CACertificateIdentifier': 'rds-ca-2015',
 'CopyTagsToSnapshot': False,

 ...

 'PendingModifiedValues': {},
 'PreferredBackupWindow': '11:39-12:09',
 'PreferredMaintenanceWindow': 'sun:07:12-sun:07:42',
 'PubliclyAccessible': True,
 'ReadReplicaDBInstanceIdentifiers': [],
 'StorageEncrypted': False,
 'StorageType': 'gp2',
 'VpcSecurityGroups': [{'Status': 'active',
   'VpcSecurityGroupId': 'sg-c511c2be'}]}
```

You can also use a version of the call that's closer to what you used with the CLI:

```
client.describe_db_instances(
    Filters=[{'Name':'db-instance-id',
             'Values':['mydatabase']}])['DBInstances'][0]
```

The output is the same either way, but the first version is shorter when you want just one instance. You can provide multiple instance identifier values, for example, when working with the second version.

Creating a Database Server

Creating a cloud-based database server works much like creating a local server except that you're performing all the tasks remotely on someone else's system. The change in venue means that you may find that some processes take longer to complete, that you may not have quite the same flexibility as you have when working locally, or that some features work differently. However, the overall workflow is the same. The following sections demonstrate how to work with a MySQL Server setup, but the techniques used with other RDBMSs are similar.

Installing a database access product

To use your new database, you need an application that can access it. For example, when you want to work with MySQL, you use the MySQL Workbench (http://dev.mysql.com/downloads/workbench/). Likewise, when working with SQL Server Express, you use the SQL Server Management Studio (https://msdn.microsoft.com/library/mt238290.aspx). No matter which DBMS you choose, you use an application outside of the RDS Management Console to manage it. You use the RDS Management Console only to control how the DBMS works with AWS. Because this chapter relies on MySQL as the DBMS, you need to download and install a copy of MySQL Workbench before proceeding with any of the other activities.

REMEMBER

This book uses the 64-bit MySQL Workbench 6.3.9 on Windows 7. If you use some other version, the screenshots are likely to differ substantially, and some procedures might not work as expected. However, the basic principles are the same across all versions (and likely across most RDBMS products). You should still be able to perform the required setups, but be aware that you obtain the best results using the 6.3.9 version.

Accessing the instance

The database instance that you created earlier will eventually become available. This means that you can interact with it. However, to interact with the database instance, you need to know its endpoint, which is essentially an address where applications can find it. When you select an instance in the RDS Management Console, a detailed view of that instance becomes visible and you can see the endpoint information, as shown in Figure 11-8.

REMEMBER

In this case, the endpoint is mydatabase.cihzb2715reh.us-west-2.rds.amazonaws.com:3306, which includes the instance name, a randomized set of letters and numbers, the instance location, and the port used to access the instance. Every endpoint is unique. If the endpoints weren't unique, you'd experience confusion trying to access them. When working through the examples in this chapter, you must use the endpoint for your database, not the endpoint for the book's example database, which appears only as an example.

FIGURE 11-8:
Find the instance endpoint so that you can access it from your management application.

When setting up a new connection in MySQL Workbench like the one shown in Figure 11-9, you need to supply the entire endpoint, except for the port, as the hostname. In this case, that means supplying `mydatabase.cempzgtjl38f.us-west-2.rds.amazonaws.com` as the hostname. You must also supply the port, which is 3306. Even though Figure 11-9 doesn't show it, you must also provide your username and password (click Store in Vault) to access the instance.

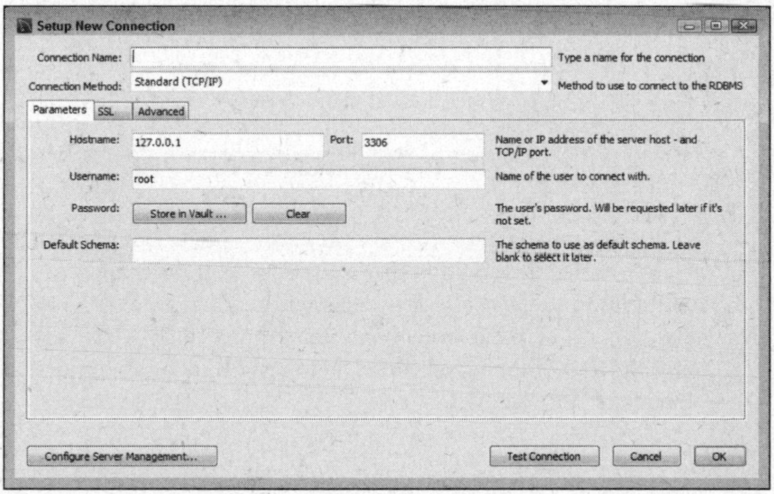

FIGURE 11-9:
Create a connection using the instance endpoint information from the RDS Management Console.

As shown in Figure 11-9, the MySQL Workbench provides a Test Connection button that you can use to determine whether the connection information will work. Most database management products provide such a button, and testing your connection before you move to the next step is a great idea. Otherwise, you can't be sure whether an error occurs because of a problem with the database or the connection to the database.

Adding tables

You work with your AWS database as you would any other database that you can access using the management tool of your choice. Everything works the same; you simply perform tasks in the cloud, rather than on your local network or on your machine. Figure 11-10 shows a typical example using MySQL Workbench. Notice that `FirstDatabase` appears in the Navigator pane, just as you'd expect, after making the connection to the RDS database.

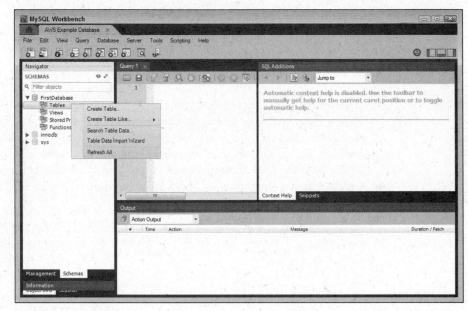

FIGURE 11-10:
Putting the database in the cloud doesn't change how your tools work.

Right-clicking the Tables entry produces a context menu in which you can choose Create Table. The creation process works as it normally does. The only difference you might note is that some tasks will require more time to complete because of the latency of the connection. Remember that you're accessing the database through a number of additional layers and that your connection speed also acts as a determining factor.

Working with other features

The tools and techniques you use depend on your role and the environment (test or production) that you find yourself using. You must make a significant separation between the database instance and the database itself:

>> **Administrator:** Addresses the needs of the production database instance using the RDS Management Console, such as by ensuring that the database is backed up or resetting the instance when it crashes.

>> **Database Administrator (DBA):** Interacts with the production database structure by using a completely different tool, such as MySQL Workbench (as demonstrated in this chapter).

>> **Developer:** Uses a combination of the tools and techniques relied upon by administrators and DBAs to set up and configure test databases, but developers may find themselves locked out of production databases. The test database must match the production database, so the developer must collaborate with both administrators and DBAs.

Because of the nature of cloud-based databases, you must consider how various administrators access tools and who can access them. The following sections detail the use of various RDS Management Console tools.

Monitoring the database instance

When working with RDS, a developer works with the database at two levels. The first level is monitoring. The detailed view always provides you with some metrics about the database. You see a log of alarms and recent events. In addition, you see the current CPU, memory, and storage use. However, these indicators are in real time, and you often need historical data to make a determination about a particular course of action.

To perform monitoring tasks, you select the database and then choose one of the monitoring options from the Show Monitoring menu of the RDS Management Console. For example, Figure 11-11 shows the multigraph view of the server data (choose Show Monitoring ⇨ Show Multi-Graph View). In this case, the graph shows the addition of a couple of connects to the database and the effect of adding a table and performing some other tasks. You'd need to look carefully at the Free Storage Space graph to detect any activity at all. Fortunately, you can click any of the graphs to expand it and get a better look. When you finish performing a monitoring task, click Hide Monitoring to see the detailed view again.

Rebooting after a crash

The Instance Actions menu lets you interact with the database instance at an administrator level. For example, when an instance does crash, you can restore it by choosing Instance Actions ⇨ Reboot.

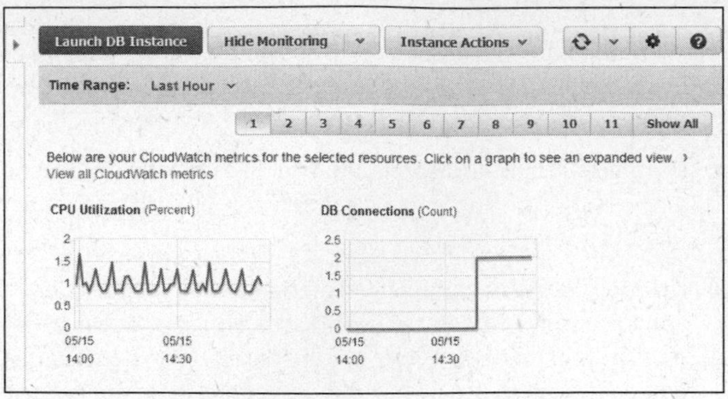

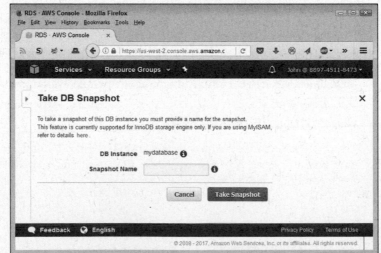

FIGURE 11-11:
Monitoring provides much-needed historical data.

Creating and deleting a snapshot

You may choose to create a read-only static view of the database (a snapshot) for archival reasons. For example, a snapshot provides a good way to restore a test database after you've played with it for a while. The capability to repeat actions using the same data is essential for development, so being able to quickly restore a database to a known configuration is important.

In this case, you choose Instance Actions ⇨ Take Snapshot. The RDS Management Console displays the Take DB Snapshot page, shown in Figure 11-12. The note about the InnoDB storage engine doesn't apply to the MySQL Community Edition because RDS supports only the InnoDB storage engine in this case. To create the snapshot, type a name (the example uses MySnapshot) in the Snapshot Name field and then click Take Snapshot. After you create the snapshot, it appears in the RDS Management Console as another snapshot (choose Snapshots in the Navigation pane) that someone can access as needed.

FIGURE 11-12:
Create a snapshot to use as a read-only source of information.

REMEMBER

Snapshots don't become usable until the Status field shows Available. Consequently, you can't create a snapshot and immediately test your code because the snapshot isn't available at that point. Wait until the Status field shows Available before testing your code.

Of course, you don't want to keep snapshots around that you're not using. Otherwise, you accumulate charges for objects you don't need. To remove a snapshot, select its entry and click Delete Snapshot.

Restoring a snapshot

The main reason to have a snapshot is for use as a backup. To restore a snapshot, select its entry in the snapshot list and then choose Snapshot Actions ⇨ Restore Snapshot. You see the Restore DB Instance page, shown in Figure 11-13. This page works much the same as the details page that you interacted when creating the initial database. However, the new database instance will contain everything found in the snapshot. It will have its own endpoint as well. Of course, you want to give the database a different instance name than the current database until you verify the snapshot's content.

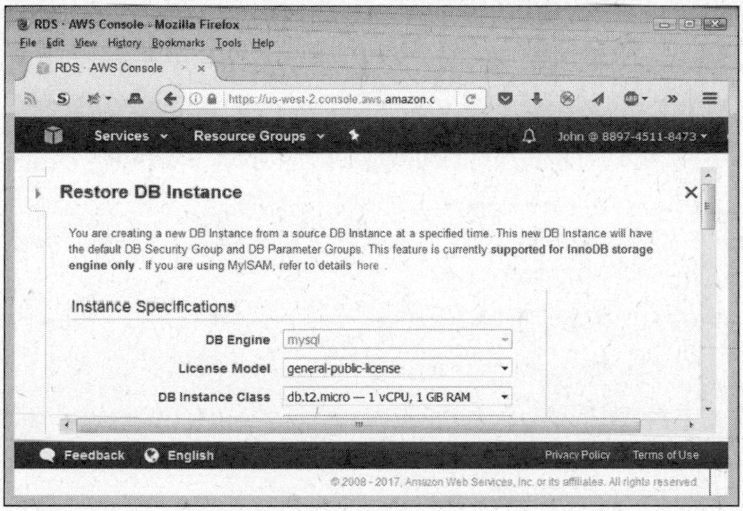

FIGURE 11-13: Specify the details of the restored snapshot to a database instance.

Verification is an important part of the process of working with any database in any situation, but especially so in the cloud. After you verify that the restored snapshot database instance contains the data you need, you can exchange it with the original database that needs repair by following these steps:

1. **Select the original database.**

You see the details for that database.

2. **Choose Instance Actions ⇨ Modify.**

You see the Modify DB Instance page, shown in Figure 11-14. This page contains all the settings you used to create the database instance initially. You can modify any of the settings as needed.

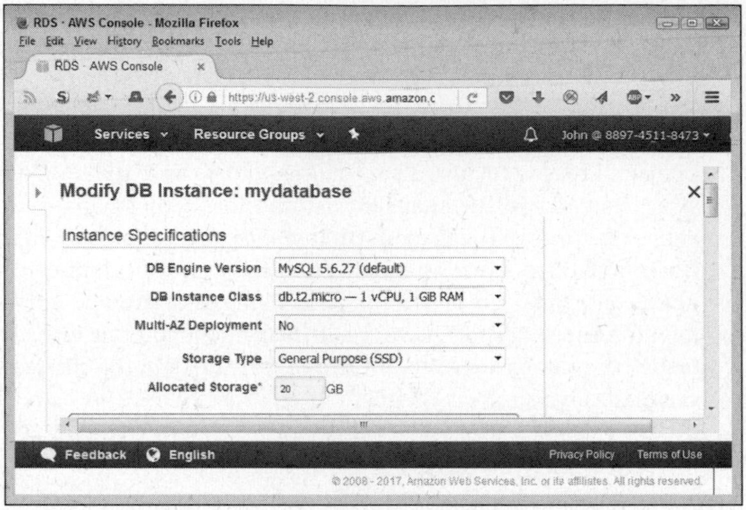

FIGURE 11-14: Change database instance settings as needed to accomplish specific tasks.

3. **Change the DB Instance Identifier field content to something new.**

4. **Select Apply Immediately and then click Continue.**

If you don't apply the change immediately, it won't take place until the next maintenance cycle. You see a summary page that shows the modifications that you want to apply.

5. **Click Modify DB Instance.**

AWS applies the changes you requested.

You must wait until AWS reboots the instance (you see Rebooting in the Status field) before the changes become permanent. When the Status field reads Available, you can move on to Step 6.

REMEMBER

6. **Perform Steps 1 through 5 for the restored snapshot database instance, except give this instance the name of the original database.**

You have now swapped the two databases and are using the restored snapshot database instance as your current database instance for applications.

Performing other modifications

The Modify DB Instance page, shown in Figure 11-14 (available through the Instance Actions ⇨ Modify command), also gives you access to a wealth of other database instance settings. For example, you can choose when backups occur and the level of monitoring provided. You can also change the database instance security settings. Anything you defined as part of the original creation process is available for modification in the Modify DB Instance page.

Adding Support to Applications

After you have a database server created and configured, you can use an application to access it. The data doesn't serve any purpose until you provide access to it. The purpose of the application in this case is to provide Create Read Update and Delete (CRUD) support for the data. Users are interested in data and what it represents; the application used to perform the task is secondary. In fact, common practice today is to provide multiple applications to perform database tasks because user needs differ so widely as a result of varying usage environments, devices, and personal preferences. The sources of these database applications can also vary. A database vendor might provide a generic application, corporate developers might supply something specific, and a third party might offer a feature-rich version of the application. The following sections discuss CRUD as it relates to working with AWS and a simple application by using the example database created earlier in the chapter.

Considering the access requirements

When working with cloud data, accessing the data requires an endpoint, just as it does for your local network or drive. As shown in the "Accessing the instance" section, earlier in this chapter, nothing really changes from a procedural perspective, except that you must now provide a different endpoint than normal. From a developer perspective, the endpoint that RDS provides for a database instance is nothing more than a URL, which means that you can use the same techniques that you use for any online data. This consideration also applies to any administrator tools used for private data. Administrators must consider the following issues as part of the application migration:

>> Verify that a connection works before attempting to use it to perform tasks on the data.

>> Assume that the connection will go down at some point, so make sure to verify that the connection is still present before each task.

DEFINING THE HYPE BEHIND CLOUD-BASED APPLICATION PERFORMANCE

There are no quick fixes to most problems. I'd go so far as to say there are no quick fixes to any problem, but someone will almost certainly e-mail me an exception to the rule. However, when it comes to performance issues, you likely can't count on a cloud-based approach to fix anything, especially performance, which consists of reliable operation in a secure manner and at the highest attainable speed. To fix performance issues, you must start with a great design, and the cloud simply can't fix design problems.

You might think that throwing more memory and processors at an application will make it perform faster. Unfortunately, as you increase memory and the number of processors, you also increase the amount of communication that occurs within the application. A poorly designed application could benefit a little from a faster environment, but not as much as you might think.

Adding auto-scaling and auto-provisioning services to your application could make it scale better, but these services won't fix inherent problems in the design. You'll get an application that provides a level performance curve, but not one that works faster. In addition, you spend a great deal more money to obtain the flatness of that curve.

Security is also an issue in the cloud. Anytime you let data out of your grasp (as you do with the cloud), you now depend on a third party to control security. In addition, cloud-based solutions won't fix the most prevalent security issue that application developers face: users. Letting your data reside in the cloud means that users will access it in all sorts of nonsecure ways, in all sorts of nonsecure environments, and potentially on all sorts of nonsecure devices. If anything, security is worse in the cloud than it could ever be on your local network.

So speed is probably going to remain about even and security is worse in the cloud. The only good news you have is that reliability is likely better. It's not as perfect, as the cloud vendor would have you believe, but it's better than having the application run in a single location, creating a single point of failure. The point is that you need a great application design before you move to the cloud, and you should have realistic expectations of what will happen when you move there.

>> Assume that someone will hack your data, no matter what security precautions you take, because the data is now available in a public venue (so have a recovery plan in place).

>> Ensure that security measures work as anticipated so that every user group can access the data within the boundaries set by company policy.

>> Define security policies for working with data in a public venue that address social hacking issues.

>> Consider legal and privacy requirements before moving the data.

>> Develop a plan for dealing with sensitive data that inadvertently makes it to your hosted database rather than staying on the local network or on a specific machine.

These precautions are in addition to the precautions you normally take when connecting an application to a database. The actual coding that you use may not change much (except for the addition of checks to address online access requirements), but the focus of how the application makes connections and performs required tasks does need to change. Otherwise, your organization might make front-page news after getting hacked and losing a lot of data to someone in another country.

Configuring the MySQL setup

To work with MySQL in any programming language, you normally need to install required library support. This is the case with Python. To install the MySQL support required for the example in this section, open a command prompt, type **pip install mysqlclient --upgrade**, and press Enter. You see the usual installation messages. The book examples use MySQL Client version 1.3.10.

TECHNICAL STUFF

You can find a wealth of libraries to support MySQL, and each of them works differently. This book uses a particular library simply to make the examples feasible. Another library may fulfill your needs better. In many cases, experimentation is the only way to determine whether a particular library meets your needs.

Interacting with the database

Depending on how you interact with the database, you might find a need to create infrastructure as part of an application process. The example in this section works with Python and MySQL. The goal is to show how you combine RDS with DBMS strategies to obtain cloud access to a database and add a table to it. Obviously, the example won't show you how to code your C# application when using SQL Server. The point of the example is the interaction, not necessarily the precise technique for adding a table. The first step of the interaction is to use RDS to obtain the endpoint that MySQL requires to access the database. (You can access the example code for this chapter in the AWS4D4D; 11; Manage Database.ipynb file in the downloadable source, as explained in the Introduction.)

```
import boto3
client = boto3.client('rds')
address = client.describe_db_instances(
    DBInstanceIdentifier='mydatabase')['DBInstances'] \
    [0]['Endpoint']['Address']
port = client.describe_db_instances(
    DBInstanceIdentifier='mydatabase')['DBInstances'] \
    [0]['Endpoint']['Port']
print('Using endpoint: ' + address + ':' + str(port))
```

When you have access to the endpoint, you can begin using the MySQL Client library to work with the database. The first step is to create a connection to the database. Note that you must supply the database name, your username, and your password rather than use any details that appear in the chapter.

```
import _mysql
conn = _mysql.connect(host=address, port=port,
                      db='FirstDatabase',
                      user='Name', passwd='Password')
print(conn.get_host_info())
```

The output from this bit of code should show the URL of the connection and define how the code made the connection. Unless you have a strange connection to AWS, the output shows that you connected using TCP/IP.

The previous steps establish a connection to the database. You'll likely use these initial steps in all your applications (or ones similar to them). The pattern is to obtain the connection to RDS, determine the connection information, and then use that connection information to connect to the actual database using a library suitable for your particular DBMS. At this point, you can start to execute commands against the database. How you execute those commands depends greatly on what you expect to achieve. The following code shows a simple scenario of creating a table after ensuring that it doesn't exist already and adding a record to it.

```
conn.query('USE FirstDatabase')
conn.query('DROP TABLE IF EXISTS MyTable')

conn.query(
    'CREATE TABLE MyTable (Field1 int, Field2 int)')

conn.query('INSERT MyTable VALUE (0, 1)')
conn.query('SELECT * FROM MyTable')
result = conn.store_result()
result.fetch_row()
```

The last steps ensure that the table, `MyTable`, actually contains the new record. Note that `conn.query()` doesn't return a result. Instead, you must store the result in a variable and then use that variable to obtain the desired information. In this case, `result.fetch_row()` shows the newly added record data.

Configuring Load Balancing and Scaling

The precise levels of load balancing and scaling that you receive with a particular RDBMS instance depends on how you configure the instance and which RDBMS you choose to use. It also depends partly on the application support you provide, how many users are accessing the database (and from where they access it), and many other factors too numerous to discuss in a single chapter of a book (or possibly in a whole shelf of books). With these caveats in mind, the following sections discuss load balancing and scaling issues in a generic way that works with all the RDBMSs that AWS supports. These discussions help you get started with both load balancing and scaling, but you may need to augment the information for your particular RDBMS to obtain a full solution to specific management needs.

Defining the purpose of load balancing

When your application gets large enough, you need multiple servers to handle the load. Of course, you don't want to configure each application instance to use a specific server; rather, you want to send the request to a general location and have it go to the server with the least load at any given time. The purpose of a load-balancing server is to

>> Act as a centralized request handler

>> Monitor the servers used to handle requests

>> Route responses to clients from the various servers

>> Determine the need for additional servers to handle increasing loads

Not all load-balancing scenarios perform all these activities, but most of them do. The point is that you use a single request point to allow access to multiple servers in order to hide the fact that a single server can't handle the load for the number of requests that users make. Using this approach enables you to scale your application across multiple servers in a transparent manner.

REMEMBER

When you're working with AWS, load balancing always occurs across multiple EC2 instances. Even though Amazon makes a point of telling you about the fault-tolerance features added through load balancing, the main focus is on the additional processing power that load balancing provides. However, if an EC2 instance does freeze or become otherwise unusable, you can substitute another EC2 instance without any problem. The application user will never see the difference.

Working with Elastic Load Balancing

When you first configure your EC2 instances, you won't have any Elastic Load Balancers configured — so you must create one. The Elastic Load Balancer must appear in the same region as the EC2 instances that it serves. The following steps help you create an Elastic Load Balancer:

1. **Sign into AWS using your administrator account.**

2. **Navigate to the EC2 Management Console at** `https://console.aws.amazon.com/ec2`.

   You see the EC2 Management Console.

3. **Verify that you have the correct region selected by choosing it in the region drop-down list at the top of the EC2 Management Console.**

4. **Select Load Balancing ⇨ Load Balancers in the Navigation pane.**

   You see the Load Balancer page, shown in Figure 11-15. Notice that the message specifies that you don't have any load balancers configured for the selected region; it doesn't say that you lack access to any load balancers.

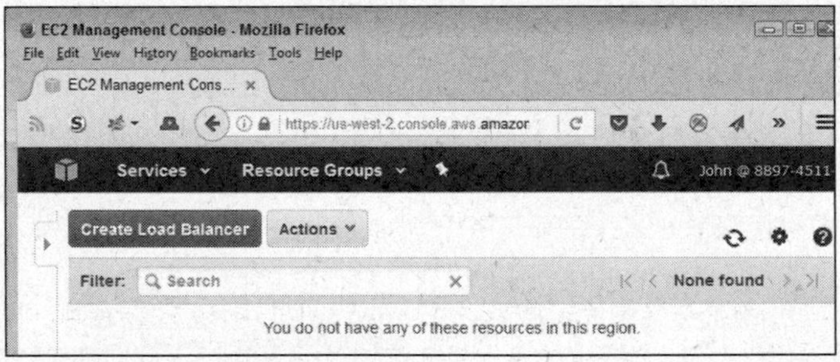

FIGURE 11-15: The Load Balancer page tells you about any load balancers you have configured.

5. **Click Create Load Balancer.**

   The wizard asks you to choose a load balancer type, as shown in Figure 11-16. The kind of load balancer you choose affects all sorts of things. The best place to get a detailed comparison is at https://www.sumologic.com/aws/elb/aws-elastic-load-balancers-classic-vs-application/. However, here is a quick overview of what to expect:

- **Classic:** The classic load balancer works at layer 4 of the OSI model, which means that it focuses on a combination of IP address and port when routing calls. The advantages of this load balancer are that it's easier to set up and configure, is generally less expensive, and differentiates between calls that use SSL and those that don't.

- **Application:** The application load balancer works at layer 7 of the OSI model, which means that it focuses application content, in addition to IP address and port. You can use rules to map how the load balancer routes information requests. The advantages of this load balancer are significantly greater flexibility, a capability to prioritize tasks, and the capability to use dynamic port mapping.

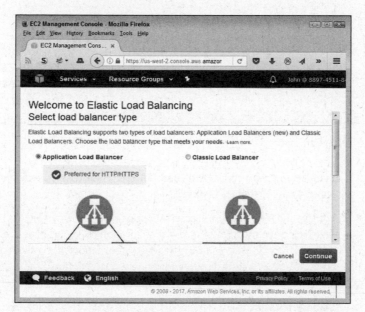

FIGURE 11-16: Choose a load balancer type based on the kind of load balancing you need.

6. **Choose a load balancer type and then click Continue.**

   The example uses the Classic Load Balancer option partly due to the EC2 setup the book uses and partly to keep the costs of working with this feature minimal.

   The wizard prompts you for a load balancer name, as shown in Figure 11-17. In addition, notice that you can add protocols for accessing the load balancer. You use the same protocols that your EC2 instances normally require. Remember that users will send requests to the load balancer instead of the EC2 instance. The load balancer will then send the request to the EC2 instance best able to handle it.

REMEMBER

If you don't provide any secure ports for your load balancer, the wizard will ask you to reconsider during the security setup step. Whether you use a secure port depends on how you're using your EC2 instances. If you don't need a secure connection for your EC2 instances, you aren't likely to need a secure connection for the load balancer.

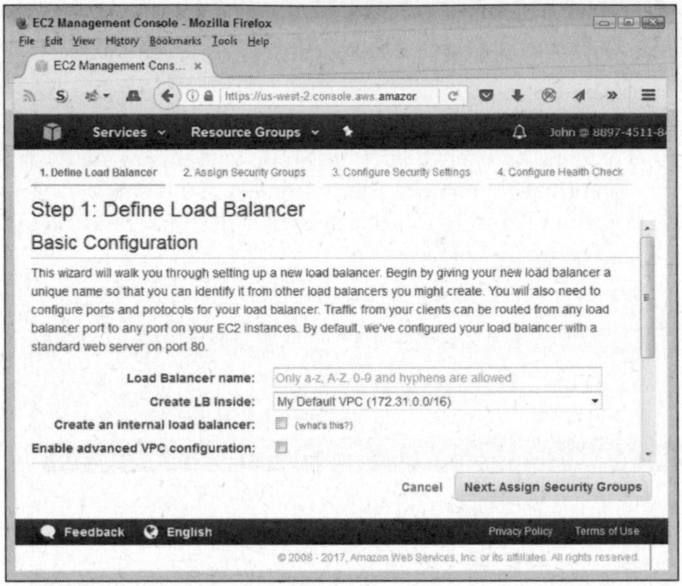

FIGURE 11-17:
Define the basic load balancer settings.

7. **Type** MyLoadBalancer **in the Load Balancer Name field and then click Next: Assign Security Groups.**

   You see the Step 2: Assign Security Groups page shown in Figure 11-18. Using an existing security group makes configuration considerably easier and reduces the risk of users failing to access applications and resources. However, creating a new security group does enable you to define a more secure environment for applications that need it.

8. **Select the Default-Launch security group and then click Next: Configure Security Settings.**

   You see a message regarding the load balancer's security. If you did select one of the secure options, the same screen asks you to provide an SSL certificate or allow AWS to generate an SSL certificate for you.

9. **Click Next: Configure Health Check.**

   You see the Step 4: Configure Health Check page, shown in Figure 11-19. This step is especially important because it ensures that the Elastic Load Balancer sends requests only to EC2 instances that are able to respond. Using this approach adds a level of reliability to your setup. The default options normally work quite well, but you can choose to change them if desired.

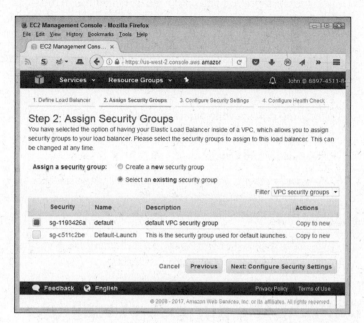

FIGURE 11-19: Define the method and timing used to verify EC2 instance health.

10. **Click Next: Add EC2 Instances.**

The wizard presents you with a list of running instances. You likely have only one such instance running now if you worked through the examples in the book. Normally, you choose as many instances as you can to help support load balancing.

11. **Select each of the EC2 instances you want to use and then click Next: Add Tags.**

The tags provide information that you can use for various organizational needs. You don't need to define any unless you use them as part of an application-programming requirement or some other need.

12. **Click Review and Create.**

The wizard presents you with a screen showing the selections you made. Make sure to check the information carefully.

13. **Click Create.**

AWS starts the Elastic Load Balancer for you and shows you the Load Balancer page, shown previously in Figure 11-15.

Defining the purpose of scaling

Load balancing generally refers to server farms, groups of servers connected through a central request point. Scaling refers to the capability to control all resources used to handle application request loads in an automated manner. When the load increases, the scaling functionality automatically increases the required resources. Likewise, a decrease on load makes the scaling functionality reduce the number of resources in use. The resources appear as part of a pool so that other applications can rely on the resources as needed. When you're working with Amazon, the resources may seem limitless, but they do truly have an end. Even so, most applications likely won't ever scratch the surface of the resources that Amazon makes available, so scaling doesn't become a problem.

REMEMBER

AWS makes a distinct difference between load balancing and scaling. The Elastic Load Balancing service is completely separate from the Auto Scaling service, even though you can coordinate the efforts of the two services to provide a robust end-user experience. Both services also deal with EC2 instances, but in different ways, so the outcomes can be different. The important difference for this book is that scaling provides a means of automatically adjusting available resources to meet specific application demands.

You can adjust the functionality and performance of Auto Scaling in a number of ways. The following methods are those that you most commonly use when working with Auto Scaling to provide database services to an application:

>> **Configuration:** The method that you use to configure Auto Scaling determines how the service reacts to EC2 events. For example, Auto Scaling automatically detects unhealthy EC2 instances and replaces them with healthy instances.

>> **Scheduling:** When you know in advance that your application will have a heavy load placed on it, you can create a schedule to ramp up the number of EC2 instances. This proactive approach may cost slightly more to use, but it always results in better application speed as long as you schedule the increased capacity at the right time.

>> **Amazon CloudWatch events:** You can create Amazon CloudWatch events that automatically react to and handle application-scaling events. This reactive approach provides adjustments as needed, but you may see a delay between the time when the event occurs and the additional resources arrive. Generally, using Amazon CloudWatch does provide faster response times than humans can provide.

>> **Elastic Load Balancing monitoring:** Combining Auto Scaling with Elastic Load Balancing helps you maintain a balanced server load, which uses resources more efficiently. You use a single set of servers to interact with a number of Auto Scaling groups to ensure that each group receives the resources it needs, but at a lower cost than when you manage each Auto Scaling group individually.

Working with Auto Scaling

In Chapters 6 and 8, you read about autoscaling, a built-in feature that automatically adjusts how your setup reacts to loads. This chapter discusses Auto Scaling, the service you use to make your RDS setup autoscale within limits that you specify. When you see the term *autoscaling*, think of the generic use of a feature (not necessarily a service) to make applications, services, and other AWS features add and remove resources as needed to make applications scale better and provide a consistent user experience. When you see *Auto Scaling*, think about the service that you specifically use to make autoscaling feasible with certain AWS services. The Auto Scaling feature enables your EC2 instances to handle loads without a lot of human intervention. The following sections tell you how to use Auto Scaling to make your AWS services provide autoscaling functionality.

Applying Auto Scaling

You have several options for applying Auto Scaling to your running EC2 instance (instances that have an Instance State other than Running won't allow you to apply Auto Scaling), but the easiest method is to select one or more EC2 instances in the Instances page and then choose Actions ⇨ Instance Settings ⇨ Attach to Auto Scaling Group. You see the Attach to Auto Scaling Group dialog box, shown in Figure 11-20.

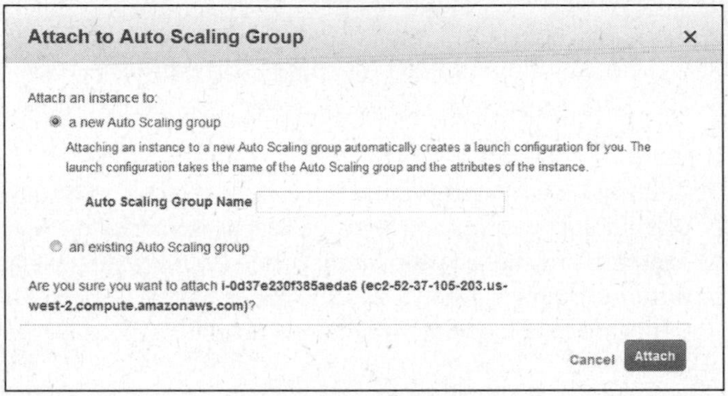

Attach to Auto Scaling Group ✕

Attach an instance to:

○ a new Auto Scaling group

Attaching an instance to a new Auto Scaling group automatically creates a launch configuration for you. The launch configuration takes the name of the Auto Scaling group and the attributes of the instance.

Auto Scaling Group Name

○ an existing Auto Scaling group

Are you sure you want to attach i-0d37e230f385aeda6 (ec2-52-37-105-203.us-west-2.compute.amazonaws.com)?

Cancel **Attach**

FIGURE 11-20:
Create a new Auto Scaling Group or use an existing one.

Because you haven't created an Auto Scaling group earlier in the book, you need to choose the A New Auto Scaling Group option, as shown. Type a name for the group in the Auto Scaling Group Name field, such as MyAutoScaleGroup, and then click Attach. AWS then automatically creates an Auto Scaling group for you that uses precisely the same settings as the selected EC2 instances.

Removing Auto Scaling

Unfortunately, you can't remove an EC2 instance from an Auto Scaling Group in the Instances page. Use the following steps to remove an EC2 instance from an Auto Scaling Group.

1. **Choose Auto Scaling ⇨ Auto Scaling Groups in the Navigation pane.**

   You see the Auto Scaling Group page. You may need to click an Auto Scaling Groups link to see the list of groups.

2. **Select the Auto Scaling Group for the EC2 instance.**

3. **Select the Instances tab of that group.**

   You see a listing of EC2 instances attached to that group, as shown in Figure 11-21.

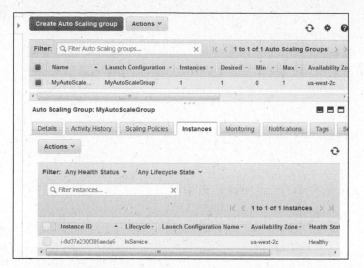

FIGURE 11-21:
Locate the EC2
instance that you
want to remove.

4. **Select the EC2 instance that you want to remove and then choose Actions ⇨ Detach in the Instances Panel.**

   Make sure that you choose the lower of the two Actions buttons. You see a Detach Instance dialog box.

5. **Click Detach Instance.**

   AWS removes the EC2 instance from the Auto Scaling Group.

WARNING

Simply deleting the Auto Scaling Group terminates the attached EC2 instance. After an EC2 instance is terminated, you can't recover it and must recreate the instance from scratch. The best way to avoid this problem is to provide your EC2 instance with termination protection by choosing Instance Settings ⇨ Change Termination Protection on the Instances page for the selected EC2 instance. You see a dialog box in which you confirm that you want to enable termination protection.

Chapter **12**

Programming Techniques for AWS and MySQL

C hapter 11 acquaints you with working with RDS and helps you get all the installation tasks done for working with MySQL. You even see a simple example of using MySQL in an application environment in the section about adding support to applications. Of course, you want to do a lot more than simply create a single table and add a single data entry to it. Consider Chapter 11 to be the start of the process.

This chapter, meanwhile, focuses more on how to get database tasks done in the cloud using a combination of RDS, MySQL, and various development techniques. This chapter isn't a primer on using MySQL or a programming language primer; it assumes that you already possess these skills. The examples are meant to demonstrate the kinds of tasks you need to perform given the differences in cloud development.

Everything you can do with a network-based database, you can do with your cloud-based database. In addition, as covered in Chapter 11, you often use the same techniques, but with a slight twist. Now you need to consider the cloud-based host in addition to the database. You often need bits of information to make RDS and MySQL work together in the same manner as you work with MySQL on a local network. This chapter helps you understand how to perform these tasks by demonstrating RDS features such as events, option groups, and parameter groups. You interact with these features using the console, Command Line Interface (CLI), and Python. However, except for a few CLI-specific tasks that the chapter tells you about, you can perform any of these tasks using any of the techniques described. The chapter provides a mix so that you can see all three methods at work.

As with a local network, you can use stored procedures and functions to automate tasks. This chapter isn't designed to help you create really exotic automation, but it does help you understand the ramifications of creating such automation in the cloud. You have some significant advantages when working in the cloud, but you also need to keep the 24/7 nature of the cloud in mind. Without local access, things all too easily happen in the remote location before you realize that they're even scheduled.

The MySQL/RDS combination also gives you access to some specialized tables that you use to help create a better development environment and to keep track of various RDS-specific events. These specialized tables are important to know about because they can help you discover issues such as when queries are slow. You can also determine when RDS-specific events occur, such as performing configuration tasks that affect MySQL.

The final sections of this chapter discuss the all-important tasks of uploading and downloading data. You usually upload data during the initial phases of placing an application in production. However, you might also need to perform uploads on other occasions, such as when performing an update. Downloads usually provide a means of obtaining a local copy of data to help improve local application performance. You might also want to create a local data backup in case of emergencies.

Interacting with RDS

Chapter 11 gives you enough information to configure a basic RDS setup using the default settings. However, RDS has more to offer than those simple settings. You should consider that these settings affect not only RDS but also — because RDS is the container for MySQL — MySQL to an extent. The following sections help you explore these settings using the console, the CLI, and Python.

Interacting with option groups using the console

Your database may come with additional features that you can manage through RDS. The features may make it easier to interact with data, manage the database, or provide additional security. The features vary by database, but here are the currently supported DBMSs:

>> MariaDB

>> Microsoft SQL Server

>> MySQL

>> Oracle

These additional features appear as RDS options, and you manage them using option groups. The sections that follow use MySQL for the example database. You can read more about the features available for individual databases at `http://docs.aws.amazon.com/AmazonRDS/latest/UserGuide/USER_WorkingWith OptionGroups.html`. Even though the features vary substantially, interacting with the option groups is the same for each of the databases, so the procedures in the following sections will work for any of the supported databases.

Defining the MySQL option groups

MySQL supports two features over the standard setup. The availability of support depends on the MySQL version. Table 12-1 summarizes these option groups.

TABLE 12-1   MySQL additional features

Option	Option ID	Supported Version	Description
MariaDB Audit Plugin Support	MARIADB_AUDIT_PLUGIN	MySQL 5.6.29 and later, and MySQL 5.7.11 and later	Records database activity, such as user logins and database accesses, so that you can better understand how applications access your database. The plugin outputs the information in a log file.
MySQL Cached Memory Support	MEMCACHED	MySQL 5.6 and later	Helps improve database performance by letting you cache key/value pairs. This feature relies on the MySQL InnoDB table functionality described at `https://dev.mysql.com/doc/refman/5.6/en/innodb-introduction.html`. Amazon recommends that you use version 5.6.21b because of bugs found in earlier versions.

REMEMBER

RDS configures a default option group for you during setup. You can't modify this option group. It provides a standard set of options for a particular DBMS. This option group also acts as the basis for any new option groups you create. The default option group name contains the word *default*, followed by the DBMS name and version in most cases. Consequently, the default option group for the example is `default:mysql-5-6`.

Creating a new option group

Before you can add new features using options to your database, you need to create an option group by following these steps:

1. **Sign into AWS using your user account.**

2. **Navigate to the RDS Management Console at** `https://console.aws.amazon.com/rds`.

   You see the RDS dashboard.

3. **Choose Option Groups in the Navigation pane.**

   AWS shows the default option group as a minimum, as shown in Figure 12-1. Note that when you select a group, the group details appear below the group listing. In addition, when selecting the default group, the Add Option, Modify Option, Delete Option, and Delete Group buttons are all disabled. This is because you can't do anything with the default option group — you must create a custom group to control anything about the option group features.

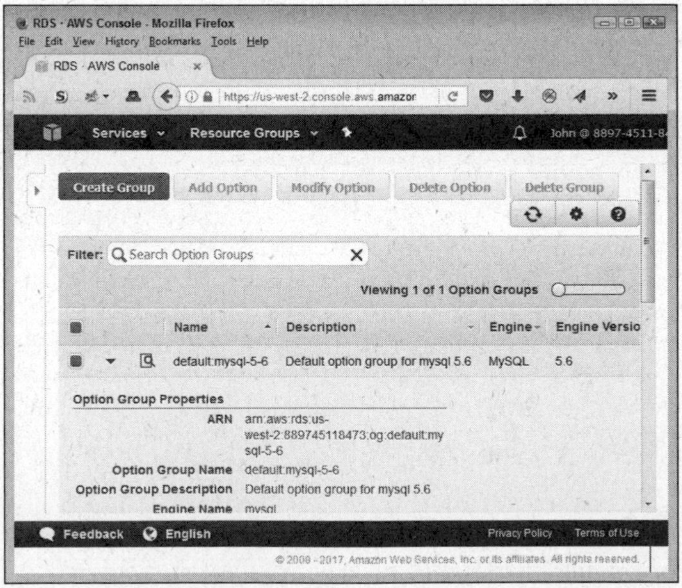

FIGURE 12-1:
The option group list contains the name of the default option group as a minimum.

4. **Click Create Group.**

   You see the Create Option Group page, shown in Figure 12-2.

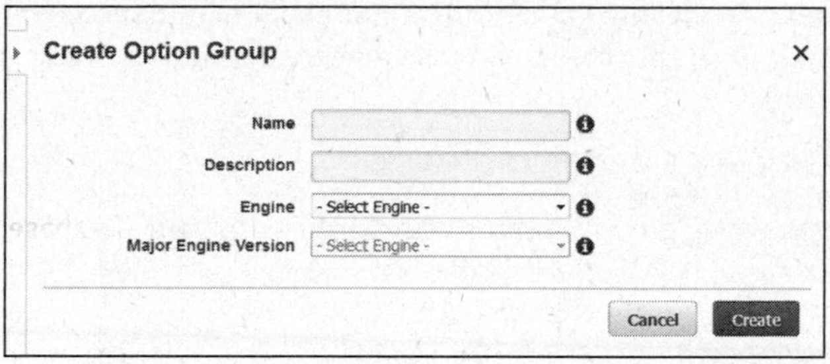

Create Option Group ✕

Name		ⓘ
Description		ⓘ
Engine	- Select Engine - ▾	ⓘ
Major Engine Version	- Select Engine - ▾	ⓘ

Cancel   Create

FIGURE 12-2:
Define the option group specifics.

5. **Type ExampleGroup in the Name field and, optionally, a description in the Description field.**

   Supplying an easily recognized option group name makes finding the option group in the list possible later. In addition, you want to be sure that you know how to use the option group.

6. **Choose mysql in the Engine field.**

   WARNING

   The Engine drop-down list contains the names of all the supported DBMSs, even if you don't currently have the DBMS installed in RDS. Consequently, you need to exercise care in choosing an engine to ensure that you make an appropriate selection. Otherwise, you might create an option group for a DBMS that you never intend to use.

7. **Choose 5.6 in the Major Engine Version field.**

   The Major Engine Version field contains the versions of the DBMSs that support options. You can't accidentally choose an older version of a DBMS that doesn't support options.

8. **Click Create.**

   You see the group added to the option group list, as shown in Figure 12-3. Note that AWS enables only the Add Option and Delete Group buttons in addition to the Create Group button that it enabled previously. Because you don't have any options added, you can't modify or delete an option. The initial setup uses the same default settings as the default group.

Copying an existing option group

There is one activity that you can't perform in the console, and that's copying an existing option group. To copy an existing option group, you rely on the CLI or the programming interface. To create a new option group called CopiedGroup, you open a command prompt or terminal window and type **aws rds copy-option-group --source-option-group-identifier examplegroup --target-option-group-identifier copygroup --target-option-group-description "Copied"**. You must provide the --target-option-group-description argument in this case, even if you provide a blank value, or the command won't succeed. Figure 12-4 shows the output from this command (the screenshot doesn't show all the typed command text).

FIGURE 12-3: AWS adds the new group to the list.

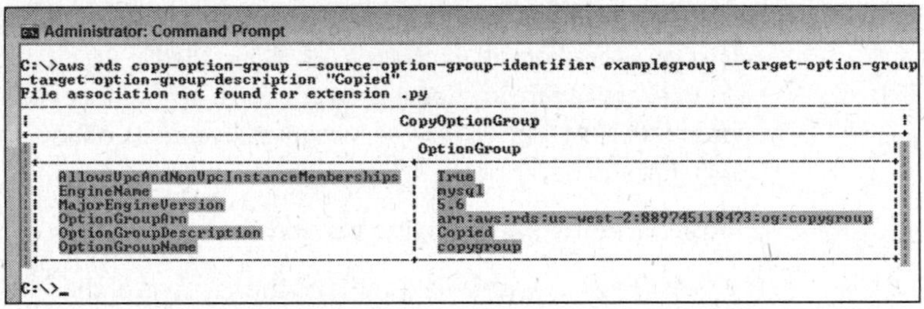

FIGURE 12-4: The output shows the particulars of the new option group you create.

Adding a new option

The purpose of creating a new option group is to assign new options (features) to it. The following steps help you add a new option to the ExampleGroup option group created in the "Creating a new option group" section, earlier in this chapter.

1. **Select the option group you want to modify in the option group list.**

You see the details for that group presented below the option group list.

2. **Click Add Option.**

AWS displays the Add Option page, shown in Figure 12-5.

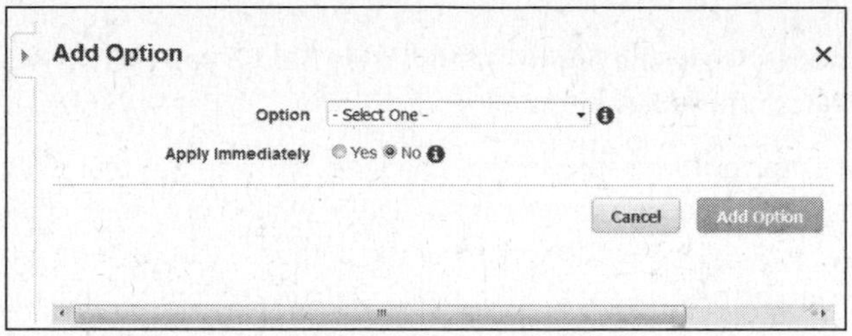

FIGURE 12-5:
Choose a new
option to add to
the option group.

3. Choose one of the options in the Option field.

The example uses the MEMCACHED option. Table 12-1 shows the options available for MySQL. Depending on the option you select, you see additional settings for that option. Figure 12-6 shows the settings for the MEMCACHED option (as described at `http://docs.aws.amazon.com/AmazonRDS/latest/UserGuide/Appendix.MySQL.Options.memcached.html`). Other options will have different settings.

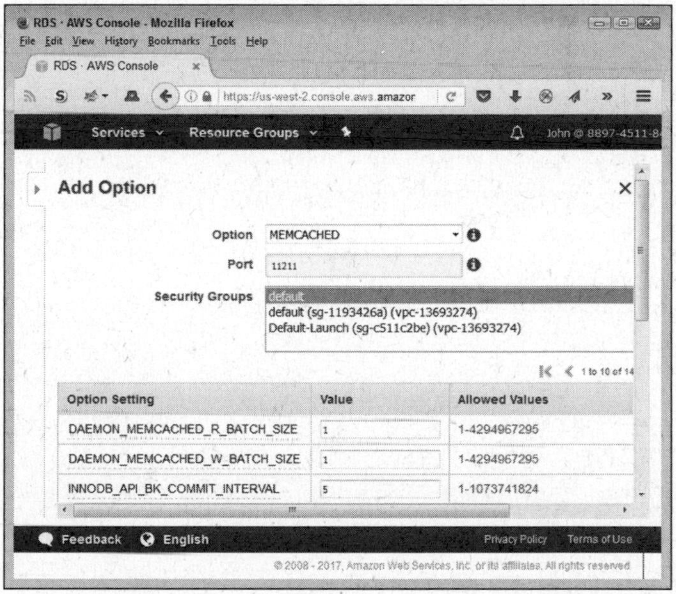

FIGURE 12-6:
Define the
settings for the
new option
group.

4. Configure the settings for the option you want to add.

For example, you must provide a port and security group when working with the MEMCACHED option.

5. **Choose Yes in the Apply Immediately field if you want AWS to apply the change immediately.**

The problem with applying the change immediately is that AWS also applies any other queued changes immediately, which could mean that your application suddenly slows down so that the database can perform a maintenance cycle. The best idea is to wait until a regularly scheduled maintenance cycle to ensure that your application continues to run as expected unless you actually do need the change immediately.

6. **Click Add Option.**

AWS adds the new option to the option group. The option name appears in the Options column of the option group list. In addition, you see the option listed below the option group list, as shown in Figure 12-7.

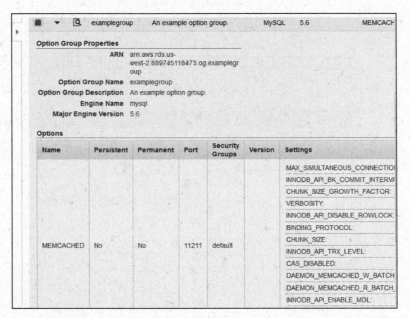

FIGURE 12-7: You see the option added to the option group.

Modifying an option group

When modifying an option, you change the option settings by using a process similar to the one used when you initially added the option. As with adding an option, you start by selecting the option group that you want to change and then click Modify Option. The Modify Option page looks similar to the one shown in Figure 12-5 for creating an option. After you select an option to change, you see the list of settings shown in Figure 12-6. Click Modify Option to make the changes permanent.

Deleting an option

Deleting an option means removing it from the option group. In this case, you choose the option group you want to modify and then click Delete Option. You see a Delete Option page like the one shown in Figure 12-8. Select one or more options to delete and then click Delete.

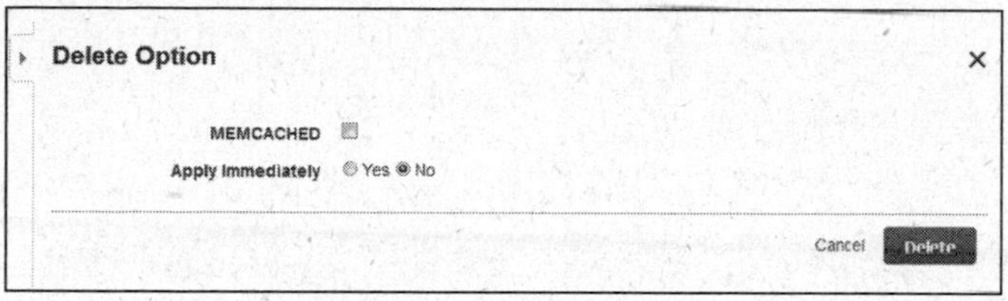

FIGURE 12-8:
Use the Delete
Option page to
remove options
from the option
group.

Delete Option   ×

MEMCACHED ☐

Apply Immediately ○ Yes ● No

Cancel **Delete**

Associating an option group with a database

Until you associate an option group with a database, it just sits there doing nothing. However, you don't perform the association in the Option Groups page. The following steps help you associate an option group with a database (the process for associating an option group with a snapshot is similar):

1. **Choose Instances in the Navigation pane.**

   You see a list of database instances.

2. **Select the instance you want to modify.**

   AWS presents the instance details below the instance list.

3. **Choose Instance Actions ⇨ Modify.**

   The Modify DB Instance page appears.

4. **Scroll down to the Database Options group.**

   You see the options shown in Figure 12-9. Note the Option Group field, in which you choose the option group you want to use.

5. **Click Continue.**

   You see a list of pending changes for the database instance. Verify that you selected the correct database instance.

6. **Click Modify DB Instance.**

   AWS makes the changes you requested (or queues them for later updates during the normal maintenance cycle).

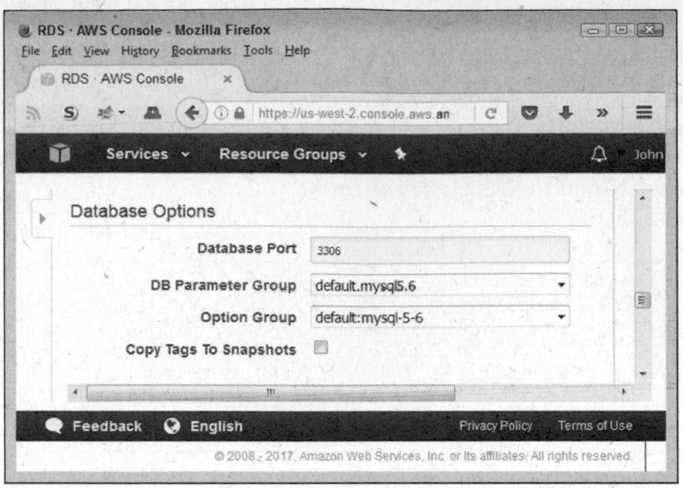

FIGURE 12-9:
Choose the option group you want to use with the database instance.

Deleting an option group

When you no longer need a particular option group, you can remove it from your configuration to help keep clutter to a minimum. To delete a group, select its entry in the option group list and then click Delete Group. AWS asks you to verify that you actually want to delete the groups. Click Delete to complete the task.

Using the CLI to work with events

AWS tracks important events associated with the database instances you create. Events tell you when AWS performs certain tasks, such as performing a database backup. You also discover status changes, such as when the database becomes temporarily unavailable or when a configuration change occurs. The page at `http://docs.aws.amazon.com/AmazonRDS/latest/UserGuide/USER_Events.html` gives a complete list of events. Even though you can interact with events by using both the console and a custom application, the following sections describe how to work with events using the CLI.

Obtaining an event listing

To see what sorts of things have happened on your server, you need to obtain an event listing. The `describe-events` command helps you perform this task.

The problem with this command is that the defaults sometimes don't help you actually see any events. For example, if you type **aws rds describe-events** and press Enter, you might think that the CLI displays a list of all events. However, the list is often blank.

To obtain a list of events, you must sometimes provide additional information. Most commonly, you need to provide a starting date using the `--start-time` argument. For example, you might decide that you want to see events starting at midnight on May 22. In this case, you type **aws rds describe-events --start-time 2017-05-22T00:00Z** and press Enter. Figure 12-10 shows an example of the output you might see.

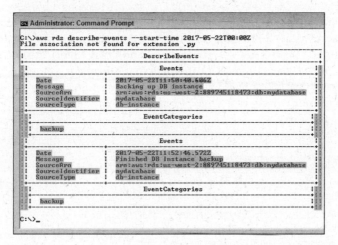

Note that the output shows the date, message, Amazon Resource Name (ARN), and other information about each event. You can find a complete list of command line arguments for this command at `http://docs.aws.amazon.com/cli/latest/reference/rds/describe-events.html`.

Subscribing to an event

Subscribing to an event means that AWS notifies you about it. Getting timely information about your RDS configuration is essential because it could mean the difference between everyone working and everyone twiddling their thumbs waiting for you to act. To subscribe to an event, you need to tell RDS where to send the event information, which means creating an entry in the Simple Notification Service (SNS). You might have noted that you automatically receive information about Elastic Beanstalk (EB) after you configure it. That's because EB automatically creates an SNS entry for you and assigns it to your EB setup. RDS doesn't provide the same service because it has no way of knowing precisely how to configure the event notifications.

To begin this process, you must create the SNS entry. An entry consists of two parts: a topic and a subscription to that topic. The topic is simply an entry that describes the kind of information that SNS passes along. To create an RDS topic, type **aws sns create-topic --name RDSAlerts** and press Enter. The output includes an ARN that you must use when creating the subscription. (You can find a list of SNS-related CLI commands at `http://docs.aws.amazon.com/cli/latest/reference/sns/`).

The subscription tells how and where to deliver content. This example assumes that you want to use email, but you have a number of options, as described at `http://docs.aws.amazon.com/cli/latest/reference/sns/subscribe.html`. To create the subscription for this example, type **aws sns subscribe --topic-arn arn:aws:sns:us-west-2:889745118473:RDSAlerts --protocol email --notification-endpoint** `john@johnmuellerbooks.com` and press Enter. The ARN is the one that AWS provides as output from the first step. Of course, you need to give your own email address as an endpoint, rather than use mine. Figure 12-11 shows typical output from these two steps (the screenshot doesn't show all of the typed command text).

```
Administrator: Command Prompt

C:\>aws sns create-topic --name RDSAlerts
File association not found for extension .py

                          CreateTopic
+----------+------------------------------------------------+
| TopicArn | arn:aws:sns:us-west-2:889745118473:RDSAlerts   |
+----------+------------------------------------------------+

C:\>aws sns subscribe --topic-arn arn:aws:sns:us-west-2:889745
john@johnmuellerbooks.com
File association not found for extension .py

                          Subscribe
+-----------------+------------------------+
| SubscriptionArn | pending confirmation   |
+-----------------+------------------------+

C:\>_
```

FIGURE 12-11: Create a topic and subscription as setup for obtaining RDS event notifications.

REMEMBER

Note that the subscription output says pending confirmation. You receive an email from AWS with a confirmation link as part of the process. Before you can receive notifications, you must confirm the subscription.

At this point, you can finally subscribe to the RDS events. A simple subscription provides you with all of the events. However, you can reduce the number of events you receive by including the options described at `http://docs.aws.amazon.com/cli/latest/reference/rds/create-event-subscription.html`. For this example, type **aws rds create-event-subscription --subscription-name GetRDSEvents --sns-topic-arn arn:aws:sns:us-west-2:889745118473:RDSAlerts** and press Enter. Again, you need to provide the ARN of the SNS topic. The subscription name in this case is the RDS subscription name, which appears in the Event Subscriptions page of the RDS dashboard. Figure 12-12 shows the output from this command (the screenshot doesn't show all of the typed command text).

FIGURE 12-12:
The RDS event subscription Is ready for use.

Obtaining a list of event subscriptions

If you have subscriptions, you also need a way to list them. To obtain a list of event subscriptions and the subscription status, type **aws rds describe-event-subscriptions** and press Enter. The output will look like Figure 12-12 in this case, except that the Status field should indicate Active. If you had more than one subscription, you'd see a list of all the RDS subscriptions (active or not). Unfortunately, the list can get really long for a complex setup, so you can use the various options described at http://docs.aws.amazon.com/cli/latest/reference/rds/describe-event-subscriptions.html to make the list manageable.

Modifying an event subscription

You may decide that an event subscription isn't working at some point. Rather than delete and recreate the subscription, you can choose to modify it instead. All the options that are available when you create a subscription are available when modifying a subscription. The page at http://docs.aws.amazon.com/cli/latest/reference/rds/modify-event-subscription.html gives you the required listing of options.

PUBLISHING YOUR OWN EVENTS

You may find it helpful to publish event information to SNS or RDS event subscribers using the SNS publish command. An event can contain a topic, message, and other information in specific formats. You can send a message globally or to just a specific topic or target ARN. Using the publish command isn't a replacement for other methods of dealing with communication issues. You should save this form of communication for specific RDS or SNS-related events — special occurrences that fall outside the normal message realm. The page at http://docs.aws.amazon.com/cli/latest/reference/sns/publish.html tells you more about the publish command.

Say that you decide that you want to limit the events to those generated by an instance. Using the previous examples as a starting point, you type **aws rds modify-event-subscription --subscription-name GetRDSEvents --source-type db-instance** and press Enter. Note that you don't use an ARN in this case, just the RDS-specific event name. Figure 12-13 shows the output of this example. Notice that the Status field now says modifying (the screenshot doesn't show all the typed command text).

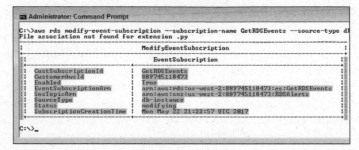

FIGURE 12-13: Modify, rather than recreate, a subscription when possible.

Deleting an event subscription

Eventually you need to remove unneeded subscriptions. At first, you might think that you would simply remove the RDS subscription, but what you really need to do is remove the RDS subscription and then potentially the SNS subscription and topic as well. Because you create the event subscription in this example using a custom SNS topic and subscription, this section shows how to remove all three. You begin by removing the RDS subscription. Type **aws rds delete-event-subscription --subscription-name GetRDSEvents** and press Enter.

To remove a subscription, you must first know the subscription ARN, which you haven't seen so far in the chapter. The SNS subscription ARN differs from the RDS subscription ARN and the SNS topic ARN. To obtain the subscription ARN, you list the subscriptions for a particular topic using the list-subscriptions-by-topic command. In this case, you type **aws sns list-subscriptions-by-topic --topic-arn arn:aws:sns:us-west-2:889745118473:RDSAlerts** and press Enter (substituting the topic ARN for your particular setup). Figure 12-14 shows typical output from this command (your data values will differ from those shown). Note the SubscriptionArn entry; this is the value you supply to remove the subscription.

Now that you have a subscription ARN, you can use the unsubscribe command to remove the subscription. Using the ARN shown in Figure 12-14 as an example, you type **aws sns unsubscribe --subscription-arn arn:aws:sns:us-west-2:889745118473:RDSAlerts:bb72051a-f95b-482a-90cd-46e427e95285** and press Enter. You won't see any output, nor will you receive a confirmation email.

To confirm that the subscription is actually gone, you need to use the list-subscriptions-by-topic command again.

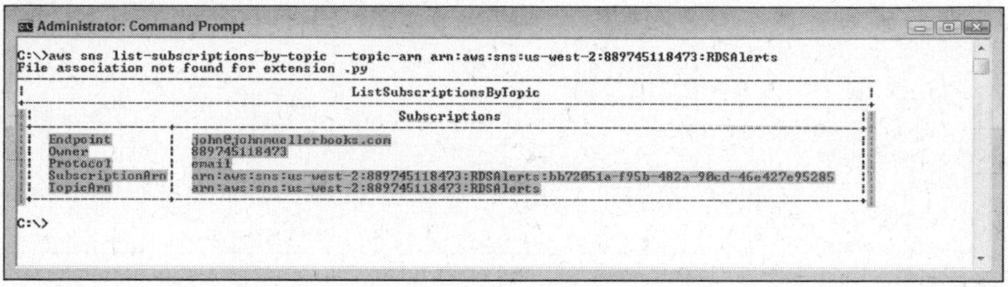

FIGURE 12-14:
Obtain the subscription ARN so that you can remove the subscription.

Removing the topic is the last step. In this case, you use the delete-topic command. Using the ARN from the previous examples, you type **aws sns delete-topic --topic-arn arn:aws:sns:us-west-2:889745118473:RDSAlerts** and press Enter. As with unsubscribing, you won't see any output. To verify that the command is successful, you type **aws sns list-topics** and press Enter. The topic no longer appears on the list.

Employing programming techniques to read and write parameter groups

Parameter groups affect the database engine configuration. You use them to change how the database engine reacts in certain circumstances. Every parameter in a parameter group has a default value based on the DBMS you use. However, when viewing the parameters, not every parameter has an actual entry.

REMEMBER

Every database instance you create has a default parameter group that contains the default settings for that database. To see the default parameters, choose Parameter Groups in the Navigation pane for the RDS Dashboard, and then click the Go to Details Page icon next to the parameter group you want to see. For example, when working with MySQL 5.6, you see a default.mysql5.6 parameter group. Figure 12-15 shows a typical example of how the parameters appear. The most important thing to remember is that you can't modify a default parameter group. Instead, you must create a custom parameter group, modify its settings, and then assign it to the database you want to affect.

You can perform all parameter group tasks using the console, the CLI, or programmatic means. The following sections demonstrate these methods using Python, but the concepts are the same no matter which path you follow. You can access the example code for this chapter in the AWS4D4D; 12, Parameter Groups. ipynb file in the downloadable source, as explained in the Introduction.

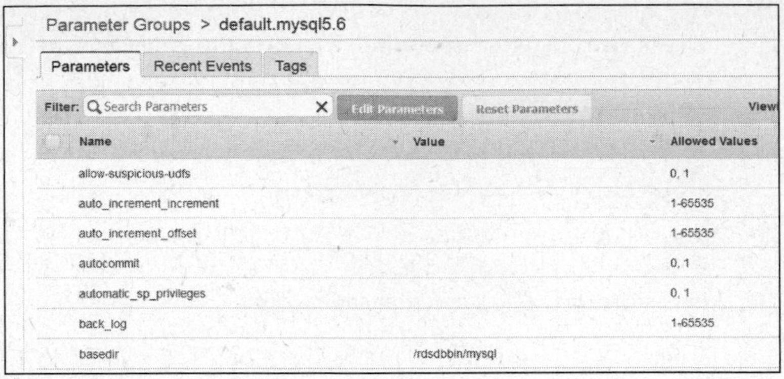

FIGURE 12-15:
Parameter groups contain parameters that affect database operation.

Creating a new parameter group

The only thing you can do with a default parameter group is to read its settings. To make changes, you must create a custom parameter group and then assign it to the database in question. Rely on the `create_db_parameter_group()` function to create new parameter groups, as shown here:

```
import boto3
client = boto3.client('rds')

client.create_db_parameter_group(
    DBParameterGroupName='MyTestGroup',
    DBParameterGroupFamily='MySQL5.6',
    Description='A test parameter group')
```

When the creation process is successful, AWS sends information about the new parameter group, as shown here:

```
{'DBParameterGroup': {'DBParameterGroupArn':
  'arn:aws:rds:us-west-2:889745118473:pg:mytestgroup',
  'DBParameterGroupFamily': 'mysql5.6',
  'DBParameterGroupName': 'mytestgroup',
  'Description': 'A test parameter group'},
 'ResponseMetadata': {'HTTPHeaders': {
   'content-length': '619',
   'content-type': 'text/xml',
   'date': 'Thu, 25 May 2017 14:54:41 GMT',
   'x-amzn-requestid':
      '14d47779-415a-11e7-a45f-7f0e0cb815c0'},
 'HTTPStatusCode': 200,
 'RequestId': '14d47779-415a-11e7-a45f-7f0e0cb815c0',
 'RetryAttempts': 0}}
```

Note the `HTTPStatusCode` is 200, which indicates success. You also get some useful additional information not found in the console, such as the new parameter group ARN.

Listing parameter groups

Depending on the size of your installation, you might need to obtain a listing of the parameter groups in use. In this case, you rely on the `describe_db_parameter_groups()` function shown here:

```
for group in client.describe_db_parameter_groups() \
    ['DBParameterGroups']:

    print(group['DBParameterGroupName'],
          '\n  ', group['Description'])
```

The code shows how to obtain all the parameter groups. However, you can provide various inputs and filters to limit the output, as described at http://boto3. readthedocs.io/en/latest/reference/services/rds.html#RDS.Client. describe_db_parameter_groups. Here's the output from this example:

```
default.mysql5.6
    Default parameter group for mysql5.6
mytestgroup
    A test parameter group
```

Assigning a parameter group to a database

Just because you create a parameter group doesn't mean that the database is actually using it. You must assign the parameter group to the database. The `modify_db_instance()` function performs this task, as shown in the following code:

```
client.modify_db_instance(
    DBInstanceIdentifier='MyDatabase',
    DBParameterGroupName='MyTestGroup') \
    ['ResponseMetadata']['HTTPStatusCode']
```

When successful, you see an output of 200 in this case. The code automatically drills down into the information you need. To verify that you have indeed changed the parameter group, use the following code:

```
client.describe_db_instances(
    DBInstanceIdentifier='MyDatabase') \
    ['DBInstances'][0]['DBParameterGroups']
```

The output should look similar to this:

```
[{'DBParameterGroupName': 'mytestgroup',
   'ParameterApplyStatus': 'pending-reboot'}]
```

Note that the `ParameterApplyStatus` entry says `pending-reboot`. To make the change current, you must reboot the database first using the `reboot_db_instance()` function. When the database is actually using the currently selected parameter group, you see a `ParameterApplyStatus` entry value of `in-sync` instead.

WARNING

Rebooting the server means that the server becomes inaccessible during the reboot cycle. Ensure that any users who are working the database log off before you perform a reboot. Otherwise, you may lose data or experience other issues.

Copying a parameter group

One task you must perform using the CLI is creating a copy of a parameter group. However, you can't create a copy of the default parameter group — you can create copies only of custom groups that you create. You use the `copy-db-parameter-group` command to perform this task. If you want to create a copy of MyTestGroup as TestCopy, you type **aws rds copy-db-parameter-group --source-db-parameter-group-identifier MyTestGroup --target-db-parameter-group-identifier Test-Copy --target-db-parameter-group-description "Copy of a custom group."** and press Enter. The command requires both the target identifier and description entries to work. Figure 12-16 shows the result of using this command (the screenshot doesn't show all of the typed command text). Note that the output does include the parameter group's ARN.

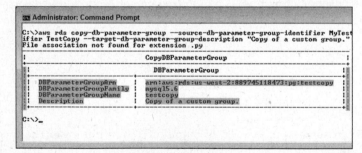

FIGURE 12-16: Use the CLI to copy an existing custom parameter group.

Reading default and custom parameters

You can see an entire list of all the parameters using the console as shown in Figure 12-15. However, the list can be overwhelming and viewing the information you actually need is hard. One of the advantages of working with parameters in code is that you can filter the output in a number of ways. The following code shows one such technique:

```
for parameter in client.describe_db_parameters(
    DBParameterGroupName='MyTestGroup') \
    ['Parameters']:

    if ('ParameterValue') in parameter:
        print(parameter['ParameterName'], ' ',
            parameter['ParameterValue'], ' ',
            parameter['IsModifiable'])
```

Note that you must use the describe_db_parameters() function to obtain the information. In this case, you end up with a list of parameters that have values assigned to them, as shown here (your list may vary):

```
basedir    /rdsdbbin/mysql    False
binlog_cache_size    32768    True
binlog_format    MIXED    True
datadir    /rdsdbdata/db/    False
default_storage_engine    InnoDB    False
explicit_defaults_for_timestamp    1    True
general_log_file
    /rdsdbdata/log/general/mysql-general.log    False
gtid-mode    OFF    False
innodb_buffer_pool_size
    {DBInstanceClassMemory*3/4}    True
innodb_data_home_dir    /rdsdbdata/db/innodb    False
innodb_file_per_table    1    True
innodb_flush_method    O_DIRECT    True
```

Using this list, you know which parameters already have values assigned and which of those you can modify. For example, you can't modify basedir, but you can modify binlog_cache_size. The reason that this code works is that the dictionary that AWS returns contains keys only for entries that have values. Consequently, when a parameter lacks an assigned value, it also lacks the ParameterValue key.

You can also use coded techniques to locate information for a specific parameter, such as `binlog_cache_size`. Here's code you can use for this task:

```
for parameters in client.describe_db_parameters(
    DBParameterGroupName='MyTestGroup') \
    ['Parameters']:

    if ('binlog_cache_size') in \
        parameters['ParameterName']:
        for k, v in parameters.items():
            print(k, ' = ', v)
```

The output in this case is

```
ParameterName  =  binlog_cache_size
ParameterValue  =  32768
Description  =  The size of the cache to hold the SQL
 statements for the binary log during a transaction.
Source  =  system
ApplyType  =  dynamic
DataType  =  integer
AllowedValues  =  4096-18446744073709547520
IsModifiable  =  True
ApplyMethod  =  pending-reboot
```

Note the `AllowedValues` entry. It tells you the range of values you can use when changing a value in code. Also notice that any changes you make to this parameter will require a reboot before they become permanent.

Writing modifiable parameters

As previously mentioned, you can't modify a default parameter group. Consequently, this section applies only to custom parameter groups that you create. To perform a modification, you use the `modify_db_parameter_group()` and supply the parameter group name and a list of one or more parameters to modify, as shown here.

```
print(client.modify_db_parameter_group(
    DBParameterGroupName='MyTestGroup',
    Parameters=
    [
        {
            'ParameterName':'binlog_cache_size',
            'ParameterValue':'65536',
```

```
            'ApplyMethod':'pending-reboot'
        },
    ],)['ResponseMetadata']['HTTPStatusCode'])

for parameters in client.describe_db_parameters(
    DBParameterGroupName='MyTestGroup') \
    ['Parameters']:
    if ('binlog_cache_size') in \
        parameters['ParameterName']:
            print(parameters['ParameterValue'])
```

Parameters always contains a list of items to change, even if you have just one item. The dictionary definition for each change must contain the ParameterName, ParameterValue, and ApplyMethod entries as shown. You can set the ApplyMethod to immediate if desired. However, an immediate change might not appear for five or more minutes, so you need to verify that the change is in place before you rely on it for your application. The output from this code is

```
200
65536
```

The 200 output shows that the change is successful and the 65536 output shows the new cache size. Always verify your changes to ensure that the change you think you made is the change you actually made.

Removing a custom parameter group

At some point, you might need to remove an existing parameter group. All you need is the delete_db_parameter_group() function with the name of the parameter group you want to remove. The following code shows how to perform this task. In addition, it shows how to add error trapping to your Python code so that it can handle failures from RDS when performing tasks.

```
from botocore.exceptions import ClientError

try:
    result = client.delete_db_parameter_group(
    DBParameterGroupName='MyTestGroup')

    print(result['ResponseMetadata']['HTTPStatusCode'])

except ClientError as e:
    if e.response['Error']['Code'] == \
        'DBParameterGroupNotFound':
```

```
        print('Parameter group is missing.')
    else:
        print("Unexpected error: %s" % e)
```

Error handling relies on the `botocore` package. You can find more about this package at `http://botocore.readthedocs.io/en/latest/index.html`. An error-handling–specific example appears at `http://botocore.readthedocs.io/en/latest/client_upgrades.html#error-handling`. In addition to the specific value shown in the code for locating the error code, you might also find these values from the exception dictionary useful:

» `['ResponseMetadata']['HTTPStatusCode']`: Provides the HTTP status code of the call.

» `['ResponseMetadata']['RequestId']`: Tells you the request identifier for the call so that you can obtain additional information from locations such as logs.

» `['Error']['Message']`: Contains the full message for the error, which you can simply repeat for unknown error types.

» `['Error']['Type']`: Provides the sender information.

Working with MySQL Code

MySQL runs within an RDS container. What you might not realize is that this means you can make calls within your stored procedures, functions, and triggers to the container. This feature is important because it lets you monitor how MySQL and RDS interact within the database itself. To use this feature, you must modify existing scripts. Of course, this sort of script modification tends to tie you into the AWS platform, so you need to consider it with care. The following sections offer insights on working with MySQL code within an RDS container.

Enabling stored procedures, functions, and triggers

In some cases, you find that you can't properly execute MySQL stored procedures, functions, and triggers within RDS. For example, this situation can occur when using binary logging. If you encounter this issue, you can use the following steps to enable use of stored procedures, functions, and triggers.

1. **Create a new custom parameter group using the technique shown in the "Creating a new parameter group" section of the chapter.**

2. Assign the parameter group to your database using the technique shown in the "Assigning a parameter group to a database" section of the chapter.

3. Modify the `log_bin_trust_function_creators` parameter as shown in the "Writing modifiable parameters" section of the chapter and set its value to 1.

4. Reboot your database server as described in the "Assigning a parameter group to a database" section of the chapter.

Using stored procedures

Your stored procedures will work as they always have from a MySQL perspective. However, because you're working with RDS, you also have RDS-specific system stored procedures that you can use. These calls all include RDS in their name, and you can see a list of them at `http://docs.aws.amazon.com/AmazonRDS/latest/UserGuide/Appendix.MySQL.SQLRef.html`. You can access the example code for this section in the `CallRDSFromMySQL.sql` file in the downloadable source, as explained in the Introduction.

To use these stored procedures, you call them as you would any other stored procedure. For example, `CALL mysql.rds_show_configuration` shows the number of hours that AWS retains the binary logs, as shown in Figure 12-17. You can obtain this information using other methods, but this call makes the information accessible to your MySQL scripts, where you can use it to ensure that your cloud application works as originally envisioned. You can read more about this call at `http://docs.aws.amazon.com/AmazonRDS/latest/UserGuide/mysql_rds_show_configuration.html`, and you can find additional uses for it at `http://docs.aws.amazon.com/AmazonRDS/latest/UserGuide/Appendix.MySQL.Common DBATasks.html`.

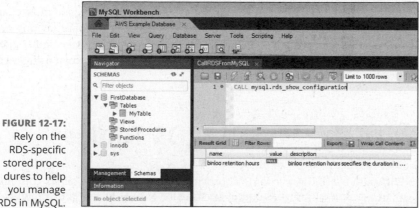

FIGURE 12-17: Rely on the RDS-specific stored procedures to help you manage RDS in MySQL.

REMEMBER

You must verify the applicable version of MySQL when using one of these calls. Many of them work only with MySQL versions 5.6 and 5.7. However, some also work with MySQL version 5.5. The important thing is to ensure that you're not trying to use a call that won't work with your version of MySQL. The documentation makes finding the version information easy — it appears as part of the Usage Notes section. In addition, you find related commands, if any, in the Related Topics section.

TIP

Fortunately, environments such as MySQL Workbench make using these special calls easier. When you type **CALL mysql.**, the application displays a list of these special commands, as shown in Figure 12-18. Double-clicking the entry you want to use adds it to the file.

FIGURE 12-18: Use MySQL Workbench functionality to make working with RDS commands easier.

Some commands, such as `mysql.rds_collect_global_status_history`, require special setup before you can use them. The information for this command appears at `http://docs.aws.amazon.com/AmazonRDS/latest/UserGuide/mysql_rds_collect_global_status_history.html`. Click the Managing the Global Status History link for details on performing the required setup. In this case, you must change a parameter in the parameter group associated with your database, among other tasks. The procedure in the "Enabling stored procedures, functions, and triggers" section, earlier in this chapter, shows how you perform this task when using certain commands.

Working with the MySQL/RDS Tables

In addition to specialized code, RDS provides access to special tables containing information about RDS functionality. MySQL also gives you access to a few cloud-related tables. For example, you can learn about RDS replication status by monitoring the entries in a table. As with using commands, MySQL Workbench helps when it comes to working with specialized MySQL and RDS tables. Type **SELECT * FROM mysql.** and you see a list of these tables. Figure 12-19 shows the special RDS tables you access by adding the letter *r* to the input.

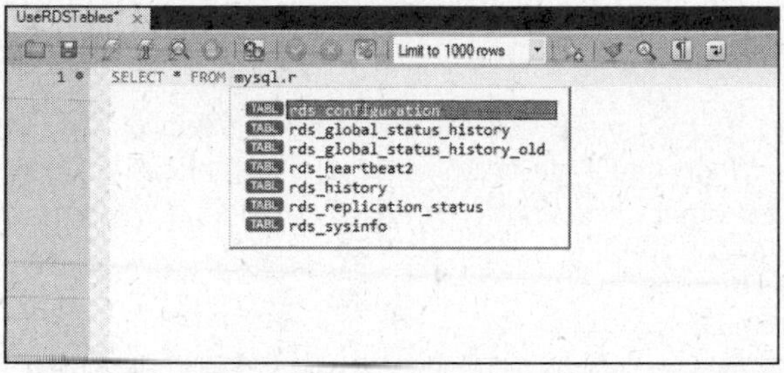

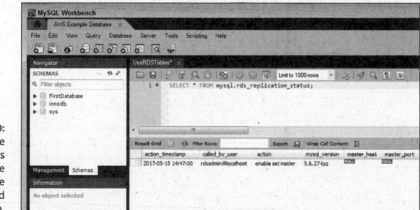

FIGURE 12-19:
Special tables
make it easier to
monitor your
cloud experience.

To see this feature in action, type **SELECT * FROM mysql.rds_replication_status;** and click Execute Script. Figure 12-20 shows typical output from this command. You can access the example code for this section in the UseRDSTables.sql file in the downloadable source, as explained in the Introduction.

FIGURE 12-20:
View the
replication status
of your database
from the
RDS-supplied
log file.

TIP

Many of the most useful pieces of information come from log files that AWS maintains as you use RDS and MySQL. You can read about these log files at http://docs.aws.amazon.com/AmazonRDS/latest/UserGuide/USER_LogAccess.Concepts.MySQL.html. For example, SELECT * FROM mysql.general_log; displays general log information for your database. However, as with many other RDS features, you must change parameters in the parameter group to enable the logs. The "Enabling stored procedures, functions, and triggers" section, earlier in this chapter, shows you how to change parameters as needed.

Interestingly enough, one of the few logs that you can't access within MySQL Workbench is probably the most important: the error log. You can access the error log from the console, the CLI, or programmatically, but not as part of a script. Follow these steps to see the error log in the console:

1. **Select a database instance in the Instances page of the RDS dashboard.**

   You see a Logs button at the bottom of the details area, as shown in Figure 12-21.

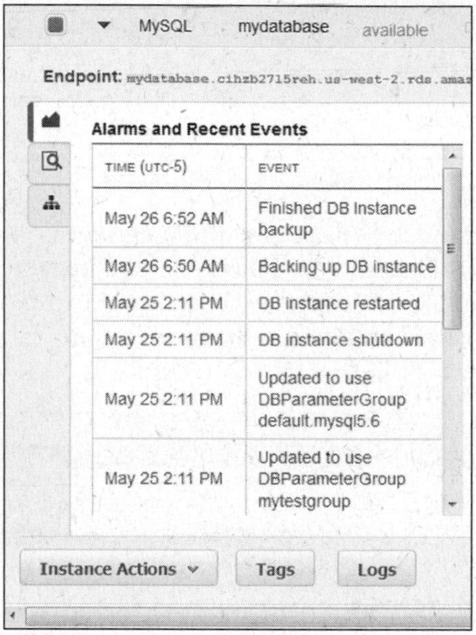

FIGURE 12-21: Locate the Logs button at the bottom of the details area.

2. **Click Logs.**

   AWS displays the Recent Events & Logs tab, shown in Figure 12-22.

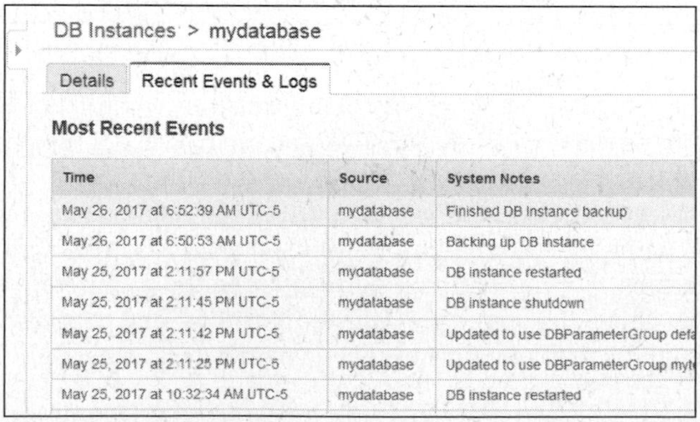

FIGURE 12-22: Display the recent events and logs page.

3. **Scroll to the Logs section and click View next to the error log that you want to see.**

AWS displays the log content, as shown in Figure 12-23. (Click Close to close the log when you finish viewing it.)

Viewing Log: error/mysql-error-running.log.16 (10.7 kB)

text: ■ background: ☐

```
2017-05-25 15:30:55 3434 [Note] /rdsdbbin/mysql/bin/mysqld:
Normal shutdown

2017-05-25 15:30:55 3434 [Note] Giving 3 client threads a chance
to die gracefully
2017-05-25 15:30:55 3434 [Note] Event Scheduler: Purging the
queue. 0 events
2017-05-25 15:30:55 3434 [Note] Shutting down slave threads
2017-05-25 15:30:57 3434 [Note] Forcefully disconnecting 2
remaining clients
2017-05-25 15:30:57 3434 [Warning] /rdsdbbin/mysql/bin/mysqld:
Forcing close of thread 2775 user: 'John'

2017-05-25 15:30:57 3434 [Warning] /rdsdbbin/mysql/bin/mysqld:
Forcing close of thread 2776 user: 'John'
```

FIGURE 12-23: The error logs show events and problems that have occurred while MySQL is running.

Performing Data Uploads

Data uploads normally occur when you initially set up and configure an application. You likely already have data that you want to use on a local network. The upload process sends the data from your local network to the cloud. Of course, you might also have other reasons to perform data uploads. No matter what the reason, this part of the chapter demonstrates how to perform a data upload by using MySQL Workbench.

TECHNICAL STUFF

The technique you see in this chapter doesn't transfer absolutely everything from your local or network hard drive to MySQL on the RDS server. It assumes that you simply want to move data. If you want to perform a complete transfer of a database, as might be done during an initial production move from a local network to RDS, you need to follow the much longer (and more convoluted) process at `http://docs.aws.amazon.com/AmazonRDS/latest/UserGuide/MySQL.Procedural.Importing.NonRDSRepl.html`. However, in general, this process is extreme overkill for the developer, and you likely won't need to perform it.

Before you begin this process, you must have a local file to use for uploading to the RDS configuration, a copy of MySQL Workbench installed, and a connection to your MySQL setup on RDS. The following steps assume that you have a local or network copy of a `.sql` file that contains everything needed to recreate your database. You must also have the rights required to access the database on RDS, which may require superuser rights (see the "Enabling stored procedures, functions, and triggers" section, earlier in this chapter, for details about overcoming problems with running scripts on RDS).

1. **Open MySQL Workbench and connect to RDS.**

   You see the connection open as normal.

2. **Choose Server ⇨ Data Import.**

   You see the Data Import page open, as shown in Figure 12-24.

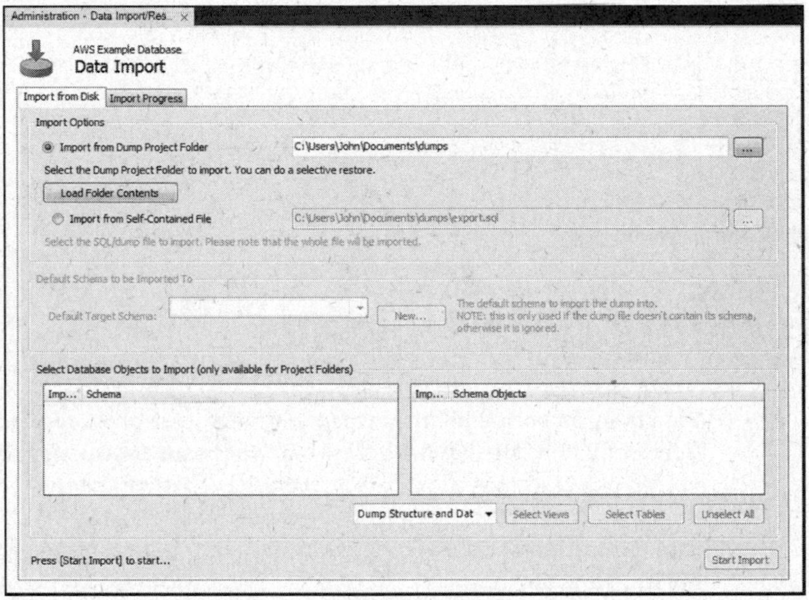

FIGURE 12-24:
Use the Data Import page to configure a data upload.

3. **Choose Import from Dump Project Folder and type a location for the folder.**

   The folder contains a series of scripts used to recreate the database schema and objects it contains.

4. **Choose the objects you want to import in the Select Database Objects to Import list.**

   This feature is available only when you use project folders.

5. **Click Start Import.**

   For a really small setup such as FirstDatabase, the process happens within a second or two.

REMEMBER

To see the new database in Navigator, you must click the Refresh button in the upper-right corner of the display. The new database and associated objects will appear after MySQL Workbench queries RDS.

Performing Data Downloads

Data downloads normally occur when you want to create a local copy of the data that you've worked with in the cloud. There are all kinds of reasons to perform this task, with backup and application performance forming the two most common needs. Normally, the data download goes into a read-only database because you don't want any local changes to the data. Otherwise, you might find yourself in the untenable position of having to referee local changes against those made by other people in the cloud (a situation that usually results in some level of data loss). This section helps you perform a data download using MySQL Workbench.

TECHNICAL STUFF

As with data uploads, you can perform data downloads that provide you with a complete, replicated copy of your MySQL database. This process can be long and a bit complicated, which is why you should avoid using it when possible. The page at `http://docs.aws.amazon.com/AmazonRDS/latest/UserGuide/MySQL.Procedural.Exporting.NonRDSRepl.html` details this longer process. Most developers, however, are more interested in actual data. If your goal is to transfer a database as an entity, which includes the tables, views, stored procedures, and functions, but not all the settings and other setup that go with the database, the shorter process in this chapter will work fine and cause you fewer problems.

Before you begin this process, make sure you have a local copy of MySQL Workbench installed and configured to access your MySQL database on RDS. These steps help you create a local or network copy of your database.

1. **Open MySQL Workbench and connect to RDS.**

   You see the connection open as normal.

2. **Choose Server ⇨ Data Export.**

   You see the Data Export page open, as shown in Figure 12-25.

3. **Select a list of schemas you want to export.**

   The example assumes that you choose FirstDatabase. However, you can export any (or all) of the schemas in the list.

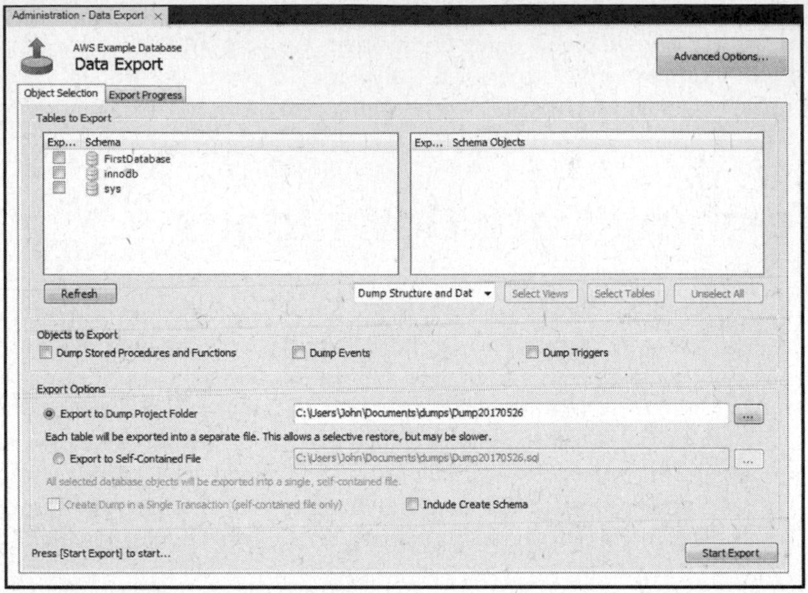

FIGURE 12-25:
Use the Data
Export page to
save a local copy
of your data.

4. **Click the schema and select all the schema entry objects you want to export.**

   The example has only MyTable to select.

5. **Select all the objects you want to export.**

   The example exports all stored procedures and functions, events, and triggers.

6. **Choose Export to Dump Project Folder and type a location for the folder.**

   A dump project folder contains a series of scripts designed to recreate the database and all its objects.

7. **Select Include Create Schema.**

   Selecting this option enables you to easily recreate the database structure in a local copy of MySQL.

8. **Click Start Export.**

   For a really small setup such as FirstDatabase, the process happens within a second or two.

Chapter **13**

Gaining NoSQL Access Using DynamoDB

The Structured Query Language (SQL) associated with relational databases (those that use tables of related data) makes up the bulk of Database Management System (DBMS) applications today. Using Relational DBMS (RDBMS) strategies makes sense for most kinds of data because information such as accounting, customer records, inventory, and a vast array of other business information naturally lends itself to the tabular form, in which columns describe the individual data elements and rows contain the individual records.

REMEMBER

However, some data, such as that used by big data or real-time applications, is harder to model using an RDBMS. Consequently, NoSQL, or non-SQL, databases become more attractive because they use other means to model data that doesn't naturally lend itself to tables. Because business, science, and other entities rely heavily on these nontraditional data sources today, NoSQL is more popular than SQL. DynamoDB is Amazon's answer to the need for a NoSQL database for various kinds of data analysis. This chapter begins by helping you understand DynamoDB so that you can better use it to address your specific NoSQL needs.

Developers often need localized access to the DBMS. With this in mind, you might find that you need a local copy of DynamoDB to use in your work. The local copy won't act as a substitute for the cloud-based version, but having it could save you considerable time as you work through various issues or try to understand how DynamoDB actually works. The chapter shows how to download a local copy of DynamoDB.

Before you can do anything substantial with DynamoDB, you need to set up and configure a copy on AWS. That's where you'll use it for the most part, after you get past the early experimentation stage, and it's where the production version of any applications your organization develops will appear. The next section of this chapter looks at the process for using DynamoDB online.

The remainder of the chapter focuses on a test database that you create locally. You develop a simple database using a local copy of DynamoDB, perform some essential tasks with it, and then upload it to your online copy of DynamoDB. You usually follow this same path when working with DynamoDB in a real-world project.

Considering the DynamoDB Features

DynamoDB provides access to all the common NoSQL features, which means that you don't need to worry about issues like creating a schema or maintaining tables. You use a NoSQL database in a free-form manner when compared to a SQL database, and NoSQL gives you the capability to work with large data with greater ease than a SQL database allows. The following sections give you an idea of just what DynamoDB provides and why NoSQL databases are important to businesses.

Getting a quick overview of NoSQL

The main reason to use NoSQL is to address the needs of modern applications. At one time, developers created applications that resided on just one or two platforms. An application development team might work on an application upgrade for months and use a limited number of data types to perform data manipulation. Today, the application environment is completely different, making the use of RDBMSs hard for modern applications. NoSQL addresses these needs in a number of ways:

>> Developers no longer limit themselves to a set number of data types. Modern applications use data types that are structured, semistructured, unstructured, and polymorphic (a data type used with a single interface that can actually work with objects of different underlying types).

>> Short development cycles make using an RDBMS hard, requiring a formal change process to update the schema and migrate the data to the new setup. A NoSQL database is flexible enough to allow ad hoc changes that are more in line with today's development cycle.

» Many applications today appear as services, rather than being installed on a particular system. The use of a Service Oriented Architecture (SOA) means that the application must be available 24 hours a day and that a user can access the same application using any sort of device. NoSQL databases can scale to meet the demands of such an application because they don't have all the underlying architecture of an RDBMS to weigh them down.

» The use of cloud computing means that data must appear in a form that works with multiple online services, even when the developers don't know the needs of those services at the time that a development cycle begins. Because NoSQL doesn't rely on formal schemas and access methodologies, you can more easily create an environment where any service, anywhere, can access the data as needed.

REMEMBER

» NoSQL supports the concept of *auto-sharding,* which lets you store data across multiple servers. When working with an RDBMS, the data normally appears on a single server to ensure that the DBMS can perform required maintenance tasks. The use of multiple servers makes NoSQL scale better and function more reliably as well, because you don't have just one failure point. DynamoDB extends the concept of auto-sharding by making cross-region replication possible (see the article at `http://docs.aws.amazon.com/amazondynamodb/latest/developerguide/Streams.CrossRegionRepl.html` for more details).

» Modern languages, such as R, provide data analysis features that rely on the flexible nature of unstructured data to perform its tasks. Because modern business makes decisions based on all sorts of analysis, it also needs modern languages that can perform the required analysis. You can find a quick R tutorial at `https://www.datacamp.com/courses/free-introduction-to-r`.

NoSQL Limitations

Even the best data storage strategy has limits and NoSQL is no exception. Actually, most of these limits exist in DynamoDB rather than NoSQL as a whole. The products you choose determine just what you can do with NoSQL, but you won't find any products today that do it all. The following list describes NoSQL limits as defined by the DynamoDB implementation:

» **Data organization:** Most NoSQL databases provide several methods of organizing data. DynamoDB doesn't support all the various types. What you get is a key-value pair setup, in which a key provides a unique reference to the data stored in the value. The key and the value are both data, but the key must provide unique data so that the database can locate a particular piece of information. A value can contain anything from a simple integer to a document to a complex description of a particular process. NoSQL doesn't place any sort of limit on what the value can contain, which makes it an extremely agile method of storing data.

>> **Specialized organizational types:** NoSQL databases typically support a number of other organizational types that DynamoDB doesn't currently support natively. For example, you can't create a graph store that shows interactions of networks of data, such as those found in social media. Examples of NoSQL databases that do provide this support are Neo4J (https://neo4j.com/) and Giraph (http://giraph.apache.org/). Fortunately, AWS recently added integration with Titan (http://titan.thinkaurelius.com/), a distributed graph database, to supply a level of this functionality.

>> **Document support:** DynamoDB also doesn't support documents such as those found in MongoDB (https://www.mongodb.com/). A document is a complex structure that can contain key-value pairs, key-array pairs (an array can contain a series of like values), and even other documents. Documents are a superset of the key-value pairs that DynamoDB does support.

>> **Wide-column data stores:** DynamoDB doesn't support the specialized wide-column data stores found in products such as Cassandra (http://cassandra.apache.org/) and HBase (https://hbase.apache.org/). These kinds of data stores find use in large dataset analysis. Using this kind of data store enables databases, such as Cassandra and HBase, to group data in columns rather than rows, which is how most databases work.

Differentiating between NoSQL and relational databases

Previous sections of the chapter may lead you to believe that RDBMS development is archaic because it lacks support for modern agile development methods. However, RDBMS and NoSQL databases actually fulfill needs in two different niches, so a business often needs access to both kinds of data storage. Of course, that's why AWS includes both (see Chapters 11 and 12 for more information about how AWS handles RDBMS requirements).

REMEMBER

Even though NoSQL provides some significant advantages, you need to consider how an RDBMS can help your organization as well. The main consideration in favor of NoSQL is whether the data is unstable or especially complex. In this case, NoSQL presents the best strategy for storing the data because it provides the best flexibility options.

However, an RDBMS offers some special features as well. For example, an RDBMS offers consistency because of the schema that seems to hold it back in other areas.

The schema ensures that the data in the database actually meets the criteria you set for it, which means that you're less likely to receive incomplete, missing, errant, or otherwise unusable data from the data source. The consistency offered by an RDBMS is a huge advantage because it means that developers spend less time coding around potential data problems — they can focus on the actual data processing, presentation, and modification.

An RDBMS usually relies on normalization to keep the data size small. When working with a NoSQL database, you can see a lot of repeated data, which consumes more resources than an equivalent RDBMS implementation. Of course, computer resources are relatively inexpensive today, but given that you're working in a cloud environment, the charges for inefficiencies can add up quickly. The thing to remember about having too much repeated data is that it also tends to slow down parsing, which means that a properly normalized RDBMS database can often find and manipulate data faster than its NoSQL counterpart can.

NoSQL and RDBMS databases offer different forms of reliability as well. Although a NoSQL database scales well and can provide superior speed by spreading itself over multiple servers, the RDBMS offers superior reliability of the intrinsic data. You can depend on the data in an RDBMS being of a certain type with specific characteristics. In addition, you get all the data or none of the data, rather than bits and pieces of the data, as is possible with a NoSQL database.

Because an RDBMS provides the data in a certain form, it can also provide more than NoSQL in the way of built-in query and analysis capabilities. Some of the major RDBMSs offer a substantial array of query and analysis capabilities so that developers don't spend a lot of time reinventing the wheel, and so that administrators can actually figure out what data is available without also getting a degree in development. When the form of the data is right (the lack of a wealth of large objects), an RDBMS can also present results faster because the organization makes parsing the information easier. DynamoDB partially offsets the enhanced query capabilities of an RDBMS by providing a secondary index capability (read more at http://docs.aws.amazon.com/amazondynamodb/latest/developerguide/SecondaryIndexes.html).

TECHNICAL STUFF

As with many data issues, no one single database solution works well in every case. Both RDBMS and NoSQL databases have definite places in an organization. In fact, that's why some vendors offer both solutions and some are working on methods to integrate the two. Interoperability between RDBMS and NoSQL databases is becoming more common with the development of APIs for products such as MongoDB by IBM (see the series of articles that begins at http://www.ibm.com/developerworks/data/library/techarticle/dm-1306nosqlforjson1/ for details). IBM is creating a data representation, query language, and wire protocol to make DB2 and MongoDB interactions relatively seamless.

Defining typical uses for DynamoDB

Most of the use cases for DynamoDB found at `https://aws.amazon.com/dynamodb/` revolve around unstructured, changeable data. One of the more interesting uses of DynamoDB is to provide language support for Duolingo (`https://www.duolingo.com/nojs/splash`), a product that helps people learn another language by using a game-like paradigm. Making learning fun generally makes it easier as well, and learning another language can be a complex task that requires as much fun as one can give it.

Obtaining a continuous stream of data is important in some cases, especially in monitoring roles. For example, BMW uses DynamoDB to collect sensor data from its cars. The use of streams in DynamoDB (see `http://docs.aws.amazon.com/amazondynamodb/latest/developerguide/Streams.html` for more information) makes this kind of application practical. Dropcam (`https://nest.com/camera/meet-nest-cam/`), a company that offers property monitoring, is another example of using streaming to provide real-time updates for an application.

DynamoDB actually provides a wide range of impressive features, which you can read about at `https://aws.amazon.com/dynamodb/details/`. The problem is finding use cases for these new features, such as ElasticMap Reduce integration, in real-world applications today. The lack of use cases is hardly surprising because most of this technology is so incredibly new. The important takeaway here is that DynamoDB has a place alongside RDS for more organizations, and you need to find the mix that works best for your needs.

Downloading a Local Copy of DynamoDB

In contrast to many of the other AWS services, you can actually get a local copy of DynamoDB that you can work with offline. Using DynamoDB offline, on your local machine, means that you can try various tasks without incurring costs or worrying about potential connectivity issues. In addition, you can use DynamoDB in a test environment, in which you use a copy of your data to mimic real-world situations. The following sections show how to obtain and install a local copy and then use your copy with Python to perform a test.

Performing the installation

To start using a local copy of DynamoDB, you need Java installed on your system because Amazon supplies DynamoDB as a `.jar` file. You can obtain a user-level version of Java at `https://www.java.com/en/download/`. However, if you plan to perform any customizations or feel you might need debugging support, then you need a developer version of Java (the Java Development Kit or JDK) that you obtain from http://www.oracle.com/technetwork/java/javase/downloads/index-jsp-138363.html. Make sure to get the latest version of Java to ensure that DynamoDB works as expected.

The next step is to download a copy of DynamoDB and extract the files in the archive. You can find links for this part of the process at http://docs.aws.amazon.com/amazondynamodb/latest/developerguide/DynamoDBLocal.html. Note that you can get versions of DynamoDB that work with Maven (see http://docs.aws.amazon.com/amazondynamodb/latest/developerguide/DynamoDBLocal.html#DynamoDBLocal.Maven) and Eclipse (see https://aws.amazon.com/eclipse/). This chapter assumes that you use the pure Java version and that you've extracted the downloaded archive to a folder named DynamoDB on your hard drive. You may need to bury the archive a level or two deep, but make sure that the path doesn't contain spaces. The main file you deal with is DynamoDBLocal.jar.

Starting DynamoDB locally

Open a command prompt or terminal window and ensure that you're in the location where you extracted the DynamoDB archive (using the CD command). Type **java -Djava.library.path=./DynamoDBLocal_lib -jar DynamoDBLocal.jar -sharedDb** and press Enter to start DynamoDB. Depending on your operating system, you see some startup messages like those shown in Figure 13-1.

```
java -Djava.library.path=./DynamoDBLocal_lib -jar DynamoDBLocal.jar -sharedDb

C:\DynamoDB>java -Djava.library.path=./DynamoDBLocal_lib -jar DynamoDBLocal.jar
-sharedDb
Initializing DynamoDB Local with the following configuration:
Port:    8000
InMemory:        false
DbPath: null
SharedDb:        true
shouldDelayTransientStatuses:    false
CorsParams:      *
```

FIGURE 13-1: DynamoDB displays some startup messages after you execute the command.

When working with Windows, you should also see the message shown in Figure 13-2 (other platforms may show other messages). This firewall message tells you that port 8000 isn't currently open. To make DyanmoDB work properly, you must allow access. If you want to change the port, use the –port command-line switch with a different port number. The page that contains the DynamoDB links also has a list of other command-line switches near the bottom, or you can use the –help command-line switch to see a listing for these command line switches locally.

Overcoming the Windows `OSError` issue

When working with Windows, you may encounter a problem that involves seeing an `OSError` message output for some Python calls, even if your code is correct. The problem is with the `tz.py` file found in the `\Users\<UserName>\Anaconda3\Lib\site-packages\dateutil\tz` folder of your Anaconda setup (the same file exists for every Python setup, but in different folders). To fix this problem, you must change the code for the `_naive_is_dst()` function so that it looks like this:

```
def _naive_is_dst(self, dt):
    # Original Code
    timestamp = _datetime_to_timestamp(dt)
    #return time.localtime(timestamp +
                        time.timezone).tm_isdst

    # Bug Fix Code
    if timestamp+time.timezone < 0:
        current_time = timestamp + time.timezone +
                    31536000
    else:
        current_time = timestamp + time.timezone

    return time.localtime(current_time).tm_isdst
```

Fortunately, you don't have to make the change yourself. You can find the updated `tz.py` file in the downloadable source, as explained in the Introduction. Just copy it to the appropriate folder on your system.

Testing your DynamoDB installation

At this point, you can begin using your local copy of DynamoDB to perform tasks. This section demonstrates how to access your local copy using Python. You can access the example code for this chapter in the AWS4D4D; 13, Local DynamoDB.ipynb file in the downloadable source, as explained in the Introduction. To start, you must create a Boto3 client, as normal, but note the use of the endpoint_url argument.

```
import boto3
client = boto3.client('dynamodb',
                      endpoint_url='http://localhost:8000')
```

TIP

The use of the endpoint_url argument lets you easily move your code to the cloud. You just need to remove the argument and you use your cloud-based copy of AWS instead of the local copy. You use the same commands as you do when accessing the AWS cloud-based copy of DynamoDB, which appear at http://boto3.readthedocs.io/en/latest/reference/services/dynamodb.html. The following code ensures that the table doesn't already exit, creates the table, and then displays its status:

```
table_list = client.list_tables()['TableNames']

if 'TestDB' in table_list:
    print('TestDB Exists')
    client.delete_table(TableName='TestDB')
    print('Deleted TestDB')

table = client.create_table(
    TableName = 'TestDB',
    KeySchema =
    [
        {
            'AttributeName': 'EmployeeID',
            'KeyType': 'HASH'
        },
        {
            'AttributeName': 'EmployeeName',
            'KeyType': 'RANGE'
        }
    ],
    AttributeDefinitions =
    [
        {
            'AttributeName': 'EmployeeID',
            'AttributeType': 'N'
        },
```

```
            {
                'AttributeName': 'EmployeeName',
                'AttributeType': 'S'
            }
        ],
        ProvisionedThroughput =
        {
            'ReadCapacityUnits': 10,
            'WriteCapacityUnits': 10
        }
    )

print(table['TableDescription']['TableStatus'])
```

The output of this code should simply say ACTIVE. The table variable contains a wealth of information about the new table, so you should explore it for additional details. To stop your local copy of DynamoDB, press Ctrl+C at the command prompt or terminal window.

REMEMBER

To get a functional setup that really does help you understand DynamoDB a bit better, you need to install other products, such as Python 2.7. You can see an example of the series of steps needed at http://docs.aws.amazon.com/amazondynamodb/ latest/developerguide/TicTacToe.Phase1.html. This tutorial covers the processes needed to build a tic-tac-toe game using DynamoDB, Python, and a few other bits and pieces.

Creating a Basic DynamoDB Setup

You have a number of ways to work with DynamoDB. For example, you can go with the local option described in the "Downloading a Local Copy of DynamoDB" section. However, the local option is really only good for experimentation. If you want to start creating a production system, you need to get onto AWS and perform the required tasks in the cloud.

Before you can do anything with DynamoDB, you must create an instance of it, just as you do for RDS. The following procedure helps you get started with DynamoDB so that you can perform some interesting tasks with it:

1. **Sign into AWS using your user account.**

2. **Navigate to the DynamoDB Management Console at** https://console. aws.amazon.com/dynamodb.

You see a Welcome page that contains interesting information about DynamoDB and what it can do for you. However, you don't see the actual console at this point. Notice the Getting Started Guide link, which you can use to obtain access to tutorials and introductory videos.

3. **Click Create Table.**

You see the Create DynamoDB Table page, shown in Figure 13-3. Amazon assumes that most people have worked with an RDBMS database, so the instructions for working with RDS are fewer and less detailed. Notice the level of detail provided for DynamoDB. The wizard explains each part of the table creation process carefully to reduce the likelihood that you will make mistakes.

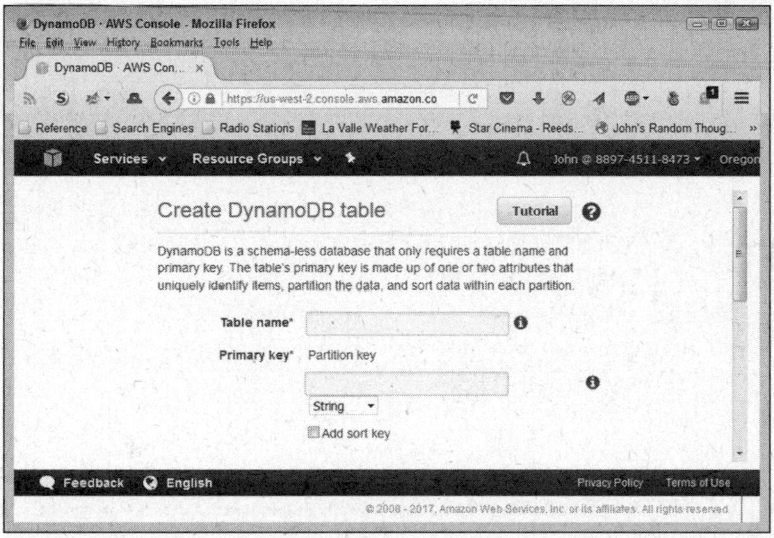

FIGURE 13-3:
Start defining the characteristics of the table you want to create.

4. **Type** TestDB **in the Table Name field.**

Pick a descriptive name for your table. In this case, you need to remember that your entire database could consist of a single, large table.

5. **Type** EmployeeID **in the Primary Key field and choose Number for its type.**

When working with a NoSQL database, you must define a unique value as the key in the key-value pair. An employee ID is likely to provide a unique value across all employees. Duplicated keys will cause problems because you can't uniquely identify a particular piece of data after the key is duplicated.

A key must also provide a simple value. When working with DynamoDB, you have a choice of making the key a number, string, or binary value. You can't use a Boolean value because you would have only a choice between true and false. Likewise, other data types won't work because they are either too complex or don't offer enough choices.

TIP

Notice the Add Sort Key check box. Selecting this option lets you add a secondary method of locating data. Using a sort key lets you locate data using more than just the primary key. For example, in addition to the employee ID, you might also want to add a sort key based on employee name. People know names; they tend not to know IDs. However, a name isn't necessarily unique: Two people can have the same name, so using a name as your primary key is a bad idea.

Not shown in Figure 13-3 is the option Use Default Settings. The default settings create a NoSQL table that lacks a secondary index, allows a specific provisioned capacity, and sets alarms for occasions when applications exceed the provisioned capacity. A provisioned capacity essentially determines the number of reads and writes that you expect per second. Given that this is a test setup, a setting of 5 reads and 5 writes should work well. You can read more about provisioned capacity at http://docs.aws.amazon.com/amazondynamodb/latest/developerguide/HowItWorks.ProvisionedThroughput.html.

6. **Select Add Sort Key.**

You see another field added for entering a sort field, as shown in Figure 13-4. Notice that this second field is connected to the first, so the two fields are essentially used together.

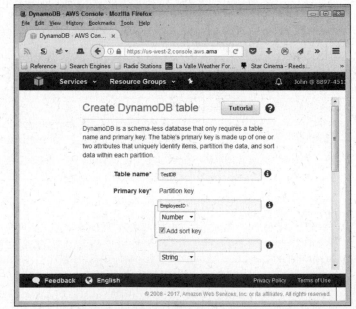

FIGURE 13-4: Choose a sort key that people will understand well.

7. **Type** EmployeeName **in the sort key field and set its type to String.**

8. **Click Create.**

You see the Tables page of the DynamoDB Management Console, shown in Figure 13-5. This figure shows the list of tables in the left pane and the details for the selected table in the right pane. Each of the tabs tells you something about the table. The More link on the right of the list of tabs tells you that more tabs are available for you to access.

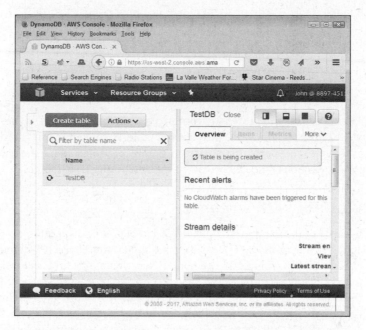

FIGURE 13-5:
The table you created appears in the Tables page.

Not shown in Figure 13-5 is the Navigation pane. Click the right-pointing arrow to show the Navigation pane, where you can choose other DynamoDB views (Dashboard and Reserved Capacity).

Developing a Basic Database

The act of creating a table doesn't necessarily mean that your database is ready for use. For one thing, even though you have the beginnings of a database, it lacks data. Also, you may need to modify some of the settings to make the database suit your needs better. For example, you may decide to include additional alarms based on metrics that you see, or to increase the capacity as the test phase progresses and more people work with the data.

Normally, you populate a database by importing data into it. The DynamoDB interface also allows you to enter data manually, which works quite well for test purposes. After the data looks the way you want it to look, you can export the data to see how the data you want to import should look. Exporting the data also allows you to move it to other locations or perform a backup outside of AWS.

REMEMBER

Databases normally contain more than one table, even NoSQL databases. Yes, creating a simple test database using a single table is possible, but multiple tables appear more often than not in a database. The examples in this chapter do rely on a single table — the one you create in the previous section. You use this table in the sections that follow to explore the techniques that DynamoDB provides for interacting with tables and the data they contain.

Configuring tables

The right pane in Figure 13-5 contains a series of tabs. Each of these tabs gives you useful information about the selected table. Because the information is table specific, you can't perform actions on groups of tables using the interface. The following sections discuss the essentials of working with tables.

Working with streams

Because of the manner in which NoSQL tables work, you often need to synchronize copies of the same data. A table in one region might receive changes that you also need to replicate in another region. In fact, you might find other reasons to provide a *log* of changes (think of the log as a detailed procedure you could use to replicate the changes) to the tables you create. A *stream* is a record of table changes (the actual data used to modify the table, rather than a procedure detailing the tasks performed, as provided by a log). Each change appears only once in the log you create, and it appears in the order in which DynamoDB received the change. The ordered list enables anyone reading the log to reconstruct table changes in another location. AWS retains this log for 24 hours, so it doesn't need to be read immediately.

The Overview tab contains a Manage Stream button in the Stream Details section that you click to set up a stream for your table, as shown in Figure 13-6. This feature isn't enabled by default (Stream Enabled will show a value of No), but you can configure it to allow the storage of specific change information. You have the following options when creating the change log:

>> **Keys Only:** Just the key portion of the key-value pair appears in the log. This option has the advantage of providing just a summary of the changes and makes the log smaller and easier to read than if both the key and the value appeared. If the receiving party wants to do something with the change, the new value can be read from the table.

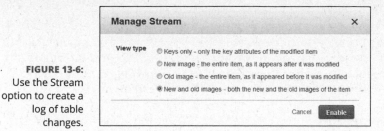

>> **New Image:** Both the new key and value of the key-value pair appear in the log. The log contains the information as it appears after the modification. This is the right option to use for replication, in that you want to copy both the new key and value to another table.

>> **Old Image:** Both the old key and the value of the key-value pair appear in the log. This log entry shows how the table entry appeared before someone modified it.

>> **New and Old Images:** The entire new and old key-value pairs appear in the log. You can use this kind of entry for verification purposes. However, realize that this approach uses the most space. The log will be much larger than the actual table because you're storing two entries for absolutely every change made to the table.

Viewing metrics

The Metrics tab contains a series of graphs, which you can expand by clicking the graphs. Metrics help you understand how well your table is working and enable you to change settings before a particular issue becomes critical. Many of the metrics tables include multiple entries. For example, in the Read Capacity metric, shown in Figure 13-7, the red line shows the provisioned read capacity and the blue line shows how much of that capacity your application consumes. When the blue line starts to approach the red line, you need to consider modifying the read capacity of the table to avoid throttled read requests, which appear in the metric to the right of the Read Capacity metric.

TIP

The *i* shown in the circle next to a metric graph tells you that you can get additional information about that graph. Hover your mouse over the *i* to see a pop-up box containing helpful information. For example, the pop-up for the Read Capacity graph tells you that small surges in reads may not appear in the graph because the graph uses averaged data. The Throttled Read Requests graph is actually a better indicator of when small surges become a problem.

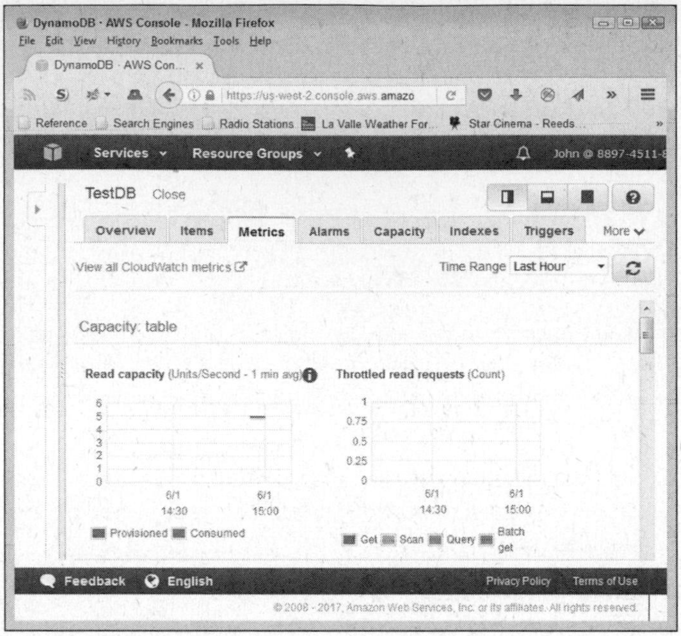

FIGURE 13-7:
Metrics help you manage your table.

Checking alarms

The Alarms tab, shown in Figure 13-8, contains the alarms that you set to monitor your table. No one can view the status of a table continuously, so alarms enable you to discover potentially problematic conditions before they cause an application crash or too many user delays. The default table setup includes two alarms: one for read capacity and another for write capacity.

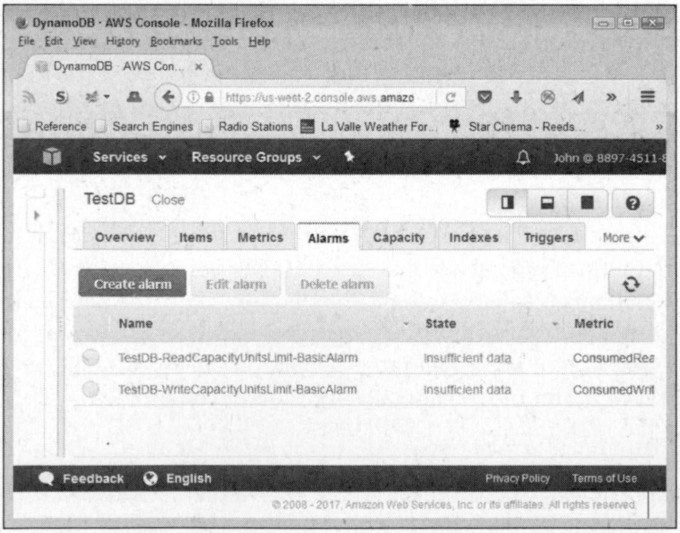

FIGURE 13-8:
Use alarms to monitor table performance when you aren't physically viewing it.

The options on the Alarms tab let you create, delete, and edit alarms. When you click one of these options, you see a dialog box similar to the one shown in Figure 13-9, in which you configure the alarm. Sending a Simple Notification Service (SNS) message lets you get a remote warning of impending problems.

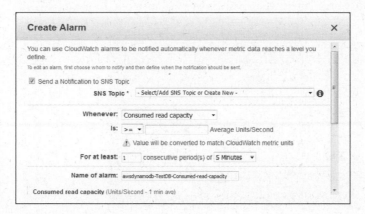

FIGURE 13-9:
Create new alarms or edit existing alarms as needed to keep tables working smoothly.

Modifying capacity

When you initially create a table, you get 5 units each of read and write capacity. As your application usage grows, you might find that these values are too small (or possibly too large). Every unit of capacity costs money, so tuning the capacity is important. The Capacity tab, shown in Figure 13-10, lets you modify the read and write capacity values for any table. You should base the amounts you use on the metrics discussed in the "Viewing metrics" section, earlier in this chapter.

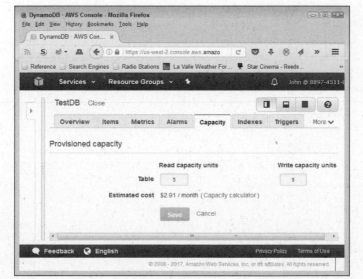

FIGURE 13-10:
Manage the read and write capacity to ensure that the application works as anticipated but costs remain low.

The tab shows an anticipated cost for the current usage level. Changing the read or write capacity will also modify the amount you pay. The Capacity Calculator link displays a Capacity Calculator that you can use to compute the amount of read and write capacity that you actually need, as shown in Figure 13-11. Simply type the amounts into the fields to obtain new read and write capacity values. Click Save to transfer these values to the Capacity tab.

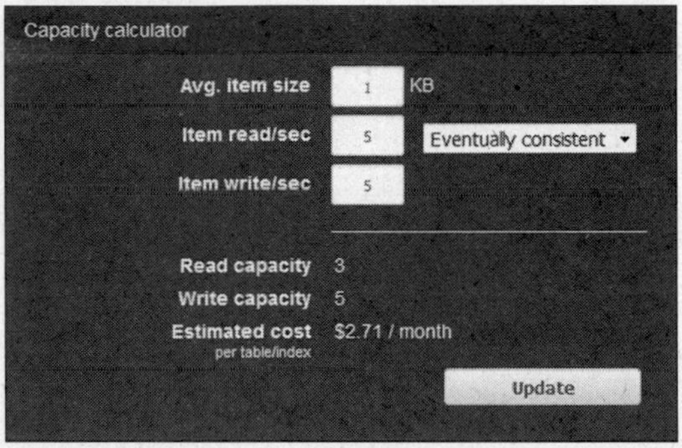

FIGURE 13-11:
The Capacity Calculator reduces the work required to compute capacity values.

Creating a secondary index

Secondary indexes make finding specific data in your table easier. Perhaps you need to find information based on something other than the primary key. For example, you can find employees based on name or ID by using the primary key for the example table. However, at some point you might also need to find employees based on their employment date. To create a secondary index, click Create Index in the Indexes tab. You see a Create Index dialog box like the one shown in Figure 13-12. (This dialog box contains sample values that you can use for experimentation purposes in the "Performing Queries" section, later in this chapter.)

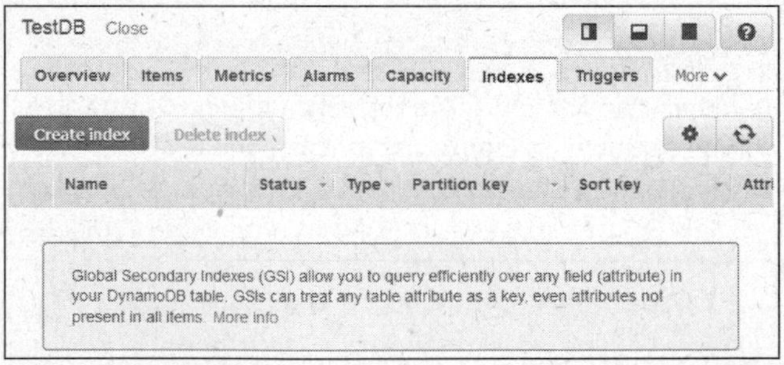

FIGURE 13-12:
Use secondary indexes to help look for data not found in the primary key.

A secondary index incurs an additional cost. You must allocate read and write capacity units that reflect the amount of usage that you expect the secondary index to receive. As with the table's capacity values, you can click the Capacity Calculator link to display the Capacity Calculator (shown in Figure 13-11) to provide an estimate of the number of units you need.

After you create a new index, you see it listed in the Indexes tab, as shown in Figure 13-13. The Status field tells you the current index condition. No option exists for editing indexes. If you find that the index you created doesn't work as anticipated, you need to delete the old index and create a new one.

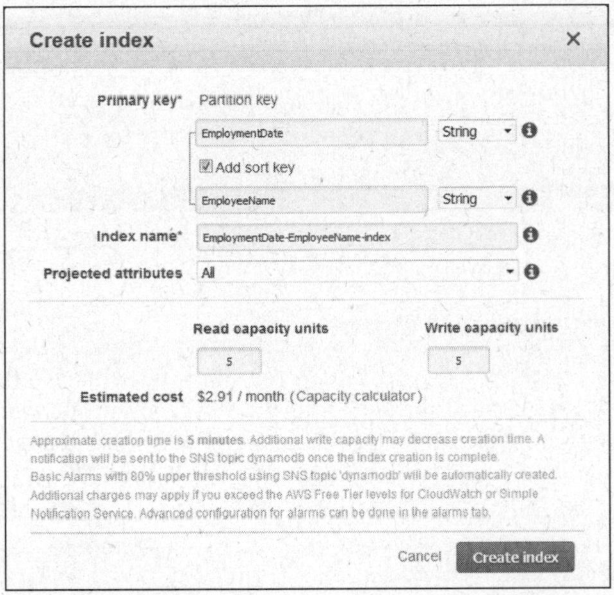

FIGURE 13-13:
The Indexes
tab provides a list
of indexes for
your table.

Adding items

After you obtain the desired setup for your table, you want to add some items to it. The Items tab, shown in Figure 13-14, can look a little daunting at first because you can use it in several different ways. This section focuses on the Create Item button, but you use the other functions as the chapter progresses.

The following sections describe how to add items to your table manually. You can also add items in bulk by importing them. Another option is to copy a table (exporting data from one table and importing it into another) or to use a stream to obtain data from another table (see the "Working with streams" section, earlier in this chapter, for details).

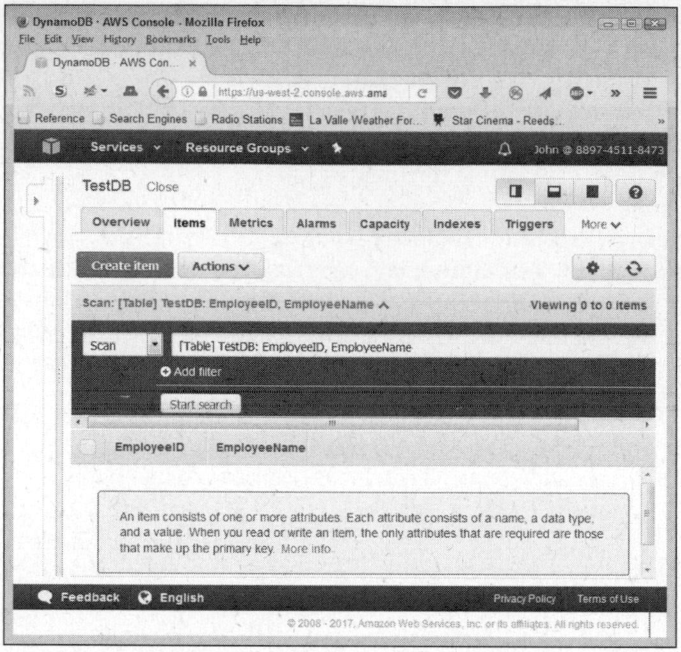

FIGURE 13-14:
The Items tab
combines a
number of tasks
into a single area.

Defining the data types

When you create an item, you initially see all the fields that you've defined in various ways, but that isn't the end of the process. You can add more fields as needed to provide a complete record. Index and key fields, those that you define using the various methods found in this chapter, have a limited number of acceptable data types: String, Binary, and Number. However, other fields can use these data types:

» **String:** A series of characters that can include letters, numbers, punctuation marks, and special characters.

» **Binary:** A series of 0s and 1s presented as Base64-encoded binary data. DynamoDB treats every value in the string as an individual, byte-coded value but stores the entire string as a single value in the table.

» **Number:** Any number that you could expect to find in other programming languages. You specify a number as a string but don't care whether the number is an integer or floating-point value. DynamoDB treats the strings you provide as numbers for math calculations.

» **StringSet:** A group of strings that work together as an array of values. Every value in the array must appear as a string. The array can have as many strings as needed to complete the information. For example, you can create a StringSet called Address. Each entry can be another line in an individual's address, which means that some entries may have just one entry, while others may have two or three entries in the array.

» **NumberSet:** A group of numeric strings that work together as an array of numeric values. Every value in the array must appear as a number, but not necessarily all as integers or floating-point values. DynamoDB treats the strings you provide as numbers for math calculations.

» **BinarySet:** A group of binary values that work together as an array of values. Every value in the array must appear as a binary value.

» **Map:** A complex data grouping that contains entries of any data type, including other maps. The entries appear as attribute-value pairs. You provide the name of an attribute and then supply a value that contains any of the data types described in this section. You can access each member of the map using its attribute name.

» **List:** A group of data of any supported DynamoDB type. A list works similarly to a set but with elements that can be of any type. A list can even contain maps. The difference between a list and a map is that you don't name the individual entries. Consequently, you access members of a list using an *index* (a numeric value that indicates the item's position in the list, starting with 0 for the first item).

» **Boolean:** A value of either true or false that indicates the truth value of the attribute.

» **Null:** A blank spot that is always set to true. You use a Null attribute to represent missing data. Other records in the table contain this data, but the data is missing for this particular record.

Creating an item

To create a new item for your table, click Create Item in the Items tab. You see a dialog box like the one shown in Figure 13-15. This dialog box automatically presents three attributes (fields). These fields are present because they represent required entries to support a primary key, sort key, or secondary index.

WARNING

The items you see when you first create an item are mandatory if you want the item to work as it should with other table items. However, you can remove the items if desired, which can lead to missing essential data in the table. DynamoDB does check for missing or duplicate key values, so you can't accidentally enter two items with the same key.

When you finish filling out the essential attributes, you can save the item (if desired) by clicking Save. DynamoDB checks the item for errors and saves it to your table. You have the option of adding other attributes, as covered in the next section.

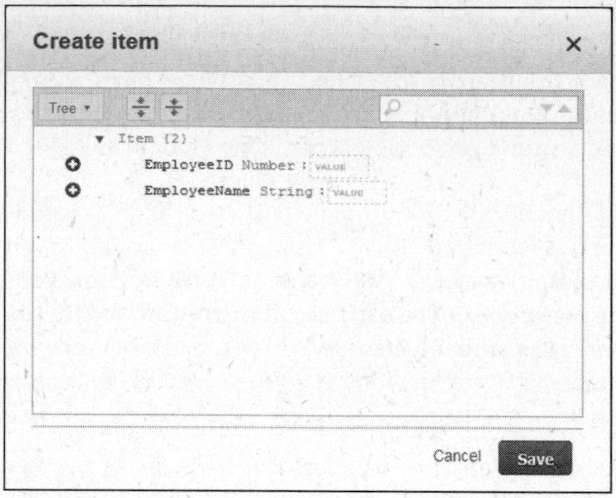

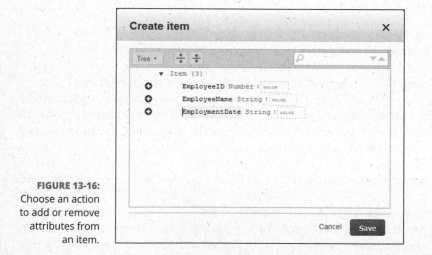

FIGURE 13-15:
Creating a
new item
automatically
adds the required
attributes for
that item.

Adding and removing attributes

Table items have key fields, sort fields, and secondary sort indexes that provide essential information to both the viewer and DynamoDB. These entries let you perform tasks such as sorting the data and looking for specific information. However, there are also informational fields that simply contain data. You don't normally sort on these attributes or use them for queries, but you can use them to obtain supplementary information. To add one of these items, you click the plus (+) sign next to an existing item and choose an action from the context menu, shown in Figure 13-16.

FIGURE 13-16:
Choose an action
to add or remove
attributes from
an item.

REMEMBER

Appending an attribute means adding it after the current attribute. Likewise, inserting an attribute means adding it before the current attribute. You can also use the menu to remove an attribute that you don't want. Use this feature with care, because you can remove attributes that you really need.

After you decide to append or insert a new attribute, you choose an attribute type that appears from the drop-down list. The "Defining the data types" section, earlier in this chapter, describes all the types. Click a type and you see a new attribute added in the correct position. Begin defining the new attribute by giving it a name. When working with a simple item, you type the value immediately after the name, as shown in Figure 13-17. If you type an incorrect value, such as when providing a string for a Boolean attribute, DynamoDB lets you know about the problem immediately.

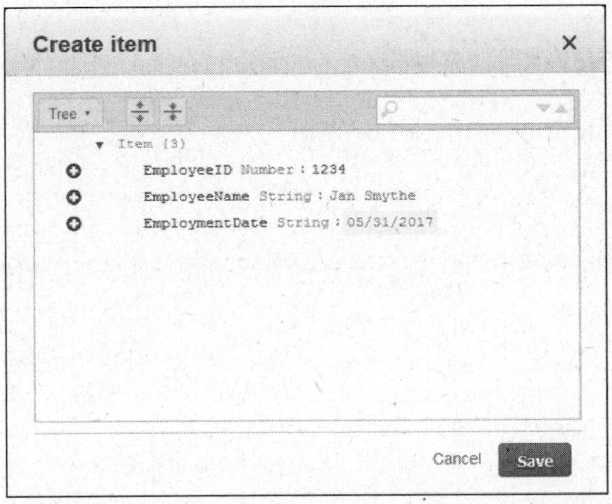

Create item   ✕

| Tree ▾ | | | ⌕ | ▾ ▲ |

▾ Item {3}
- EmployeeID Number : 1234
- EmployeeName String : Jan Smythe
- EmploymentDate String : 05/31/2017

Cancel   **Save**

FIGURE 13-17:
Attributes
appear as
attribute-
value pairs.

Adding complex attributes take a little more time and thought. Figure 13-18 shows a map entry. Note how the attribute-value pairs appear indented. If this map had contained other complex types, such as a set, list, or map, the new data would appear indented at another level to the right. The map automatically keeps track of the number of map entries for you.

It isn't apparent from the figure, but you use a slightly different technique to work with attributes in this case. When you want to add a new attribute, one that's at the same level as the map, you actually click the plus sign (+) next to the map entry, which is Address in Figure 13-18. However, if you want to add a new entry to the map, you must click the + next to one of the map entries, such as Address1.

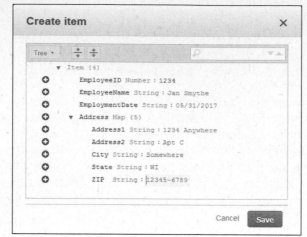

FIGURE 13-18:
Complex data appears as indented entries.

Modifying items

Several methods are available for modifying items. If you want to modify all or most of the entries in the item, select the item's entry in the list and choose Actions ⇨ Edit. You see a dialog box, similar to the one shown in Figure 13-18, in which you can edit the information as needed. (If the information appears with just the complex data shown, click the Expand All Fields button at the top of the dialog box.)

To modify just one or two attributes of an item, hover your mouse over that item's entry in the Items tab. Attributes that you can change appear with a pencil next to them when you have the mouse in the correct position. Click the pencil icon, and you can enter new information for the selected attribute.

Copying items

You may have two items with almost the same information, or you might want to use one of the items as a template for creating other items. You don't need to perform this task manually. Select the item you want to copy and choose Actions ⇨ Duplicate in the Items tab. You see a Copy Item dialog box that looks similar to the dialog box shown in Figure 13-18. Change the attributes that you need to change (especially the primary key, sort key, and secondary indexes) and click Save to create the new item. This approach is far faster than duplicating everything manually each time you want to create a new item, especially when you have complex data entries to work with.

Deleting items

To remove one or more items from the table, select each item that you want to remove and then choose Actions ➪ Delete. DynamoDB displays a Delete Items dialog box, which asks whether you're sure about removing the data. Click Delete to complete the task.

Deleting a table

At some point, you may not want your table any longer. To remove the table from DynamoDB, select the name of the table you want to remove and then choose Actions ➪ Delete Table in the Tables page. DynamoDB displays a Delete Table dialog box that asks whether you're sure you want to delete the table. Click Delete to complete the action.

As part of the table deletion process, you can also delete all the alarms associated with the table. DynamoDB selects the Delete All CloudWatch Alarms for this Table entry in the Delete Table dialog box by default. If you decide that you want to keep the alarms, you can always deselect the check box to maintain them.

Performing Queries

CRUD involves creating, reading, updating, and deleting data items. However, the task that users perform the most is reading the data. Of course, you could read the entire database, but that wouldn't be time efficient, especially when you need just one entry. That's where queries come into play. A query makes accessing a subset of the entries possible without manually reading them all. The following sections detail several methods for performing queries against a DynamoDB database.

Using the console

Finding data that you need can become problematic. A few records, or even a few hundred records, might not prove to be much of a problem. However, hundreds of thousands of records would be a nightmare to search individually, so you need to have some method of finding the data quickly. This assistance comes in the form of a query. DynamoDB actually supports two query types:

» **Scan:** Uses a filtering approach to find entries that match your criteria.

» **Query:** Looks for specific attribute entries.

The examples in this section employ two test entries in the TestDB table. The essential entries are the EmployeeID, EmployeeName, and EmploymentDate attributes, shown here:

EmployeeID	EmployeeName	EmploymentDate
1234	Jan Smythe	05/31/2017
1235	Hal Jones	02/28/2015

The two methods of querying data have advantages and disadvantages, but what you use normally comes down to a matter of personal preference. The following sections describe both approaches.

Using a scan

Scans have the advantage of being a bit more free-form than queries. You filter data based on any field you want to use. To scan the data, you choose either a [Table] entry that contains the primary key and sort key, or an [Index] entry that sorts the data based on a secondary index that you create, as shown in Figure 13-19.

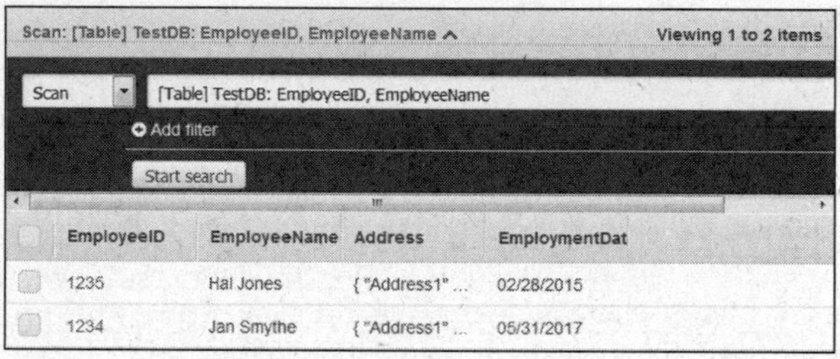

FIGURE 13-19: Scans employ filters to locate data.

Using a scan means deciding on what kind of filtering to use to get a desired result. The following steps give you a template for a quick method of performing a scan. (Your steps will vary because you need to provide specific information to make the procedure work.)

1. **Choose Scan in the first field.**

2. **Select either a [Table] or [Index] entry in the second field.**

   The entry you choose determines the output's sort order. In addition, using the correct entry speeds the search because DynamoDB will have a quick method of finding the data.

3. **Click Add Filter (if necessary) to add a new filter entry.**

   You can remove filters by clicking the *X* on the right side of the filter's entry.

4. **Choose an attribute, such as in the first Filter field.**

5. **Select the attribute's type in the second Filter field.**

6. **Specify a logical relationship in the third Filter field.**

   This entry can be tricky, especially when working with strings. For example, if you want to find all the entries that begin with the name George, you choose the Begins With entry in this field. However, if you want to find all the employees hired after 11/08/2016, use the > entry instead.

7. **Type a value for the fourth Filter field, such as George.**

8. **Click Start Search.**

   You see the entries that match your filter criteria. You can use as many filters as desired to whittle the data down to just those items you really want to see. Simply repeat Steps 3 through 8 to achieve the desired result.

Using a query

Queries are stricter and more precise than scans. When you perform a query, you look for specific values, as shown in Figure 13-20. Notice that the key value is precise. You can't look for a range of employment dates; instead, you must look for a specific employment date. In addition, the employment date is a mandatory entry; you can't perform the query without it. However, you can also choose an optional sort key and add filtering (as found with scans) as well.

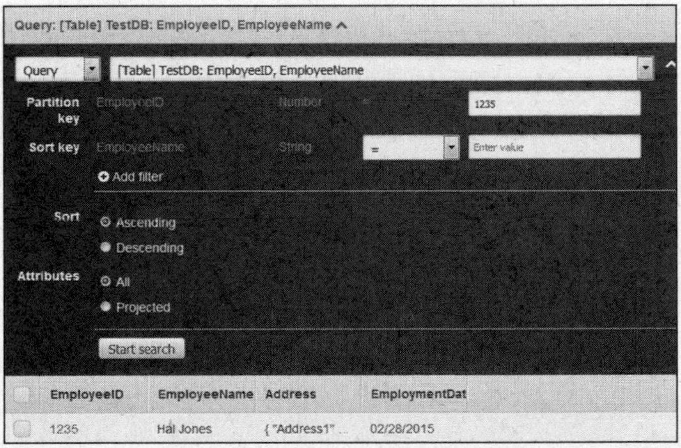

FIGURE 13-20: Queries use specific values to find information.

Using a query is like asking a specific question. You can ask which employees, who were hired on 02/28/2015, have a name that begins with Hal. In this case, you see just one record. Scans can produce the same result by employing multiple filters. The advantage of a query is that it forces you to think in a particular way; also, because you use attributes that are indexed, using a query is faster than a scan.

Querying the database programmatically

As with the console, you can perform both scans and queries using languages such as Python. Using the console actually helps you understand what you need to provide in order to obtain the correct results. The following code demonstrates both a scan and a query. You can access the example code for this chapter in the AWS4D4D; 13, Scans and Queries.ipynb file in the downloadable source, as explained in the Introduction.

```python
import boto3
client = boto3.client('dynamodb')

result = client.scan(
    TableName = 'TestDB',
    ScanFilter =
    {
        'EmployeeName':
        {
            'AttributeValueList':
            [
                {
                    'S': 'Jan Smythe'
                }
            ],
            'ComparisonOperator': 'EQ'
        }
    })

for item in result['Items']:
    print(
    'Employee ID: ', item['EmployeeID']['N'],
    '\nEmployee Name: ', item['EmployeeName']['S'])
```

```
result = client.query(
    TableName = 'TestDB',
    KeyConditions =
    {
        'EmployeeID':
        {
            'AttributeValueList':
            [
                {
                    'N': '1234'
                }
            ],
            'ComparisonOperator': 'EQ'
        }
    })

for item in result['Items']:
    print(
    'Employee ID: ', item['EmployeeID']['N'],
    '\nEmployee Name: ', item['EmployeeName']['S'])
```

The `client.scan()` function doesn't require any input except `TableName`. The `ScanFilter` argument is optional. On the other hand, `client.query()` does require both `TableName` and `KeyConditions`. In both cases, you must supply the data type and value of the conditions, plus a `ComparisonOperator` used to interpret the input. The output of both the scan and the query is

```
Employee ID:  1234
Employee Name:  Jan Smythe
```

5

The Part of Tens

Chapter **14**

Ten Ways to Create AWS Applications Quickly

t's deadline time and you've been struggling to complete your AWS application before the boss arrives to make life interesting. Fortunately, you have this chapter to help you work faster (beating the deadline so that you can just smile as the boss walks by). Of course, you didn't have to get so close to the deadline in the first place. By using these techniques, you can make AWS application development faster and easier.

Working at the Console

The GUI is slow, the GUI is cumbersome, the GUI is for someone else — someone less experienced with computers than you. Of course, you can keep telling yourself these less-than-truthful memes or you can come to the decision that the GUI really can help you understand AWS better. Sometimes, the fastest way to determine how to perform a task using the Command Line Interface (CLI) or within a program is to determine how the console does it. The console can show you the process that AWS prefers when performing certain tasks. In many cases, going through the process and keeping notes can help you write applications that work much faster than a trial-and-error approach.

Another reason to use the console is to determine what values AWS actually wants. Many of the examples in this book have you go to the console to obtain a required value. For example, trying to find the Amazon Resource Number (ARN) for an object can prove nearly impossible when using CLI or code, but finding it in the console is usually quite easy. Rather than spend an afternoon fiddling with code to retrieve an ARN, you can simply hard code it while working through the specifics of the application. Later you can work through the code required to obtain the ARN you need.

REMEMBER

The console also provides monitoring, which is possibly the most important of the developer tools it provides. Monitoring can help you detect issues such as code that takes too long to execute. However, monitoring is important because it also tells you when your code isn't at fault. When developing applications for the cloud, you need to remember that you have an Internet connection to consider, along with AWS. In fact, you have a wealth of failure points to consider that have nothing to do with your code. So instead of spending hours looking for a problem that doesn't actually exist, you can spend time monitoring the application to determine the true origin of the problem.

Using Example Source Code

Most developers spend a great deal of time looking at other people's code. It's sort of like viewing your neighbor's sheet during a test in school, except this kind of cheating is perfectly legal. In fact, it's encouraged. Here are a few places you might want to try when looking for an example that completely squashes that problem you're having:

>> **AWS Sample Code and Libraries:** https://aws.amazon.com/code

>> **AWS Documentation (check the individual services and SDKs):** https://aws.amazon.com/documentation/

>> **GitHub:** https://github.com/search?q=AWS

TIP

You can also find other sources of example code. For example, places such as SitePoint (https://www.sitepoint.com/) provide interesting articles that include a wealth of example sources you can use. In addition, Amazon provides some *living* examples, through which you can try the example code using a form and then seeing the underlying source. One such example is the S3 demonstration at https://s3.amazonaws.com/doc/s3-example-code/post/post_sample.html. The biggest problem with the Amazon examples is that you can find them everywhere. You might remember seeing an example at some point, but it's nearly impossible to determine just where unless you actually remember that it did appear somewhere in the documentation.

Don't forget to check the documentation for any SDKs or add-on libraries you use. For example, Python developers will definitely want to check the Boto3 documentation at `https://boto3.readthedocs.io/en/latest/`. These sites often contain separate example application sections that you can use to get started faster.

Combining Trial-and-Error Techniques

This book shows you at least three different ways to accomplish most tasks. It might seem like overkill at first, but sometimes working with AWS doesn't sink in by using only one technique. The three most common techniques you should use to perform trial-and-error methods when discovering a new way to interact with AWS are

» Use the consoles

» Use the CLI

» Use your own application code

It isn't random chance that this book relies on Anaconda to perform most programmatic tasks. The combination of Python and Anaconda Notebooks provides an exceptionally friendly environment in which to write code and see what happens. Because the feedback is instantaneous and you can work in a piecemeal fashion, the Notebook environment gives you immediate and detailed feedback. You don't have to keep going through the write ⇨ debug ⇨ run cycle with Python — you just write code and execute it.

Watching the Videos

Watching a video and then practicing what the video shows you offers you two methods of learning that have nothing to do with the usual trial-and-error coding techniques. A change of pace can help you discover that nuanced technique that you completely missed by using other methods. Every developer has had the experience of someone else checking code to find a really obvious error that the developer should have seen but didn't. Videos work the same way, giving you a different perspective on the whole configuration and coding process so that an obvious error actually does become obvious.

Videos can also provide a needed break and a change of pace. It's hardly surprising when you continue to attack a problem using precisely the same methods and continue to fail. There is likely nothing wrong with the method, but you become tired and stop thinking through the process correctly. You need a different viewpoint. With this in mind, here are some places to look for AWS videos that help you get a fresh start on that problem you're currently trying to solve:

>> **Amazon Instructional Videos and Labs:** `https://aws.amazon.com/training/intro_series/`

>> **YouTube (AWS-specific):** `https://www.youtube.com/user/AmazonWeb Services`

>> **YouTube (other sources):** `https://www.youtube.com/results?search_query=AWS`

>> **FreeVideoLectures:** `http://freevideolectures.com/Course/3649/Cloud-Computing/`

REMEMBER

You can also find sites that list video collections. For example, you can find an article on the top 100 Amazon videos (at least in the opinion of the author) on the RoboPsychology site at `http://meta-guide.com/videography/100-best-amazon-aws-tutorial-videos`. The most useful aspect of these articles is that they often supply clues as to the quality and content of the videos so that you don't have to wade through hundreds of videos to find the one you need.

Attending the Webinars

Webinars involve attending a short course without actually going anywhere. You get the kind of instruction you might get from a seminar but get to be in your usual comfortable seat and drink coffee from your own mug. For many developers, it's pure heaven because they can replay sections of the webinar as needed and don't suffer the discomfort of going to an unfamiliar location. Viewing a webinar can help you learn new techniques that are too complex for other sorts of learning, such as videos. Here are some places you can look for AWS webinars to meet your every need:

>> **AWS Monthly Webinar Series:** `https://aws.amazon.com/about-aws/events/monthlywebinarseries/`

>> **AWS Monthly Webinar Series Archive:** `https://aws.amazon.com/about-aws/events/monthlywebinarseries/archive/`

- » **Events and Webinars:** https://aws.amazon.com/about-aws/events/

- » **AWS Partner Webinar Series:** https://aws.amazon.com/webinars/partner-webinar-series/

- » **AWS Webinar YouTube Channel:** https://www.youtube.com/user/AWSwebinars

TIP

You can also find webinars from other companies online. For example, Cloud Academy (https://cloudacademy.com/webinars/) and OneLogin (https://www.onelogin.com/resources/webinars) both provide AWS-related webinars. However, these webinars require payment or a subscription. The best option is to go with the free resources first and then use the paid resources if the free resources don't quite tell you everything you need to know.

Discovering Others Efforts

Case studies don't necessarily provide you with that amazing bit of code you absolutely have to have to complete your application, but they can impart ideas. By the end of most days, developers have mush for brains because they've tried every idea — more than once — and sometimes to the point of being absurd. In fact, the last few hours of your workday might not even prove productive, except in improving your skills at Solitaire. That's why the case studies at https://aws.amazon.com/websites/ are so important. By seeing how other developers deal with problems, you might get some insights into dealing with your own. Even in the worst-case scenario, reading about other people's successes can help inspire you a lot more than yet another game of Solitaire will.

REMEMBER

One of the most important features of these case studies is that you see block diagrams of how other developers have used AWS services to create a complete solution. The block diagrams and accompanying discussion can help you see new ways in which to use AWS to create a solution that requires less coding and maintenance to create a reliable application.

Depending on Peer Support

Anyone who works with open source products knows the benefits of using peer support to answer the tough questions. The same principle might not seem to apply to AWS, but it does. You can often get just the right answer from someone who has already been where you are now through an online peer resource. Some of the most popular places to get AWS-specific help are

>> **Amazon Developer:** https://developer.amazon.com/support

>> **Quora:** https://www.quora.com/

>> **GitHub:** https://github.com/

WARNING

Unfortunately, peer support also comes with a few issues. For example, you don't really know who is on the other end of the line; it could be a troll whose only happiness is ruining your day. In addition, you can't always trust that someone is actually from Amazon, even if the email address suggests they are. For that matter, even if they are from Amazon, you don't know that they're an expert in the problem that you have. The point is that you need to exercise care when using peer support. Often, the support really does work, but all it takes is one or two instances when it doesn't to cause you considerable woe in your current development project.

Working with Blogs

Blogs can be helpful because many authors are quite knowledgeable about AWS. A blog can provide you with a process for performing a configuration or some special coding technique to use with Lambda. Blog posts can also tell you about caveats and supply fixes that Amazon sometimes buries on a page that no one visits.

WARNING

Realize, though, that although they can be useful, blogs can also become outdated quite fast because AWS moves at the speed of light. In addition, the author might not have as much knowledge as originally thought. Don't rely on blog posts that are more than a year or so old because AWS has likely changed in that time. In addition, read the posts carefully to see how much of the information you already know and how well it agrees with your knowledge before using the blog information to go into unknown territory. With all this in mind, here are some blogs that you might try when looking for the ultimate in setup or coding techniques:

>> **SearchAWS:** https://developer.amazon.com/support

>> **CloudThat:** https://blog.cloudthat.com/category/aws/

>> **Hacker Noon:** https://hackernoon.com/tagged/aws

Using Alternative Sources

You can sometimes find answers in surprising places, and it pays to look hard sometimes rather than waste days with a problem someone else has already solved. One of the alternative sources you might try is other vendor sites. For example, you can occasionally find useful information on the MSDN forums (`https://social.msdn.microsoft.com/Forums/`). Not long ago, a thread appeared on MSDN about running the MSDN subscription on AWS (to make accessing it everywhere easier). Odd bits of information like this can be elusive to find, so don't limit your search to just one location; look everywhere.

Sites such as SlideShare (`https://www.slideshare.net/`) can also prove excellent resources. For example, when considering the previous MSDN license-hosting question, you can find information on that topic on SlideShare at `https://www.slideshare.net/AmazonWebServices/leveraging-amazon-web-services-to-host-msdn-licenses`. YouTube (`https://www.youtube.com/`) also offers a wealth of videos to check out. Some of these videos are listed at `https://www.youtube.com/results?search_query=AWS`. If everyone learned precisely the same way, you wouldn't need to check out these other resources, but when you're in a bind, looking into alternatives really does pay. Perhaps a coding example presented in the traditional way just isn't enough to solve that horrifying problem that threatens your weekend.

Going Back to Tutorials

This book is one of your main sources of information. However, even as informative as this book is, it can't contain absolutely every piece of information about AWS in every possible form. A lot of people rely on tutorials to fill in gaps. Even the experts do (sometimes, especially the experts). Tutorials are fast and often present information in ways that you wouldn't otherwise consider. Of course, you have all the Amazon-specific tutorials to consider as well. Every main service page contains a listing of tutorials to try. In addition, check out the tutorials at these locations:

>> **Amazon 10-Minute Tutorials:** `https://aws.amazon.com/getting-started/tutorials/`

>> **AWS Tutorials:** `http://docs.aws.amazon.com/gettingstarted/latest/awsgsg-intro/gsg-aws-tutorials.html`

>> **AWS Tutorial Series:** `https://www.youtube.com/user/awstutorialseries`

Amazon likely has other tutorials for you to try, but these locations give you just about everything you could ask for in the way of quick information. Of course, many third parties are also involved with AWS. Here are some of the more interesting sites to try:

>> **TutorialsPoint:** `https://www.tutorialspoint.com/amazon_web_services/index.htm`

>> **Guru99:** `http://www.guru99.com/aws-tutorial.html`

>> **PluralSight (free trial only):** `https://www.pluralsight.com/browse/software-development/python` and `https://www.pluralsight.com/courses/aws-developer-introduction-aws-lambda`.

TIP

You can also locate specific topic tutorials, and you shouldn't discount them as you search. For example, if you really need to learn more about Convolutional Neural Networks (and who doesn't these days?), check out the tutorial at `http://cs231n.github.io/aws-tutorial/`. A possibly less esoteric topic is machine learning, which you can find at `https://www.analyticsvidhya.com/blog/2016/05/comprehensive-guide-ml-amazon-web-services-aws/`. Some tutorials are presented as combination blog posts and tutorials presented as a series, such as the one on Node.js at `https://hackernoon.com/tutorial-creating-and-managing-a-node-js-server-on-aws-part-1-d67367ac5171`. The point is that you can probably find a tutorial of the right type, presented in the right way, somewhere on the Internet.

Chapter **15**

Ten AWS Tools Every Developer Needs

Tools take a wide variety of forms, and you need to consider them all if you want to make your AWS setup everything you need it to be. When asked about tools, many developers narrow their focus to the development environment. They consider add-on libraries that make coding easier, or IDE add-ons that make the development process faster. However, when working in the cloud, the concept of a tool becomes much larger than just the development environment. You must also consider the cloud environment.

REMEMBER

The cloud environment encompasses quite a broad range of potential tool candidates. You consider not only the AWS services but also third-party entities, such as web services. The cloud brings with it the possibility of accessing code, data, and services from all over the world in ways that localized development could never entertain. Consequently, you may find some of the entries in this chapter a little surprising because they most definitely won't fit into the traditional IDE or programming language categories. In fact, given the broad range of programming languages that AWS supports, covering programming language-specific tools to any depth in a single chapter (especially not one that has a ten-entry limit) would be nearly impossible.

Obtaining Additional Amazon Offerings

Because of the way Amazon has set up its site, you can easily miss those special offerings that might make the difference between an easy project and a hair-pulling one. The following sections offer some Amazon-specific solutions that you might not have considered.

Enhancing ASW services directly

Many of the AWS services give you the means to update their functionality directly. The update falls outside the range of AWS configuration. For example, when working with EC2, you can install localized programming languages and associated libraries. The additional functionality enables you to upload applications and run those applications from within EC2. For example, you can create a custom web service that runs like the web services you use locally, but have a cloud-based approach that makes them more accessible and achieve greater reliability.

TIP

Of the various services, EC2 is the most flexible in its capability to accept third-party enhancements directly. Consequently, EC2 is the service that you should try working with first when it comes to adding functionality directly. The article at `http://docs.aws.amazon.com/AWSEC2/latest/UserGuide/find-software.html` supplies the details on how to locate new software for your EC2 setup. The article at `http://docs.aws.amazon.com/AWSEC2/latest/UserGuide/install-software.html` tells you how to install the packages after you find them. You should try to find and install a package that can prove useful in your development efforts, and then experiment with it to see what is possible to address your specific needs.

Employing Tools for Amazon Web Services

The Tools for Amazon Web services page (`https://aws.amazon.com/tools/`) offers a complete list of all the tools that Amazon provides, not just those that have appeared in the book. This page actually contains links to four kinds of tools that you can use to make your development experience better:

>> **Developer tools:** These tools all help you develop applications in some way: storage, version control, building, testing, or deploying.

>> **SDKs:** Each SDK applies to a specific language, and Amazon supports most of the popular languages used today. The individual SDK entries include links that let you install the SDK, see its associated documentation, and learn more about what the SDK can do for you.

>> **IDE toolkits:** Each toolkit augments an Integrated Development Environment (IDE) regardless of language used. The two IDEs supported now are Eclipse and Visual Studio (both of which support multiple languages), but you may see more IDEs in the future. As with SDKs, the IDE entries include links that let you install the extended support, see its associated documentation, and learn more about what the toolkit can do for you.

>> **Command-line tools:** This book concentrates on using the standard Command Line Interface (CLI) tools because most platforms support these tools. Amazon also provides support for Windows PowerShell. As with SDKs, the command line tool entries include links that let you install the extended support, see its associated documentation, and learn more about what the command-line tools can do for you.

Wandering through Amazon Marketplace

Amazon Marketplace (https://aws.amazon.com/marketplace/b/2649276011) helps you locate third-party tools that you need based on search criteria you provide. As shown in Figure 15-1, you have a lot of choices to make in the Amazon Marketplace. Some of the choices aren't apparent unless you spend time playing with the interface. For example, you can choose between AMI & SaaS (as shown in the figure) or Desktop in the search field.

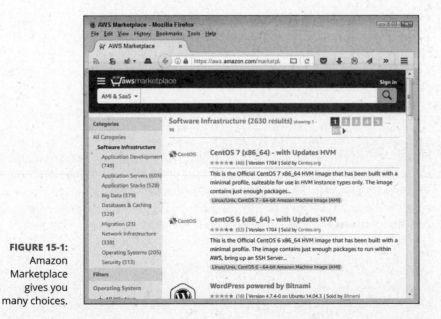

FIGURE 15-1: Amazon Marketplace gives you many choices.

The search filters also offer a great many choices. You can choose the software category, operating system, pricing plan, support type, free trial offering, delivery method, average rating, architecture (32-bit or 64-bit), region, and instance type. The software descriptions also provide you with the vendor name, product name, rating, version number, description, and all sorts of other useful information. Click one of the product links and you see even more information about that product, plus links to perform tasks such as downloading the software, when the option is available.

If the page shown in Figure 15-1 seems a little daunting, you can always try the Amazon Marketplace home page (https://aws.amazon.com/marketplace). This page offers a gentler interface that lets you choose from the most popular offerings. In other words, Amazon offers to filter some of the options for you.

Getting Amazon-supported peer help

Amazon provides a wealth of forums on which you can ask for peer support with your AWS-specific issue. You can find a list of these forums at https://forums.aws.amazon.com/index.jspa. Many of the forums give language-specific support. In addition, Amazon developers do sometimes visit the forums to offer additional help beyond that normally offered by peers. Obviously, the level of support, even with Amazon employee help, doesn't quite match the paid support option at https://aws.amazon.com/premiumsupport/.

Fortunately, you don't have to deal with English-only peer support. The Amazon forums support the Japanese, German, Portuguese, and Korean languages as well. You also have the option to review feeds using RSS, so you can keep up with what other developers are asking about as well (finding the answer that you need before you actually need it).

Partnering with a Third Party

You may decide to employ the shortcut of partnering with a third party to get your application up and running faster. The partner brings expertise to your organization that takes considerable time and effort to build.

The AWS Partner Programs page at https://aws.amazon.com/partners/programs/ describes the long list of partner types, any of which could be helpful to your development effort. However, the most useful developer options appear in the Technology Partner Programs location on the page. For example, members of the AWS SaaS Partner Program (https://aws.amazon.com/partners/saas/)

help you build, launch, and grow your application — allowing you to better focus on getting a working application put together.

TECHNICAL STUFF

You may decide that a technique, process, tool, or application that you develop is generalized and useful enough to sell to others. If this is the case, you may want to become an Amazon partner. The details appear on the main partner page at `https://aws.amazon.com/partners/`. Amazon actively supports developers who create solutions in a broad range of categories.

Developing New Knowledge

Knowledge is power. If you want to power your way through the various issues you face when working through code, you need to find the knowledge that other developers already possess. After all, you may not know that certain tools exist, that they have certain features that you need, or that you can use them in unexpected ways. All these sorts of knowledge require that you either experiment to obtain the information on your own or get it from someone else. The following sections assume that you want to go the fast route and get it from someone else.

Getting an education

Going to school, which is essentially what taking any kind of course amounts to, won't answer any immediate questions or help you use the tools better today. However, taking a course will help you over the long term to develop a better grasp of precisely how AWS works and how to employ various tools to make your development tasks easier. Third-party sites, such as Linux Academy (`https://linuxacademy.com/amazon-web-services/courses`), enable you to get the education you need quickly and easily. Interestingly enough, you can even take a course on AWS Developer Tools at `https://linuxacademy.com/amazon-web-services/training/course/name/manage-and-deploy-code-with-aws-developer-tools`.

When looking for an online course, make sure you choose sites that offer multiple methods of learning the material. Otherwise, you might find THAT the one learning method offered by a site doesn't help you much. Sites that contain the following types of educational experiences tend to work best (obviously, some types of offerings, such as instructor-led training, cost more):

>> Videos

>> Hands-on labs

- » Downloadable source code
- » Sample tests
- » Slide shows
- » Text-based training
- » Instructor-led training

Locating online blogs and note sources

A number of online sites provide an interesting sort of information source, notes. For example, Compute Patterns (http://www.computepatterns.com/aws-notes/) is a site that specializes in putting out bite-sized pieces of information that you can easily consume and then get right back to work.

Some blogs are also specialized and offer content in short bits. For example, the AWS Startup Collection (https://medium.com/aws-activate-startup-blog) presents this sort of information.

If you want to find an ultimate source of AWS blog posts on every subject imaginable, check out the AWS Labs site at https://github.com/awslabs/. This is actually a good place to discover what Amazon has in mind for the future. You can use these various information sources to get up and running quickly without having to waste time in classes when you need just one answer.

One of the more interesting blog entries you can find online is Chef Supermarket. The cookbooks you find here (https://supermarket.chef.io/cookbooks/) give instructions for performing various tasks in an extremely terse but efficient manner. For example, check out the AWS developer tools post at https://supermarket.chef.io/cookbooks/aws_developer_tools.

Rely on an information repository

A few sites online contain repositories of information. One such site is the StratoScale wiki at http://www.stratoscale.com/wiki/display/privatecloud/Amazon+Web+Services. The site categorizes various repositories for you, and the developer-related posts generally appear in the Operations and Management category at http://www.stratoscale.com/wiki/display/privatecloud/AWS+Operations+and+Management. For example, check out the listing of AWS APIs, SDKs, and Developer Tools at http://www.stratoscale.com/wiki/display/privatecloud/AWS+APIs%2C+SDKs+and+Developer+Tools.

REMEMBER

A potential down side of using repositories is that some links do become outdated, so you need to exercise care in believing everything you read. However, repositories can also save considerable time trying to research a topic on your own. You don't have to dig through every available link that turns up when you Google a topic because a repository does the heavy lifting for you.

Using Bitnami Developer Tools-

Going to the Bitnami site (`https://bitnami.com/stacks/developer-tools`) is a bit like going to a candy store. You like everything you see and have no idea what to pick first. The Bitnami site (`https://bitnami.com/`) acts as a library for server-based software of all sorts, not just developer tools. In fact, you can find just about anything you can imagine and more than a few things that you didn't know existed. The site can seem overwhelming, but using the stacks entries (`https://bitnami.com/stacks`) makes it easier to manage.

TIP

Keep your eyes on the Coming Soon area at the bottom of each page. These entries appear on the Bitnami wish list. However, Bitnami can't implement all of them at the same time — the list is just too long. Consequently, you can click your favorite applications in this area to cast your vote for the applications that Bitnami adds next.

Relying on Device Emulators

In all the discussions you read, most of them leave out one essential fact: You can't see how your application works on other devices unless you own those devices or rely on an emulator. You definitely won't own all the devices that your users employ unless you have a vault of money stashed somewhere, so the emulator route is the one that most developers use. Taking the shotgun approach to emulators isn't a good idea, either, because trying to test your application against every emulator out there just won't work. Here are some tips for working with emulators:

>> Obtain a list of devices that your users actually have.

>> Categorize the devices so that you can create a reasonable list of useful emulators.

>> Locate well-supported emulators (those that have support plans) when you can.

>> Use the version of the device that most of your users have, rather than the newest version.

>> Upgrade your emulator test suite as user choices change (which entails performing surveys regularly).

>> Avoid using emulators that simply check for application parameters and functionality; you want to see how the application will look.

Index

Symbols

A

About the Author

John Mueller is a freelance author and technical editor. He has writing in his blood, having produced 103 books and more than 600 articles to date. The topics range from networking to artificial intelligence and from database management to heads-down programming. Some of his current works include a book about machine learning, a couple of Python books, and a book about MATLAB. He has also written *AWS For Admins For Dummies,* which provides administrators a great place to start with AWS. His technical editing skills have helped more than 63 authors refine the content of their manuscripts. John has provided technical editing services to both *Data Based Advisor* and *Coast Compute* magazines. John has had an interest in Amazon Web Services (AWS) since its inception. In fact, he wrote *Mining Amazon Web Services* based on that humble beginning. AWS has come a long way since that time. Be sure to read John's blog at `http://blog.johnmuellerbooks.com/`.

When John isn't working at the computer, you can find him outside in the garden, cutting wood, or generally enjoying nature. John also likes making wine, baking cookies, and knitting. When not occupied with anything else, he makes glycerin soap and candles, which come in handy for gift baskets. You can reach John on the Internet at `John@JohnMuellerBooks.com`. John is also setting up a website at `http://www.johnmuellerbooks.com/`. Feel free to take a look and make suggestions on how he can improve it.

Dedication

Every day I look around and see unacknowledged heroes everywhere — all those people, from farmers, to librarians, to the teller at the bank, who never seem to receive thanks for their contribution to making my writing possible. This book is dedicated to them. Even if I don't always say it, I do appreciate all the hard work others put in to make life possible and happy.

Acknowledgments

Thanks to my wife, Rebecca. Even though she is gone now, her spirit is in every book I write, in every word that appears on the page. She believed in me when no one else would.

Russ Mullen deserves thanks for his technical edit of this book. He greatly added to the accuracy and depth of the material you see here. Russ worked exceptionally hard helping with the research for this book by locating hard-to-find URLs and also offering a lot of suggestions. This was also an especially difficult book from a testing perspective, and Russ was there to help me try various methods to obtain specific goals.

Matt Wagner, my agent, deserves credit for helping me get the contract in the first place and taking care of all the details that most authors don't really consider. I always appreciate his assistance. It's good to know that someone wants to help.

A number of people read all or part of this book to help me refine the approach, test scripts, and generally provide input that all readers wish they could have. These unpaid volunteers helped in ways too numerous to mention here. I especially appreciate the efforts of Eva Beattie and Luca Massaron, who provided general input, read the entire book, and selflessly devoted themselves to this project.

Finally, I would like to thank Katie Mohr, Susan Christophersen, and the rest of the editorial and production staff for their unparalleled support of this writing effort.

Publisher's Acknowledgments

Acquisitions Editor: Katie Mohr
Project and Copy Editor: Susan Christophersen
Technical Editor: Russ Mullen
Sr. Editorial Assistant: Cherie Case

Production Editor: Vasanth Koilraj
Cover Image: © PowerUp/Shutterstock